RAGNARÖK

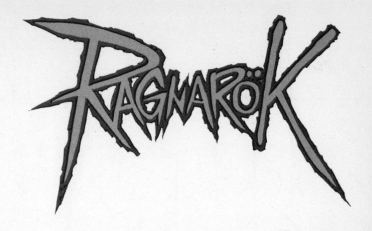

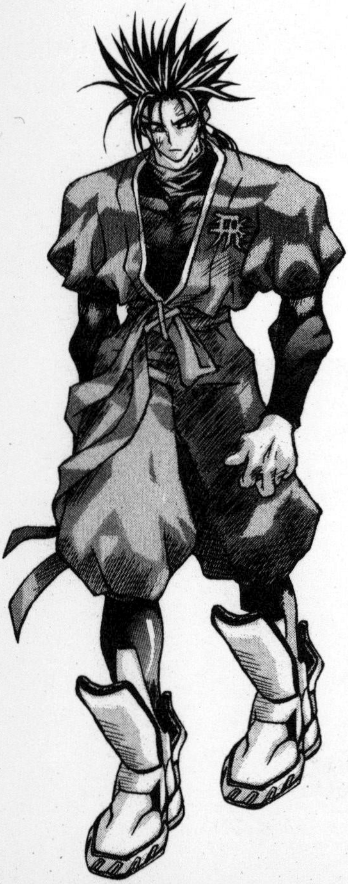
飛

Volume 3:
Night of Blood

By
Myung-Jin Lee

English Version
by
Richard A. Knaak

Los Angeles • Tokyo • London

Graphic Designer - Anna Kernbaum
Retouch & Lettering - Monalisa J. de Asis

Editor - Jake Forbes
Managing Editor - Jill Freshney
Production Coordinator - Antonio DePietro
Production Manager - Jennifer Miller
Art Director - Matt Alford
Editorial Director - Jeremy Ross
VP of Production - Ron Klamert
President & C.O.O. - John Parker
Publisher & C.E.O. - Stuart Levy

Email: editor@TOKYOPOP.com
Come visit us online at www.TOKYOPOP.com

A  Manga

TOKYOPOP Inc.
5900 Wilshire Blvd. Suite 2000
Los Angeles, CA 90036

RAGNAROK VOLUME 3

ISBN: 1-931514-75-5

First TOKYOPOP Printing: August 2002

14 13 12 11 10

Printed in the USA

Bonus Supplement

RAGNARÖK

Players Handbook

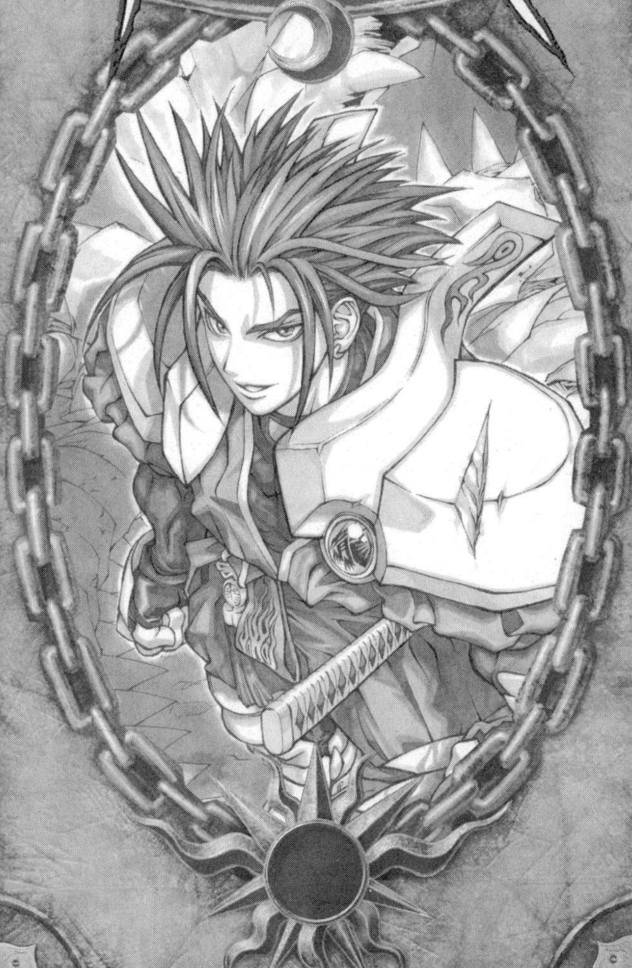

A complete guide to the characters and story for novice adventurers.

HEROES

NOTE: THE FOLLOWING STATISTICS ARE INSPIRED BY THE MANGA, BUT ARE DO NOT REFLECT ANY OFFICIAL RAGNAROK RPG. – EDITOR

NAME: Chaos
Class: Rune Knight
Level: 8
Alignment: Chaotic Good
STR: 17
DEX: 10
CON: 15
INT: 12
WIS: 14
CHR: 16

Equipment:
Vision- Enchanted sword- STR +2

Rune Armor- AC -4, 20% bonus
saving throw vs. magical attacks

Notes:
A warrior with no memories, Chaos searches
for the truth about his past. He might very
well hold the key to humanity's salvation.

NAME: Iris Irine
Class: Cleric
Level: 4
Alignment: Lawful Good
STR: 7
DEX: 12
CON: 9
INT: 13
WIS: 16
CHR: 16

Equipment:
Chernryongdo- Enchanted dagger-
STR +1, DEX +1, 1D4 damage if
anyone but her touches it.

Irine Family Armor- AC -5, WIS +1

Notes:
The heir to city of Fayon and the powers of the Four
Constellations. She is currently training with Chaos
to become a great leader like her father.

HEROES

NAME: Fenris Fenrir
Class: Warlock
Level: 9
Alignment: Neutral Good
STR: 14
DEX: 15
CON: 13
INT: 16
WIS: 12
CHR: 14

Equipment:
Psychic Medallion: Magic compass
which leads its bearer to whatever
their heart most desires.

Laevatein, Rod of Destruction- STR+1, extends
to staff on command.

Notes:
The reincarnation of the Wolf God, Fenris
searches the land for Balder so that they can
prevent gods and demons from taking control
of Midgard.

NAME: Loki
Class: Assassin
Level: 8
Alignment:Lawful Neutral
STR: 14
DEX: 18
CON: 12
INT: 12
WIS: 14
CHR: 10

Equipment:
Sword of Shadows: + 4 to hit, damage +2

Bone Armor: AC -5, STR +2

Notes:
Greatest of the assassins, Loki's anonymity is
a testament to his skill at going unseen. His
ability to keep a level-head under stress
makes him ideal for leading assault teams.

ENEMIES

NAME: Sara Irine
Class: Valkyrie
Level: 7
Alignment: Chaotic Neutral
STR: 14
DEX: 12
CON: 13
INT: 14
WIS: 15
CHR: 17

Equipment:
Haeryongdo, Sword of Retribution-
STR+2

Enchanted Parchments x 24

Notes:
One of the 12 Valkyries of Valhalla,
Sara Irine was sent to prevent Fenris
from completing her quest. She also
seeks revenge on the city of her birth
that abandoned her.

NAME: Skurai
Class: Cursed Prosecutor
Level: 12
Alignment: Chaotic Evil
STR: 17
DEX: 16
CON: 19
INT: 15
WIS: 8
CHR: 12

Equipment:
Talatusu- Cursed sword- STR+2, HP
+12- cannot be discarded unless it
tastes the blood it is looking for.

Notes:
Skurai follows the will of his sword,
Talatsu, who seeks the one blood that
will quench his thirst. He has an
enormous bounty on his head.

NPC's

Muninn and Huginn

Odin's Beholders, these messengers can take the form of crows. They seem to be manipulating events, but to what end remains a mystery.

Assassins

The ancient order of Assassins have maintained the balance of power in Midgard for centuries. A truly neutral organization, when any one group tips the scales with bloodshed, the assassins repay in kind.

The story so far...

Welcome back, friends, to the world of Midgard, where ancient gods and mortal men vie for control of destiny. 'Tis an epic tale, spread over many a weathered tome, so if memory fails you, or if this is your first journey to Midgard, this should help you get up to speed...

Twelve years ago a terrible act was committed in the city of Fayon. Lord Irine's eldest daughter, Sara, was to be sacrificed and a new heir proclaimed. But things didn't go as planned—the child escaped and was adopted into Freya's army of Valkyries. Now the prodigal daughter has returned to wreak her vengence on the entire city.

Other warriors have converged on Fayon as well. Skurai, a swordsman with a cursed blade, has come in search of the blood that will set him free. Chaos, a rune knight with no memories, would like to make the town his home. Fenris Fenrir came in search of Balder, the fallen god who will help her bring about Ragnarok, who she believes was reincarnated as Chaos.

When Sara Irine and her army of giants descended on the town, no one was spared. Those who weren't killed by Sara were picked up by the bloodthirsty Skurai. The entire town and everyone in it should have been destroyed, but for a miracle. Chaos found within his heart the power to summon Nidhogg, the Eater Beneath the Tree, greatest of all dragons.

Meanwhile, in the Morroc Desert to the west, an elite band of assassins have been sent to take out a madman who is sacrificing children to the demon lord, Surt. When they encounter a guard of demons, it appears as if they may be too late, as they are about to discover in *Ragnarok Vol.3: Night of Blood...*

TOKYOPOP

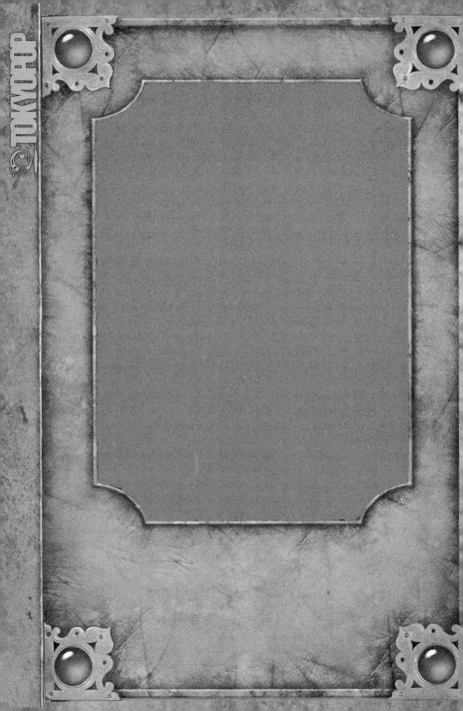

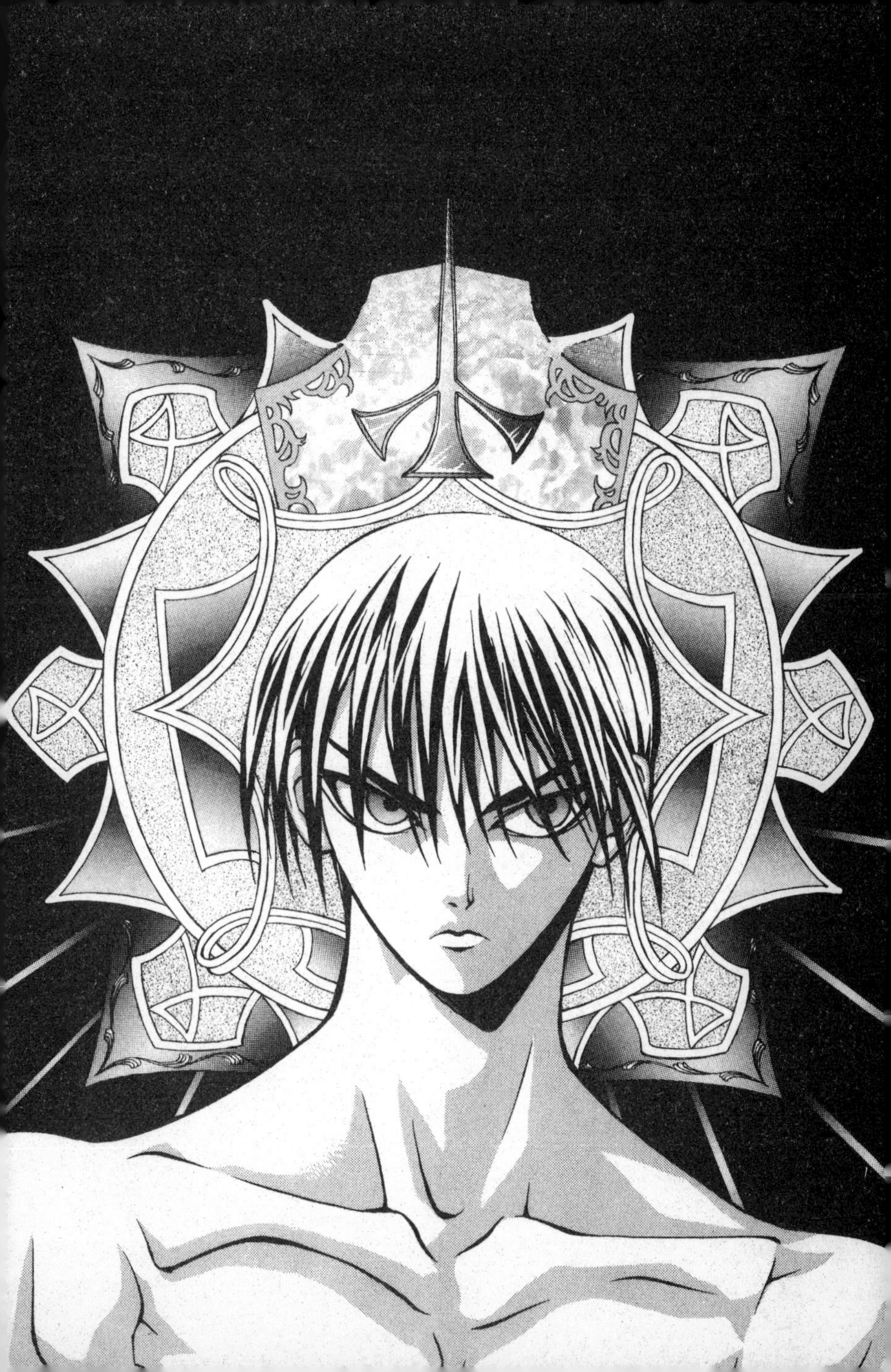

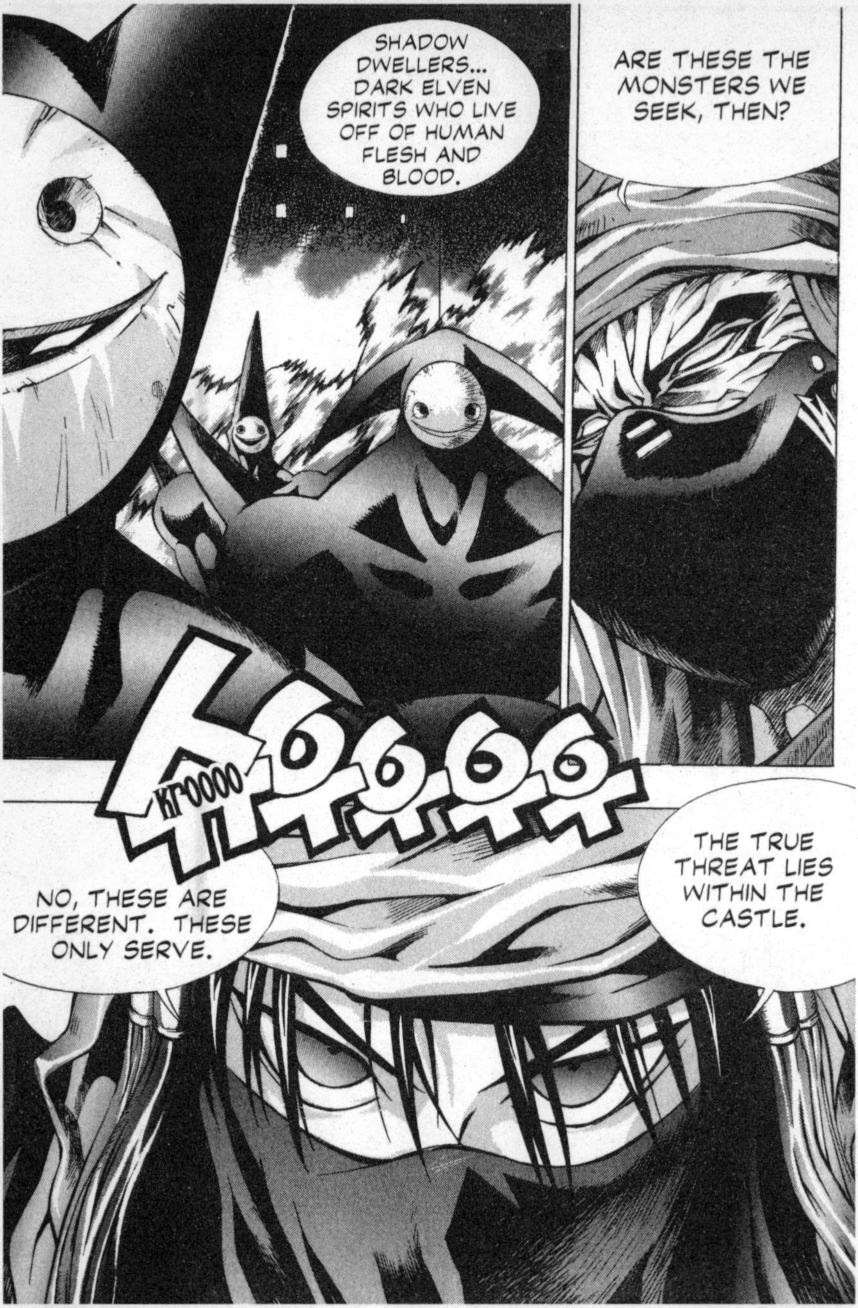
SHADOW DWELLERS... DARK ELVEN SPIRITS WHO LIVE OFF OF HUMAN FLESH AND BLOOD.
ARE THESE THE MONSTERS WE SEEK, THEN?
KROOOO
NO, THESE ARE DIFFERENT. THESE ONLY SERVE.
THE TRUE THREAT LIES WITHIN THE CASTLE.

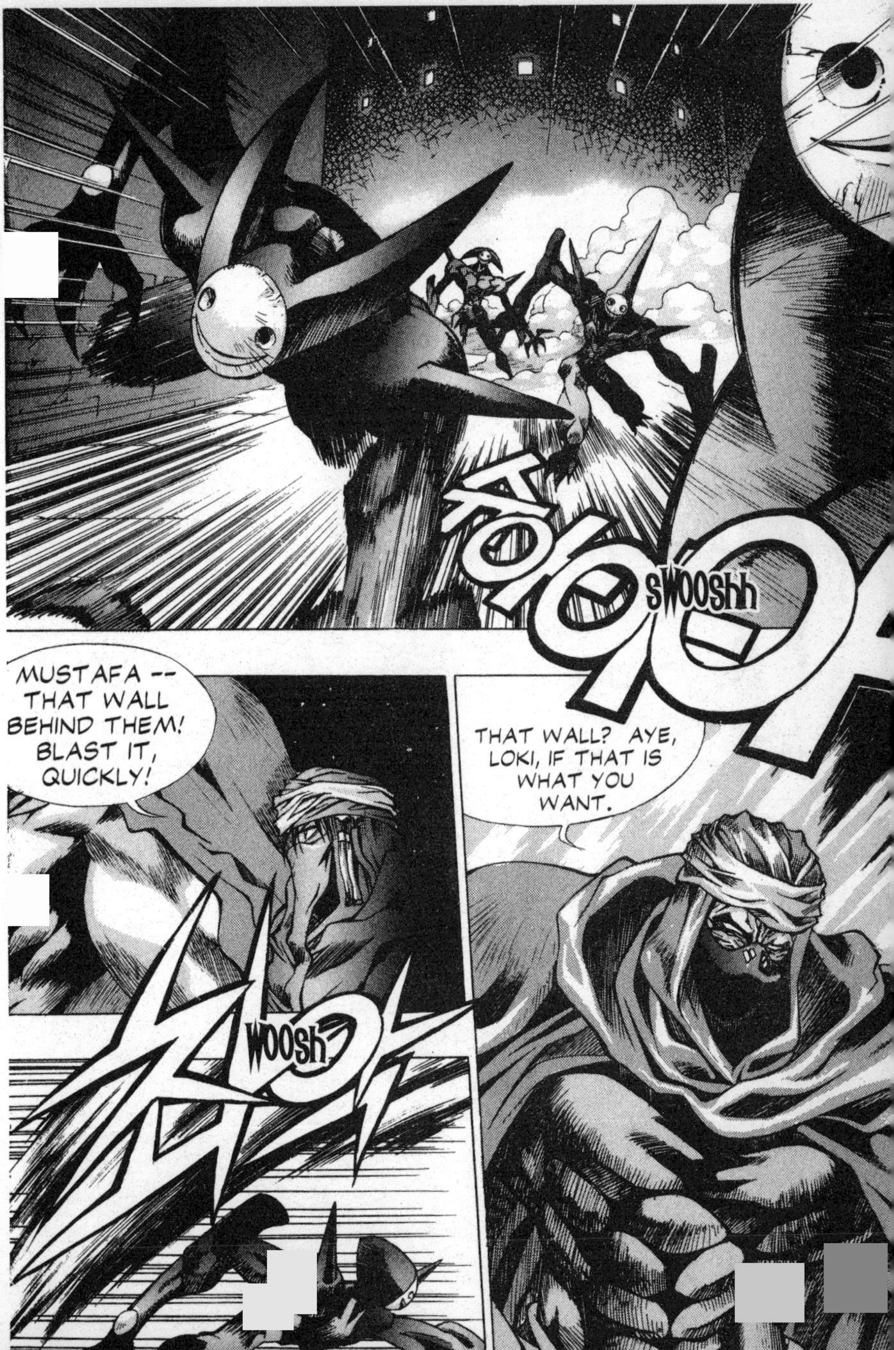
sWOOShh
MUSTAFA -- THAT WALL BEHIND THEM! BLAST IT, QUICKLY!
THAT WALL? AYE, LOKI, IF THAT IS WHAT YOU WANT.
WOOSH

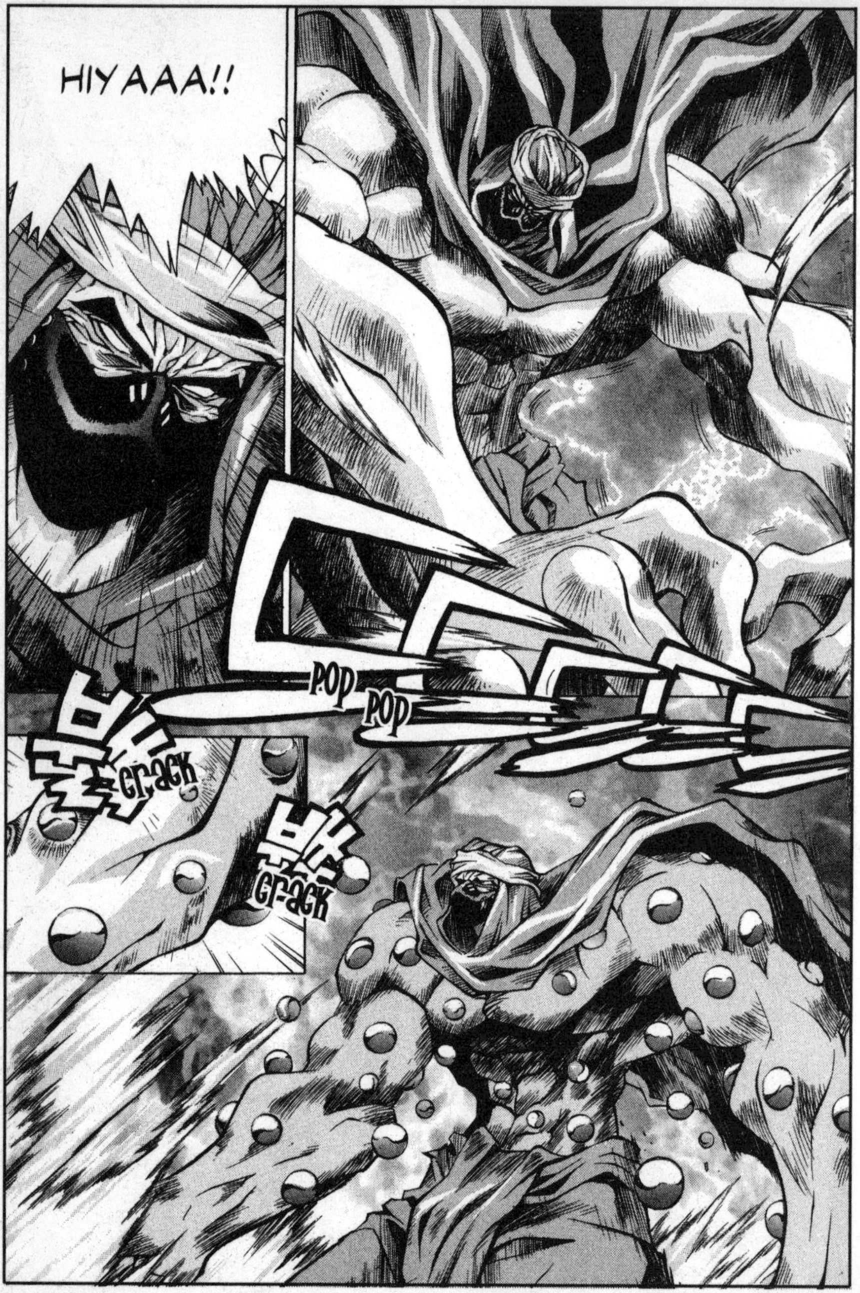
HIYAAA!!
POP
POP
crack
crack

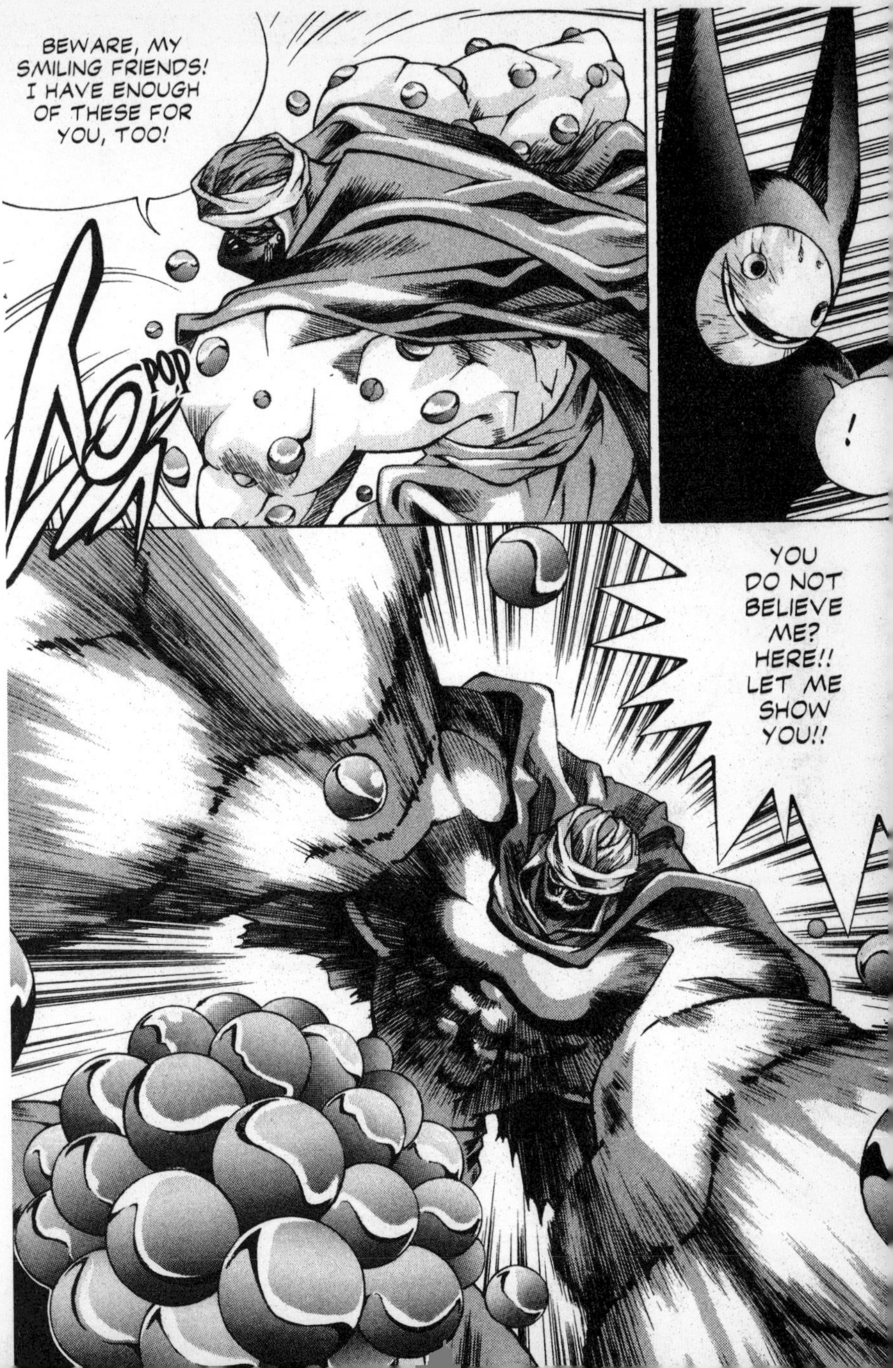
BEWARE, MY SMILING FRIENDS! I HAVE ENOUGH OF THESE FOR YOU, TOO!
POP
!
YOU DO NOT BELIEVE ME? HERE!! LET ME SHOW YOU!!

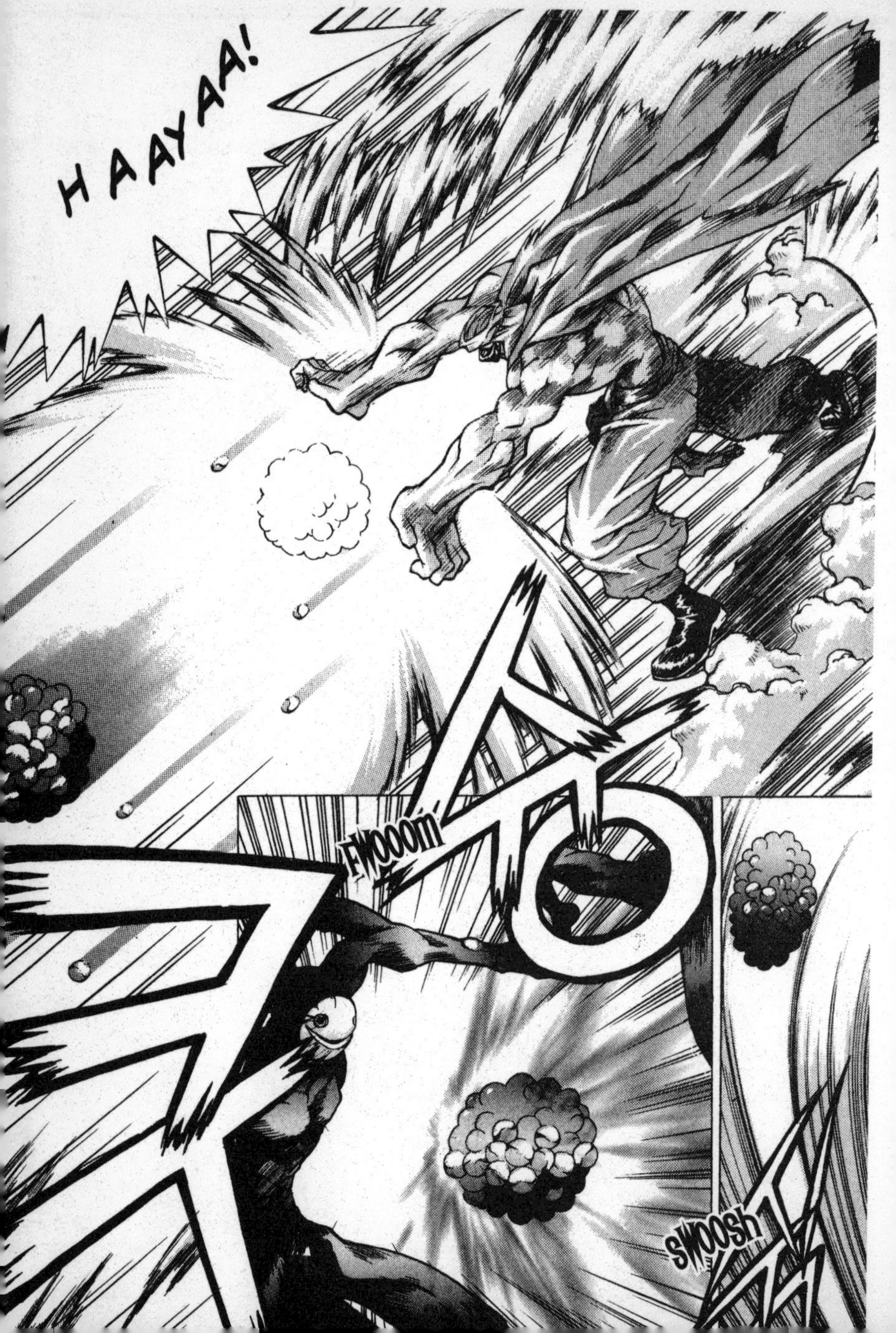
HAAYAA!
FWOOOm
SWOOSh

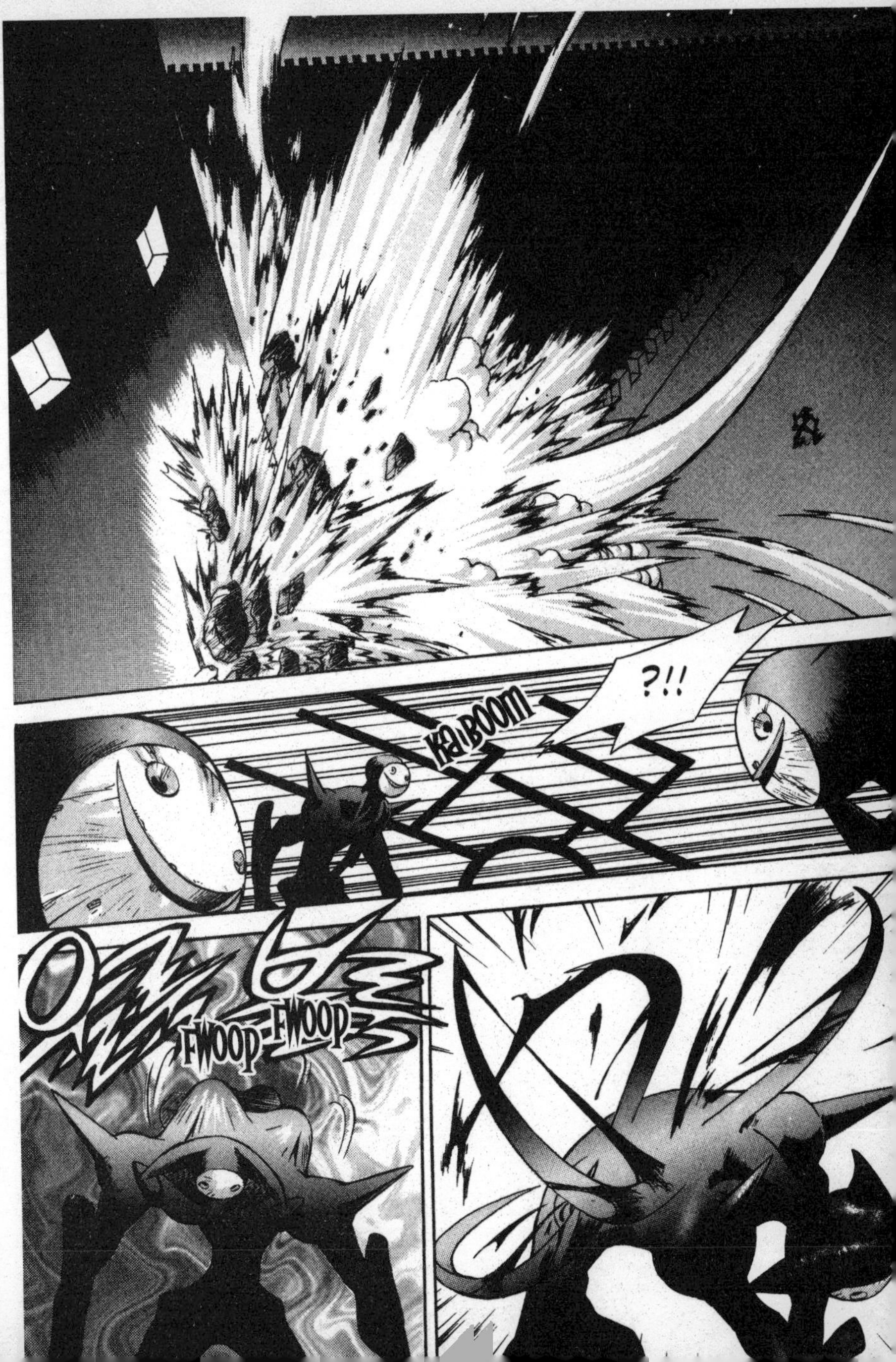
KA-BOOM
?!!
FWOOP-FWOOP

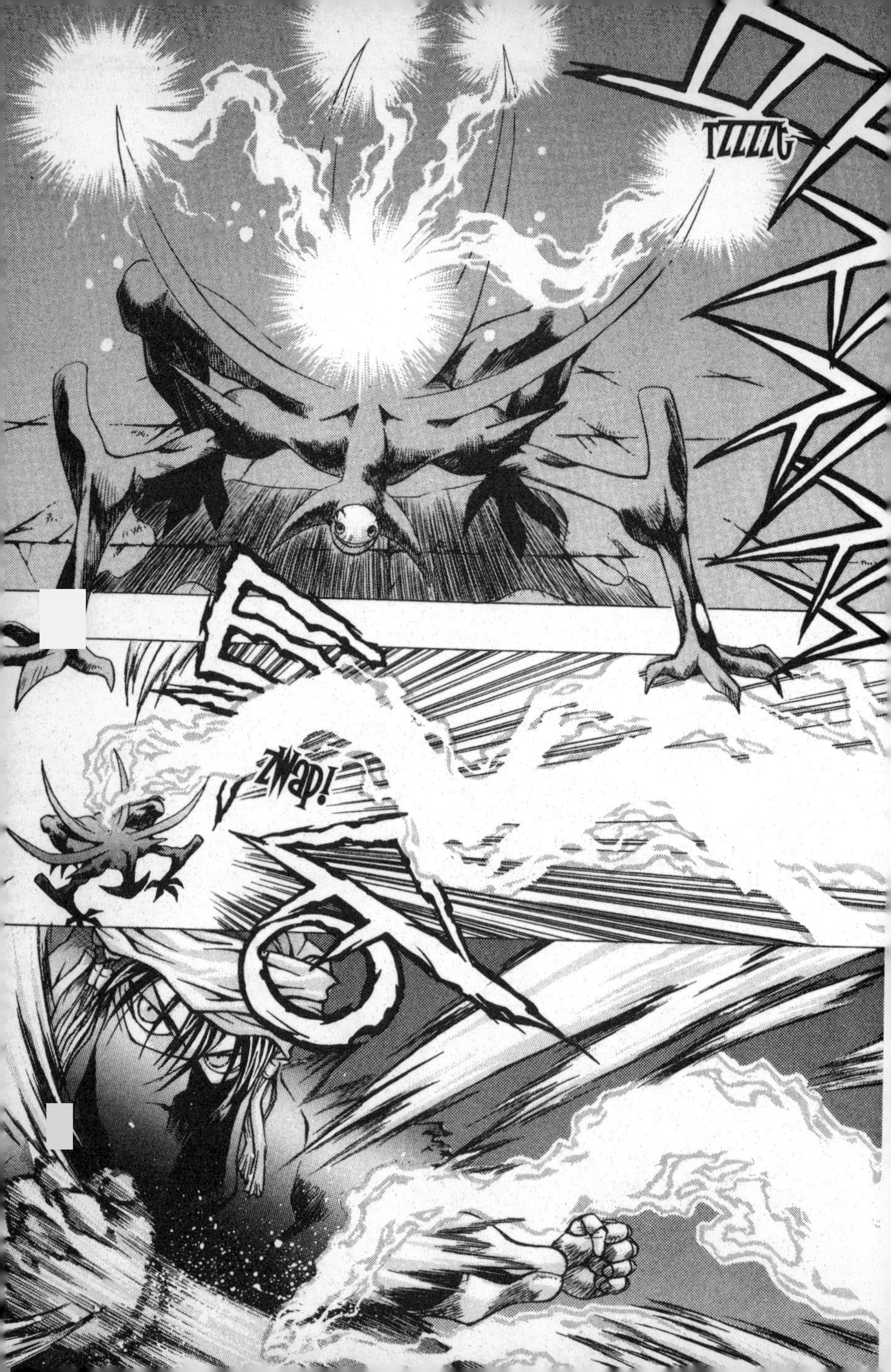
TZZZZG
ZWAP!

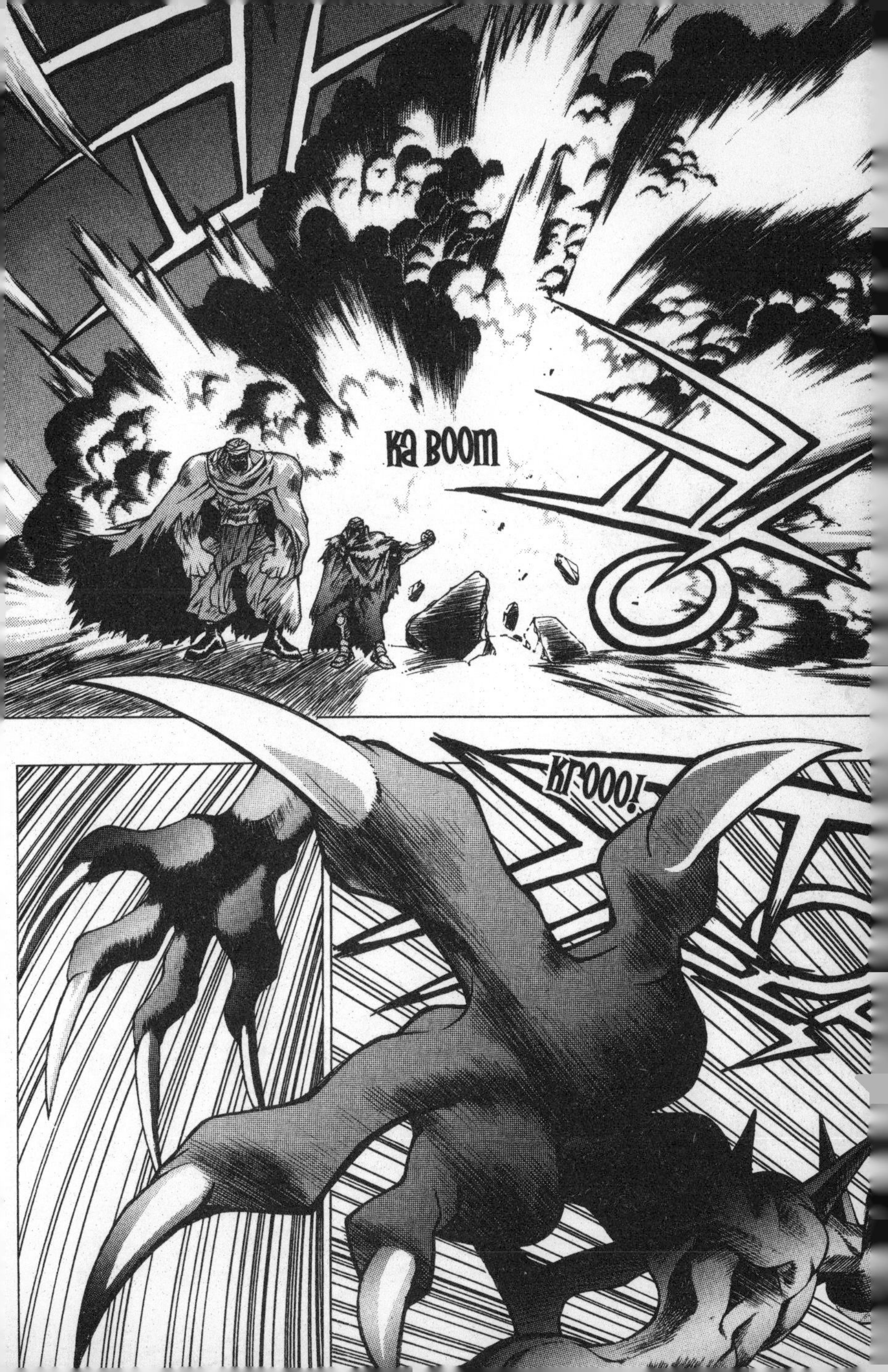
KA BOOM
KI-OOO!

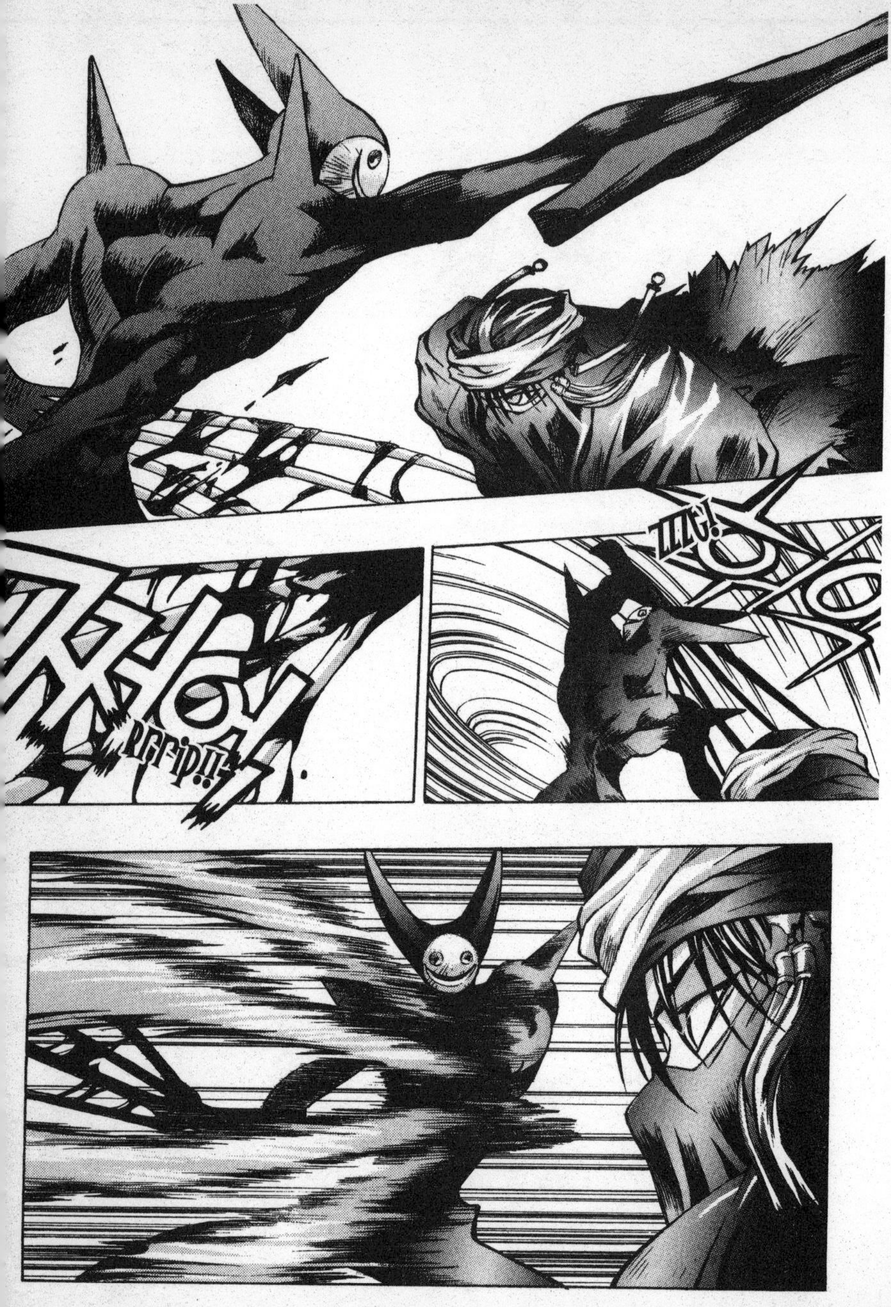
RRRIP!!
ZZZG!

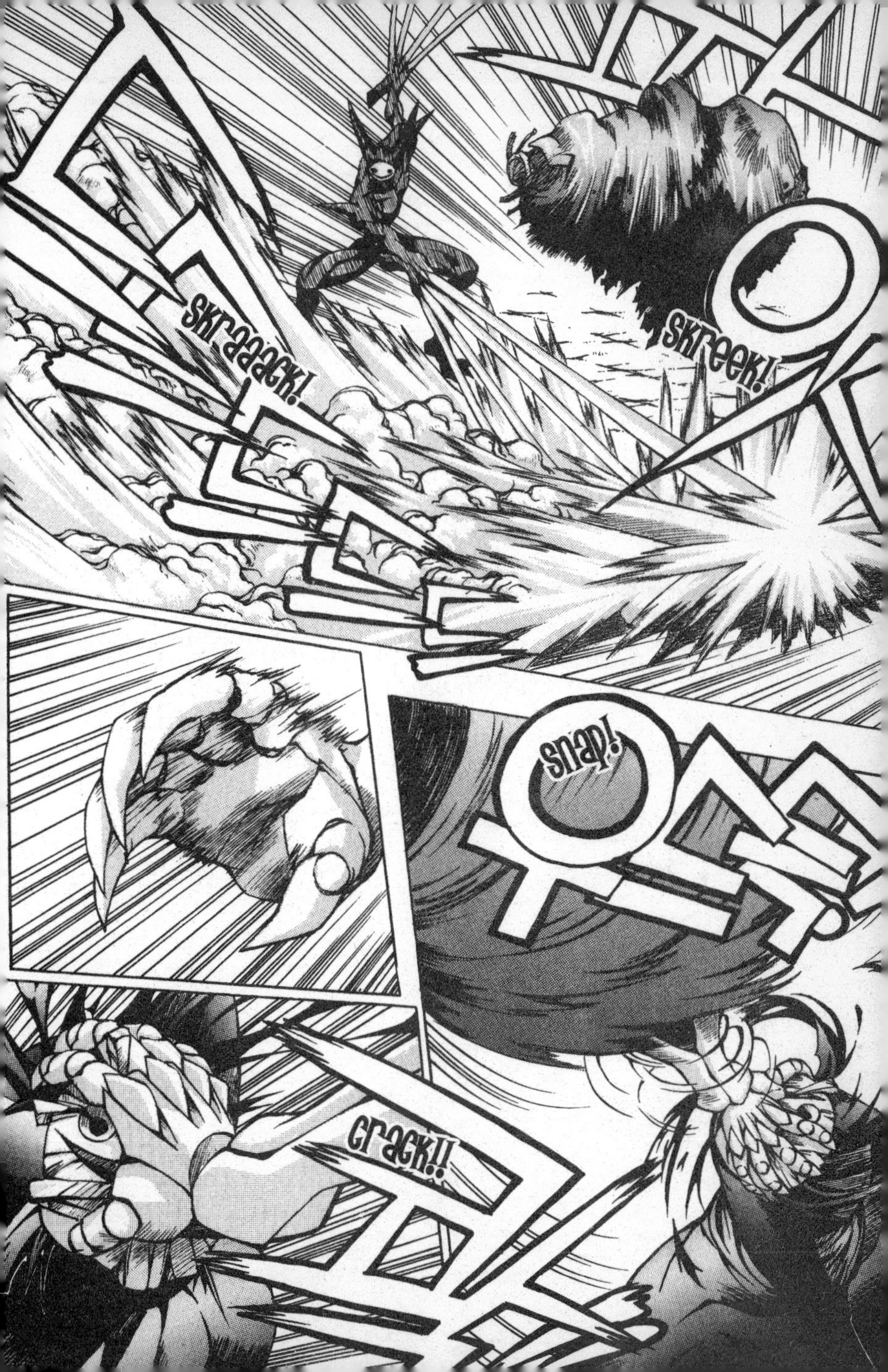
skraaack!
skreek!
snap!
crack!!

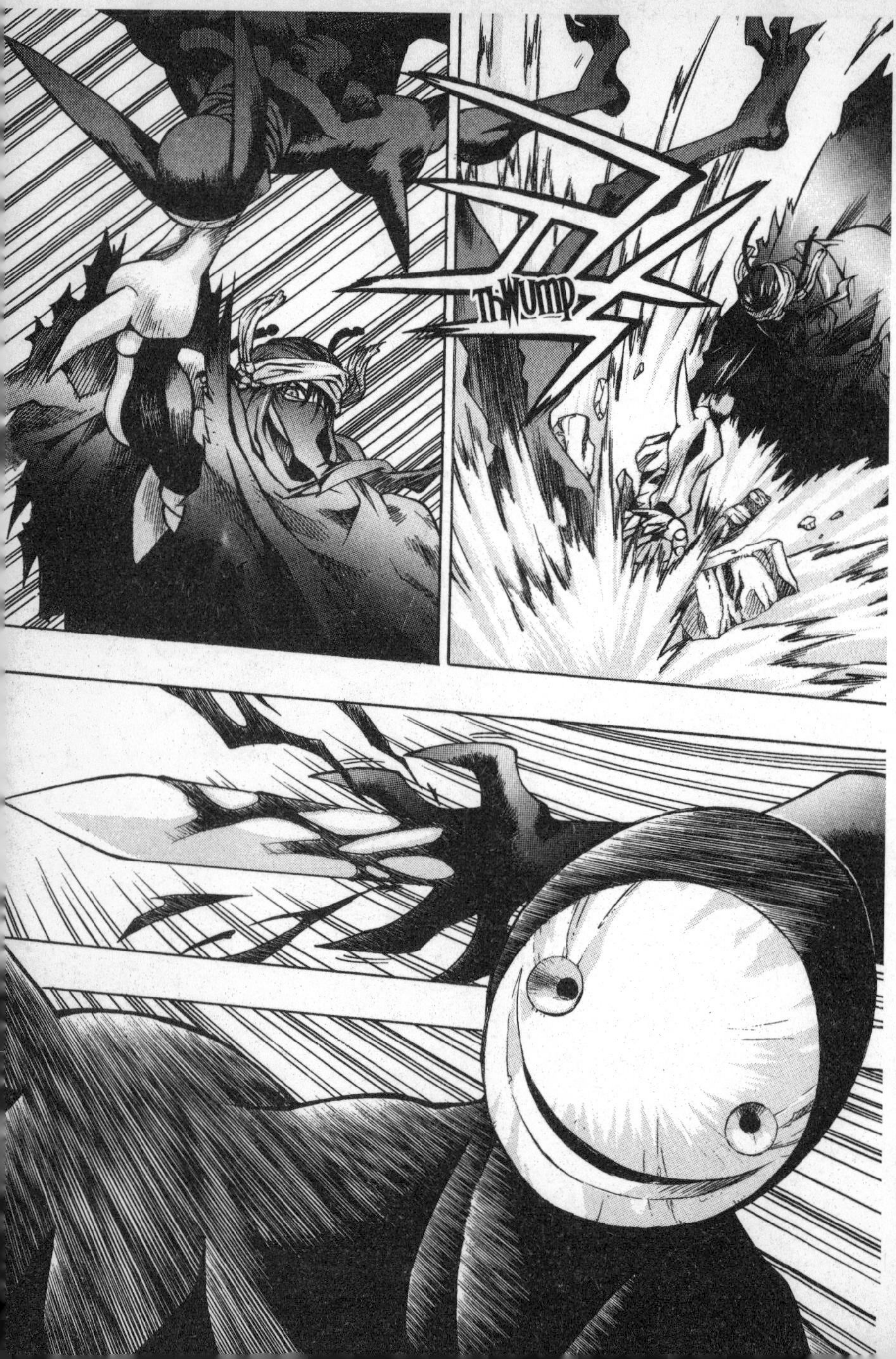
THWUMP

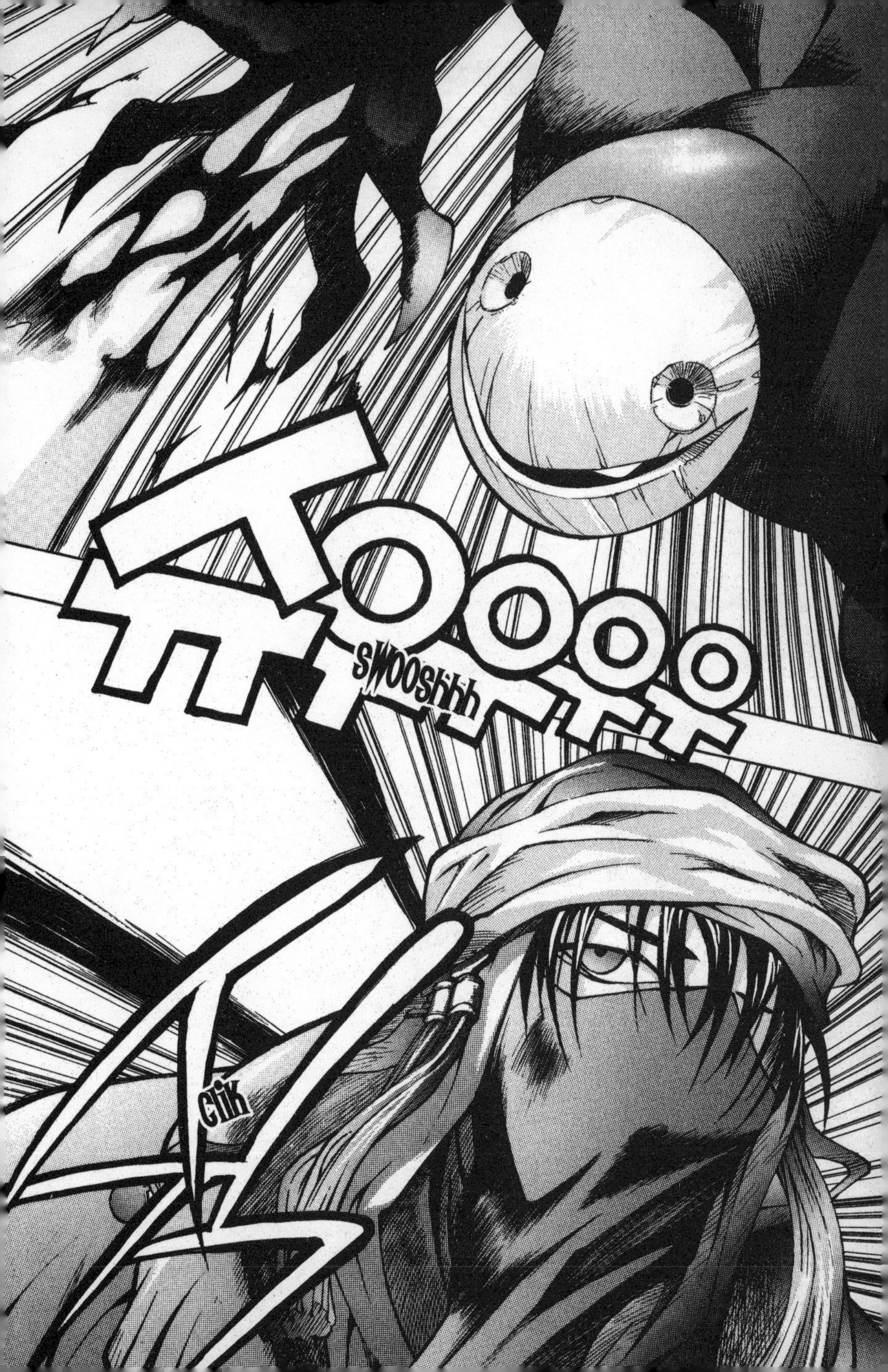
sWOOshhh
cliK

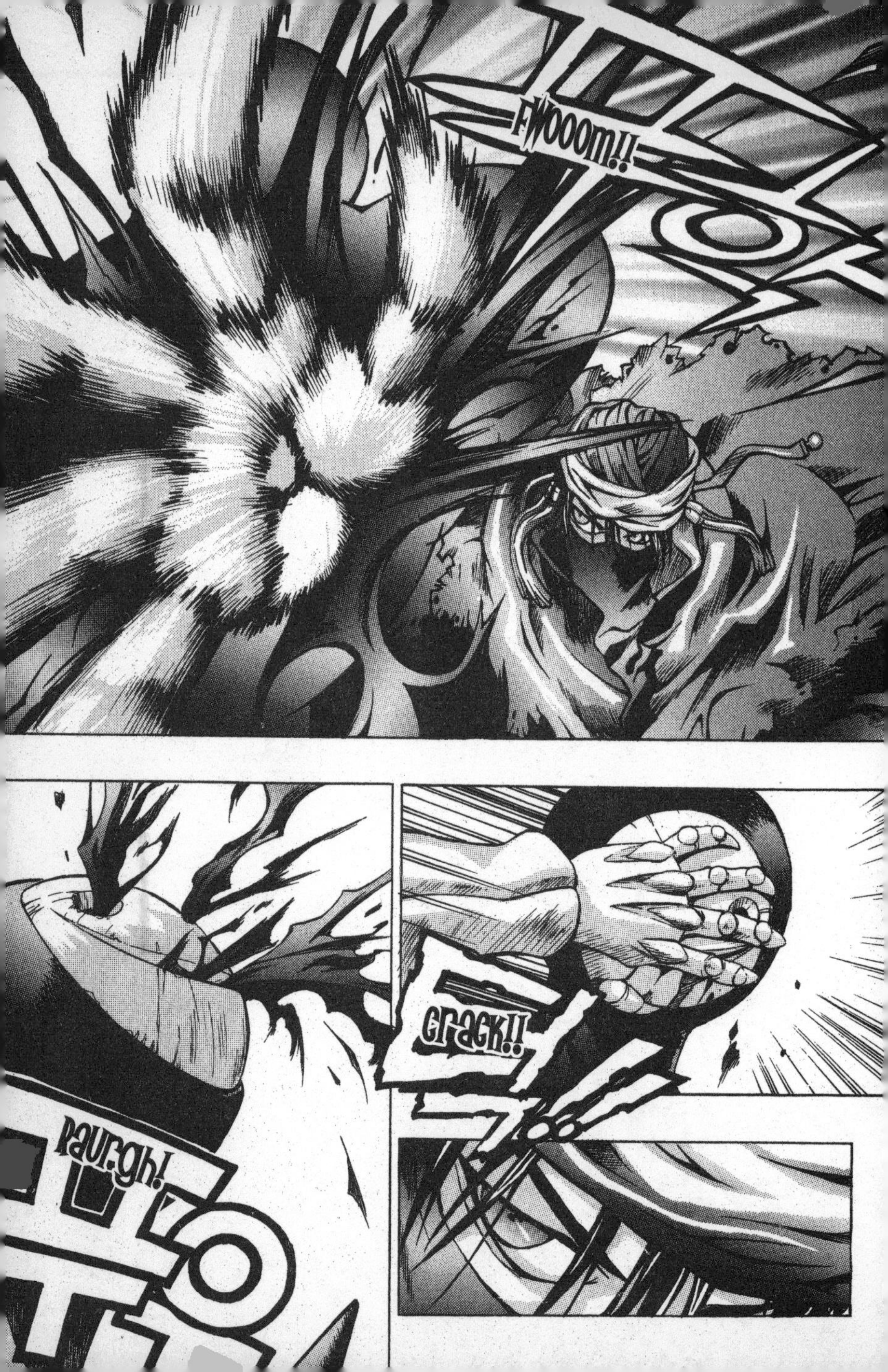
FWOOOM!!
PAURGH!
CRACK!!

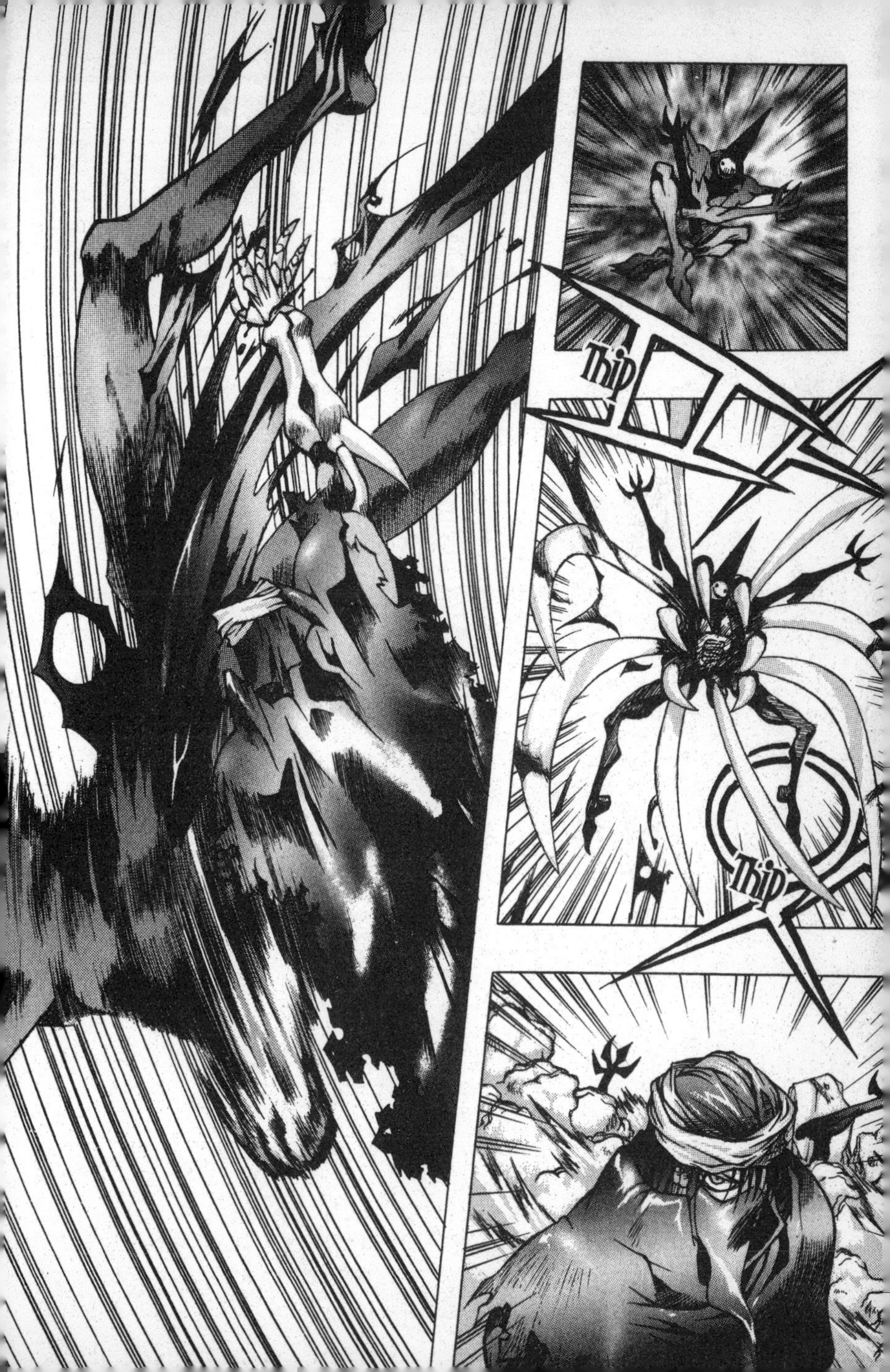
Thip
Thip

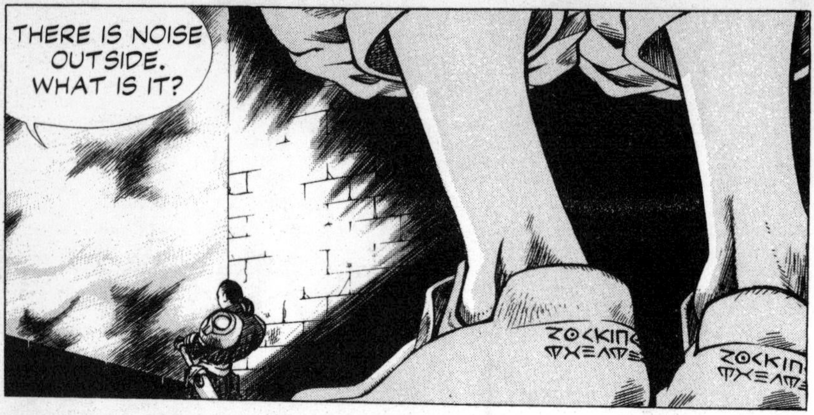
THERE IS NOISE OUTSIDE. WHAT IS IT?
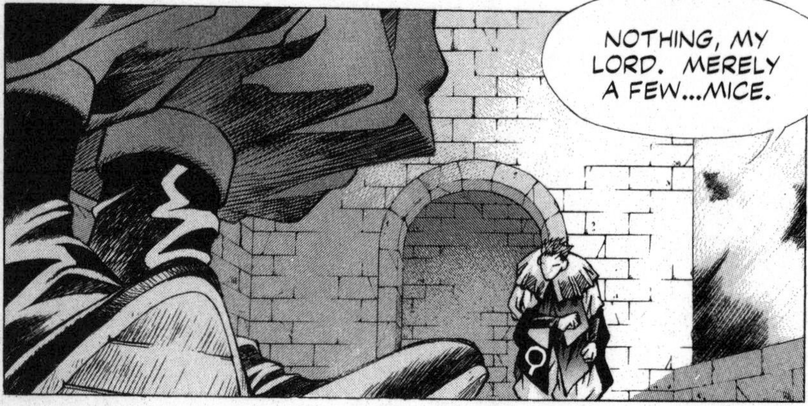
NOTHING, MY LORD. MERELY A FEW...MICE.
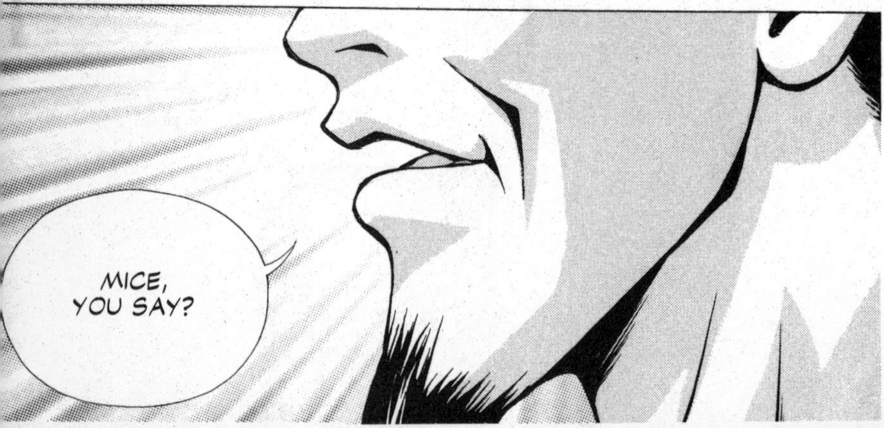
MICE, YOU SAY?

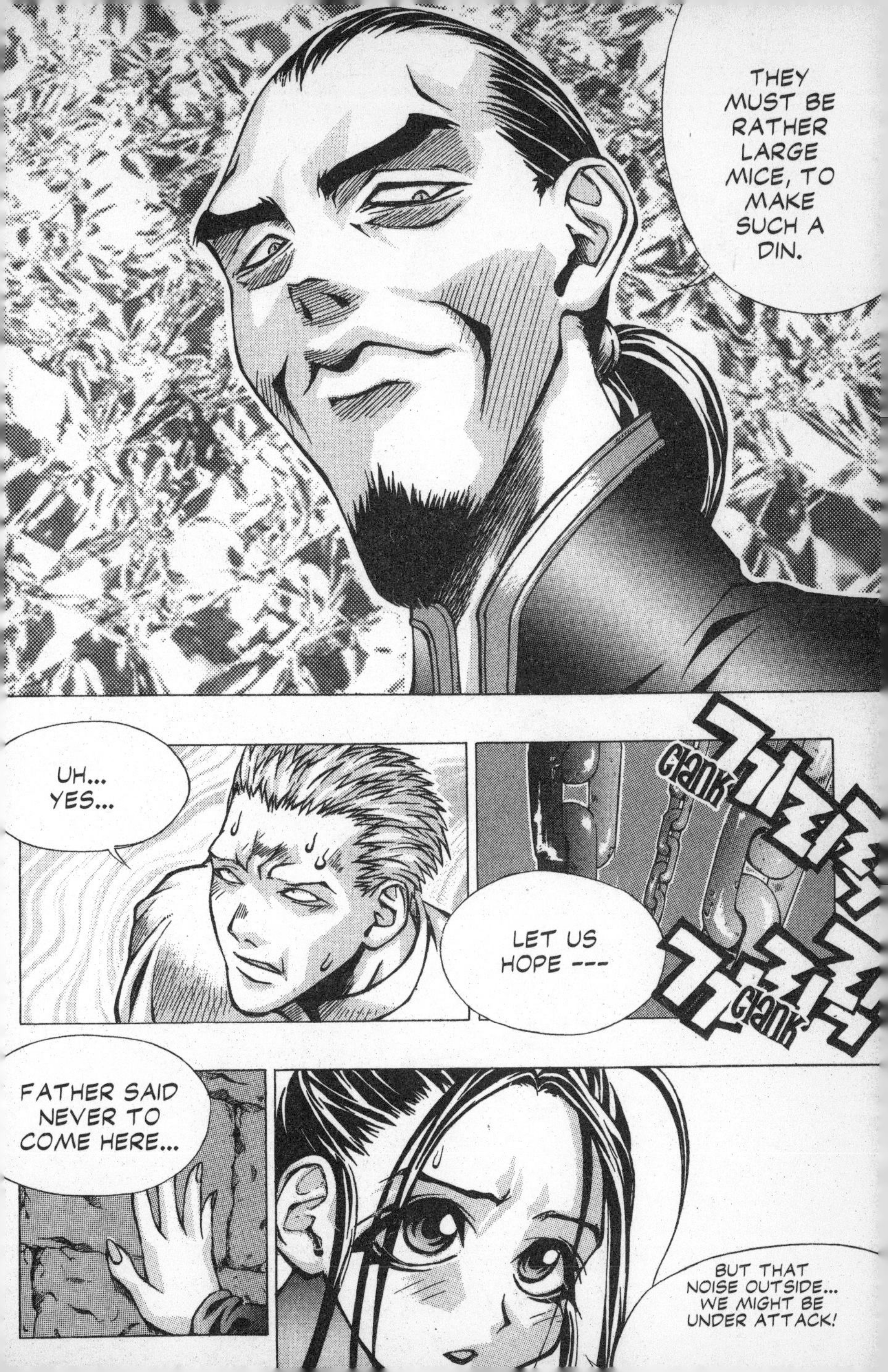
THEY MUST BE RATHER LARGE MICE, TO MAKE SUCH A DIN.
UH... YES...
LET US HOPE ---
CLANK
CLANK
FATHER SAID NEVER TO COME HERE...
BUT THAT NOISE OUTSIDE... WE MIGHT BE UNDER ATTACK!

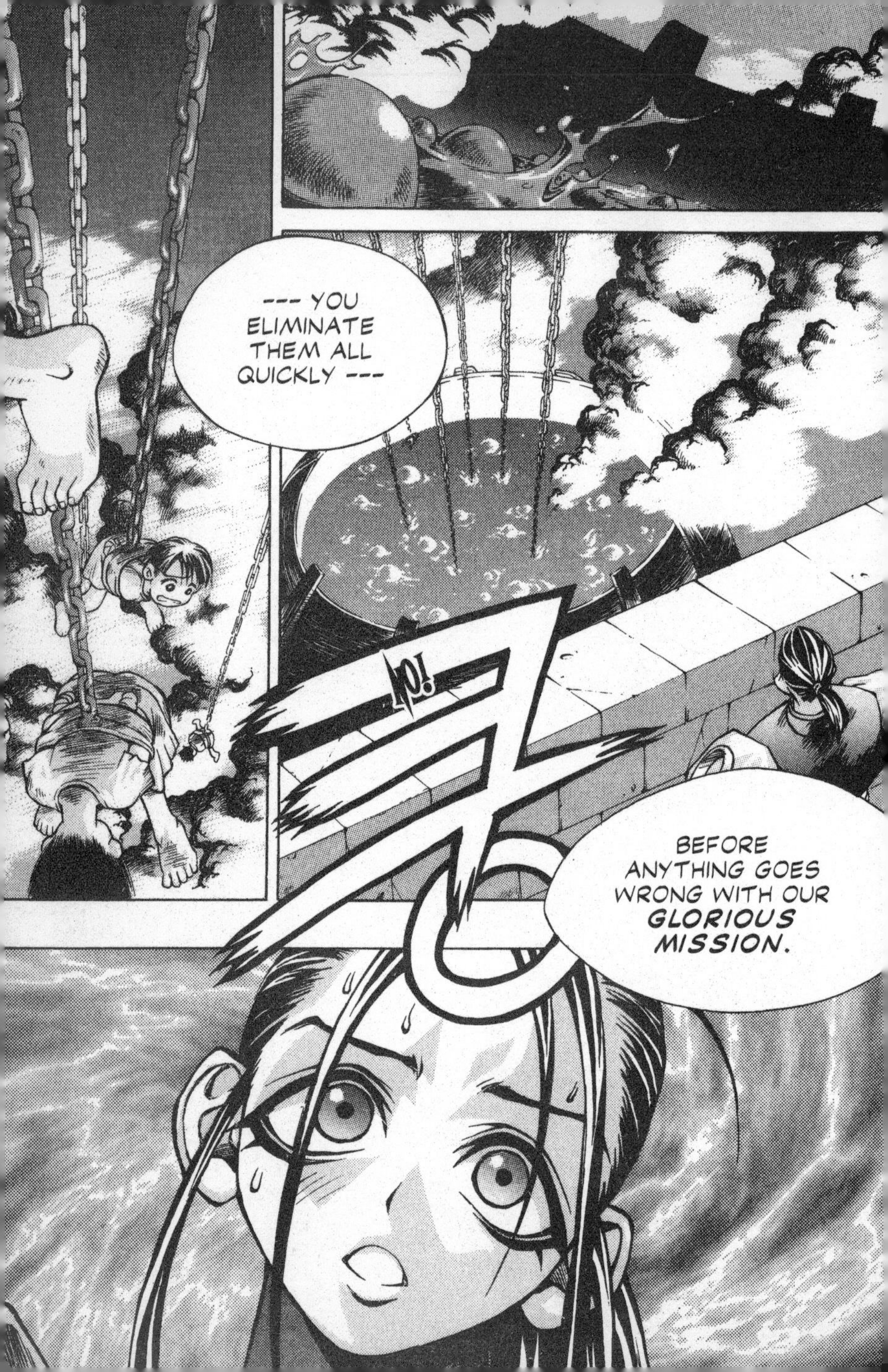
--- YOU ELIMINATE THEM ALL QUICKLY ---
!?!
BEFORE ANYTHING GOES WRONG WITH OUR GLORIOUS MISSION.

RAGNAROK
라그나로크
IN TO THE ABYSS

音樂

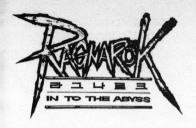

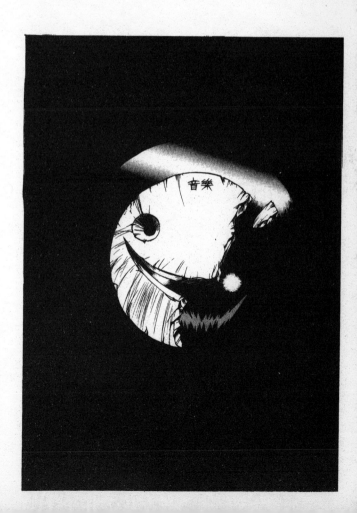

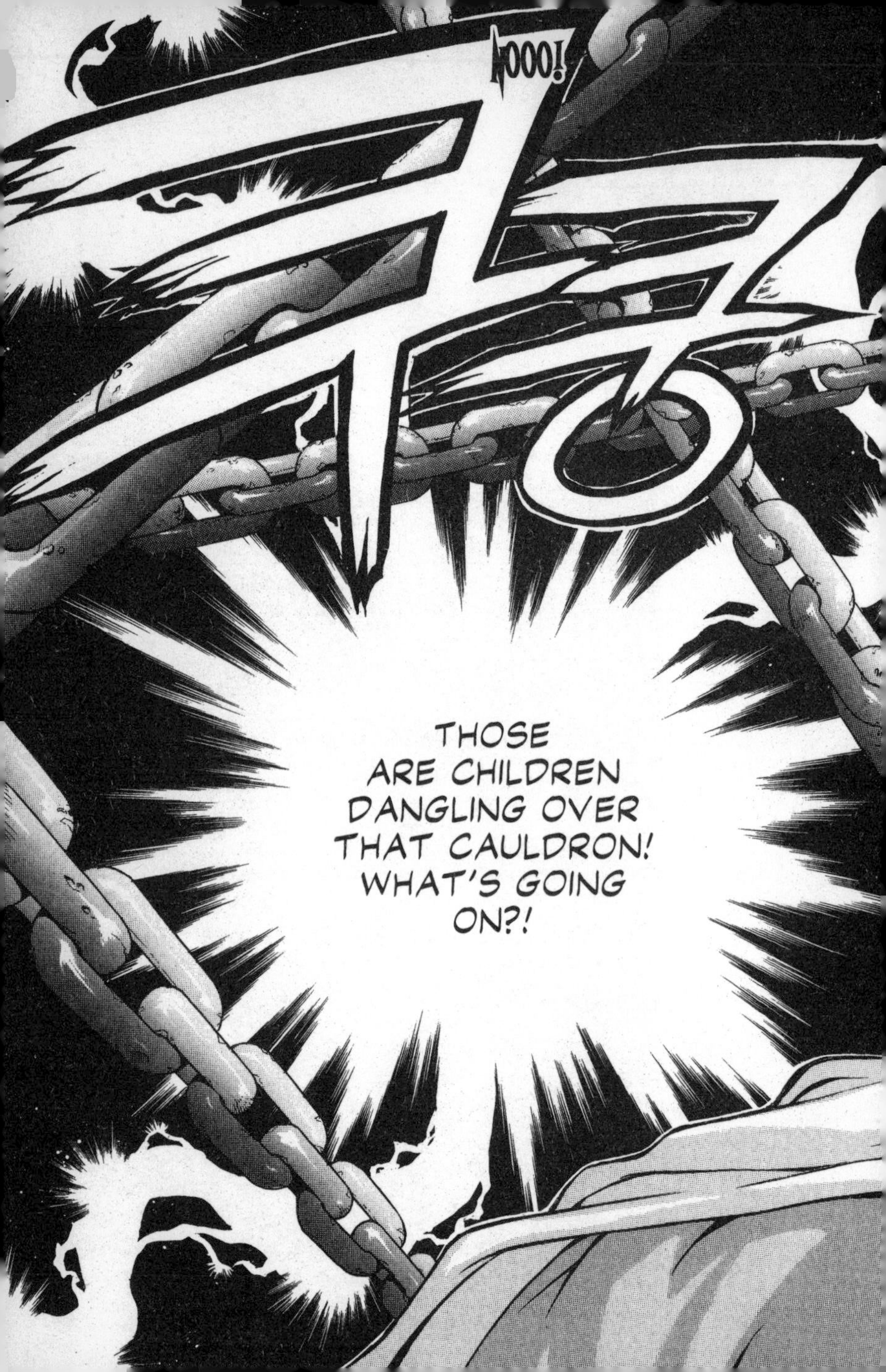
NOOO!
THOSE ARE CHILDREN DANGLING OVER THAT CAULDRON! WHAT'S GOING ON?!

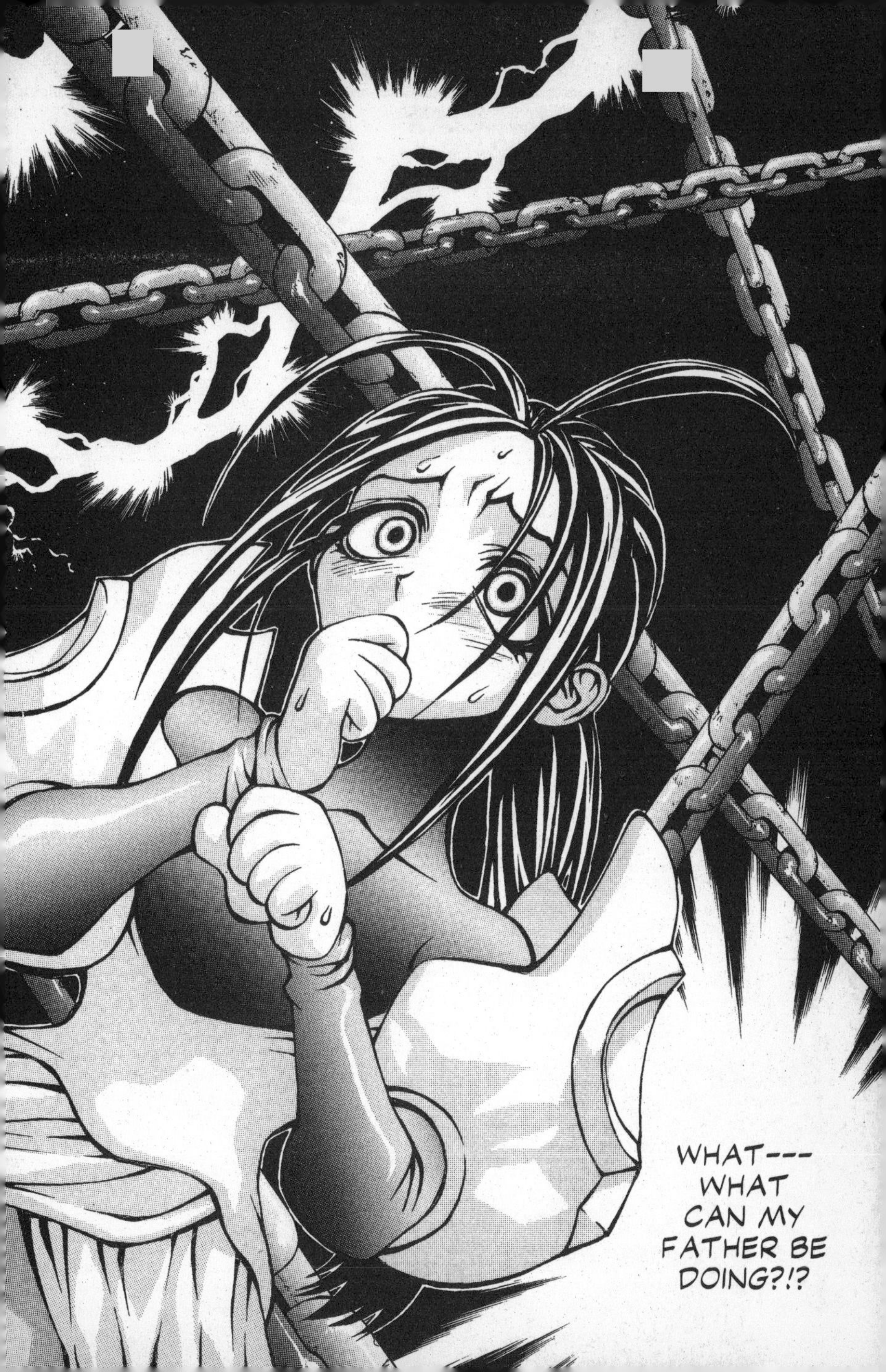
WHAT--- WHAT CAN MY FATHER BE DOING?!?

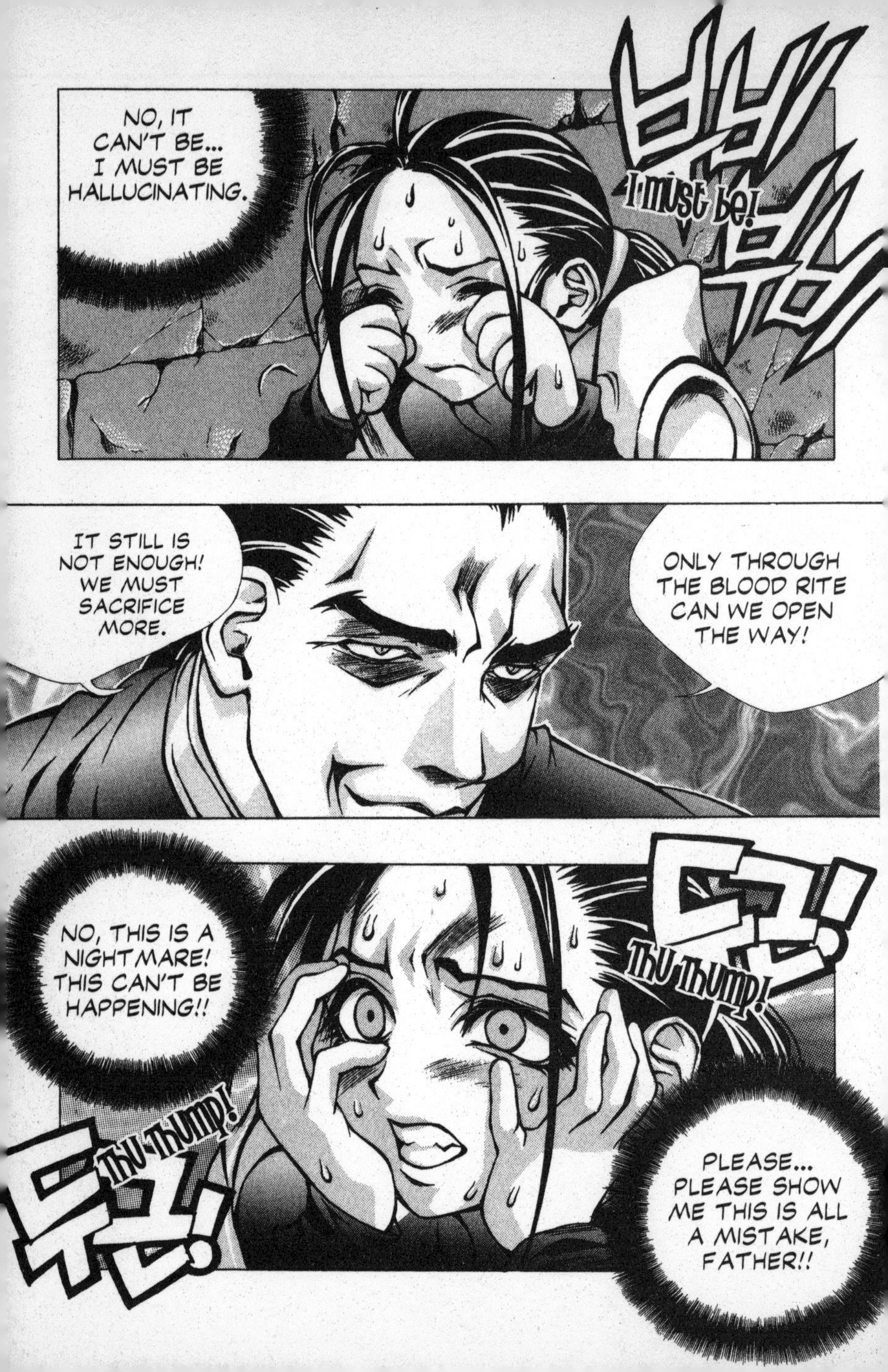
NO, IT CAN'T BE... I MUST BE HALLUCINATING.
I must be!
IT STILL IS NOT ENOUGH! WE MUST SACRIFICE MORE.
ONLY THROUGH THE BLOOD RITE CAN WE OPEN THE WAY!
NO, THIS IS A NIGHTMARE! THIS CAN'T BE HAPPENING!!
THU THUMP!
THU THUMP!
PLEASE... PLEASE SHOW ME THIS IS ALL A MISTAKE, FATHER!!

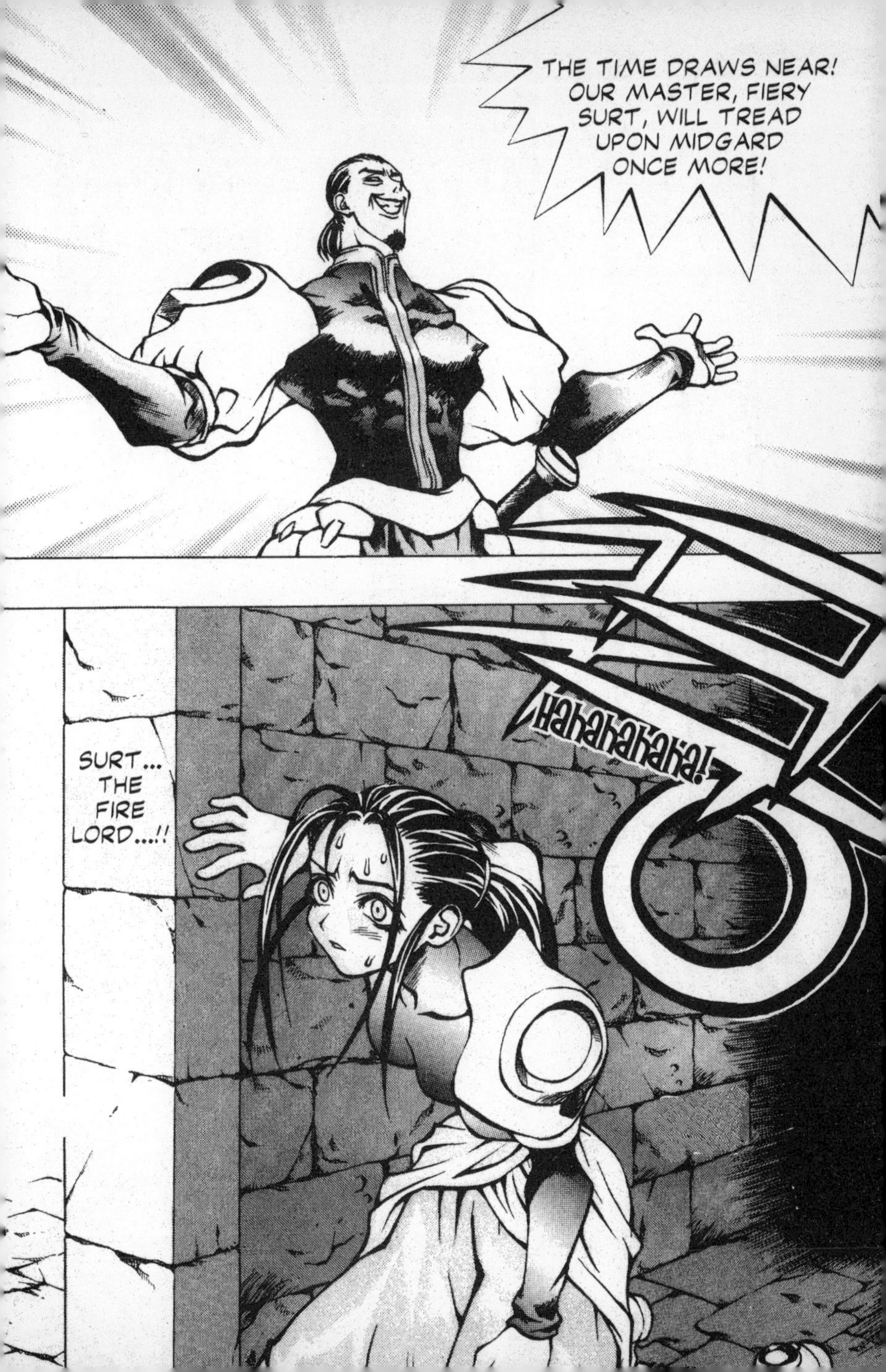

THE TIME DRAWS NEAR! OUR MASTER, FIERY SURT, WILL TREAD UPON MIDGARD ONCE MORE!
SURT... THE FIRE LORD...!!
HAHAHAHAHAHA!

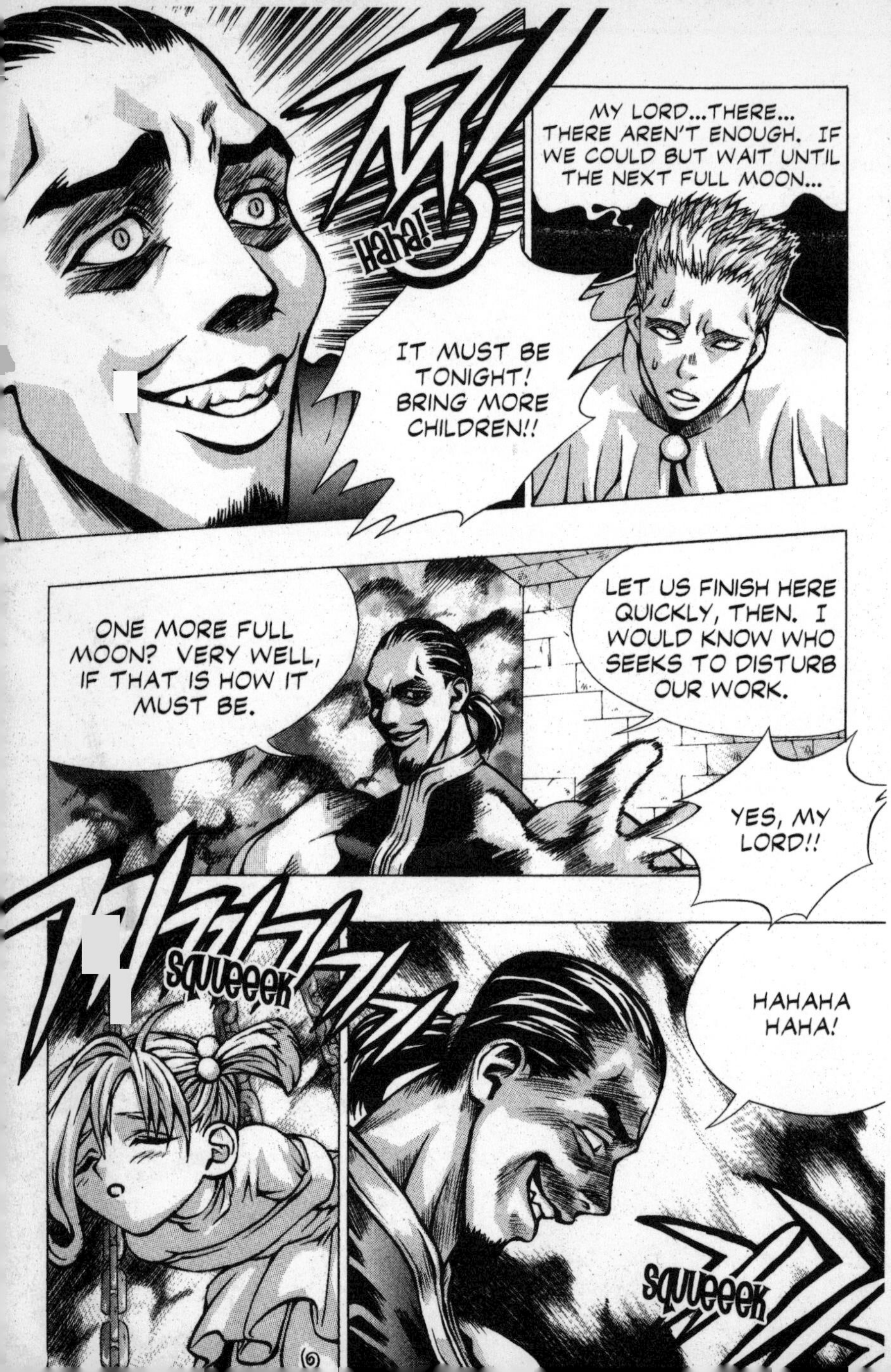
HAHA!
IT MUST BE TONIGHT! BRING MORE CHILDREN!!
MY LORD...THERE... THERE AREN'T ENOUGH. IF WE COULD BUT WAIT UNTIL THE NEXT FULL MOON...
ONE MORE FULL MOON? VERY WELL, IF THAT IS HOW IT MUST BE.
LET US FINISH HERE QUICKLY, THEN. I WOULD KNOW WHO SEEKS TO DISTURB OUR WORK.
YES, MY LORD!!
SQUEEEEK
HAHAHA HAHA!
SQUEEEEK

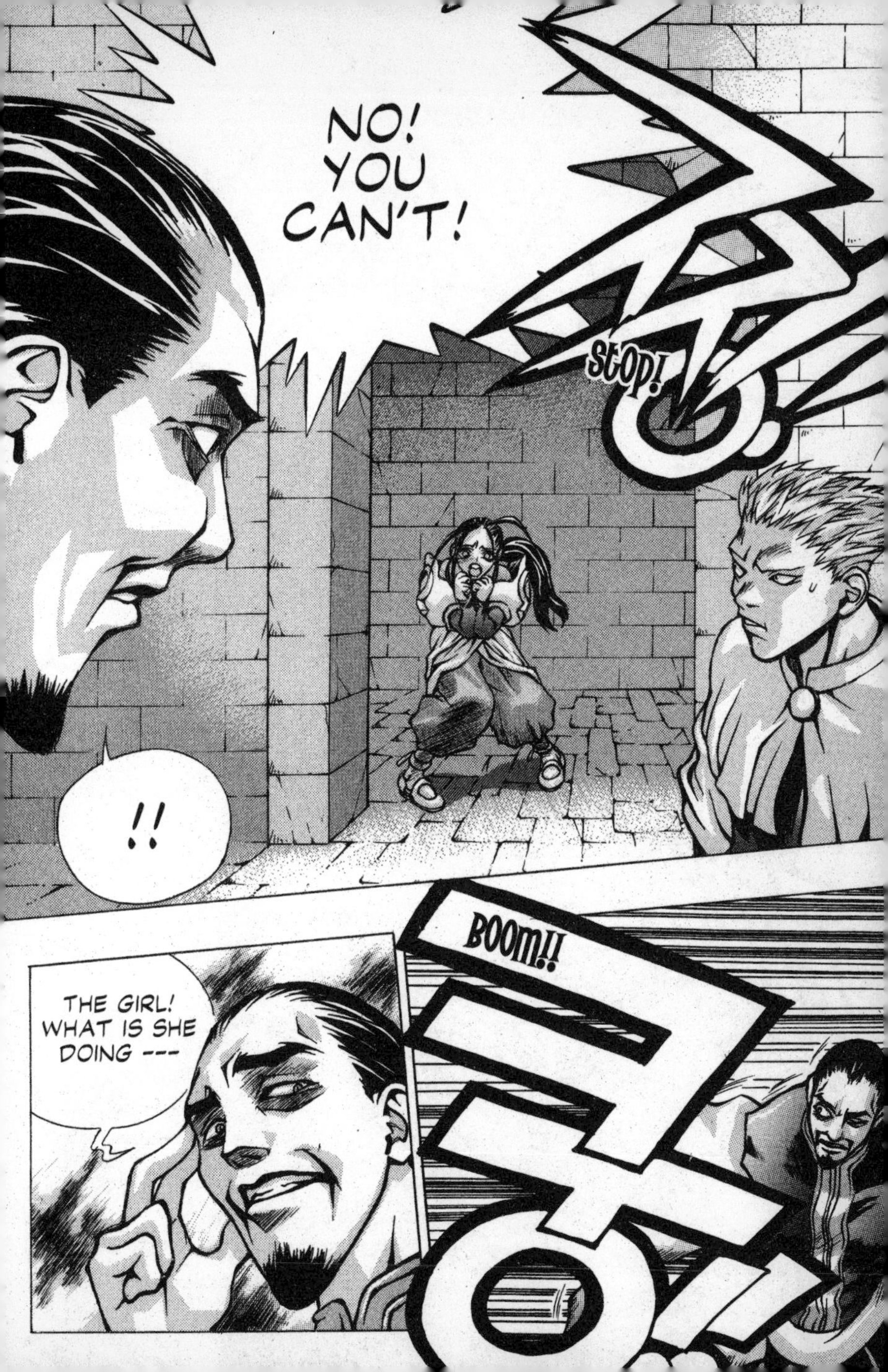
NO! YOU CAN'T!
STOP!
!!
THE GIRL! WHAT IS SHE DOING ---
BOOM!!

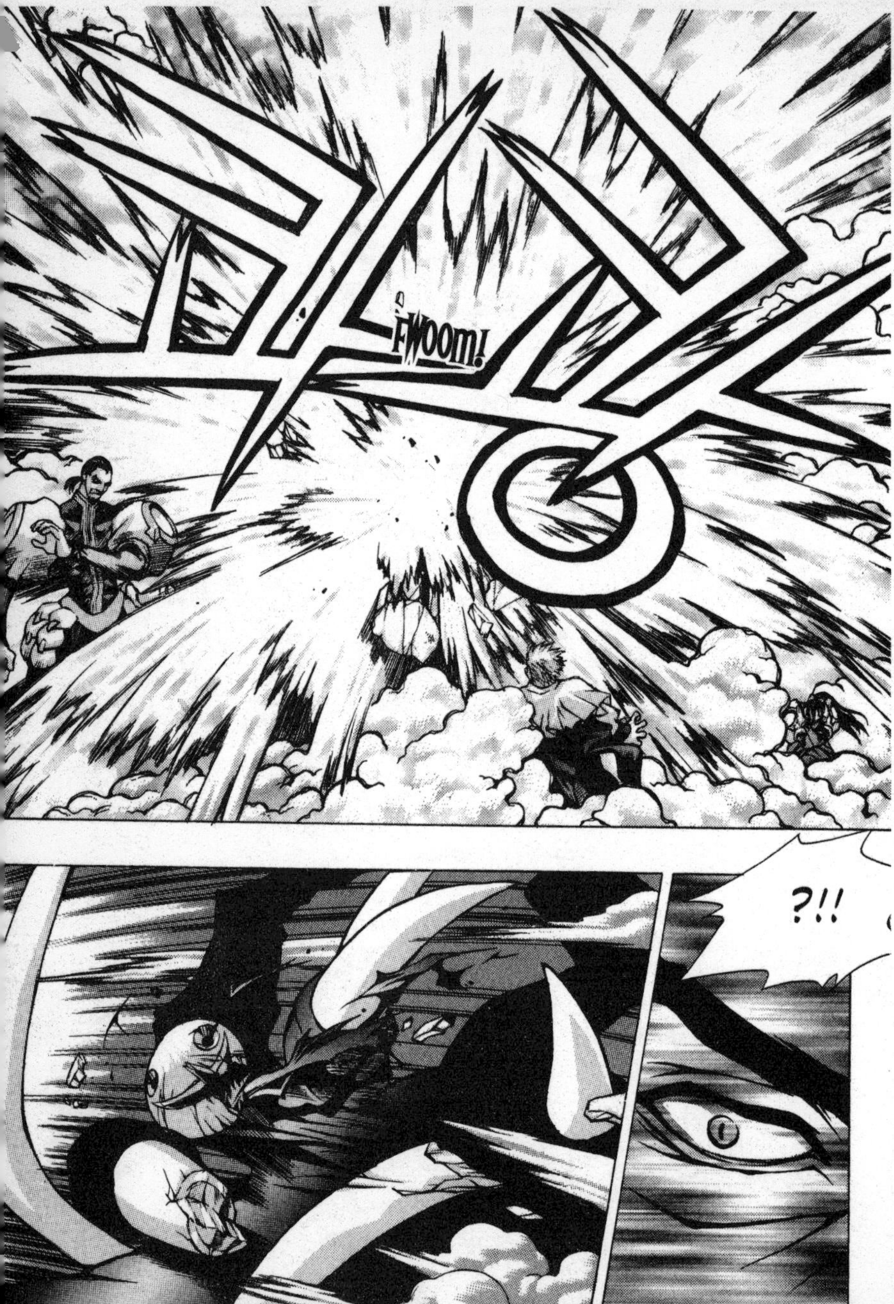
FWOOM!
?!!

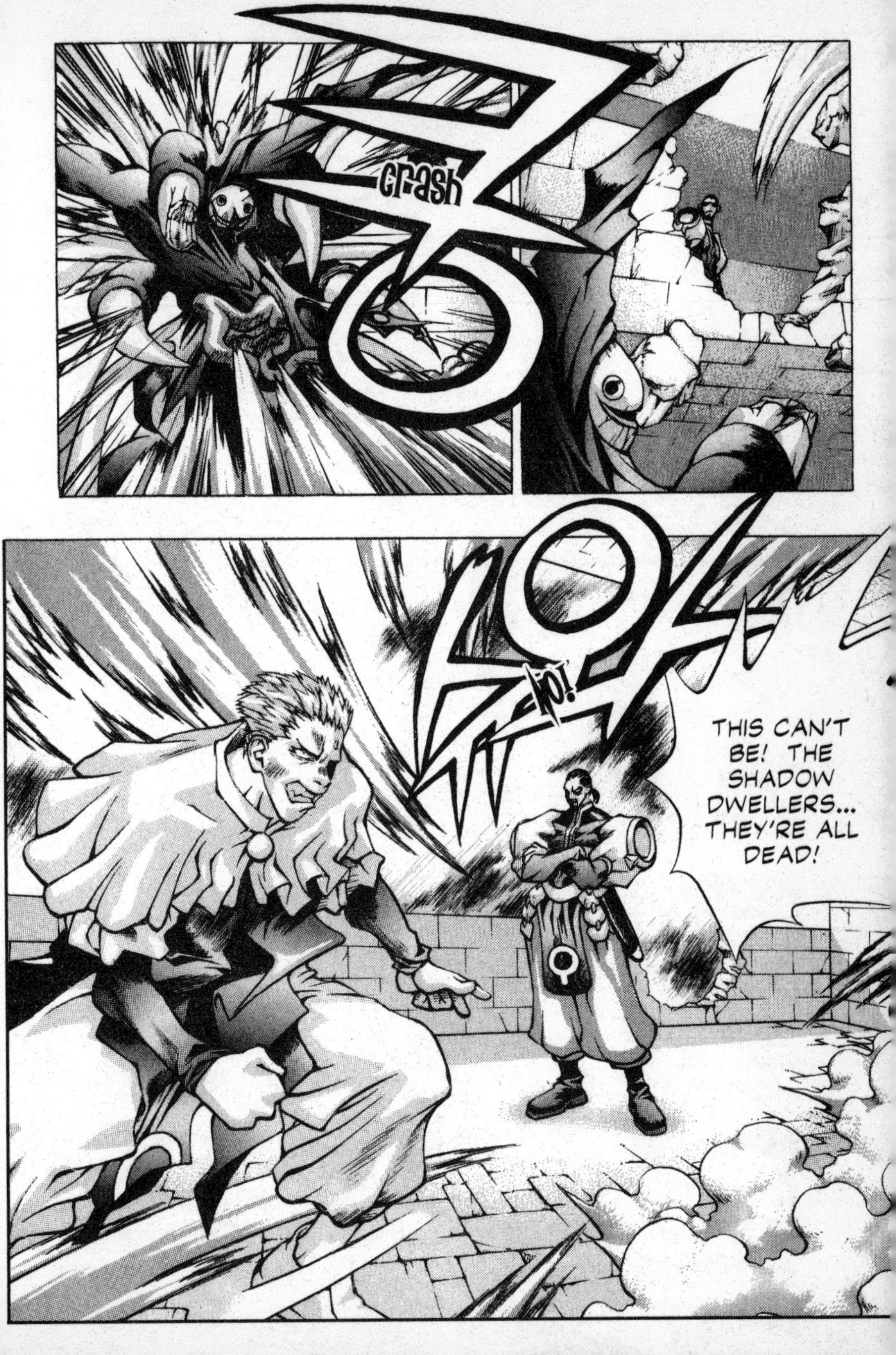
crash
KO!
THIS CAN'T BE! THE SHADOW DWELLERS... THEY'RE ALL DEAD!

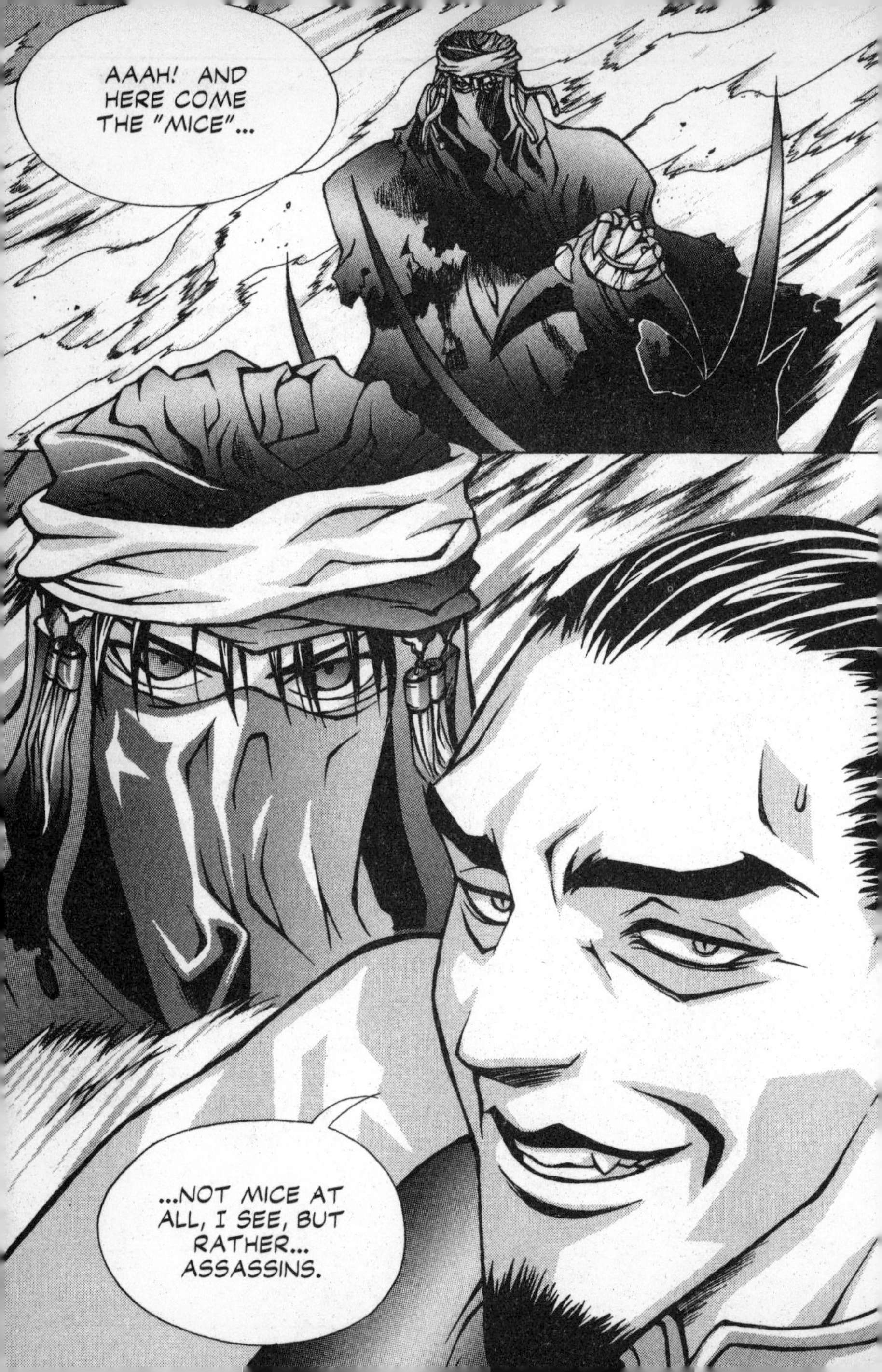
AAAH! AND HERE COME THE "MICE"...
...NOT MICE AT ALL, I SEE, BUT RATHER... ASSASSINS.

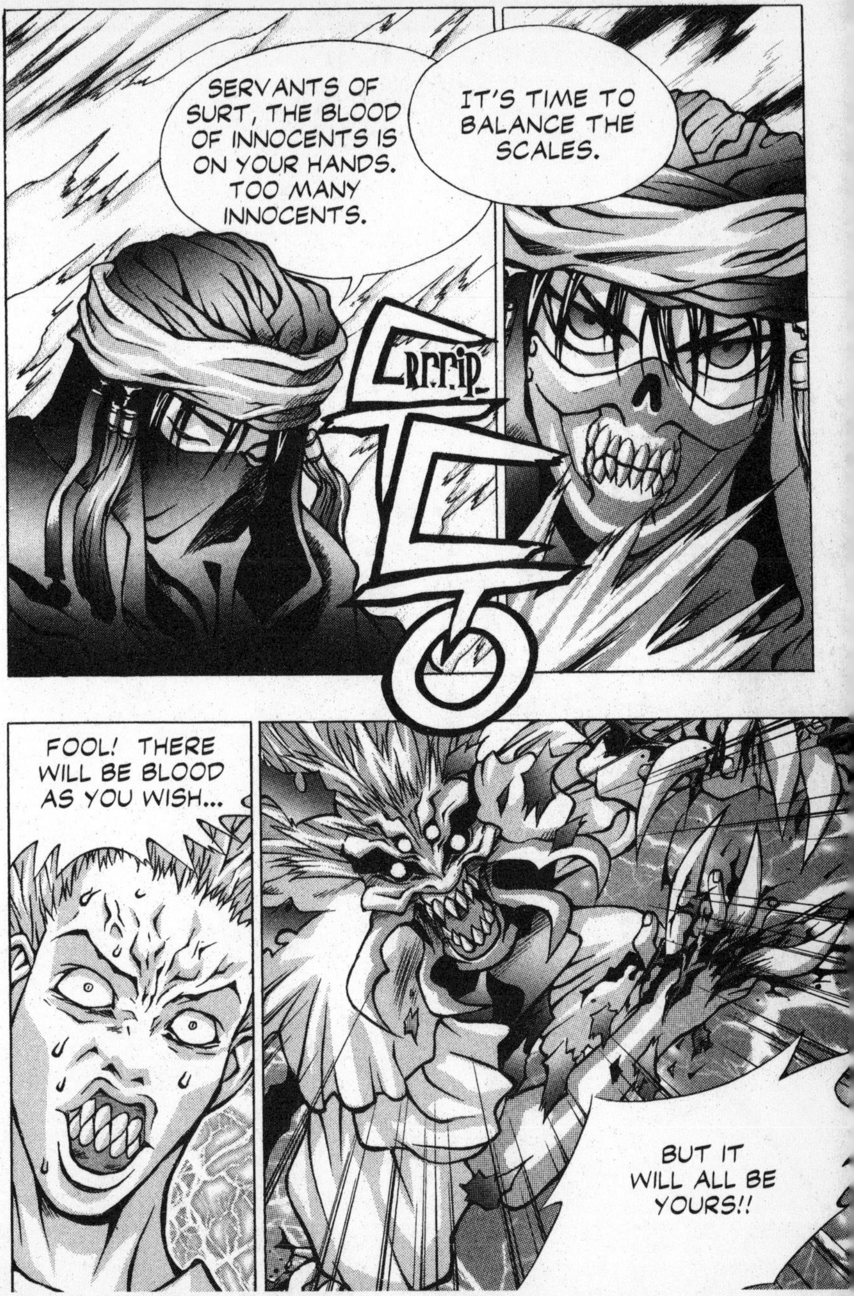
SERVANTS OF SURT, THE BLOOD OF INNOCENTS IS ON YOUR HANDS. TOO MANY INNOCENTS.
IT'S TIME TO BALANCE THE SCALES.
CRRRIP
FOOL! THERE WILL BE BLOOD AS YOU WISH...
BUT IT WILL ALL BE YOURS!!

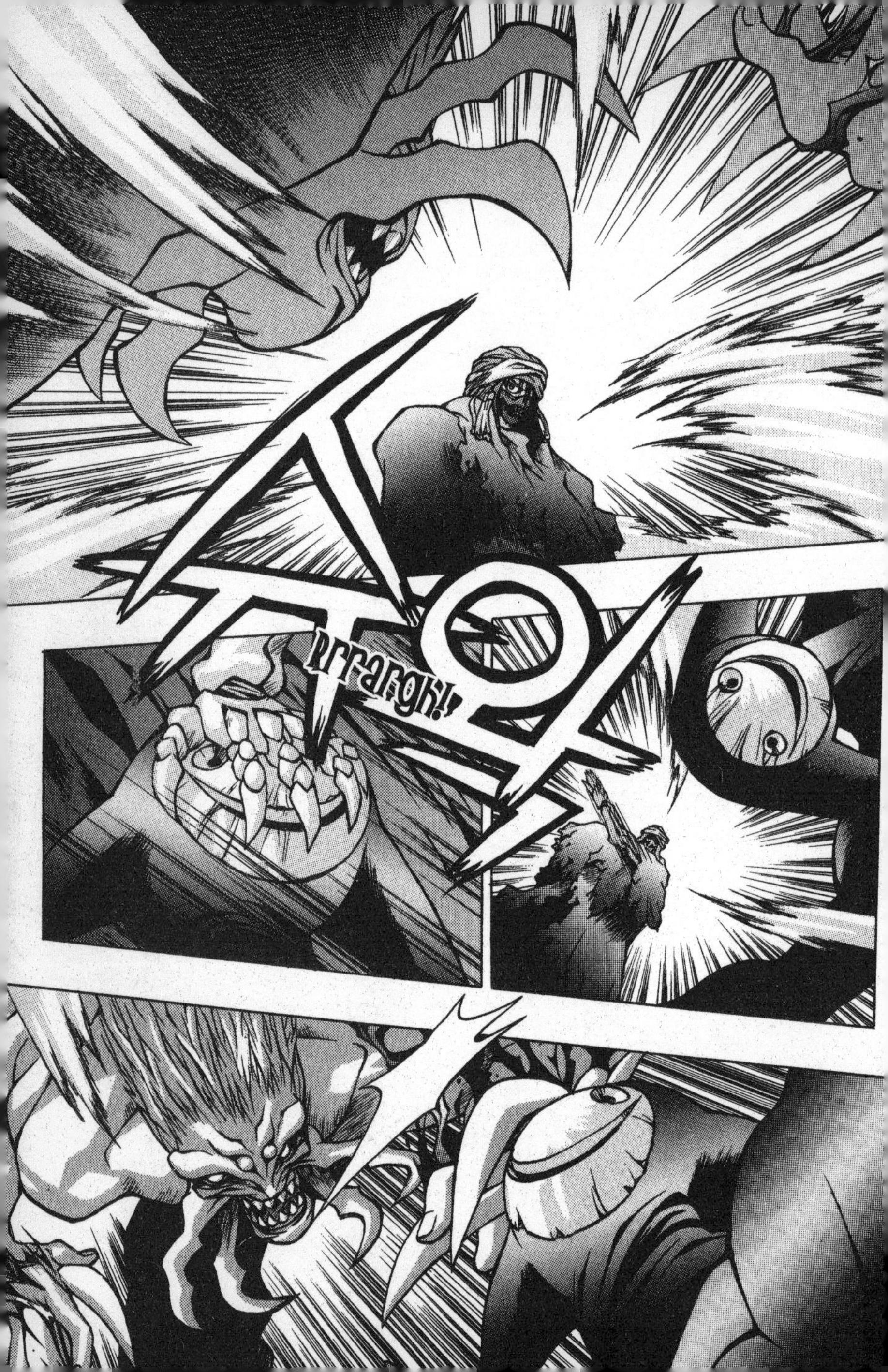
Rrrargh!

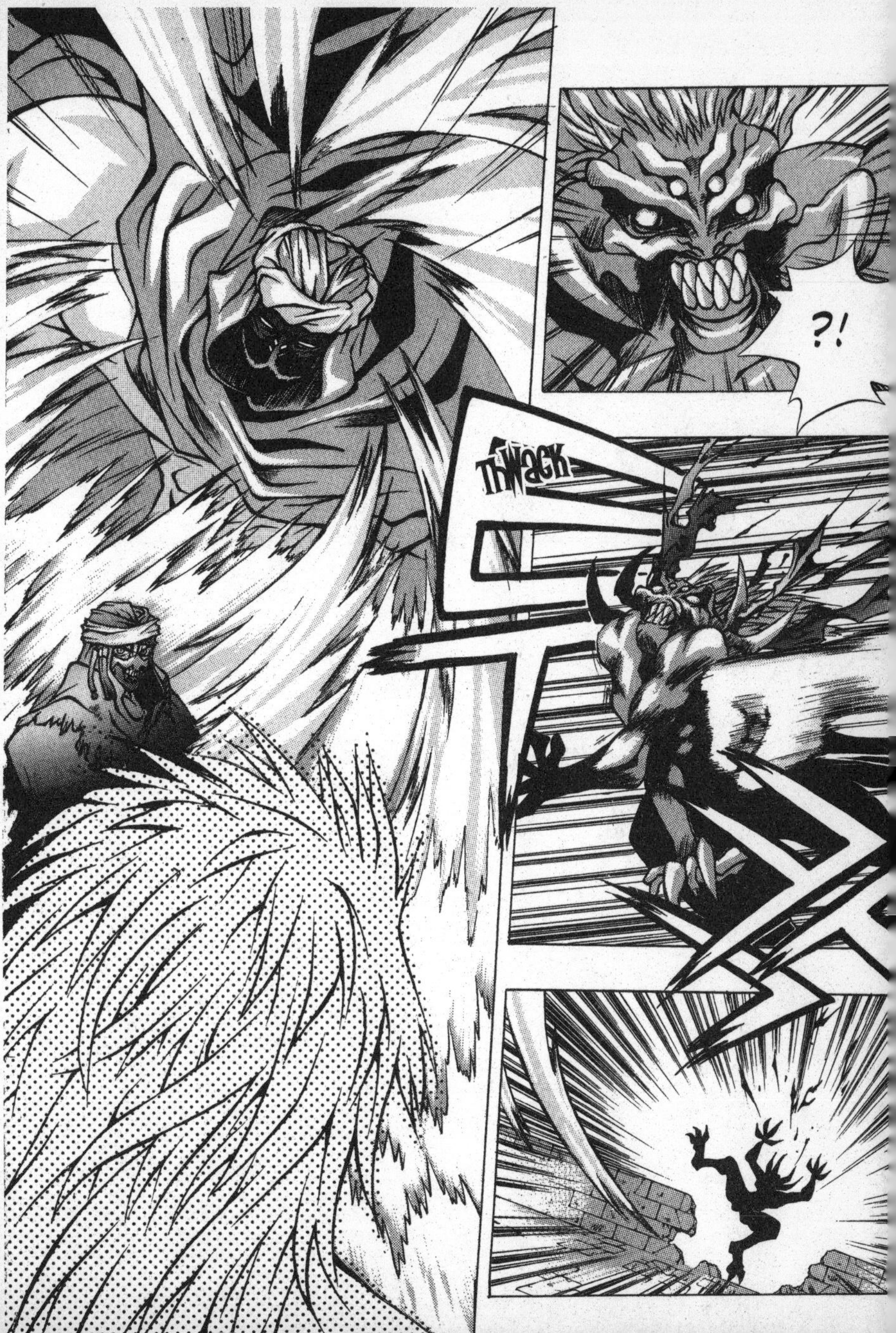
?!
THWACK

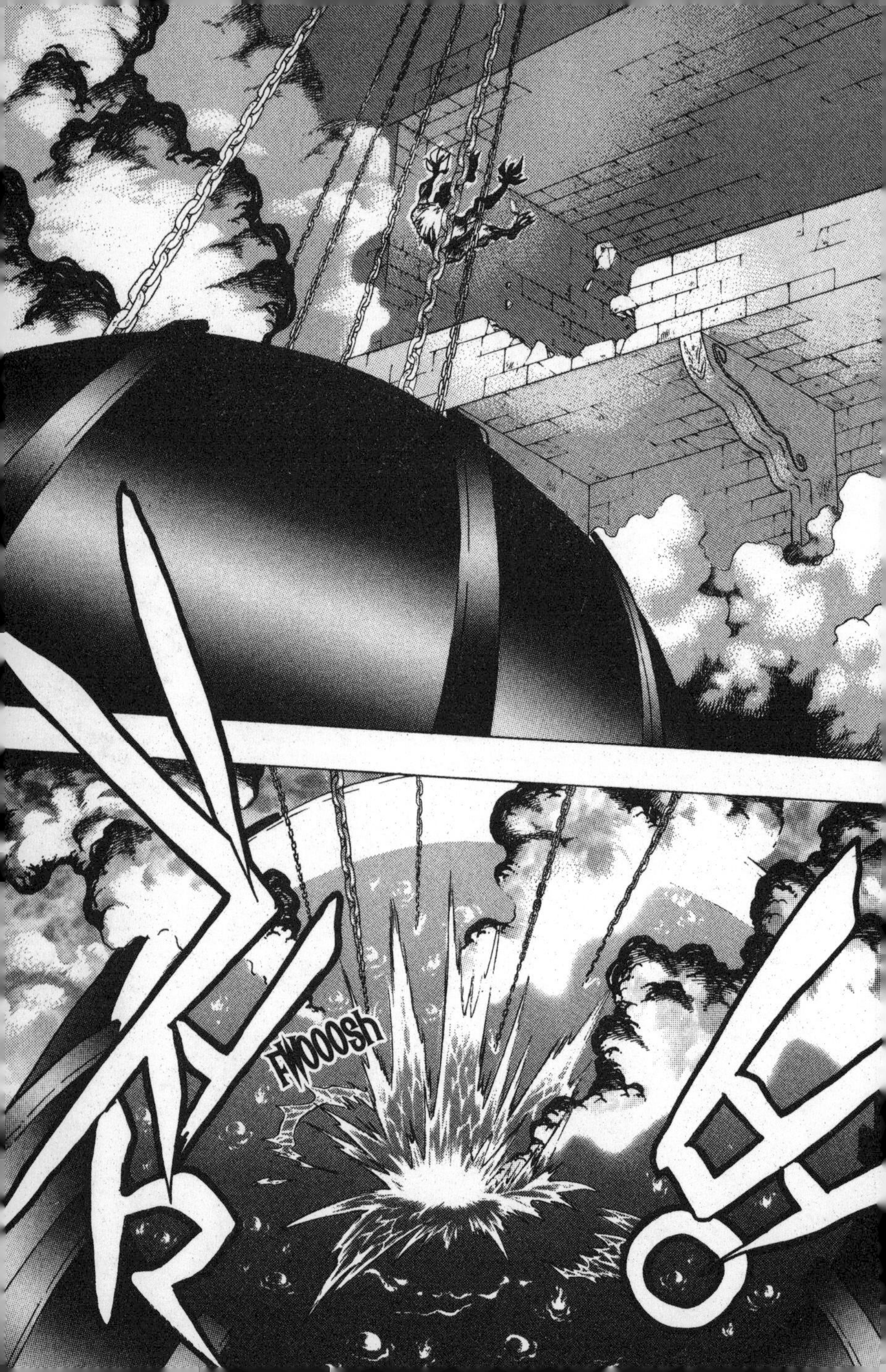
FWOOOSH

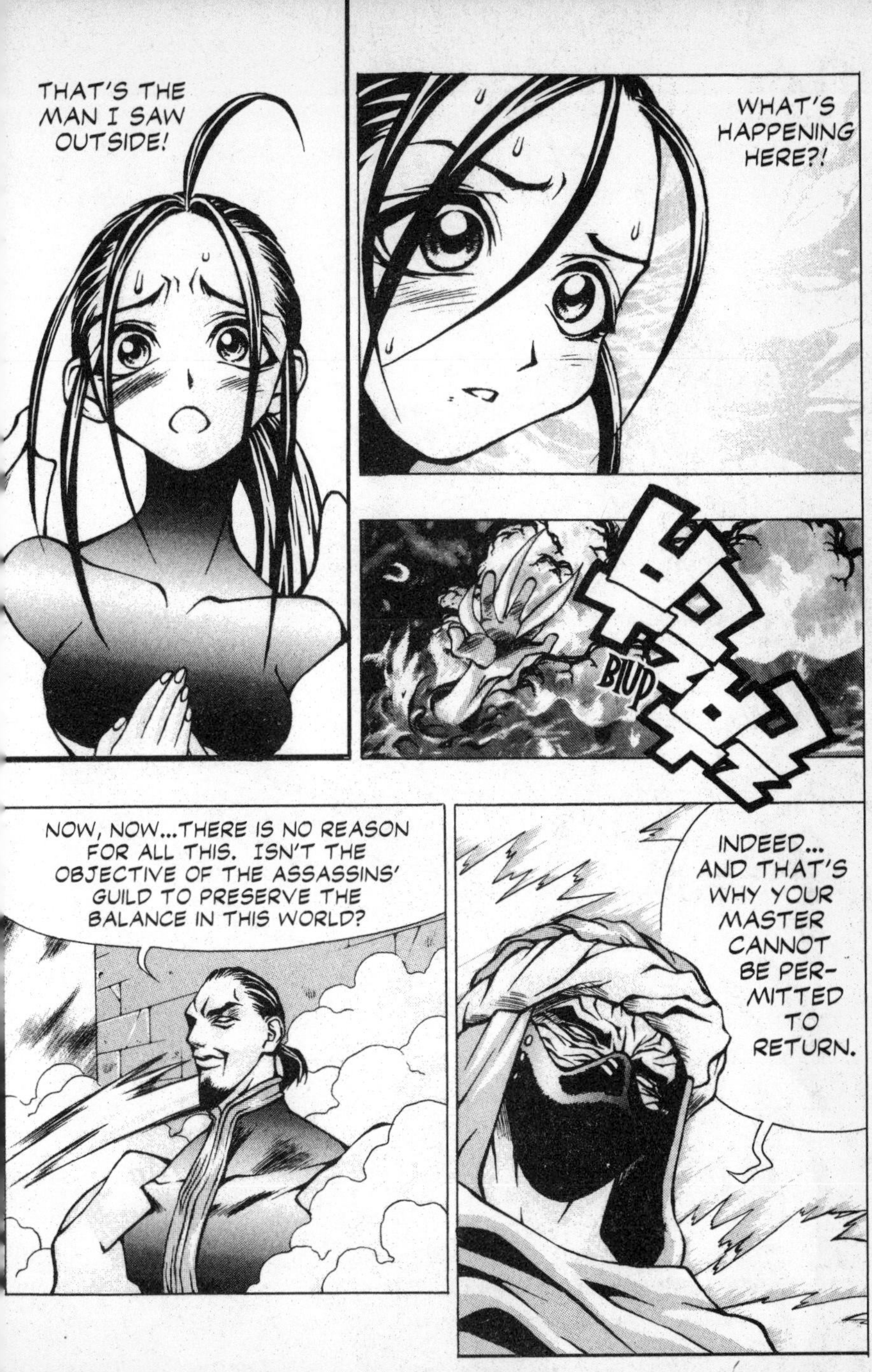
THAT'S THE MAN I SAW OUTSIDE!
WHAT'S HAPPENING HERE?!
BLUP
NOW, NOW...THERE IS NO REASON FOR ALL THIS. ISN'T THE OBJECTIVE OF THE ASSASSINS' GUILD TO PRESERVE THE BALANCE IN THIS WORLD?
INDEED... AND THAT'S WHY YOUR MASTER CANNOT BE PER-MITTED TO RETURN.

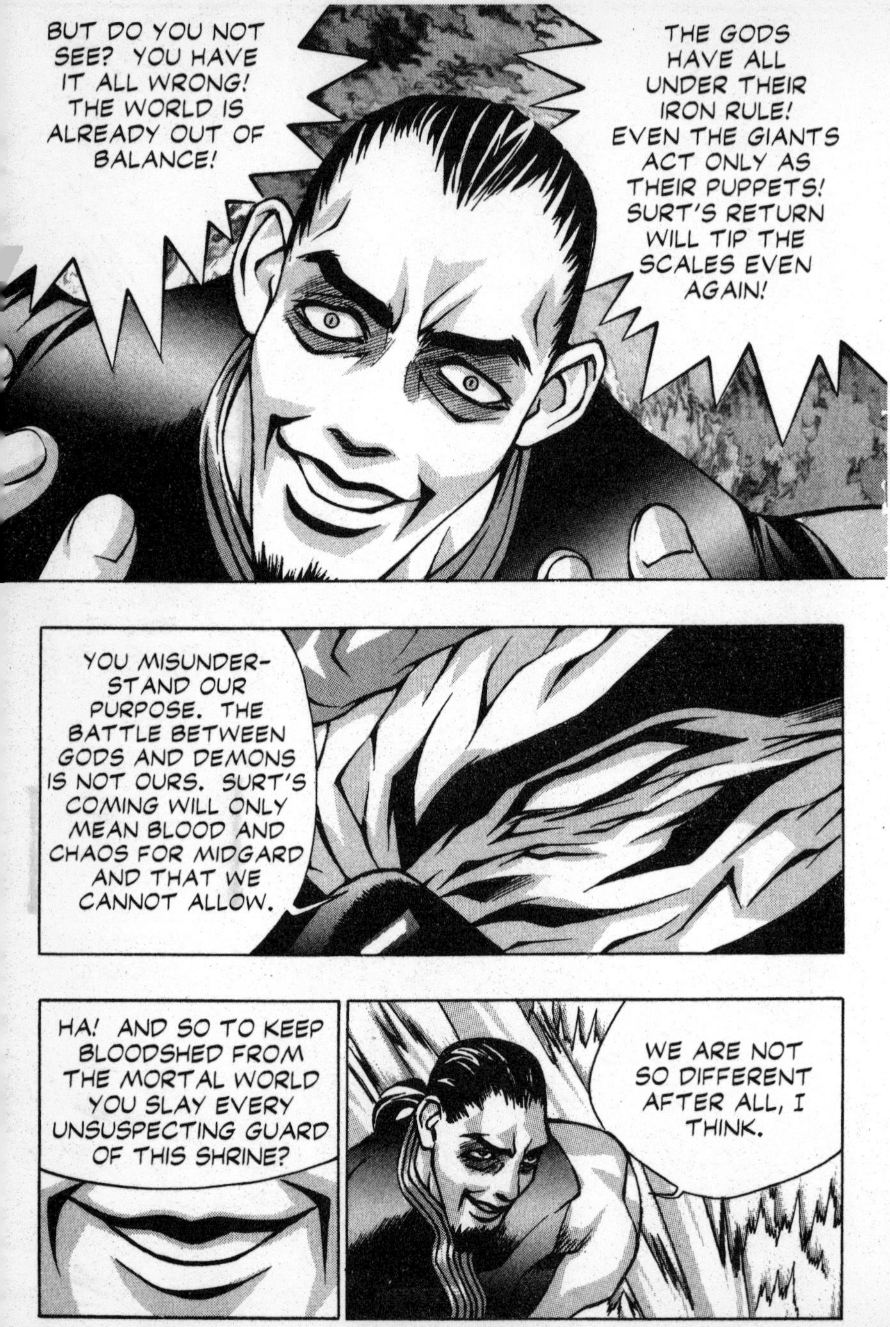
BUT DO YOU NOT SEE? YOU HAVE IT ALL WRONG! THE WORLD IS ALREADY OUT OF BALANCE!
THE GODS HAVE ALL UNDER THEIR IRON RULE! EVEN THE GIANTS ACT ONLY AS THEIR PUPPETS! SURT'S RETURN WILL TIP THE SCALES EVEN AGAIN!
YOU MISUNDER-STAND OUR PURPOSE. THE BATTLE BETWEEN GODS AND DEMONS IS NOT OURS. SURT'S COMING WILL ONLY MEAN BLOOD AND CHAOS FOR MIDGARD AND THAT WE CANNOT ALLOW.
HA! AND SO TO KEEP BLOODSHED FROM THE MORTAL WORLD YOU SLAY EVERY UNSUSPECTING GUARD OF THIS SHRINE?
WE ARE NOT SO DIFFERENT AFTER ALL, I THINK.

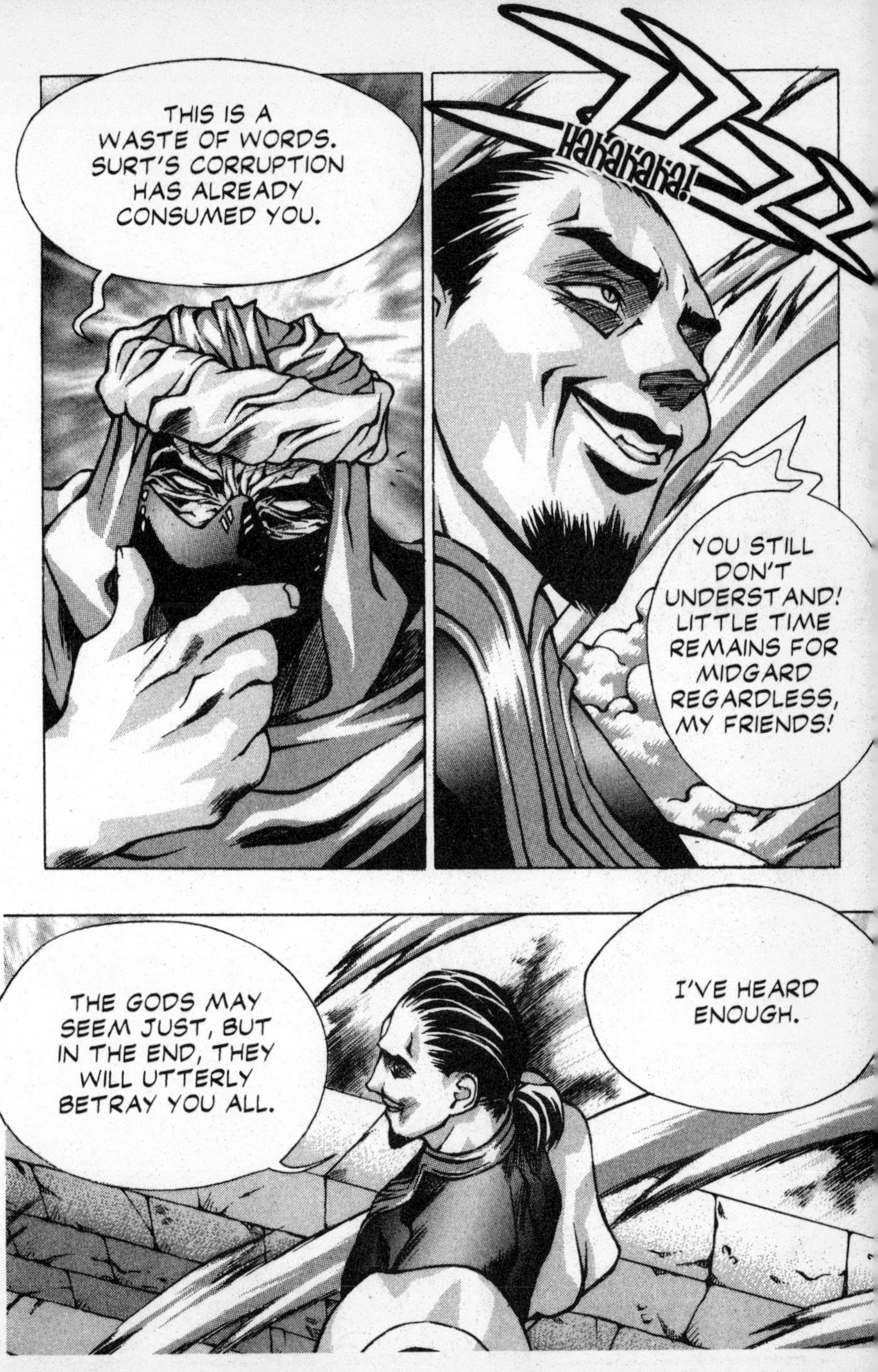
THIS IS A WASTE OF WORDS. SURT'S CORRUPTION HAS ALREADY CONSUMED YOU.
HAHAHAHA!
YOU STILL DON'T UNDERSTAND! LITTLE TIME REMAINS FOR MIDGARD REGARDLESS, MY FRIENDS!
THE GODS MAY SEEM JUST, BUT IN THE END, THEY WILL UTTERLY BETRAY YOU ALL.
I'VE HEARD ENOUGH.

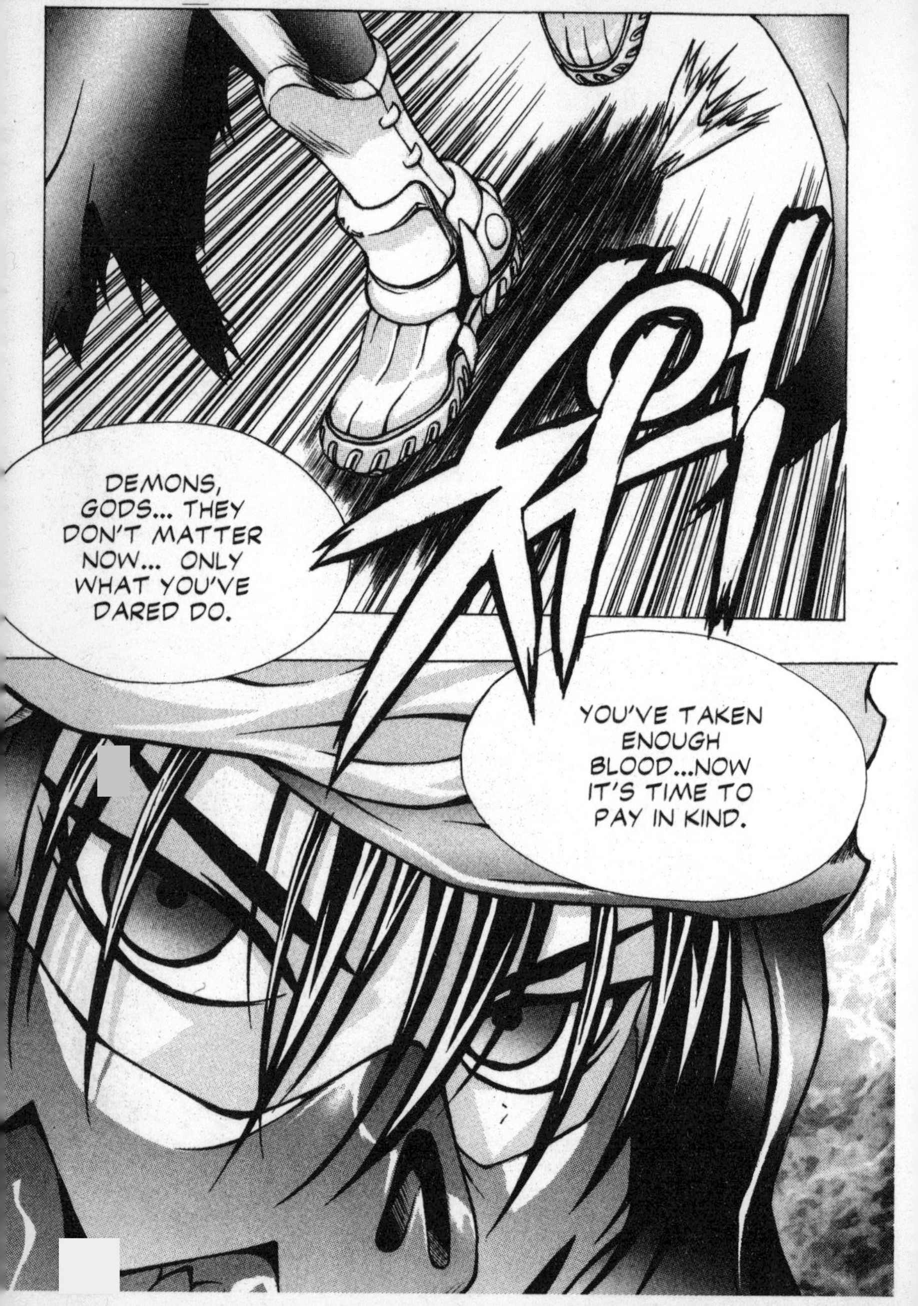
DEMONS, GODS... THEY DON'T MATTER NOW... ONLY WHAT YOU'VE DARED DO.
YOU'VE TAKEN ENOUGH BLOOD...NOW IT'S TIME TO PAY IN KIND.

RAGNAROK

라그나로크

IN TO THE ABYSS

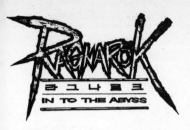

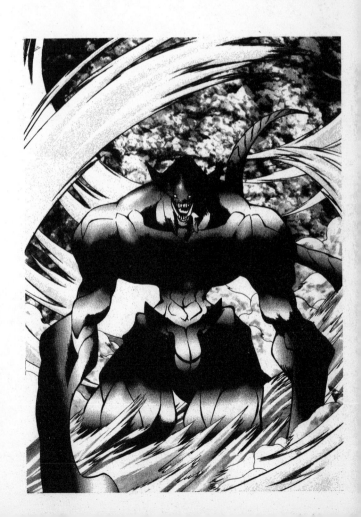

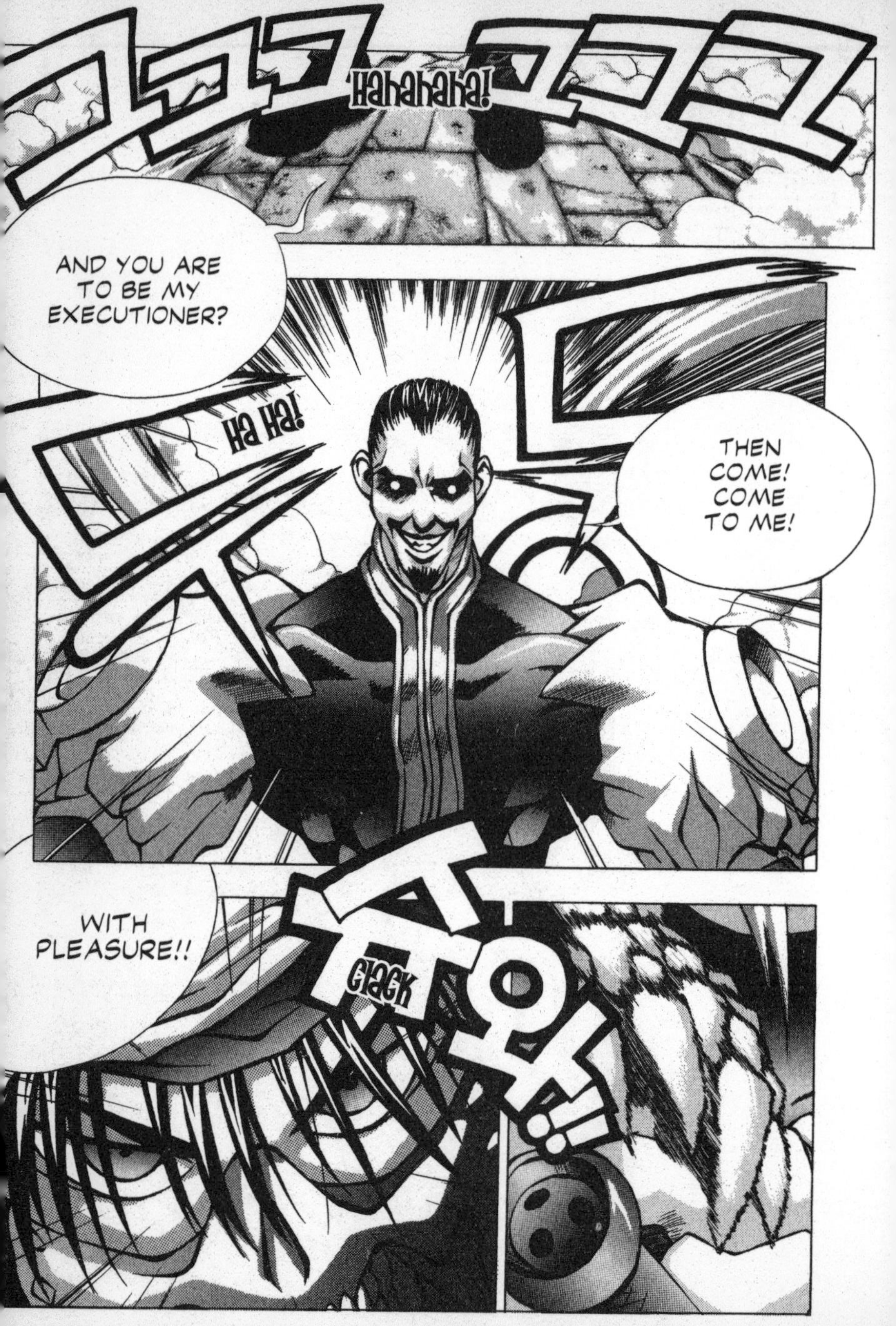
HAHAHAHA!
AND YOU ARE TO BE MY EXECUTIONER?
HA HA!
THEN COME! COME TO ME!
WITH PLEASURE!!
CLACK

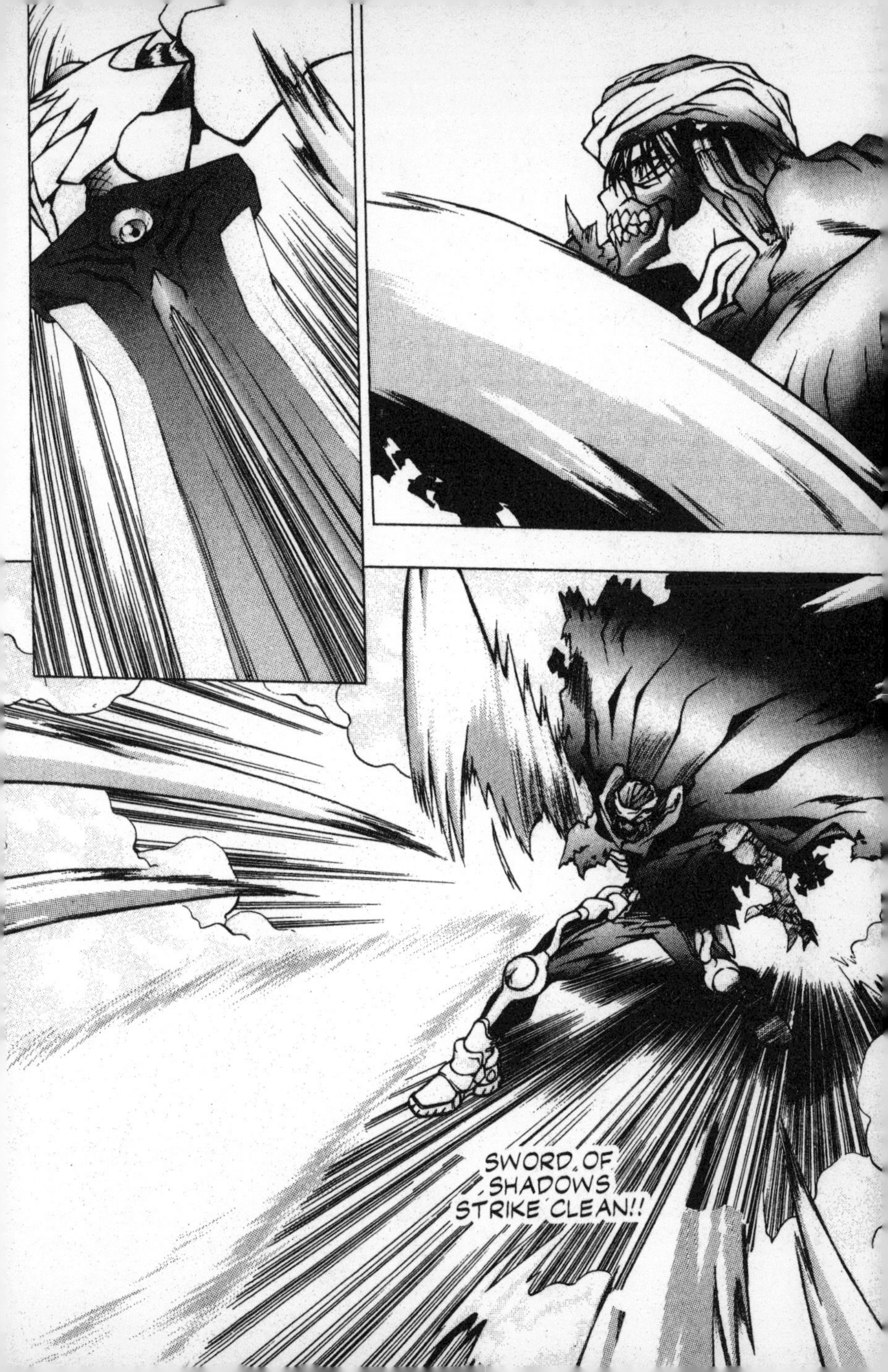
SWORD OF SHADOWS STRIKE CLEAN!!

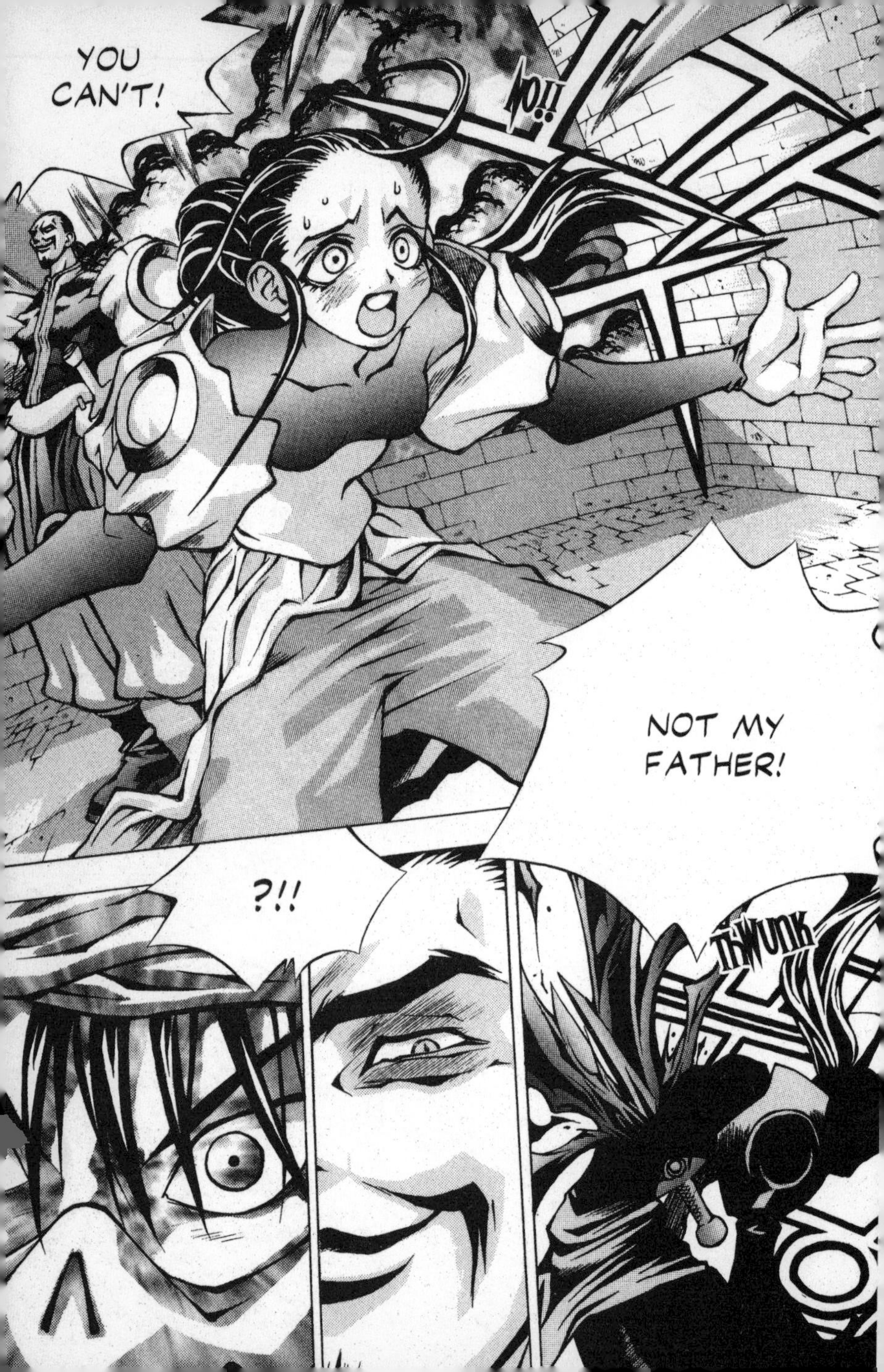
YOU CAN'T!
NO!!
NOT MY FATHER!
?!!
THWUNK

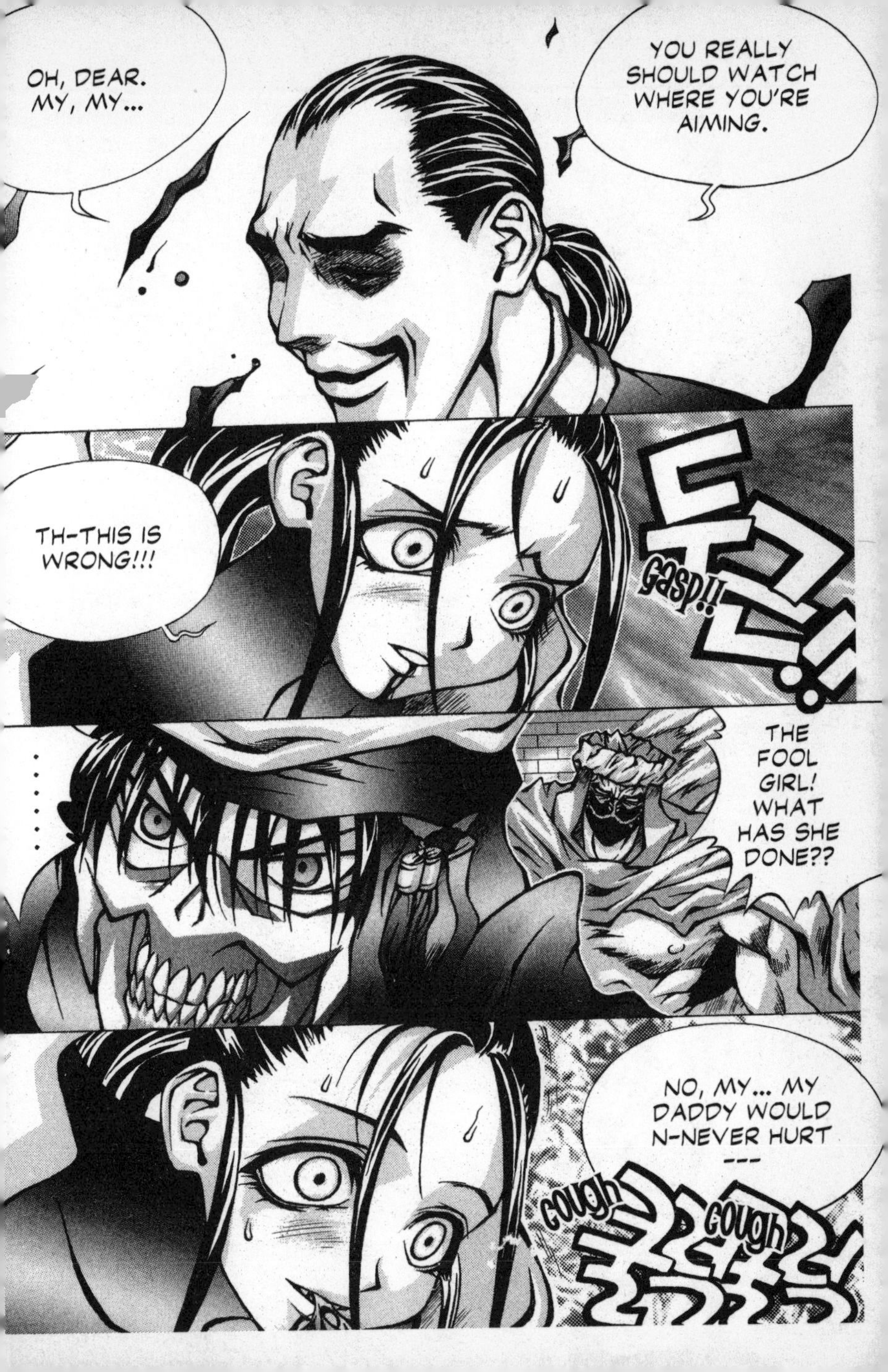

OH, DEAR. MY, MY...
YOU REALLY SHOULD WATCH WHERE YOU'RE AIMING.
TH-THIS IS WRONG!!!
GASP!!
......
THE FOOL GIRL! WHAT HAS SHE DONE??
NO, MY... MY DADDY WOULD N-NEVER HURT ---
COUGH
COUGH

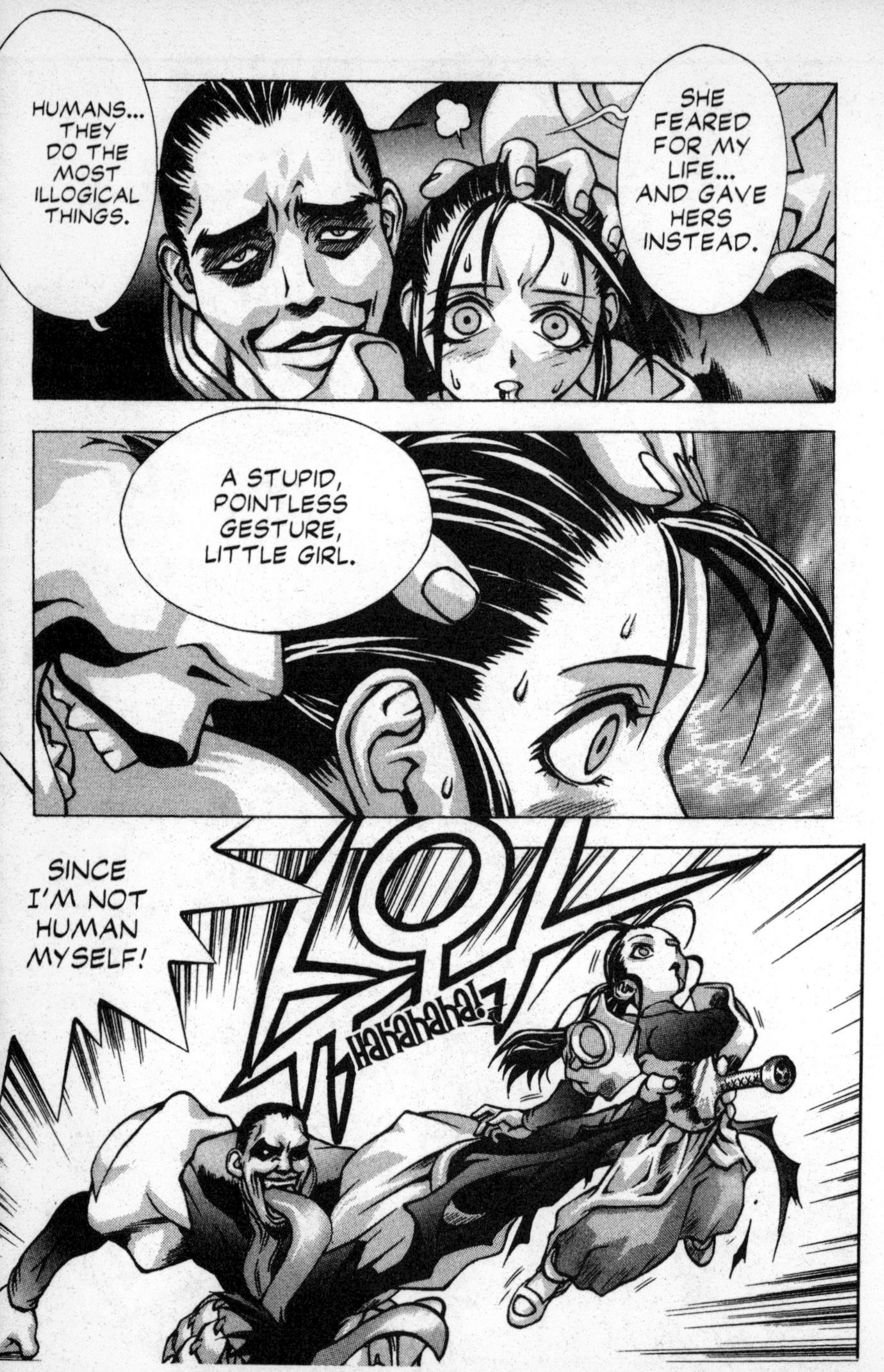
HUMANS... THEY DO THE MOST ILLOGICAL THINGS.
SHE FEARED FOR MY LIFE... AND GAVE HERS INSTEAD.
A STUPID, POINTLESS GESTURE, LITTLE GIRL.
SINCE I'M NOT HUMAN MYSELF!
HAHAHAHA!

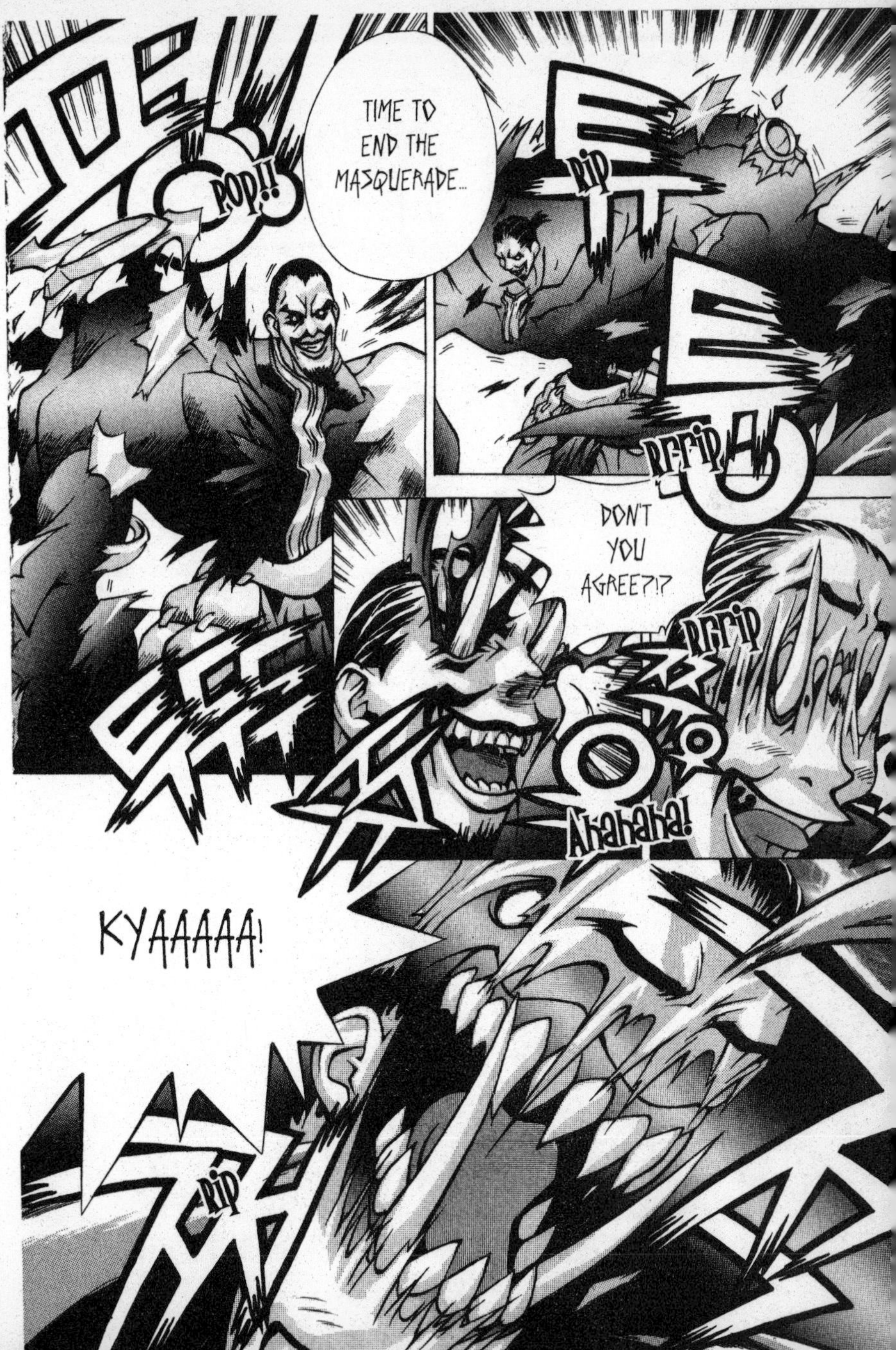
POP!!
TIME TO END THE MASQUERADE...
RIP
RRRIP
DON'T YOU AGREE?!?
RRRIP
AHAHAHA!
KYAAAAA!
RIP

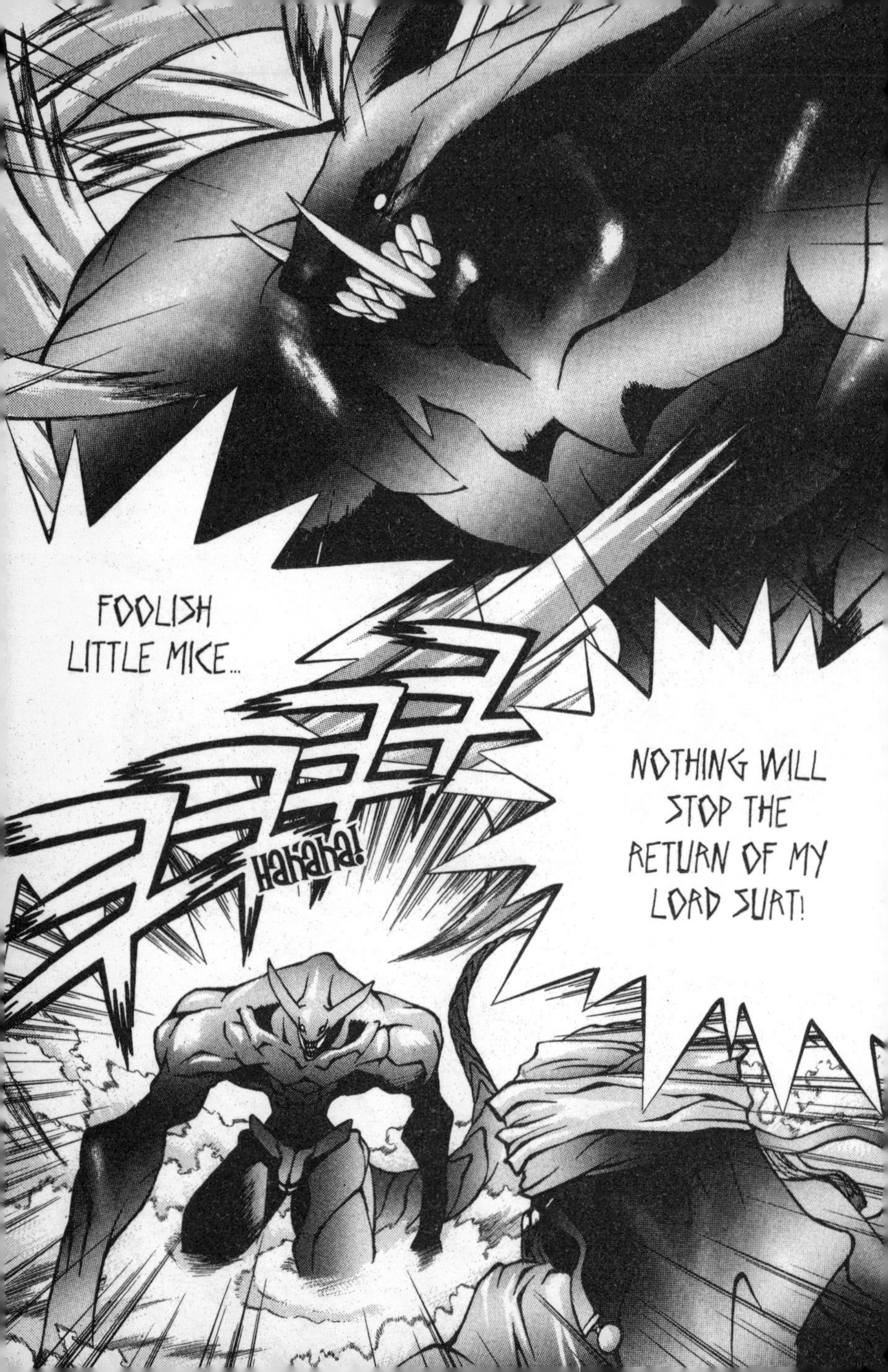
FOOLISH LITTLE MICE...
HAHAHA!
NOTHING WILL STOP THE RETURN OF MY LORD SURT!

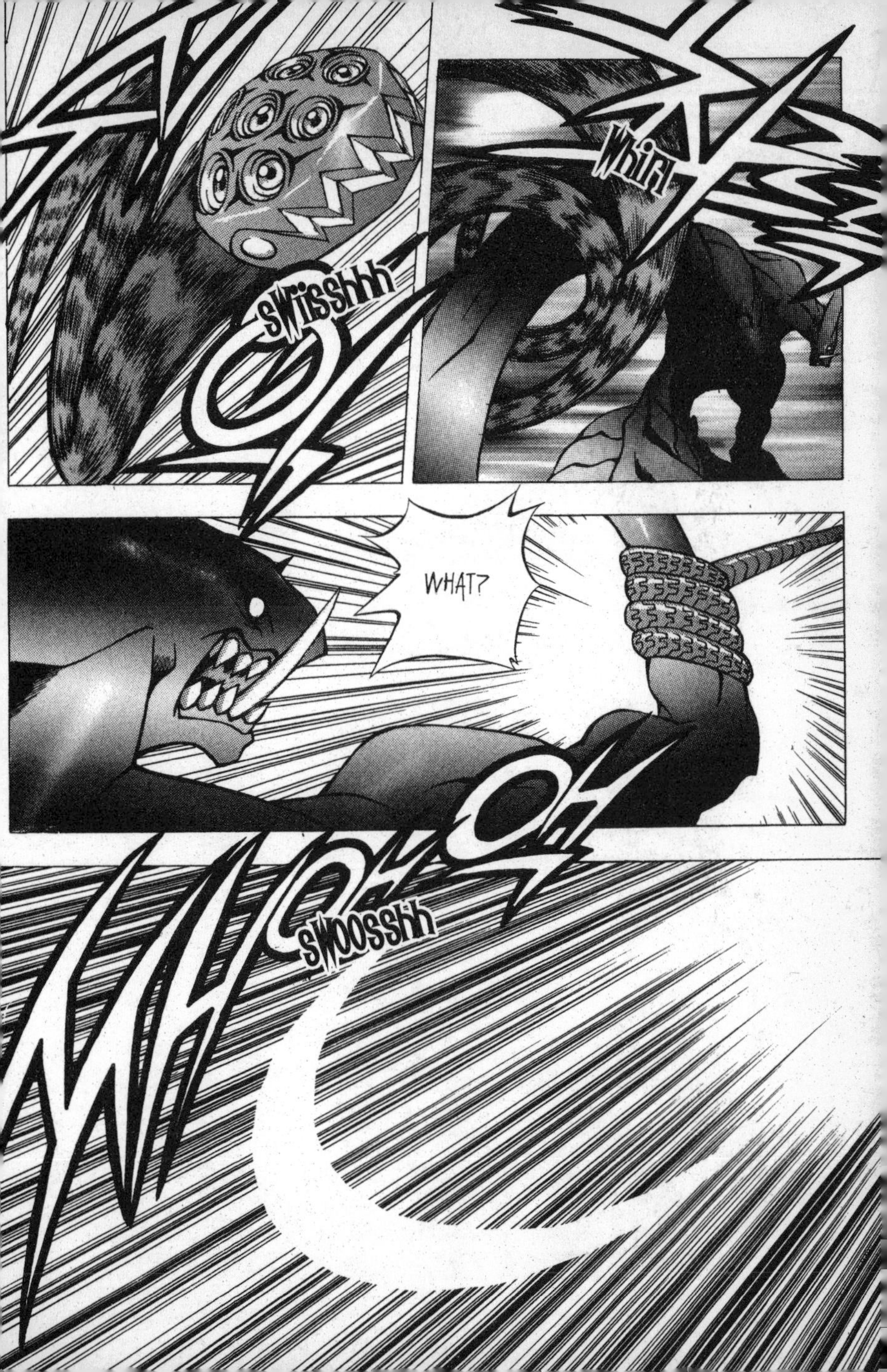
Whirl
Swisshhh
WHAT?
Swoosshh

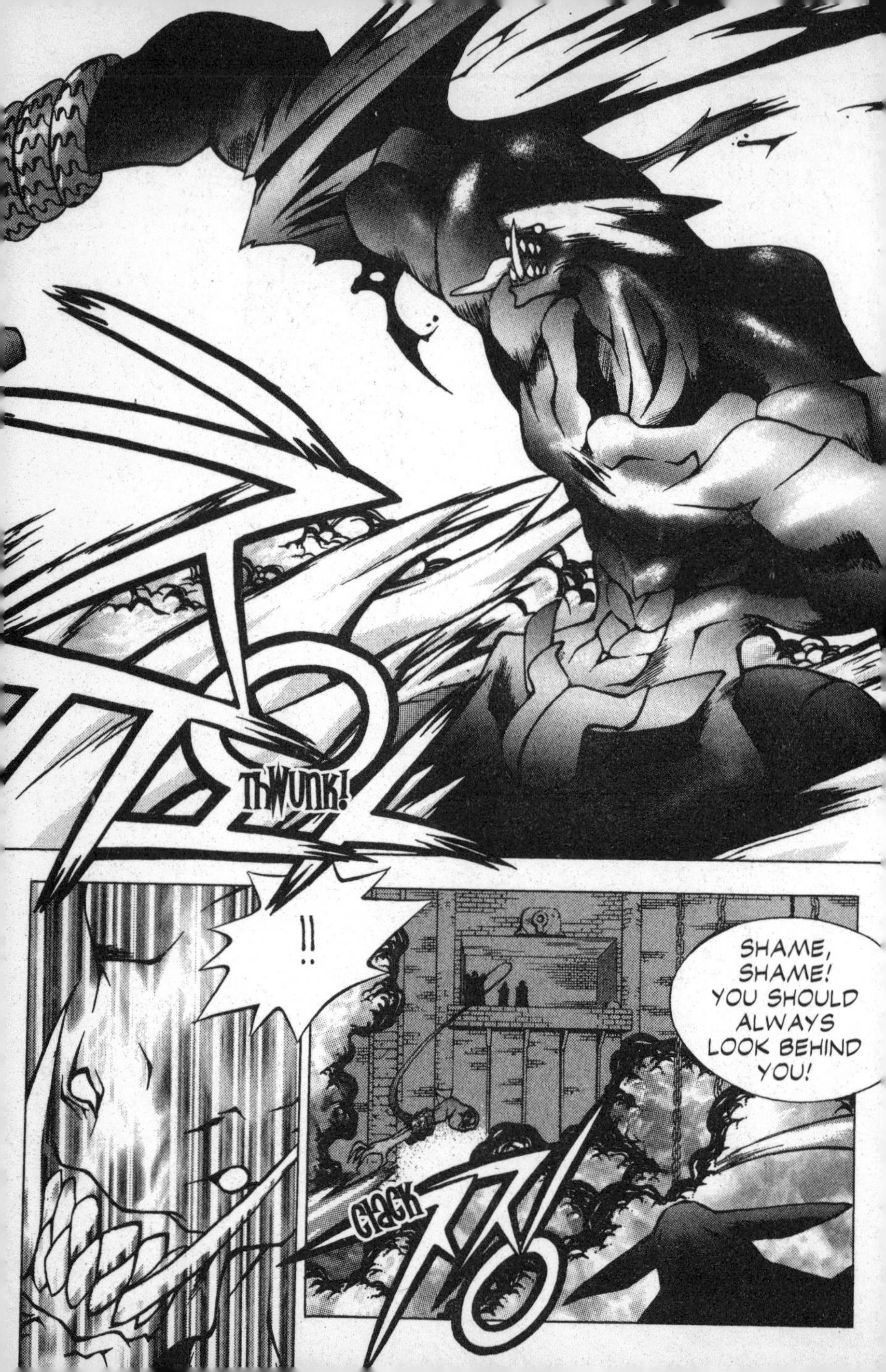
THWUNK!
!!
SHAME, SHAME! YOU SHOULD ALWAYS LOOK BEHIND YOU!
CRACK

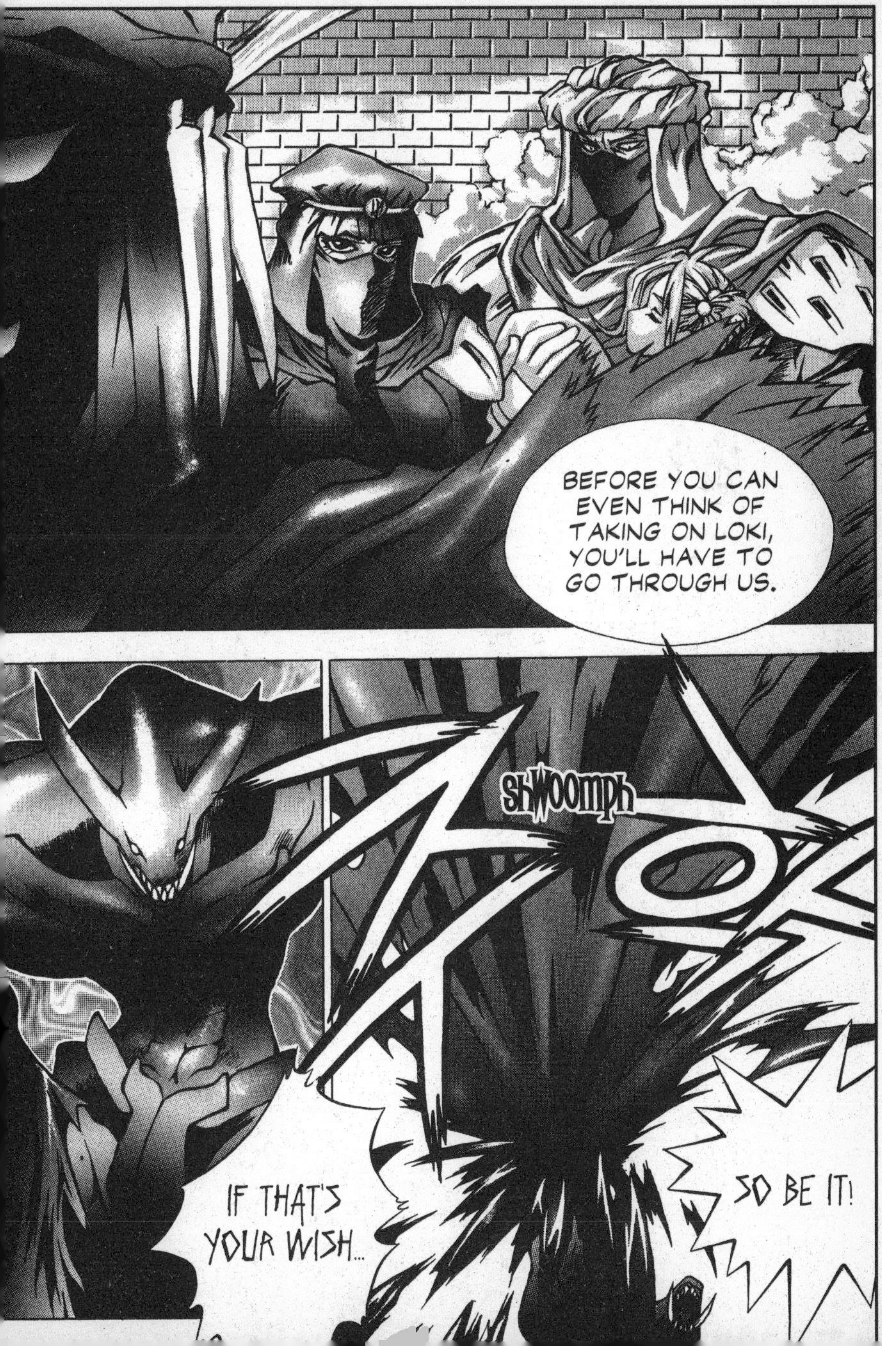
BEFORE YOU CAN EVEN THINK OF TAKING ON LOKI, YOU'LL HAVE TO GO THROUGH US.
SHWOOMPH
IF THAT'S YOUR WISH...
SO BE IT!

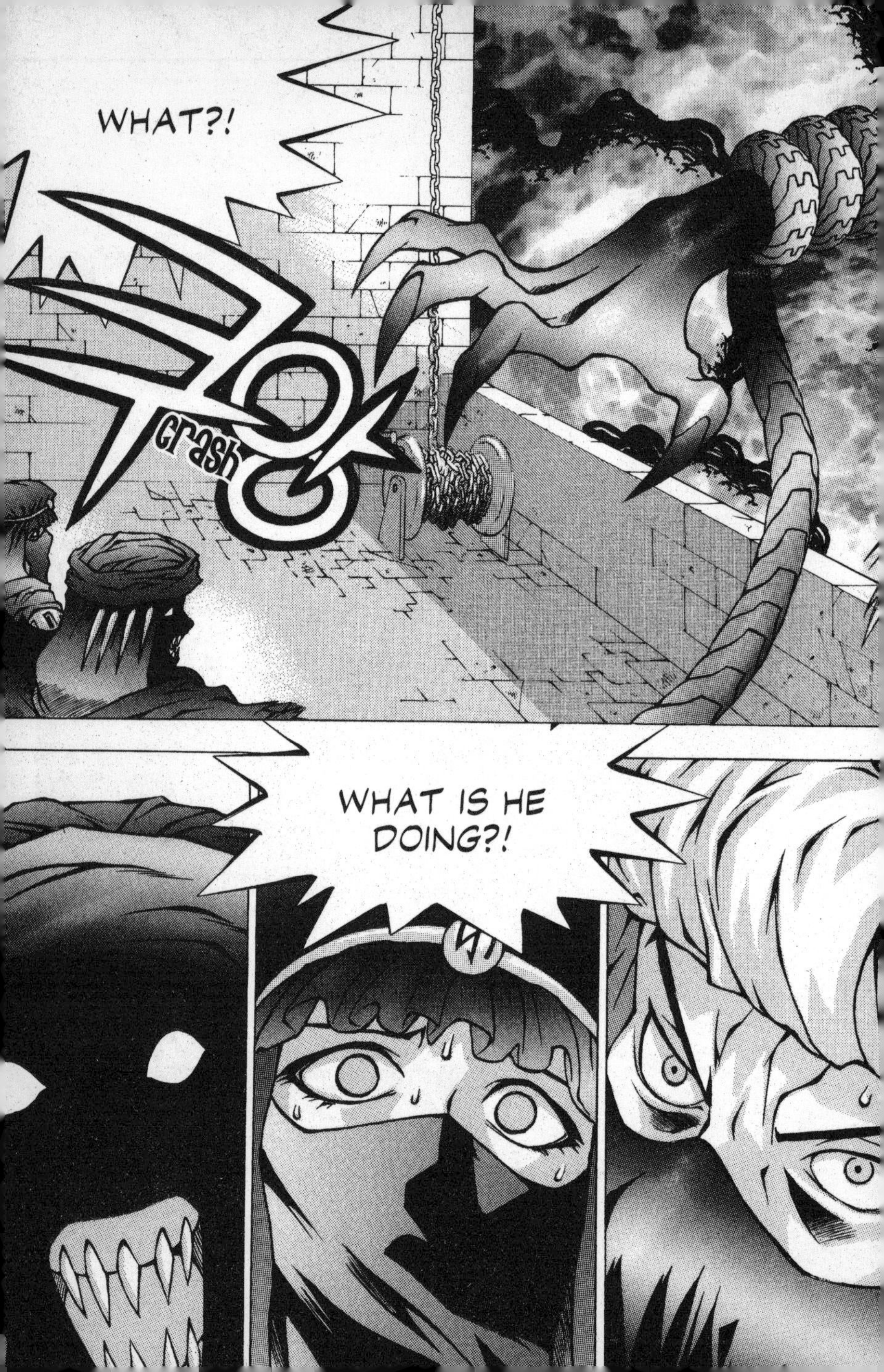
WHAT?!
crash
WHAT IS HE DOING?!

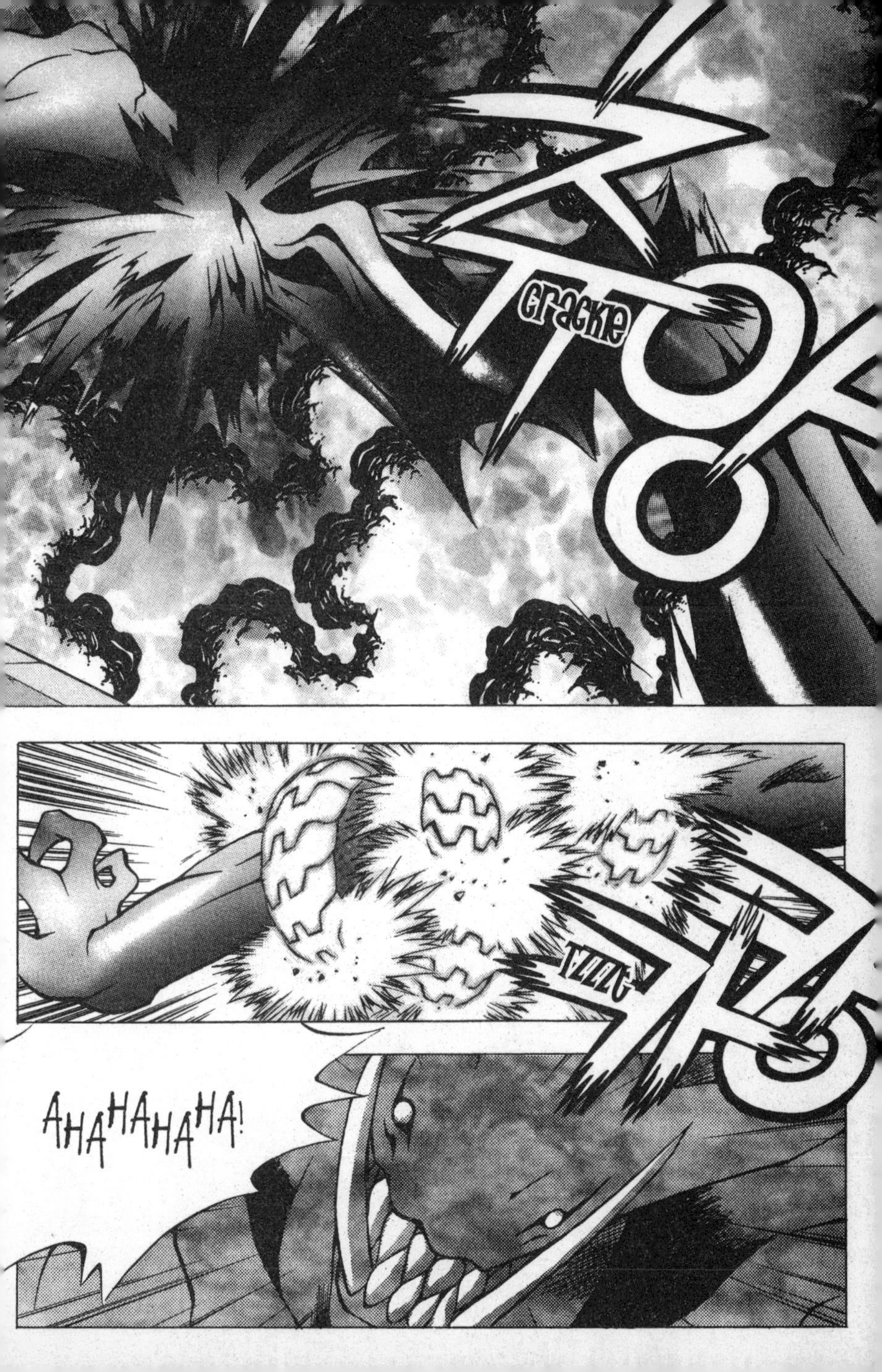
crackle
AHAHAHAHA!

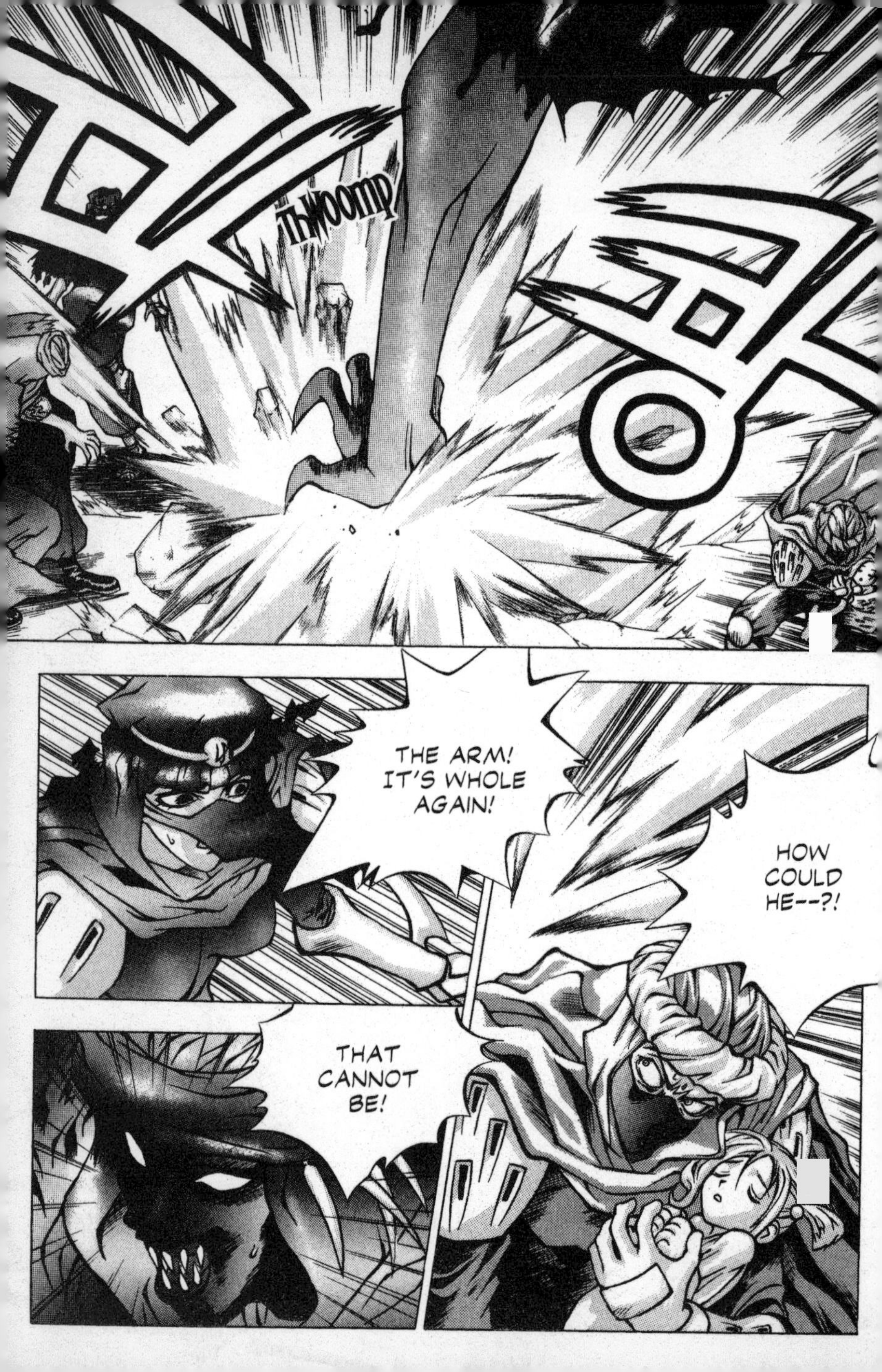
THWOOMP
THE ARM! IT'S WHOLE AGAIN!
HOW COULD HE--?!
THAT CANNOT BE!

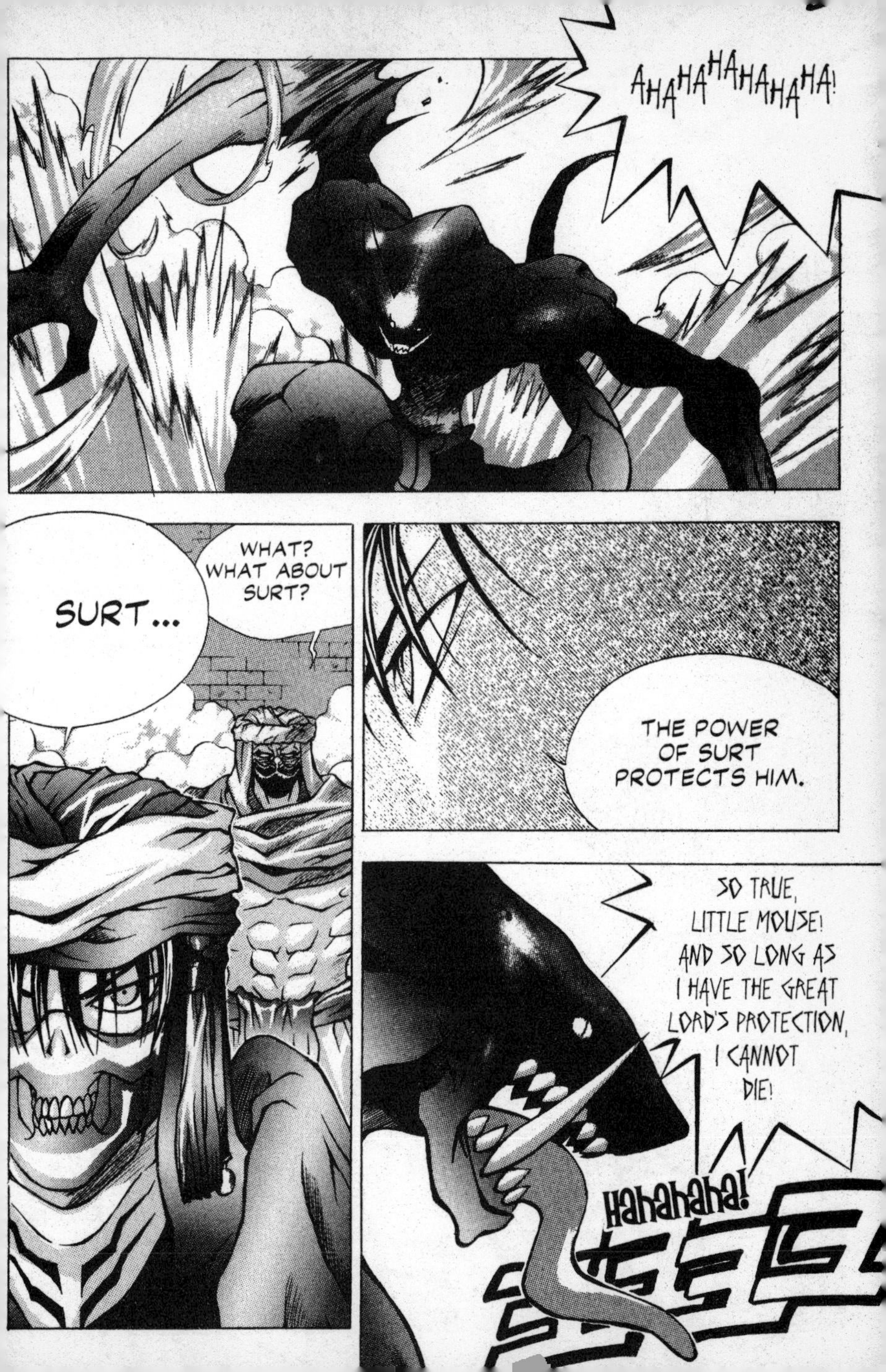
AHAHAHAHAHAHAHAHA!
SURT...
WHAT? WHAT ABOUT SURT?
THE POWER OF SURT PROTECTS HIM.
SO TRUE, LITTLE MOUSE! AND SO LONG AS I HAVE THE GREAT LORD'S PROTECTION, I CANNOT DIE!
HAHAHAHA!

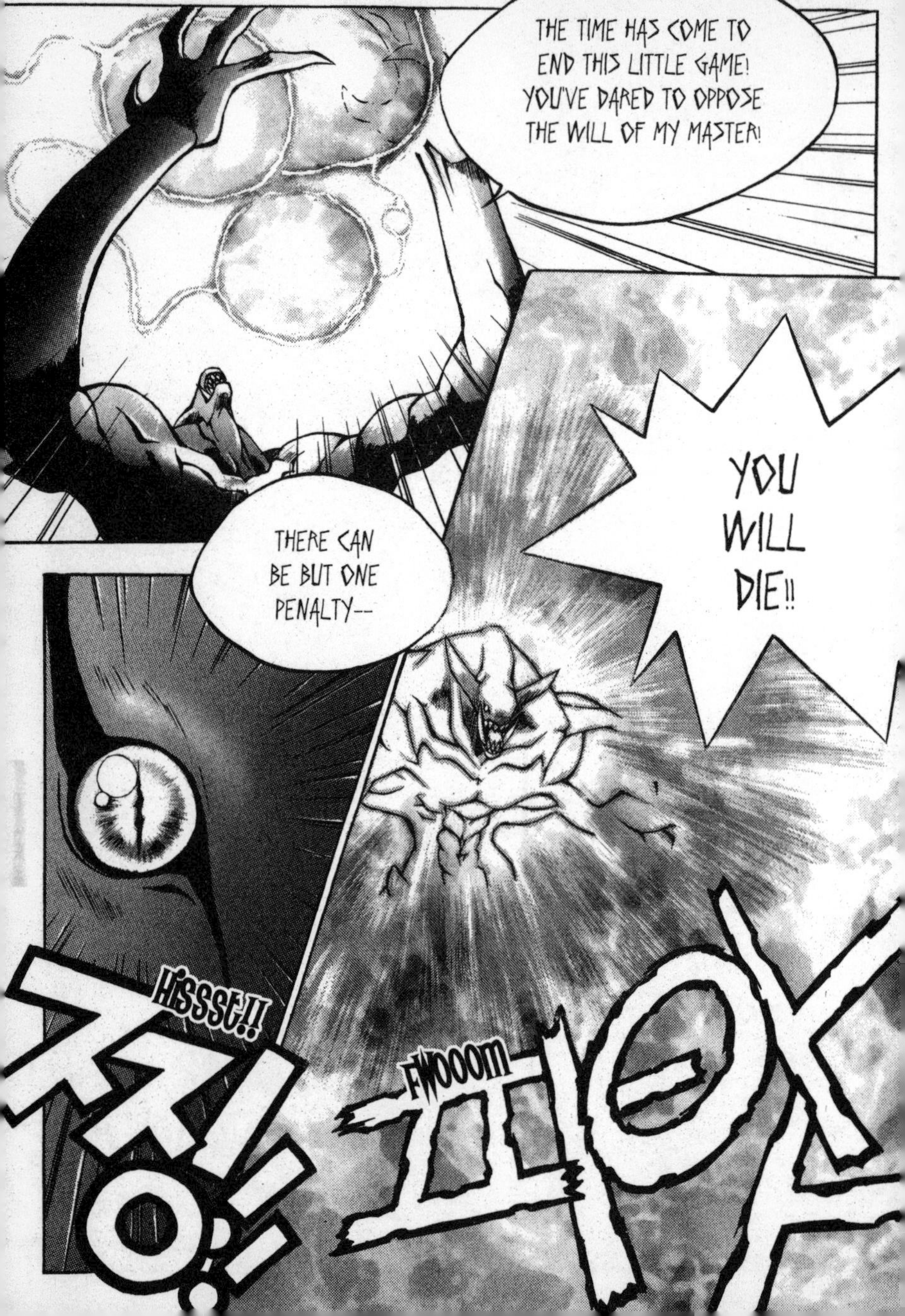
THE TIME HAS COME TO END THIS LITTLE GAME! YOU'VE DARED TO OPPOSE THE WILL OF MY MASTER!
THERE CAN BE BUT ONE PENALTY--
YOU WILL DIE!!
HISSST!!
FWOOOM

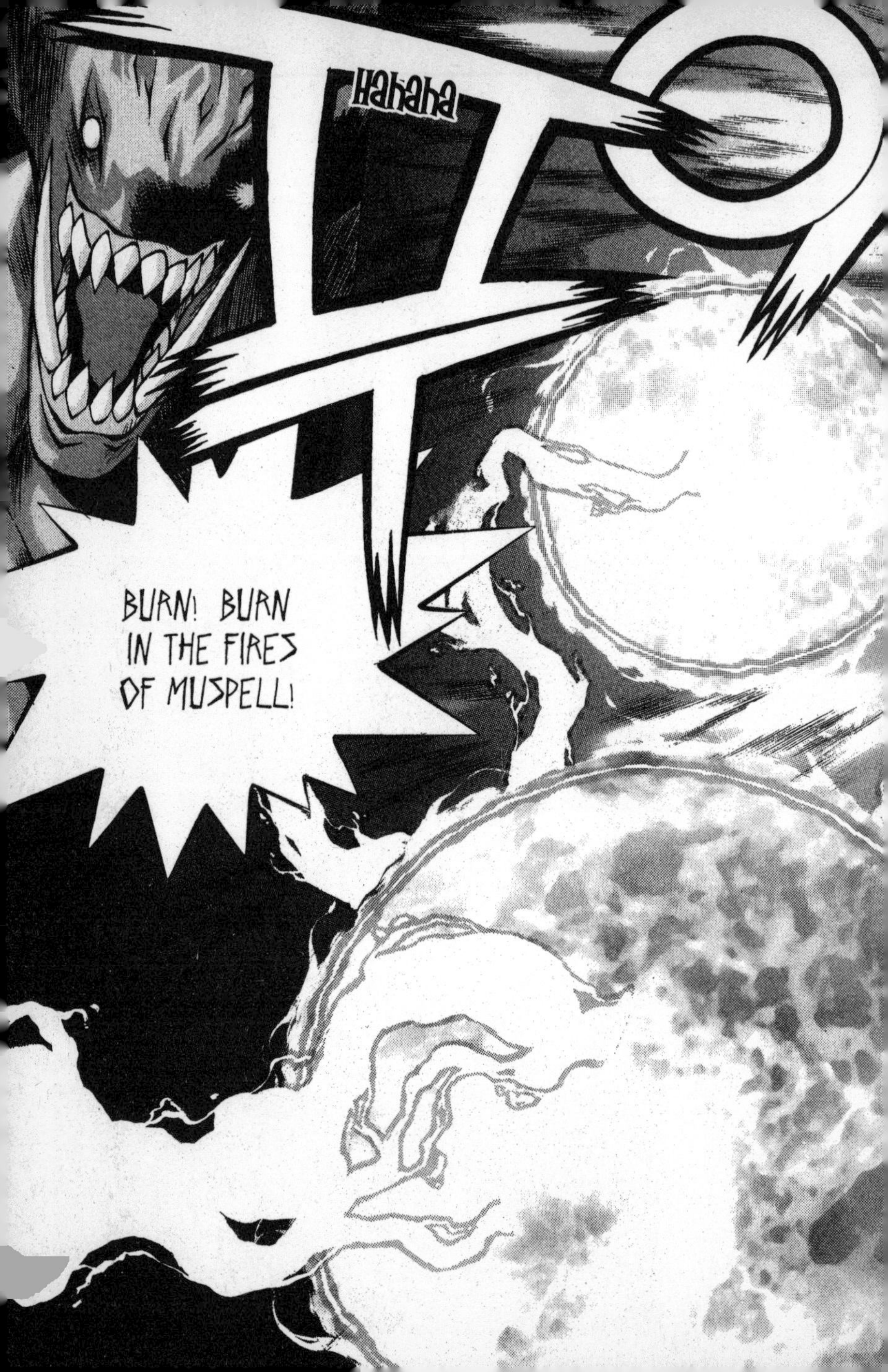
HAHAHA
BURN! BURN IN THE FIRES OF MUSPELL!

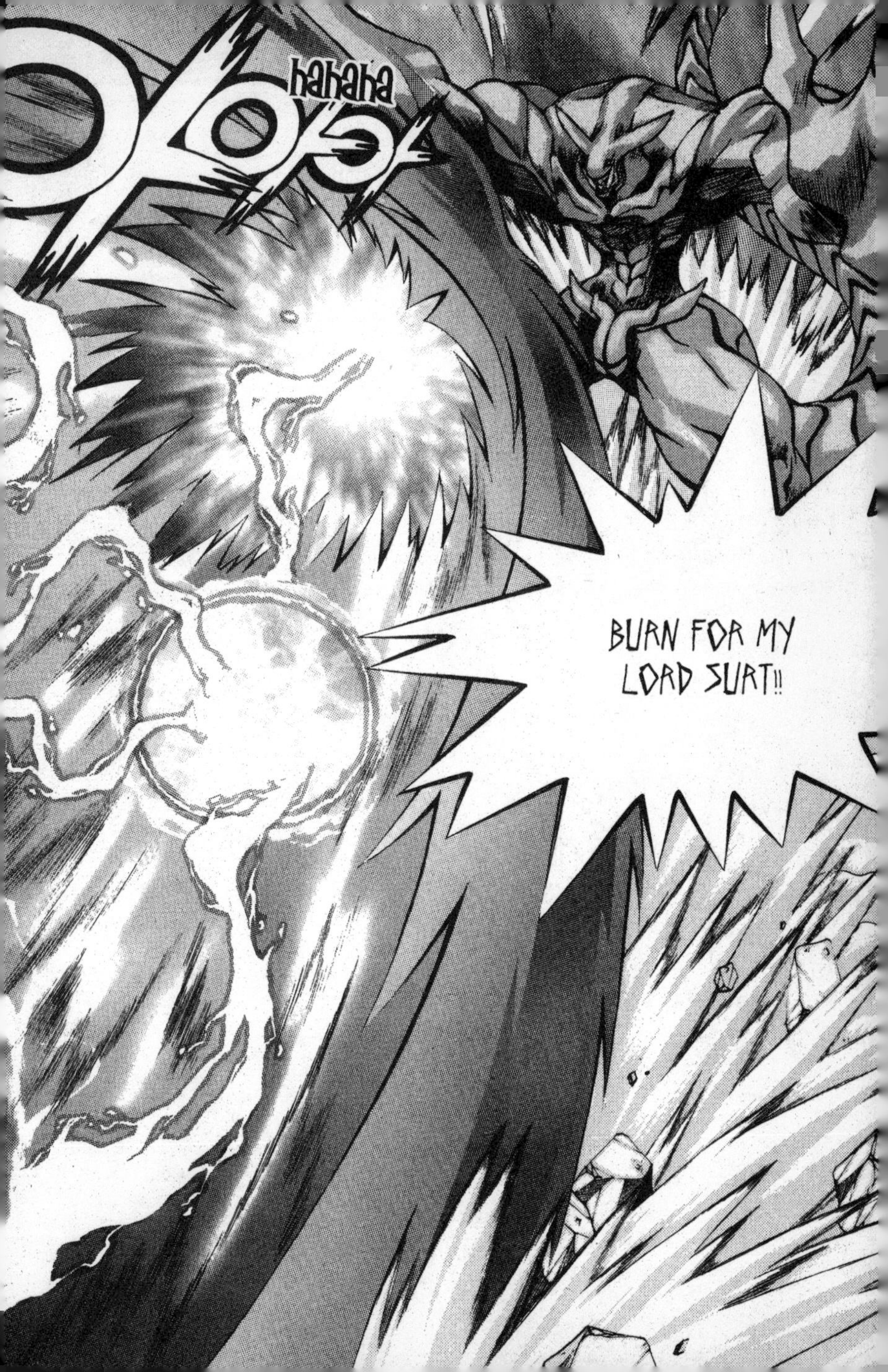
hahaha
BURN FOR MY LORD SURT!!

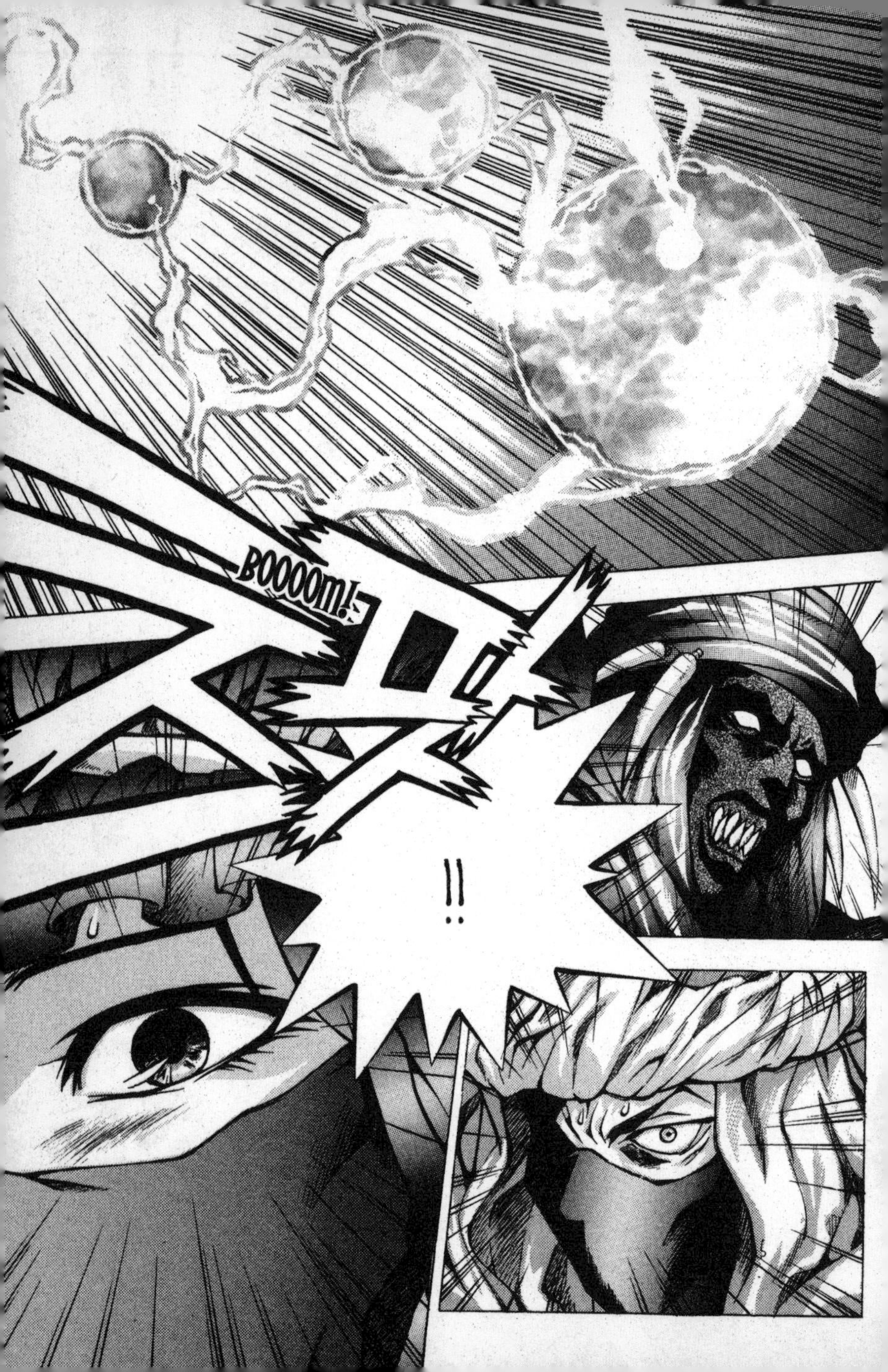
BOOOOm!
!!

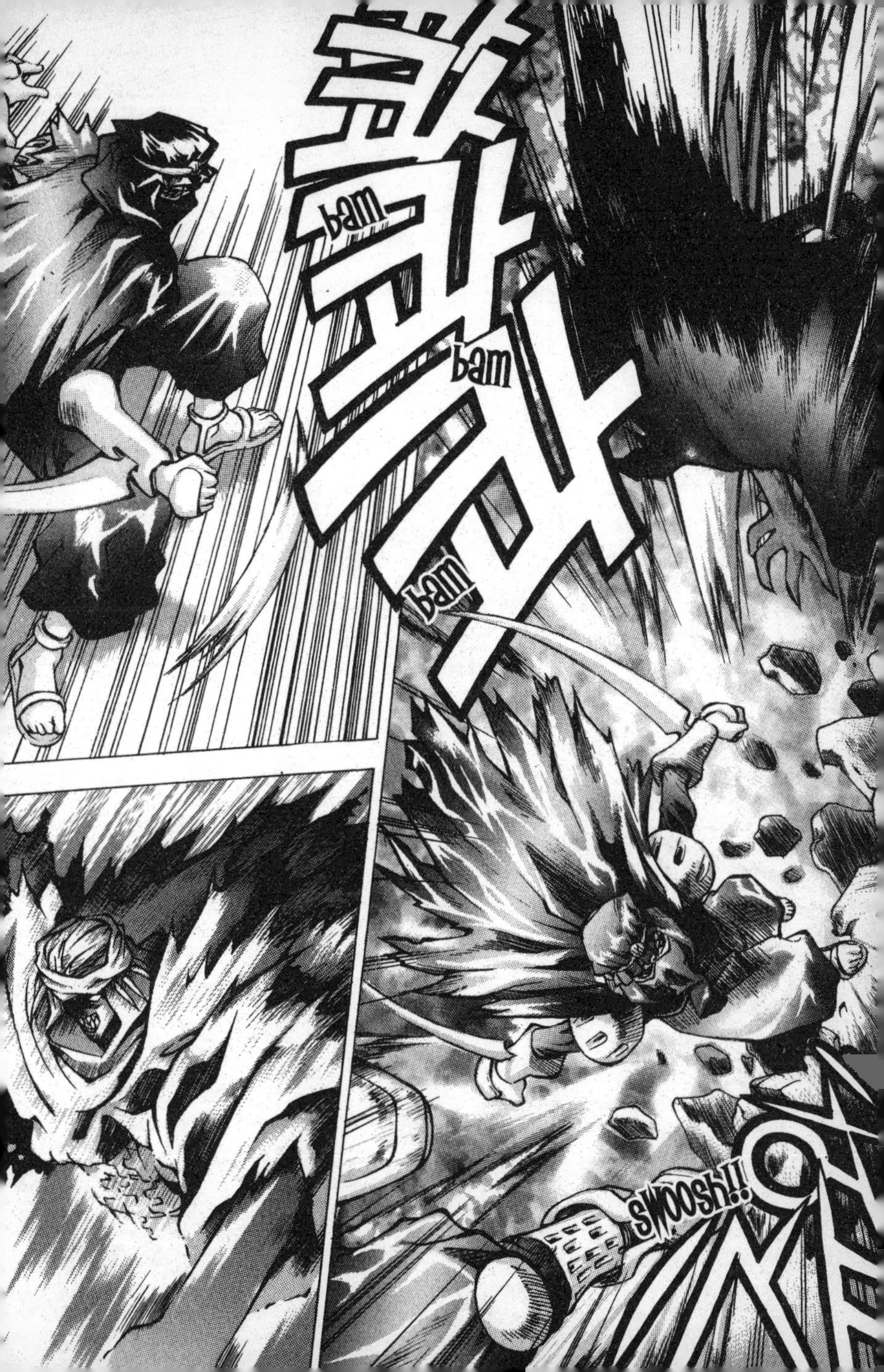
bam
bam
bam
SWOOSH!!

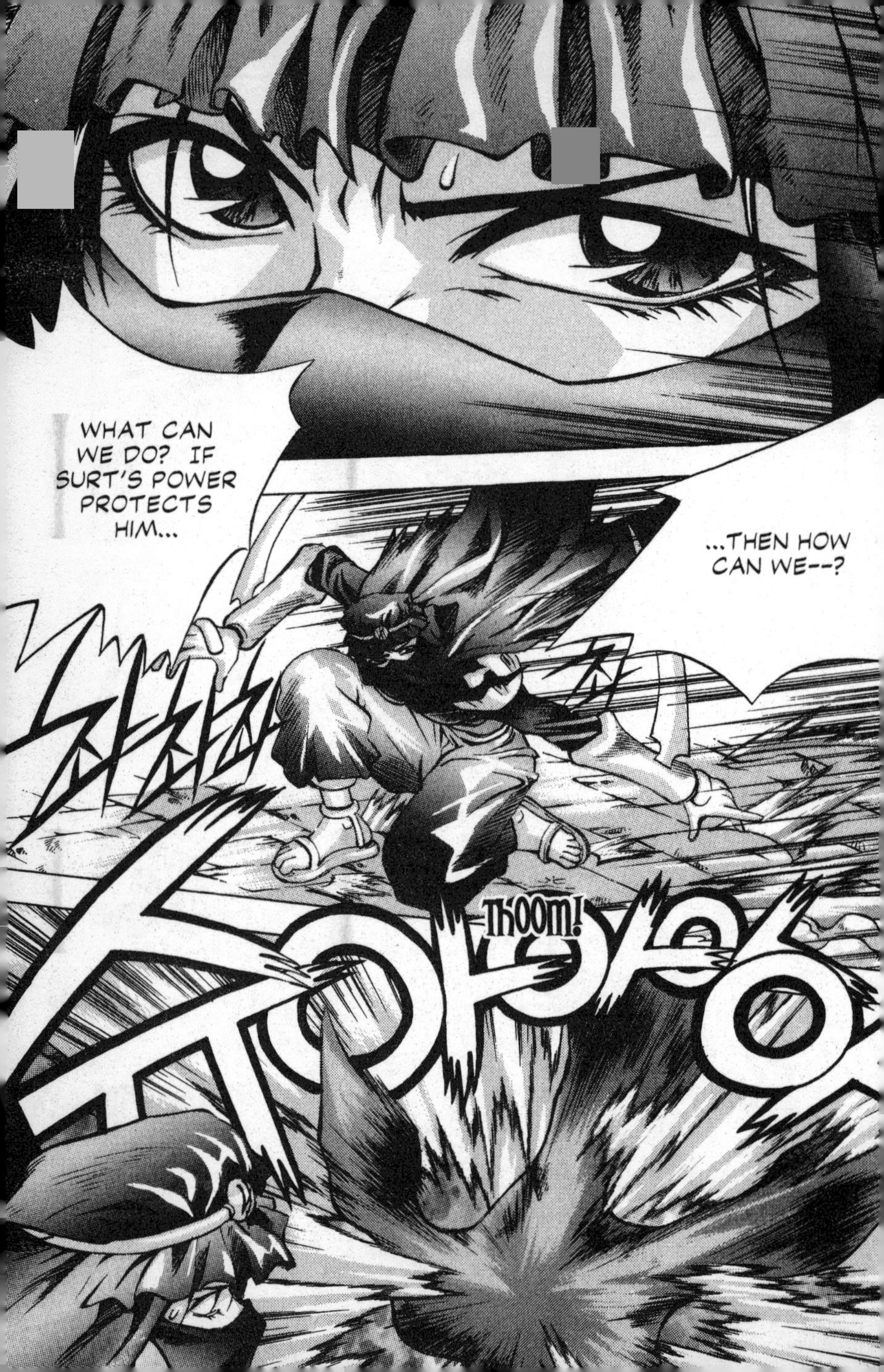
WHAT CAN WE DO? IF SURT'S POWER PROTECTS HIM...
...THEN HOW CAN WE--?
THOOM!

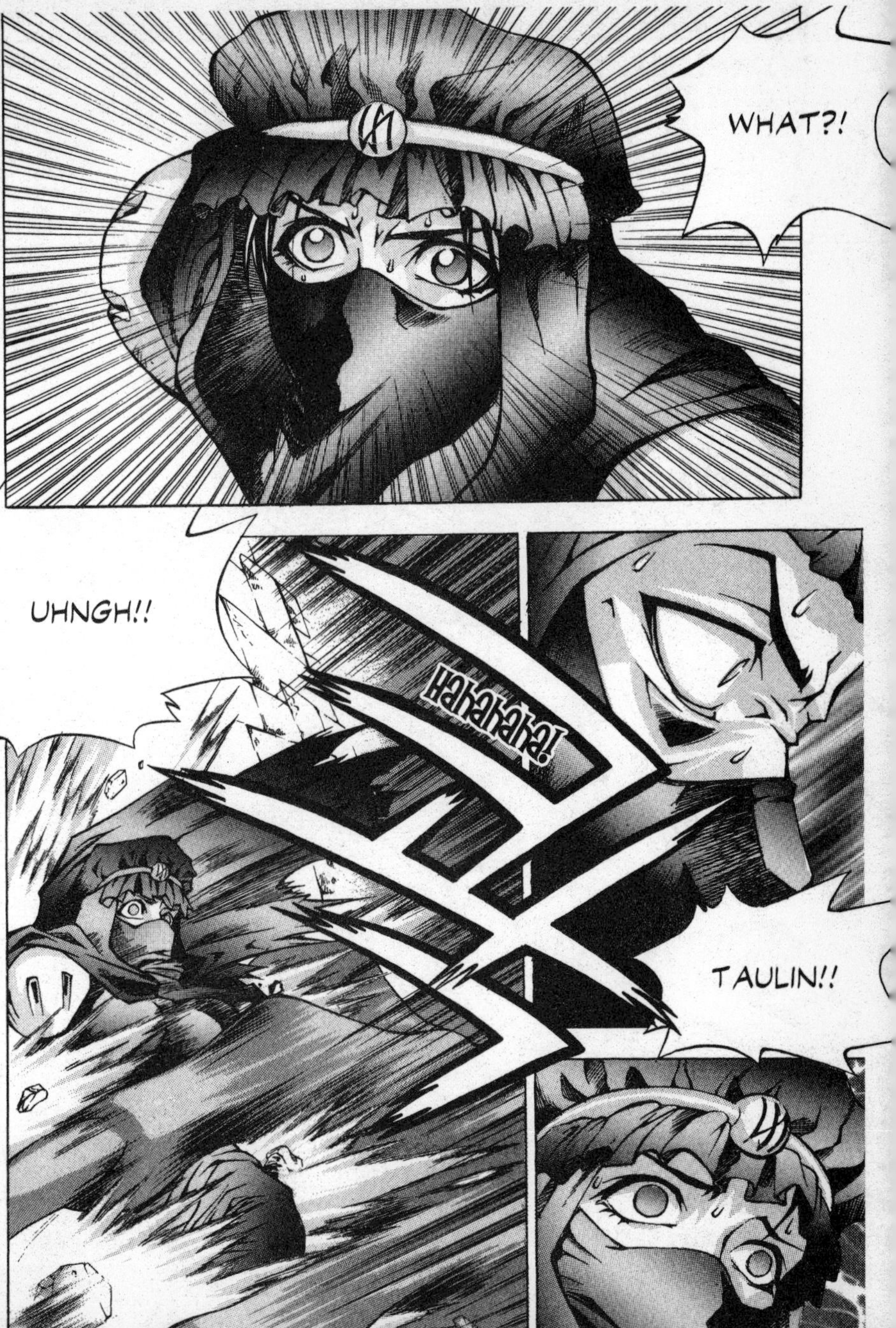
WHAT?!
UHNGH!!
HAHAHAHA!
TAULIN!!

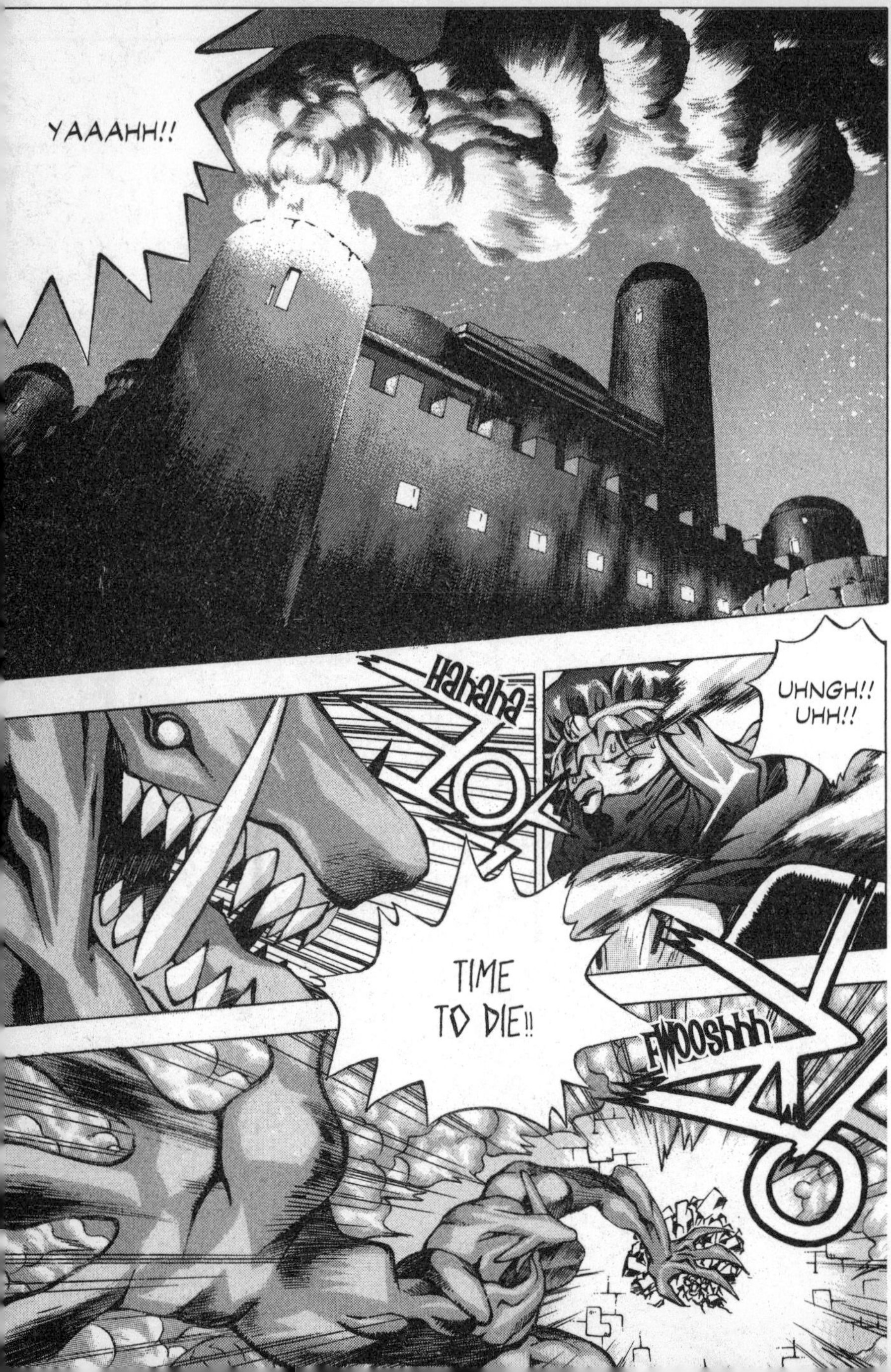
YAAAHH!!
Hahaha
UHNGH!! UHH!!
TIME TO DIE!!
FWOOSHHH

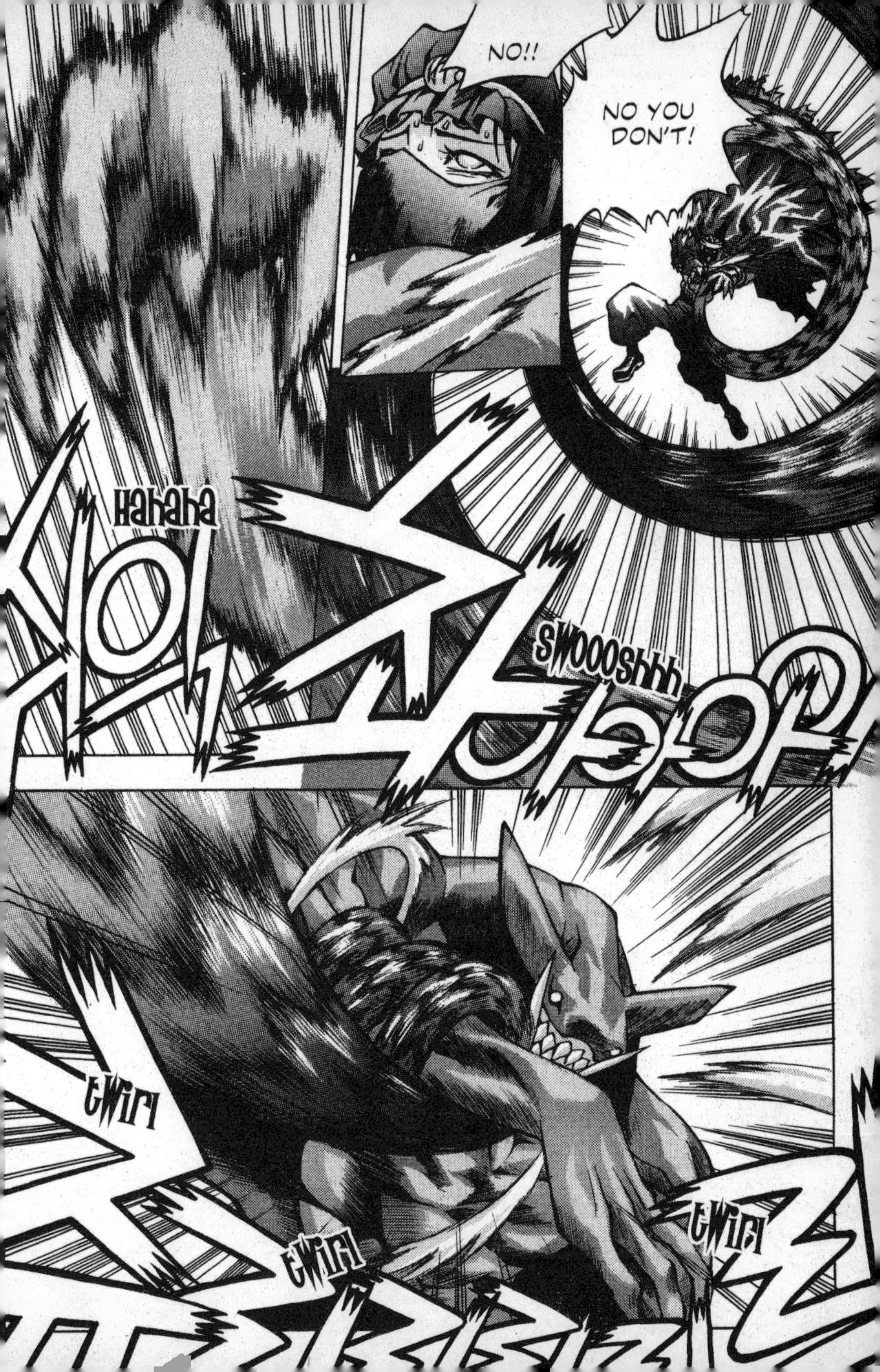
NO!!
NO YOU DON'T!
Hahaha
SWOOOShhh
twirl
twirl
twirl

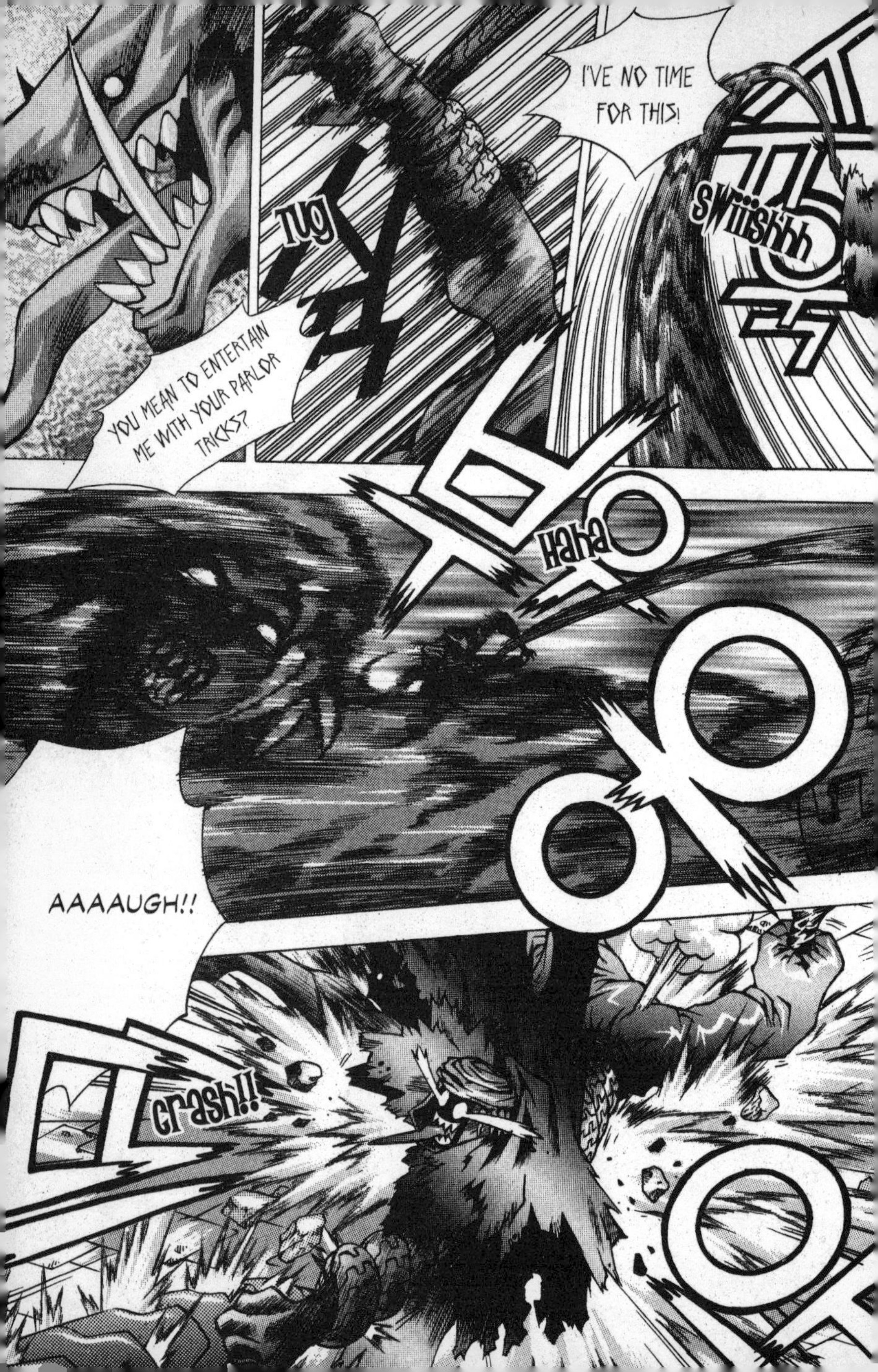
I'VE NO TIME FOR THIS!
SWIISHHH
TUG
YOU MEAN TO ENTERTAIN ME WITH YOUR PARLOR TRICKS?
HAHA
AAAAUGH!!
CRASH!!

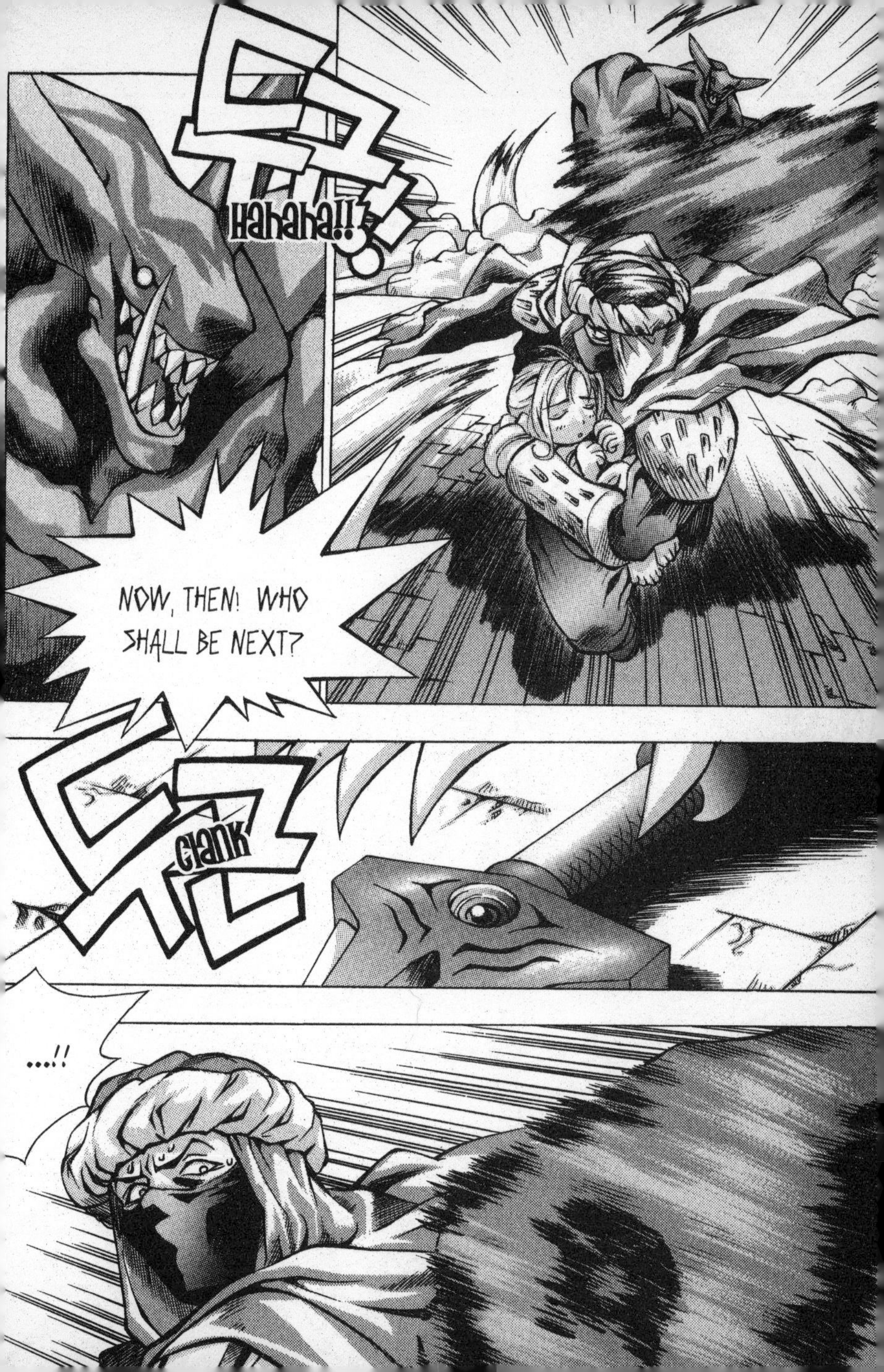

HAHAHA!!
NOW, THEN! WHO SHALL BE NEXT?
CLANK
...!!

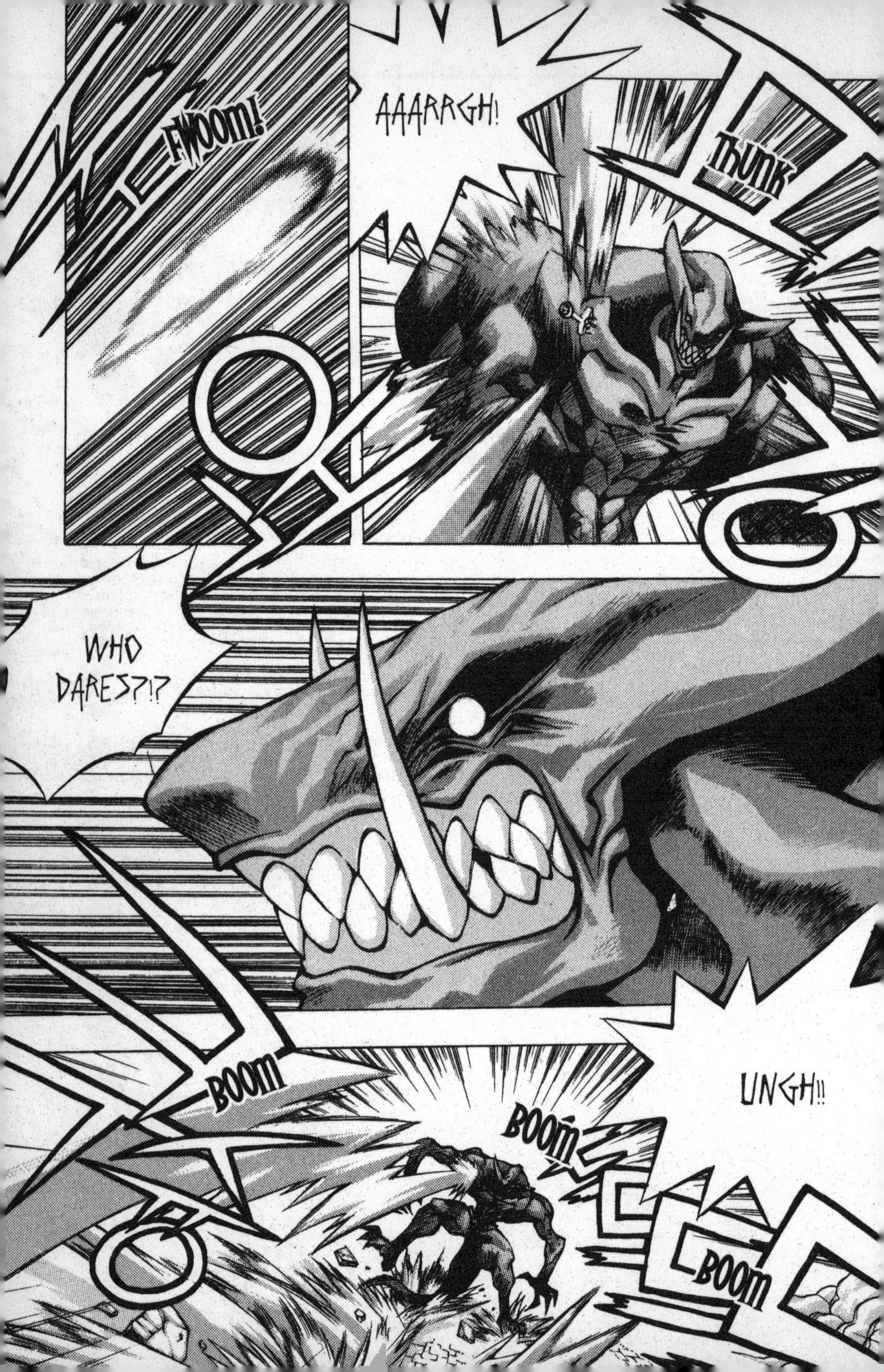
THUNK
AAARRGH!
FWOOM!
WHO DARES?!?
UNGH!!
BOOM
BOOM
BOOM

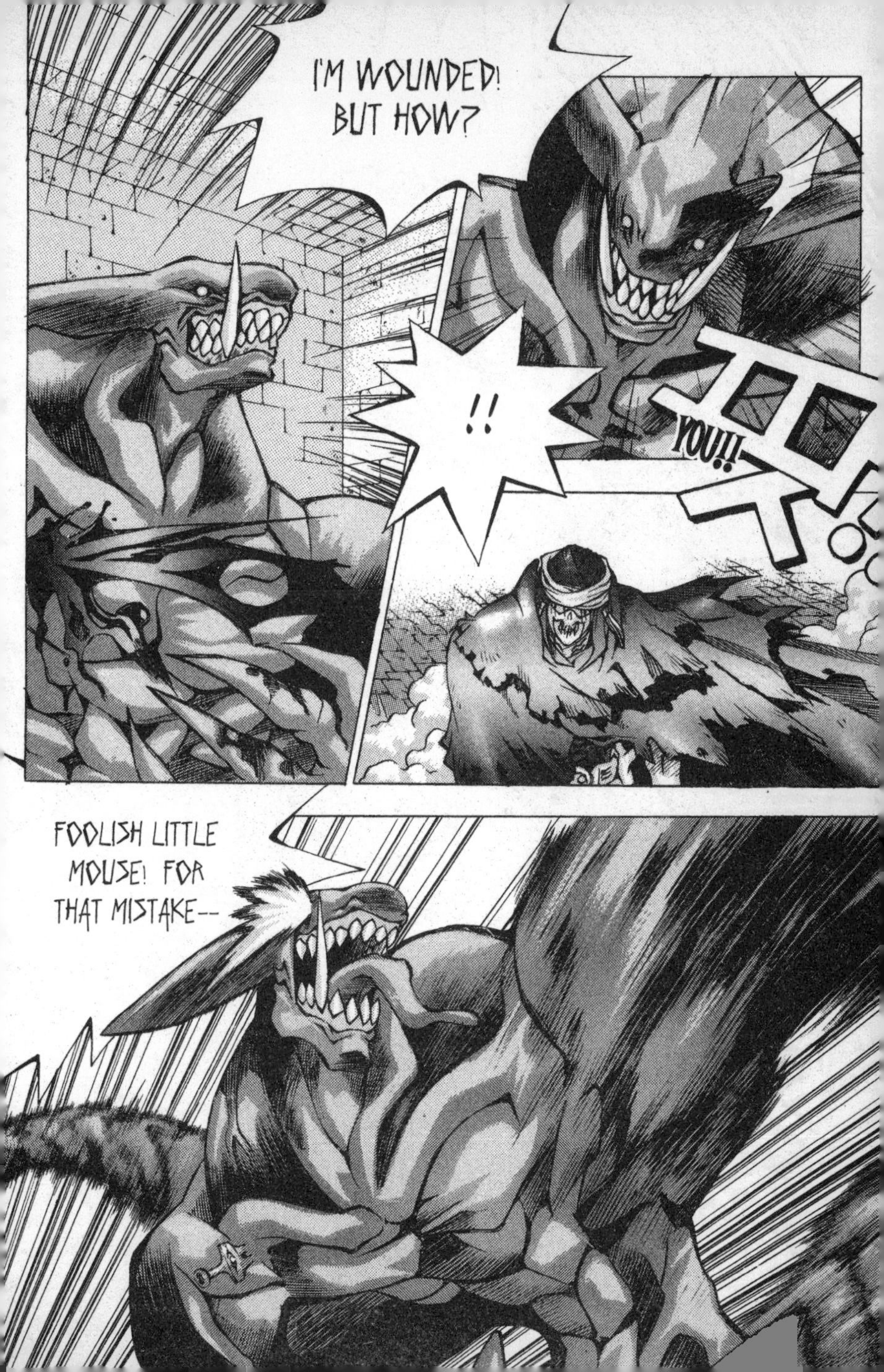
I'M WOUNDED! BUT HOW?
!!
YOU!!
FOOLISH LITTLE MOUSE! FOR THAT MISTAKE--

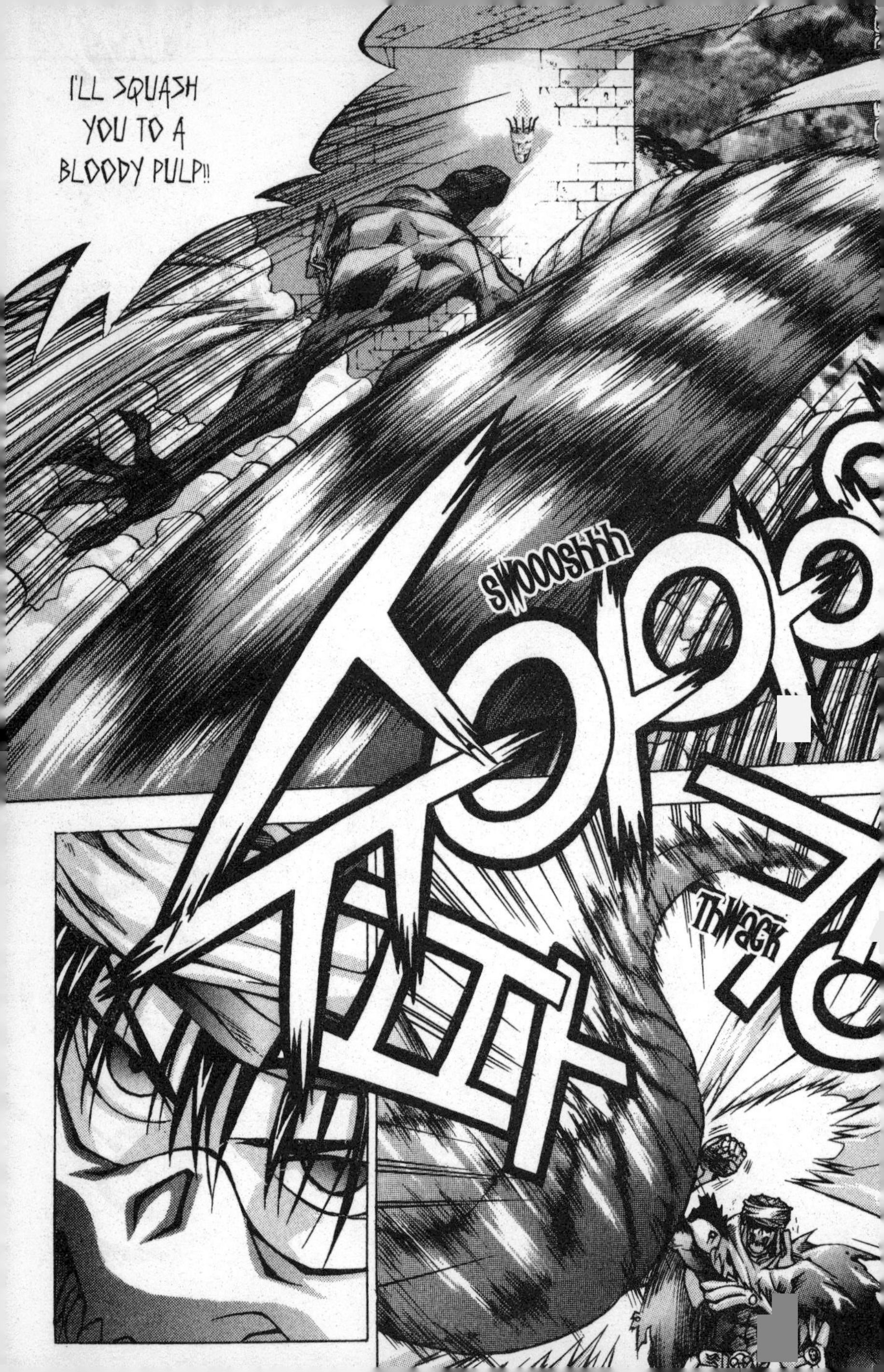
I'LL SQUASH YOU TO A BLOODY PULP!!
SWOOOSHHH
THWACK

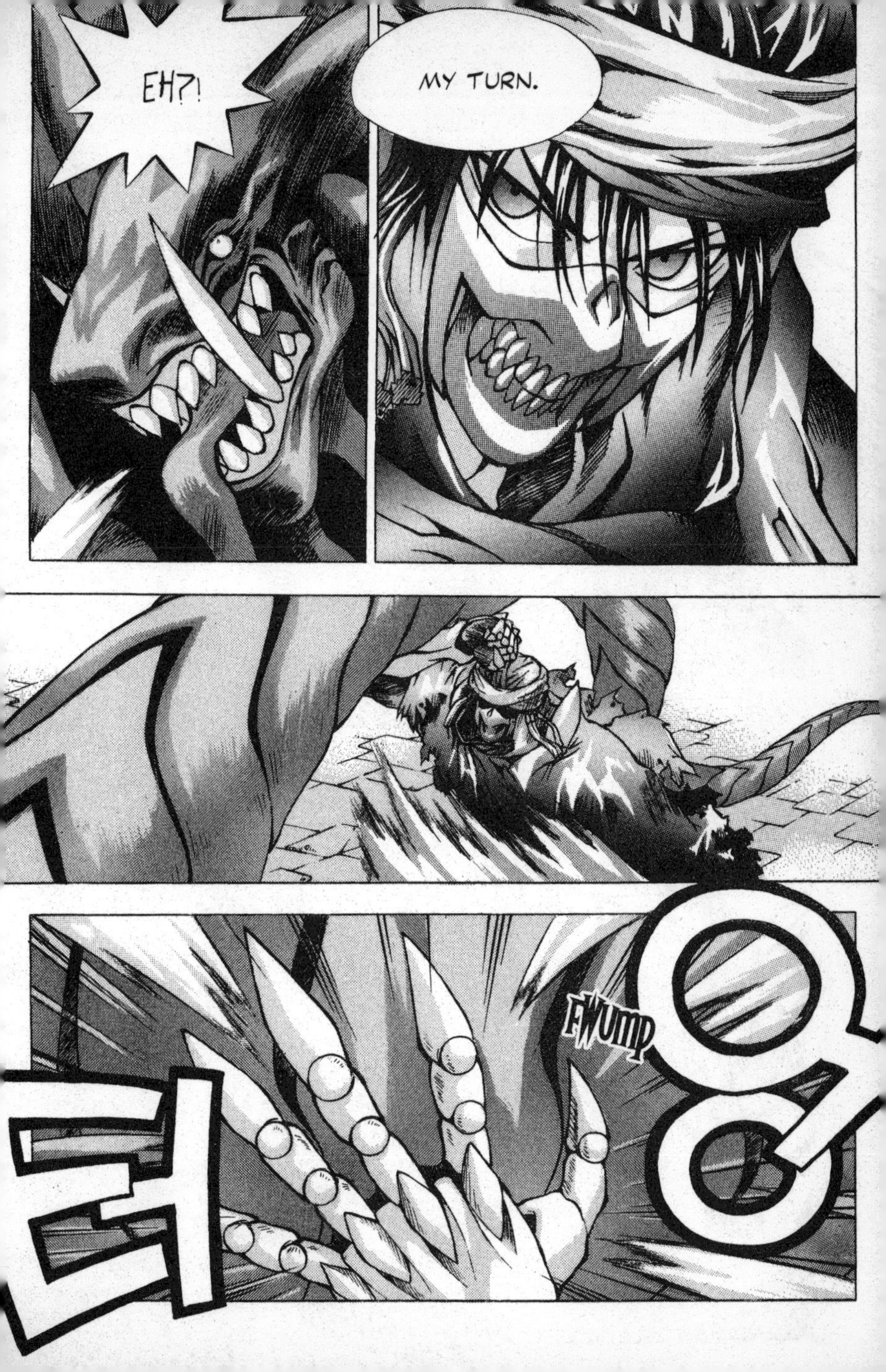
EH?!
MY TURN.
FWUMP

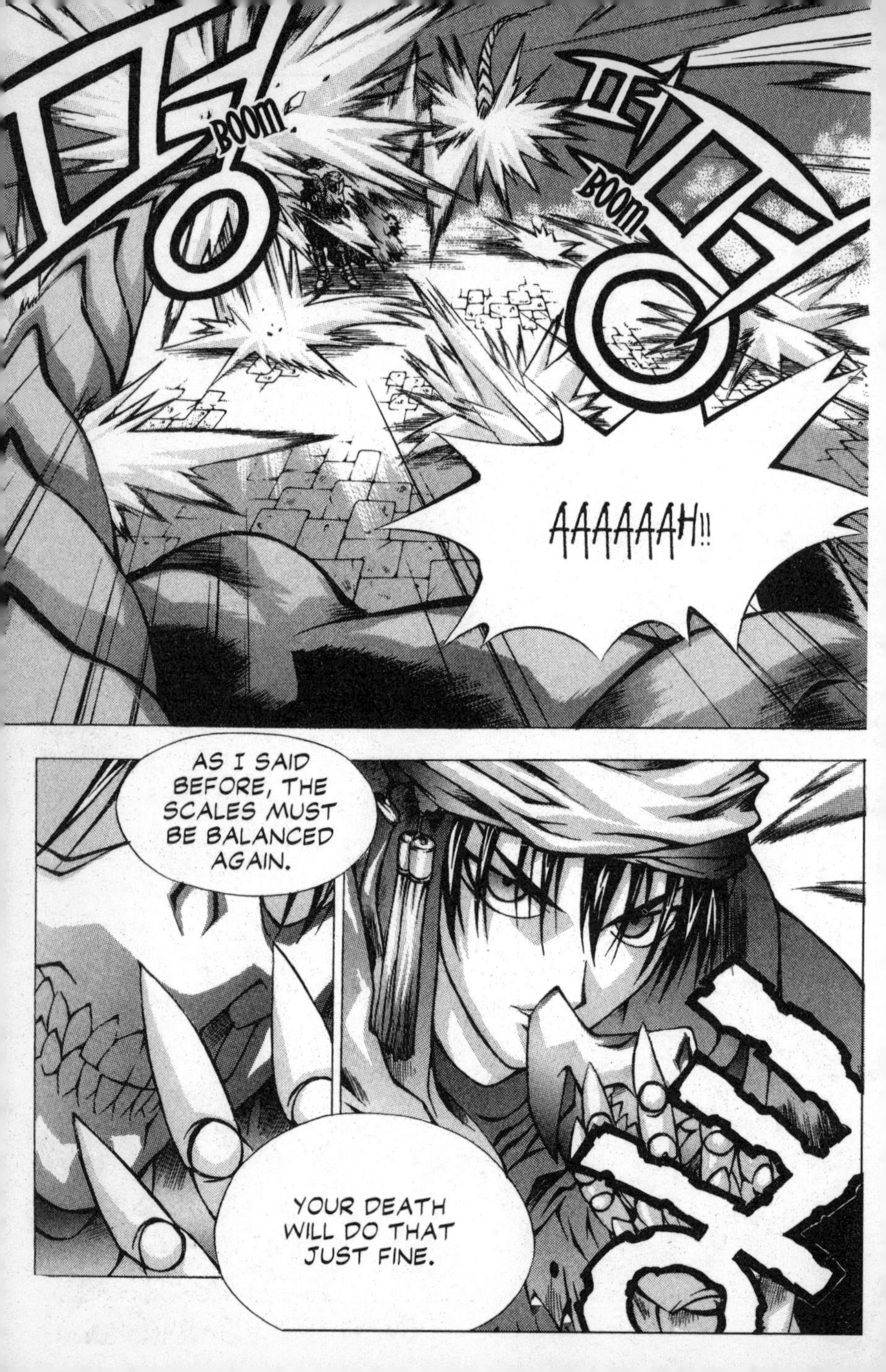
BOOM
BOOM
AAAAAAH!!
AS I SAID BEFORE, THE SCALES MUST BE BALANCED AGAIN.
YOUR DEATH WILL DO THAT JUST FINE.

RAGNAROK
라그나로크
IN TO THE ABYSS

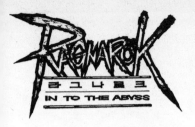

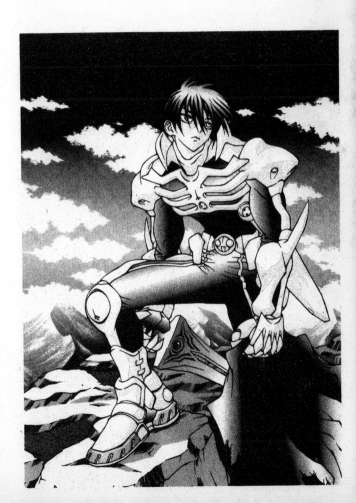

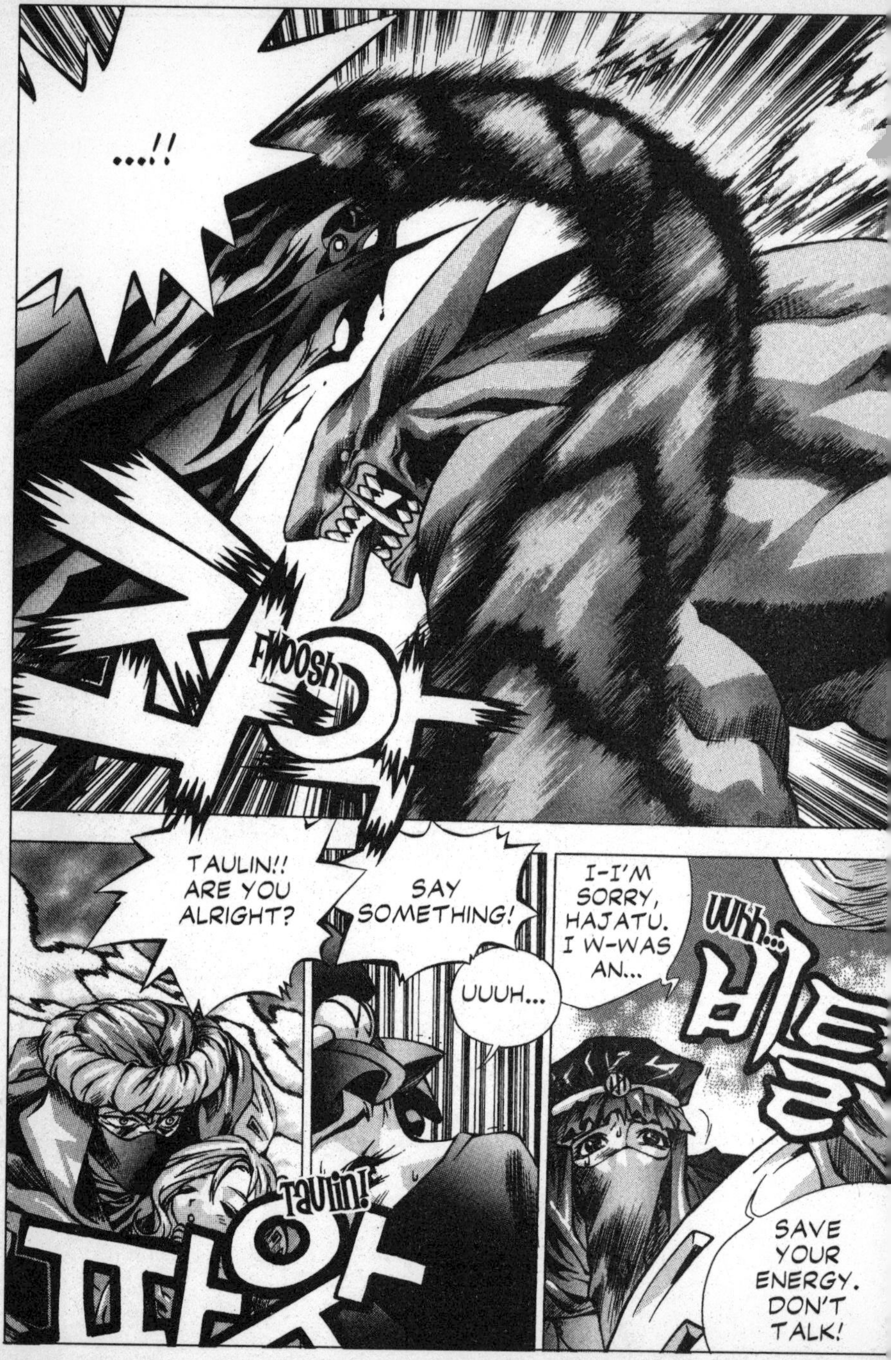
...!!
FWOOSH
TAULIN!! ARE YOU ALRIGHT?
SAY SOMETHING!
UUUH...
TAULIN!
I-I'M SORRY, HAJATU. I W-WAS AN...
Whh...
SAVE YOUR ENERGY. DON'T TALK!

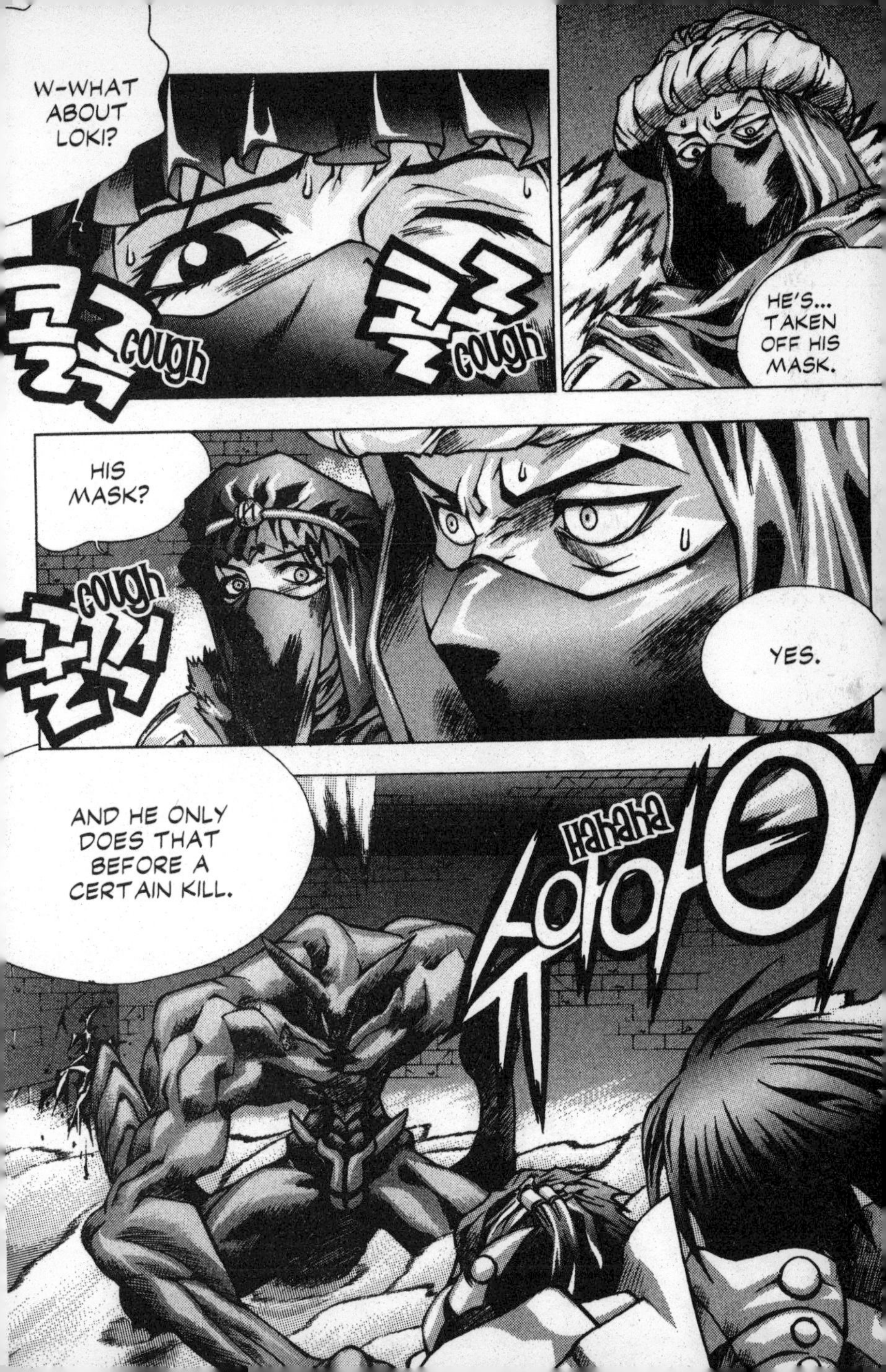
W-WHAT ABOUT LOKI?
cough
cough
HE'S... TAKEN OFF HIS MASK.
HIS MASK?
cough
YES.
AND HE ONLY DOES THAT BEFORE A CERTAIN KILL.
Hahaha

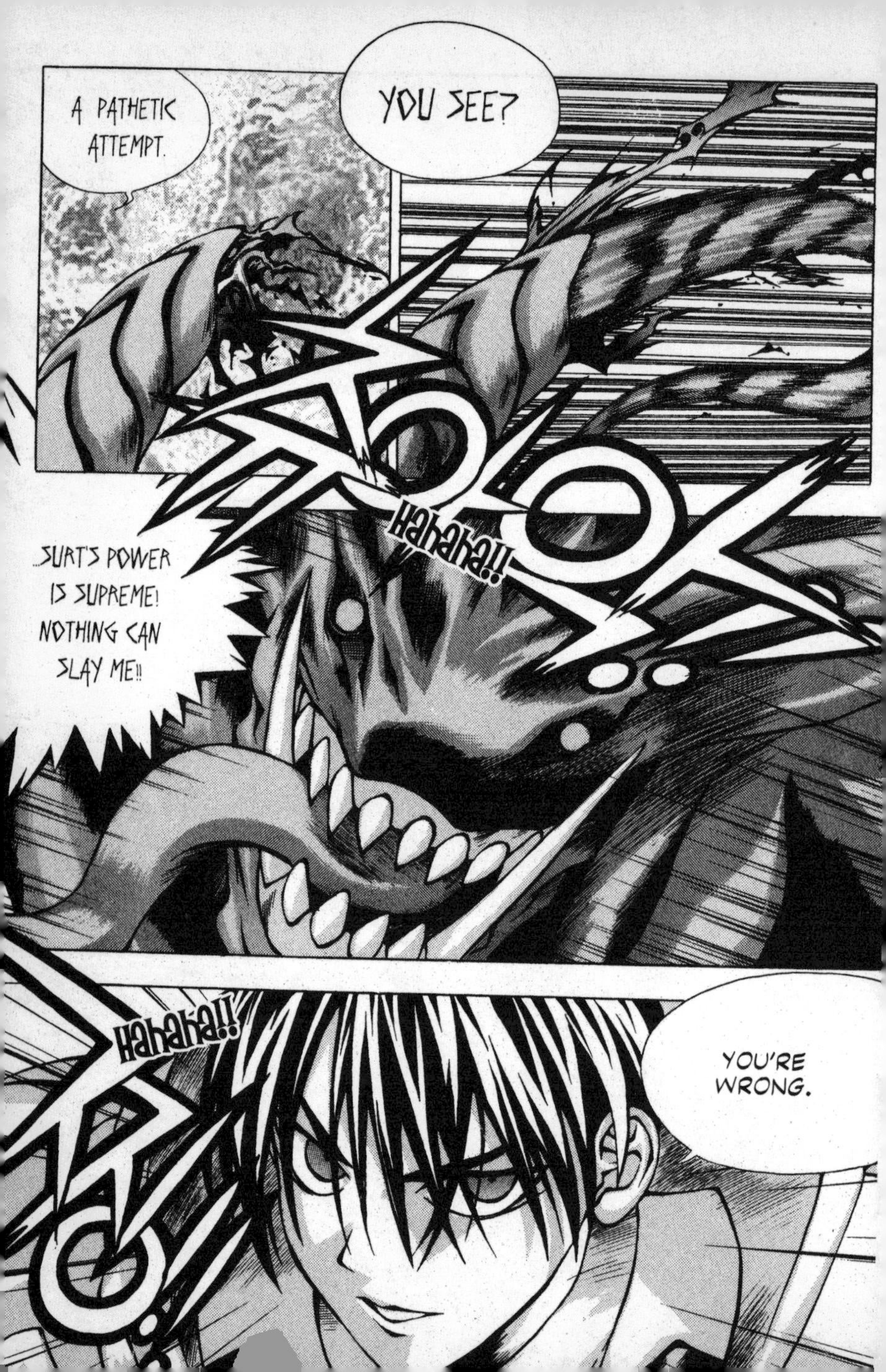
A PATHETIC ATTEMPT.
YOU SEE?
HAHAHA!!
...SURT'S POWER IS SUPREME! NOTHING CAN SLAY ME!!
HAHAHA!!
YOU'RE WRONG.

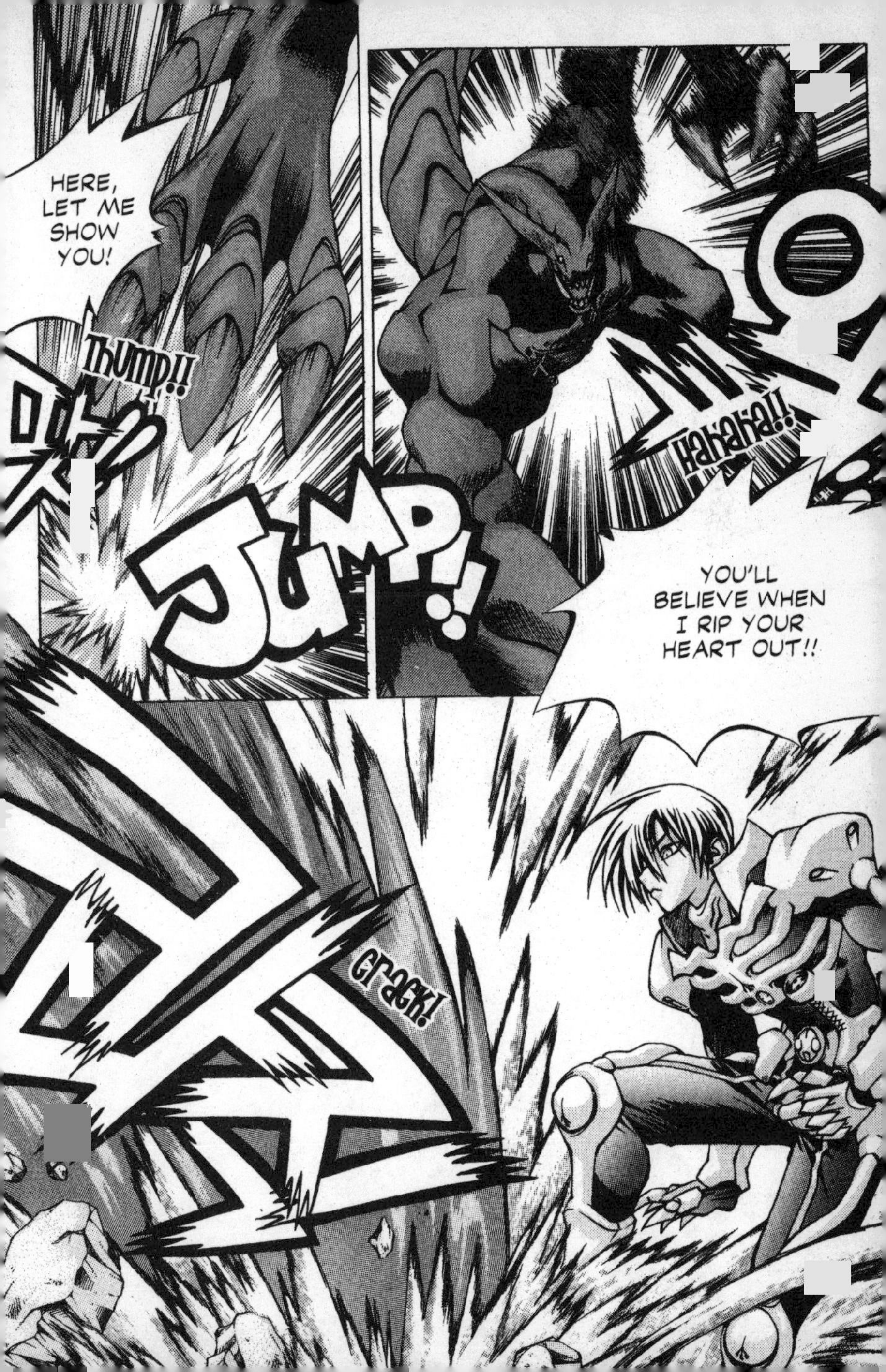
HERE, LET ME SHOW YOU!
THUMP!!
JUMP!!
HAHAHA!!
YOU'LL BELIEVE WHEN I RIP YOUR HEART OUT!!
CRACK!

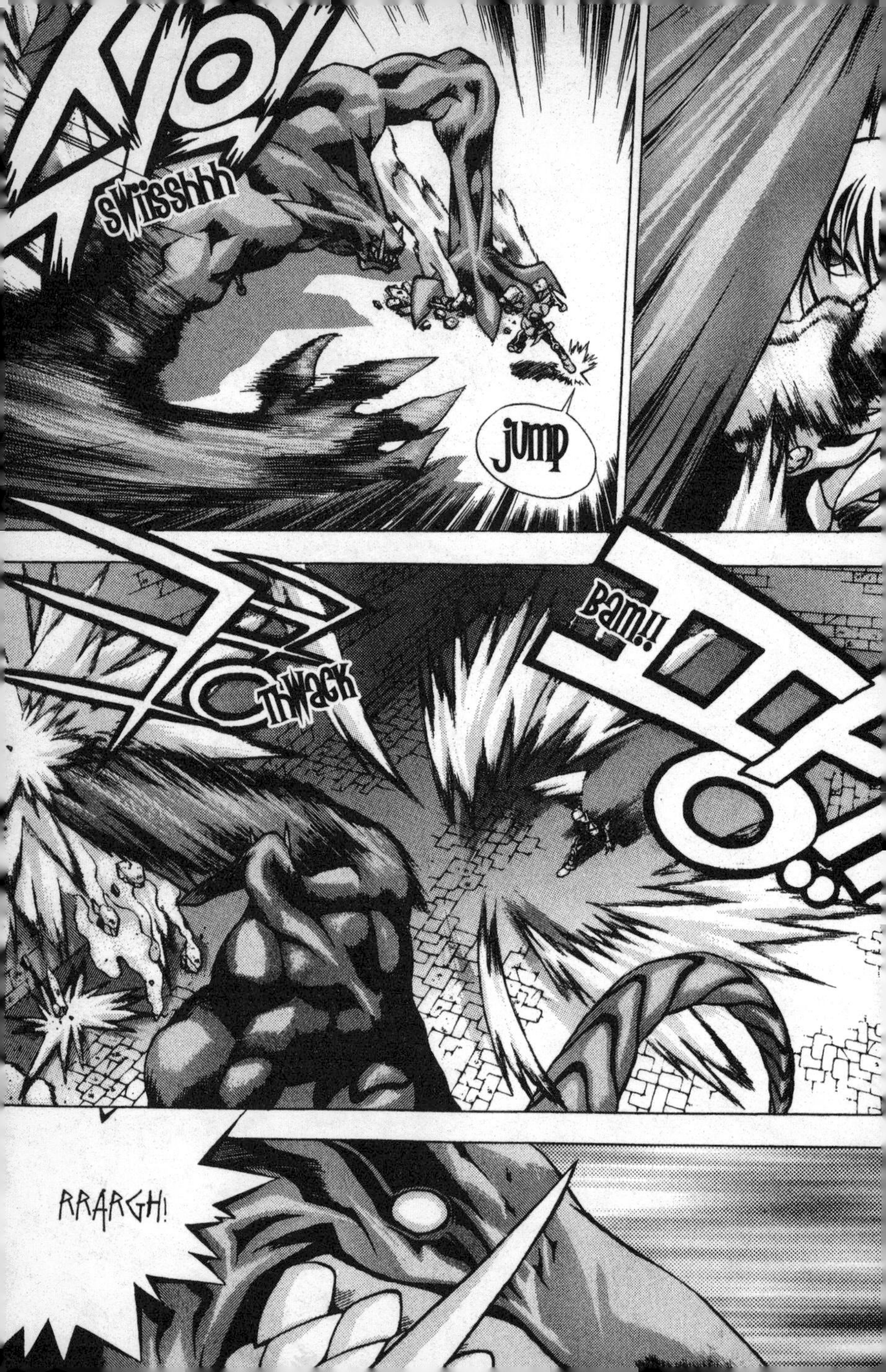
SWISSHHH
JUMP
THWACK
BAM!!
RRARGH!

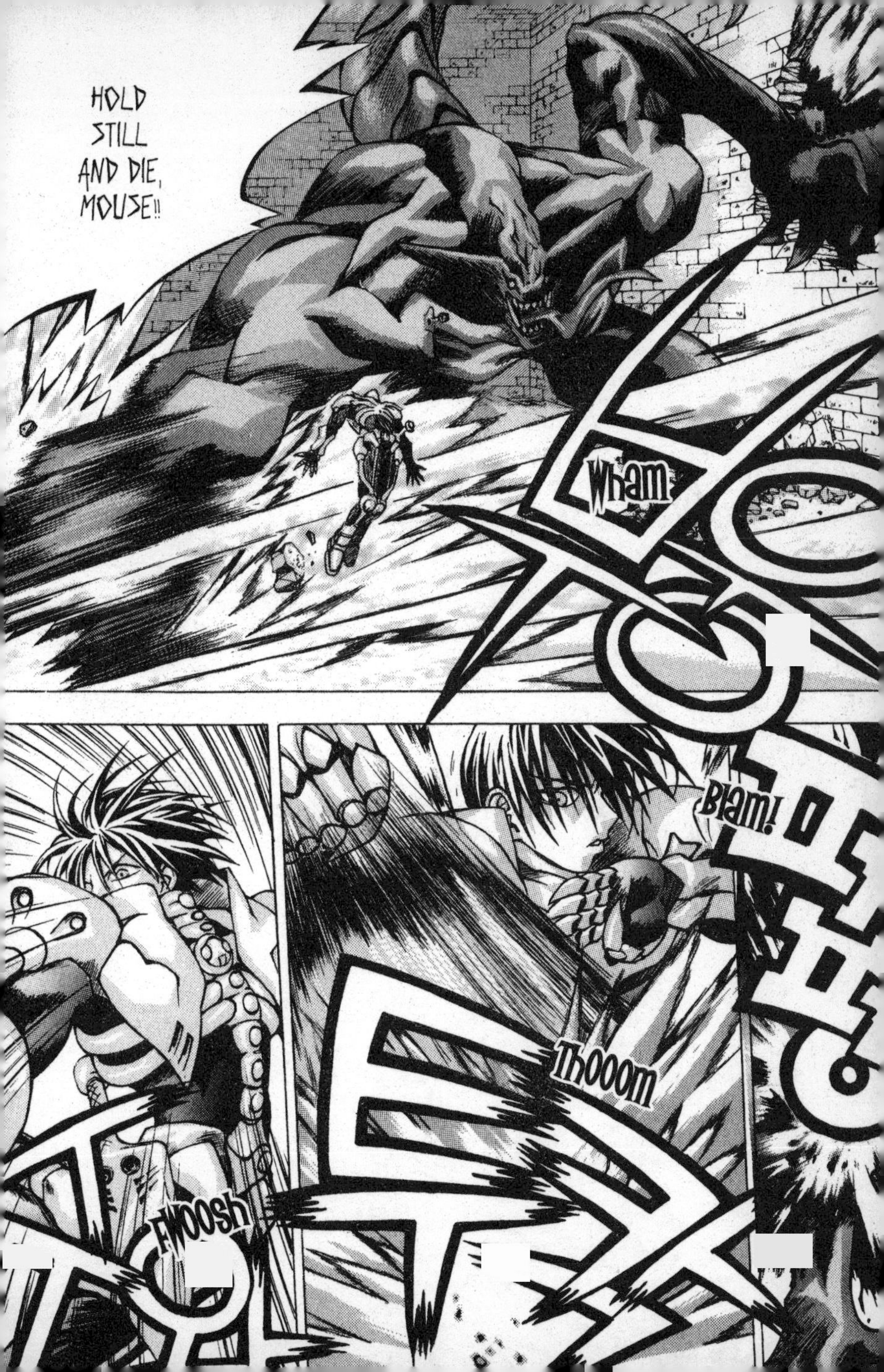
HOLD STILL AND DIE, MOUSE!!
Wham
FWOOSH
Blam!
ThOOOM

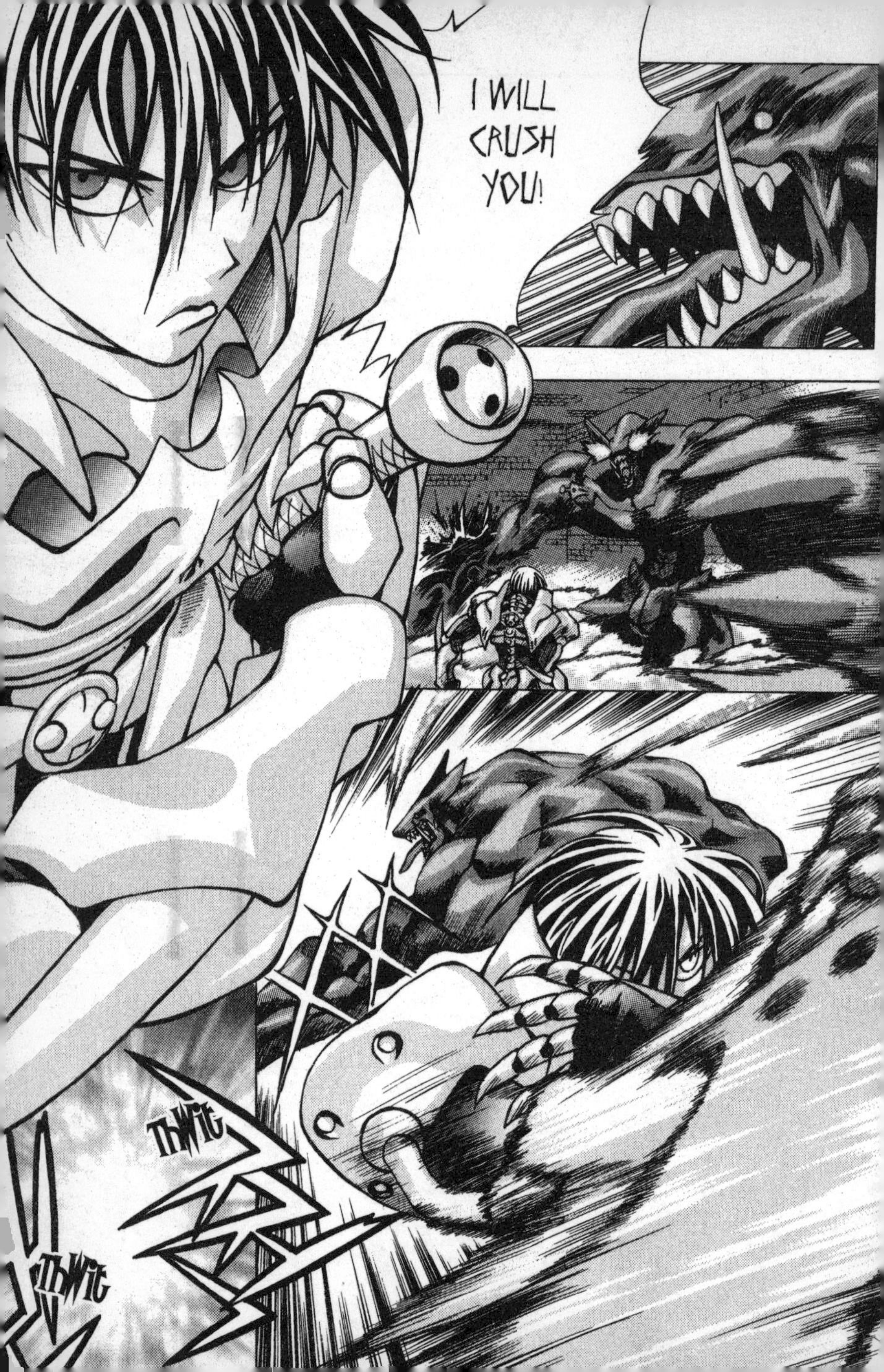
I WILL CRUSH YOU!
THWIT
THWIT

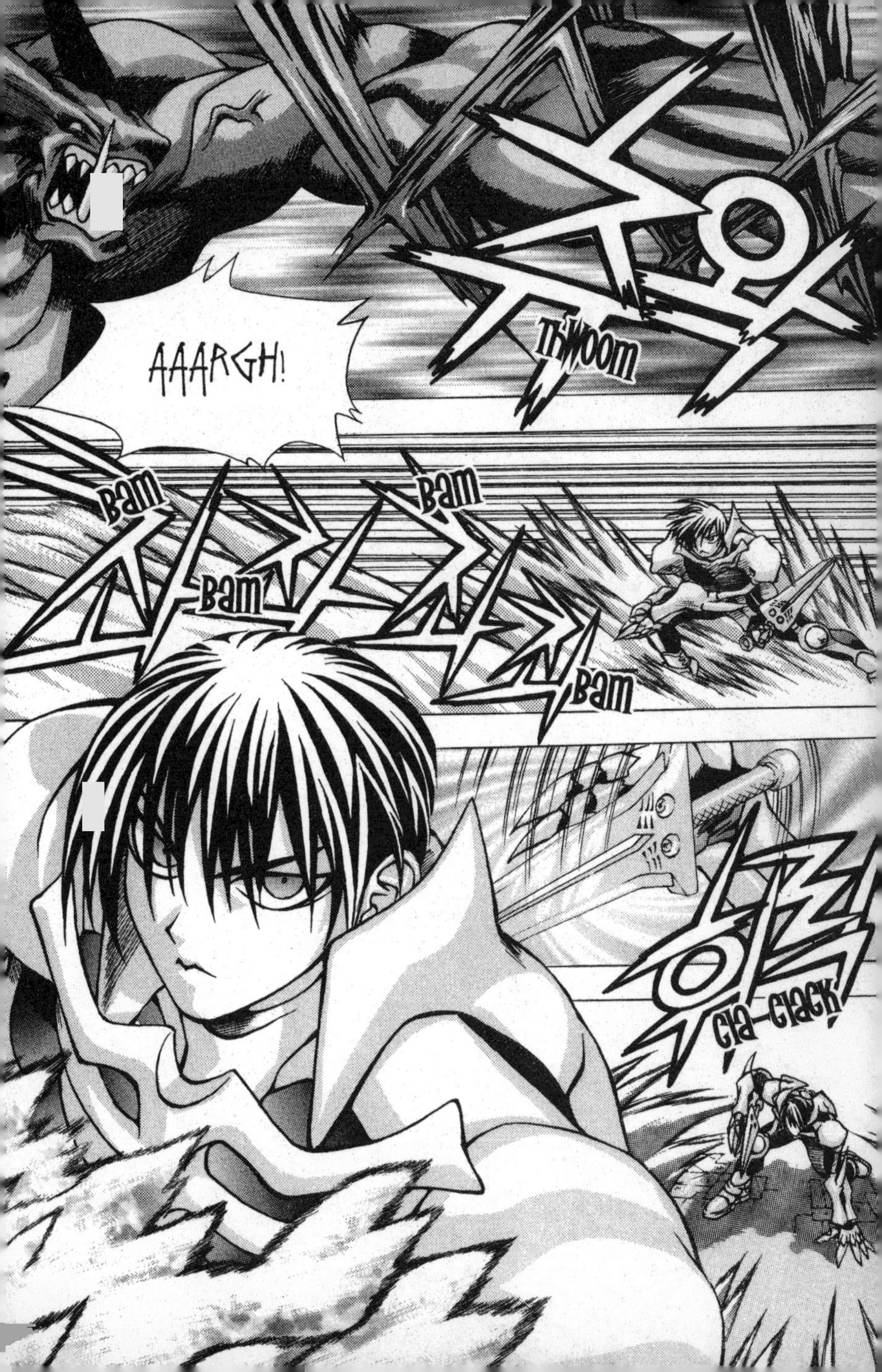
AAARGH!
THWOOM
BAM
BAM
BAM
BAM
CLA-CLACK!

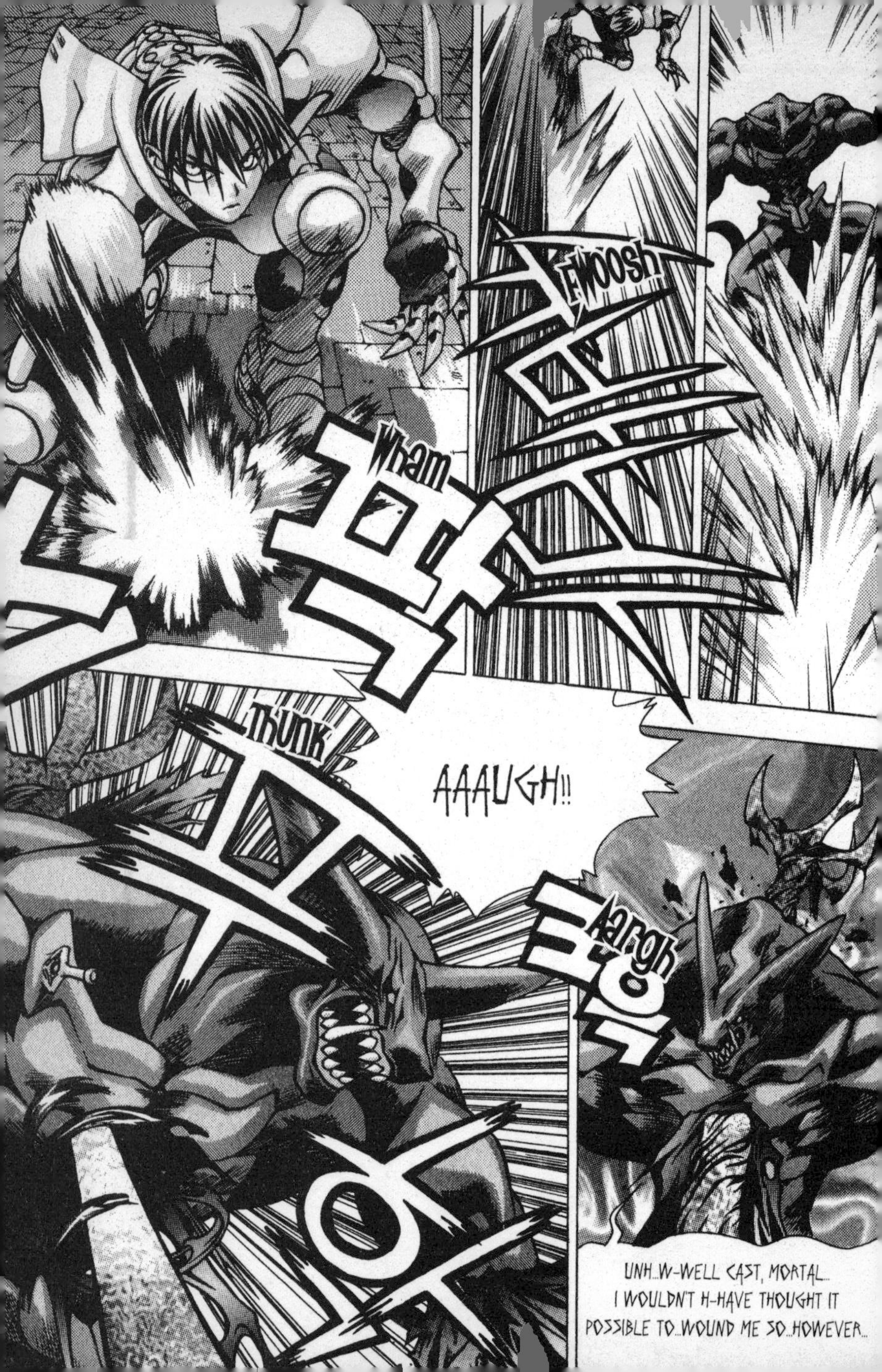
Wham
Whoosh
Thunk
AAAUGH!!
Aargh
UNH...W-WELL CAST, MORTAL... I WOULDN'T H-HAVE THOUGHT IT POSSIBLE TO...WOUND ME SO...HOWEVER...

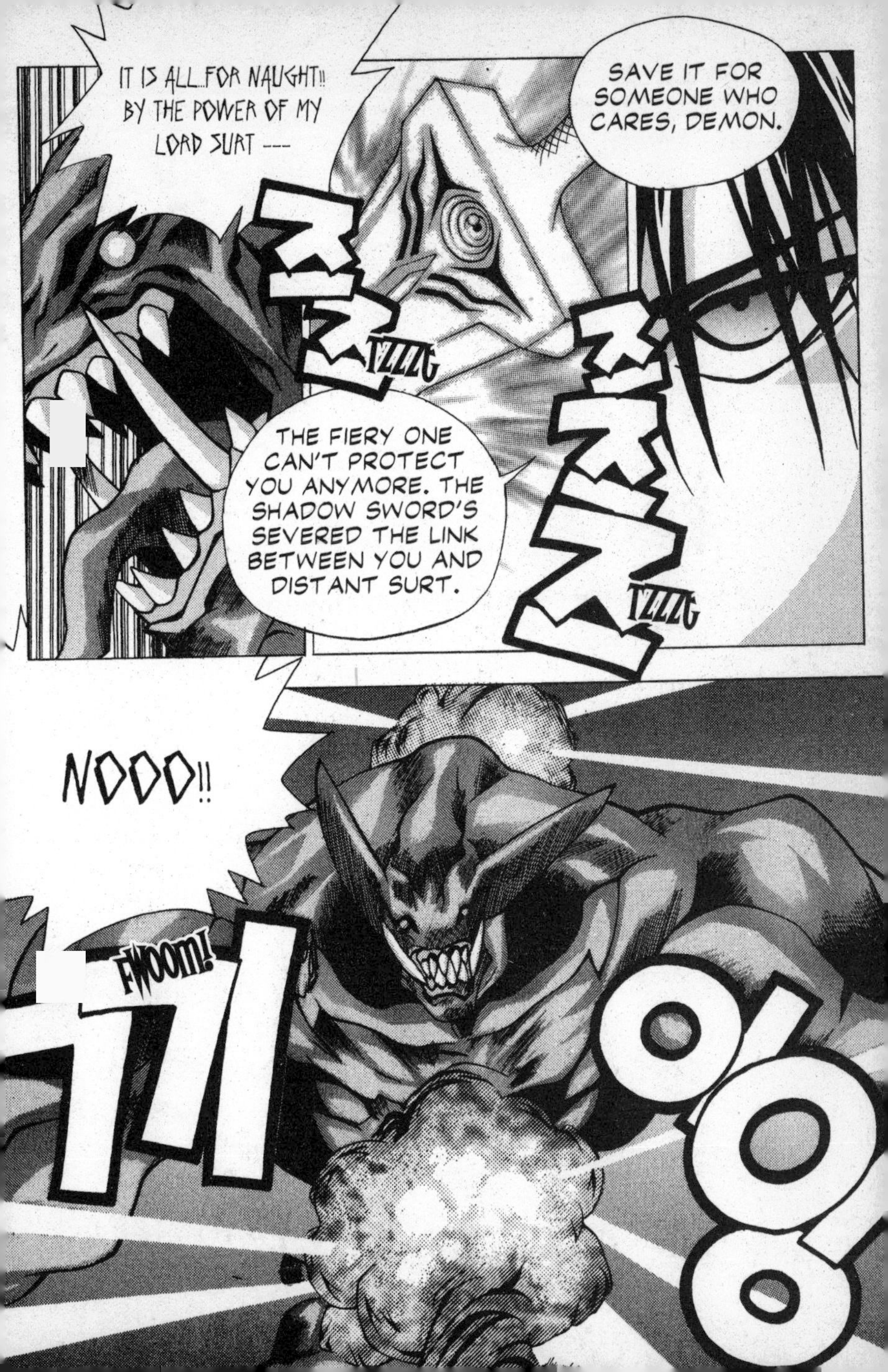
IT IS ALL...FOR NAUGHT!! BY THE POWER OF MY LORD SURT ---
SAVE IT FOR SOMEONE WHO CARES, DEMON.
TZZZG
THE FIERY ONE CAN'T PROTECT YOU ANYMORE. THE SHADOW SWORD'S SEVERED THE LINK BETWEEN YOU AND DISTANT SURT.
TZZZG
NOOO!!
FWOOM!

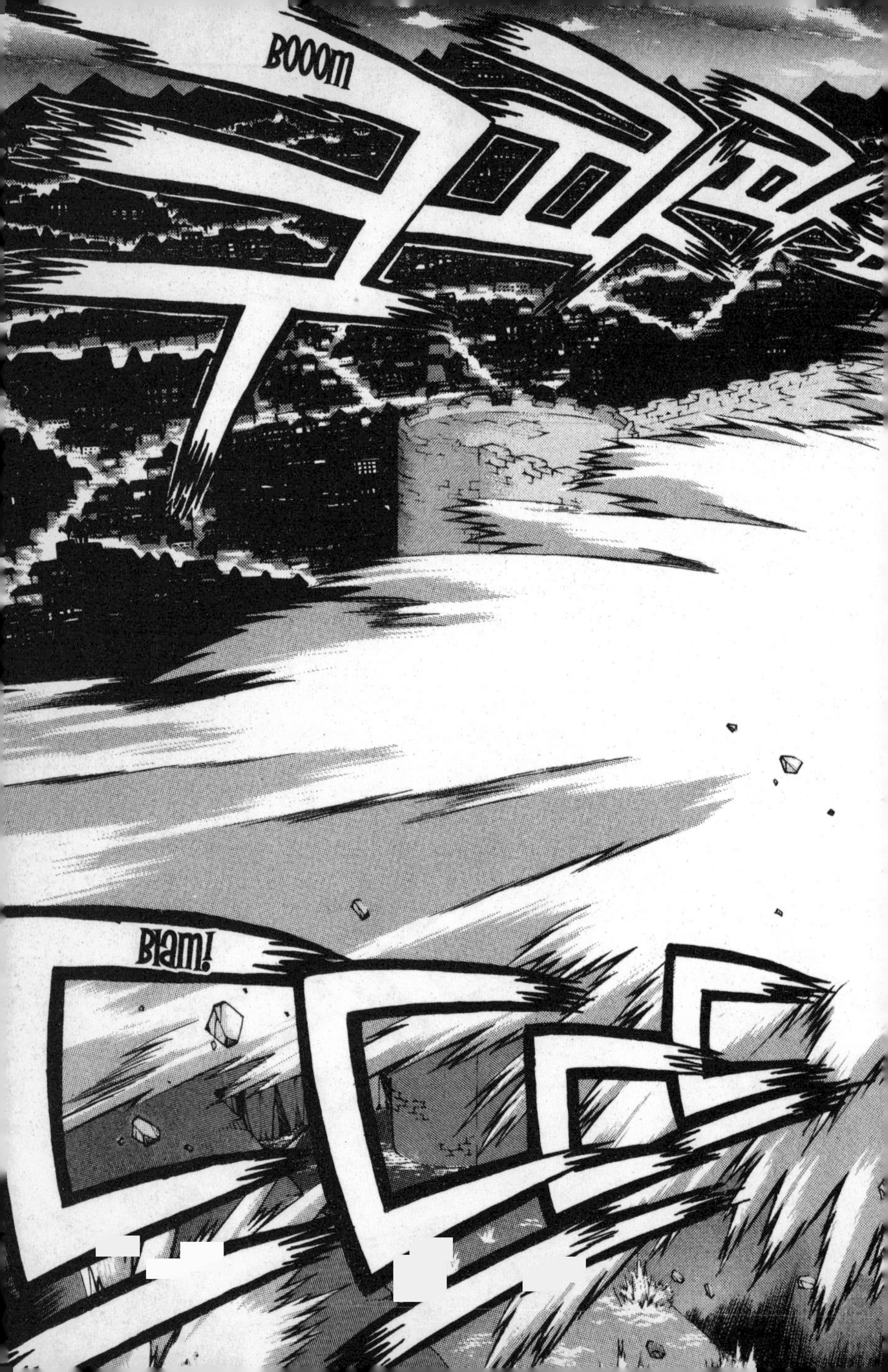
BOOOM
BLAM!

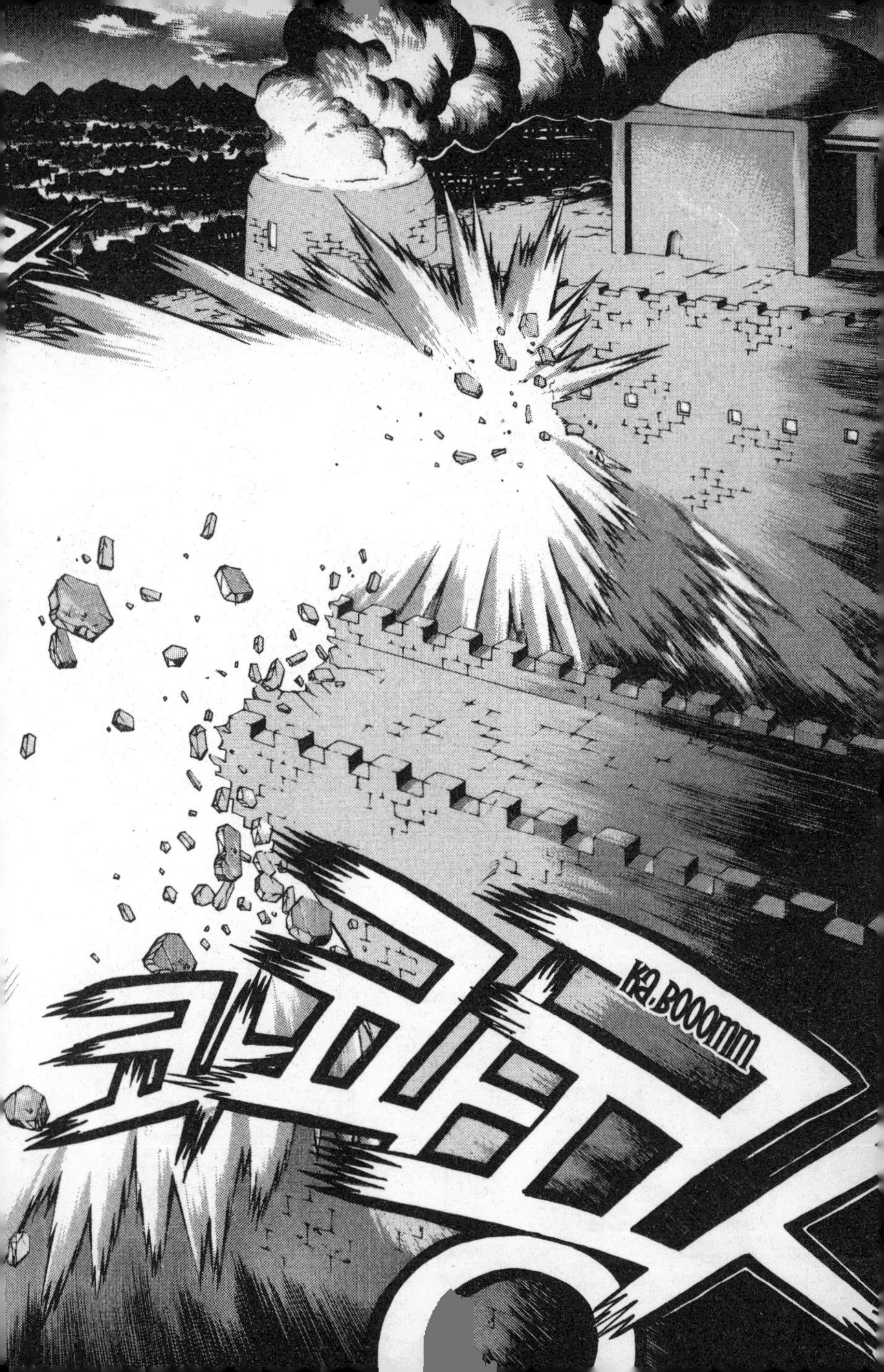
ka.BOOOmm

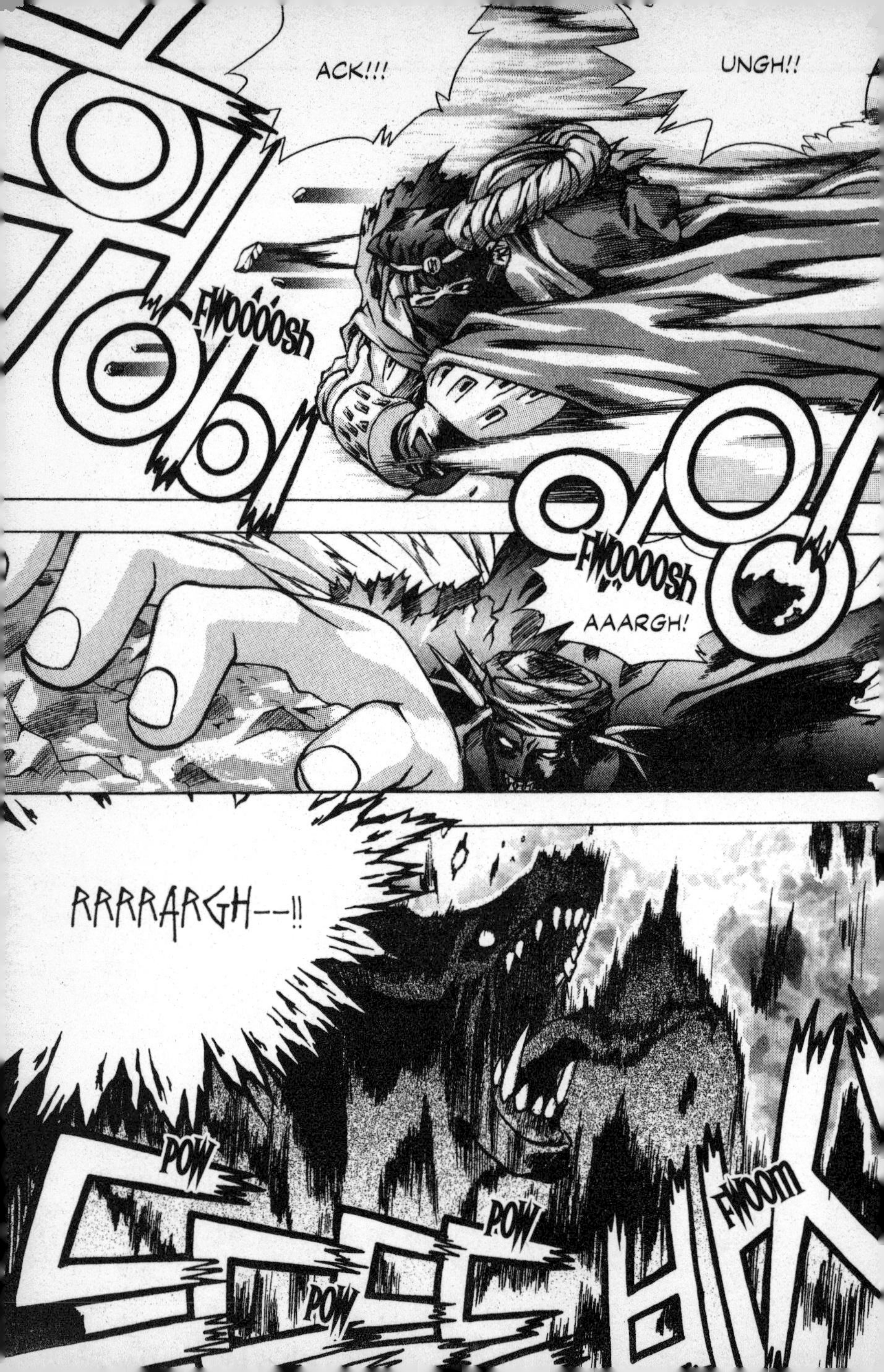
ACK!!!
UNGH!!
FWOOOOsh
FWOOOOsh
AAARGH!
RRRRARGH--!!
POW
POW
POW
FWOOM

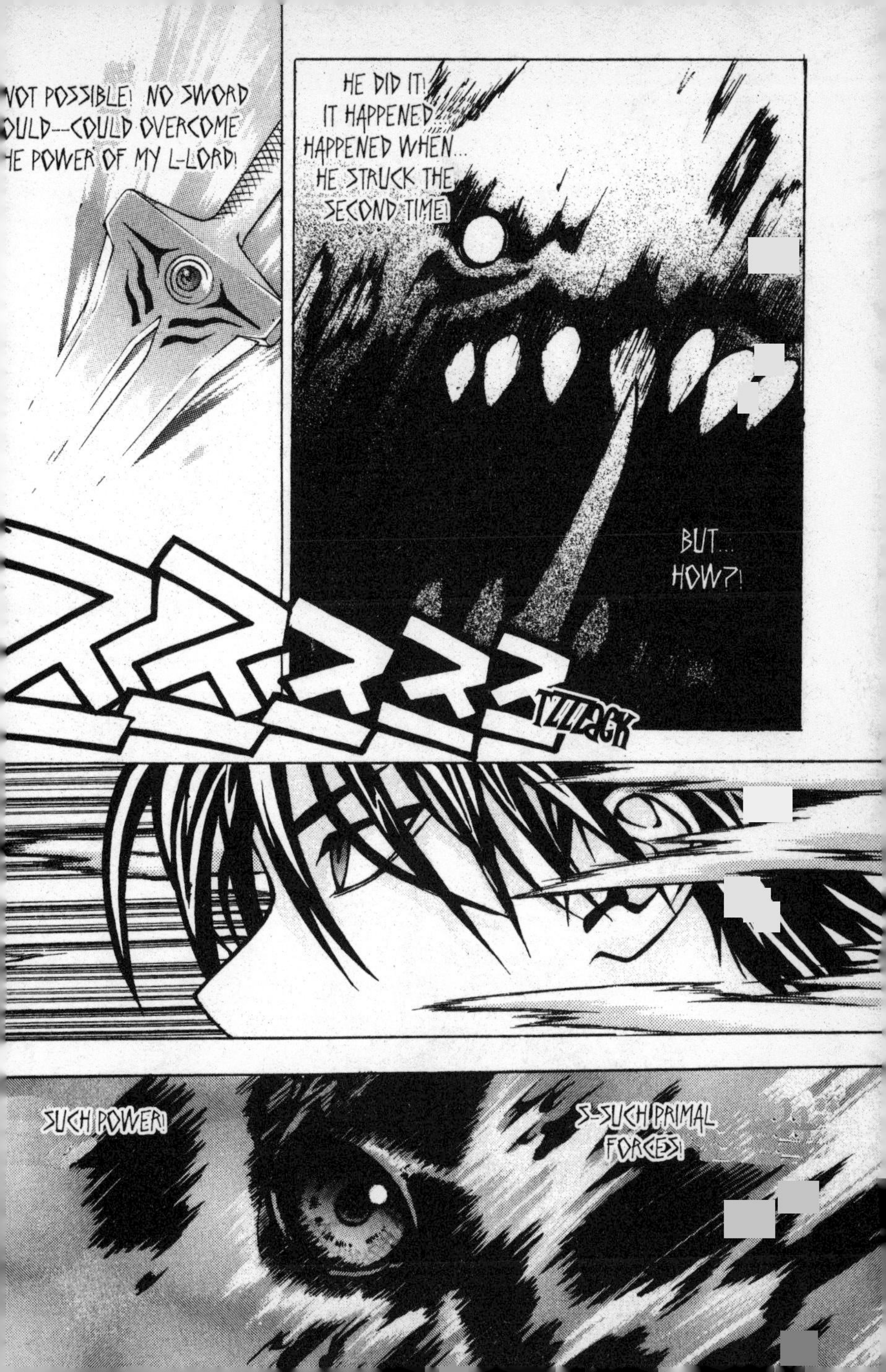
NOT POSSIBLE! NO SWORD COULD--COULD OVERCOME THE POWER OF MY L-LORD!
HE DID IT! IT HAPPENED... HAPPENED WHEN... HE STRUCK THE SECOND TIME!
BUT... HOW?!
TZZZACK
SUCH POWER!
S-SUCH PRIMAL FORCES!

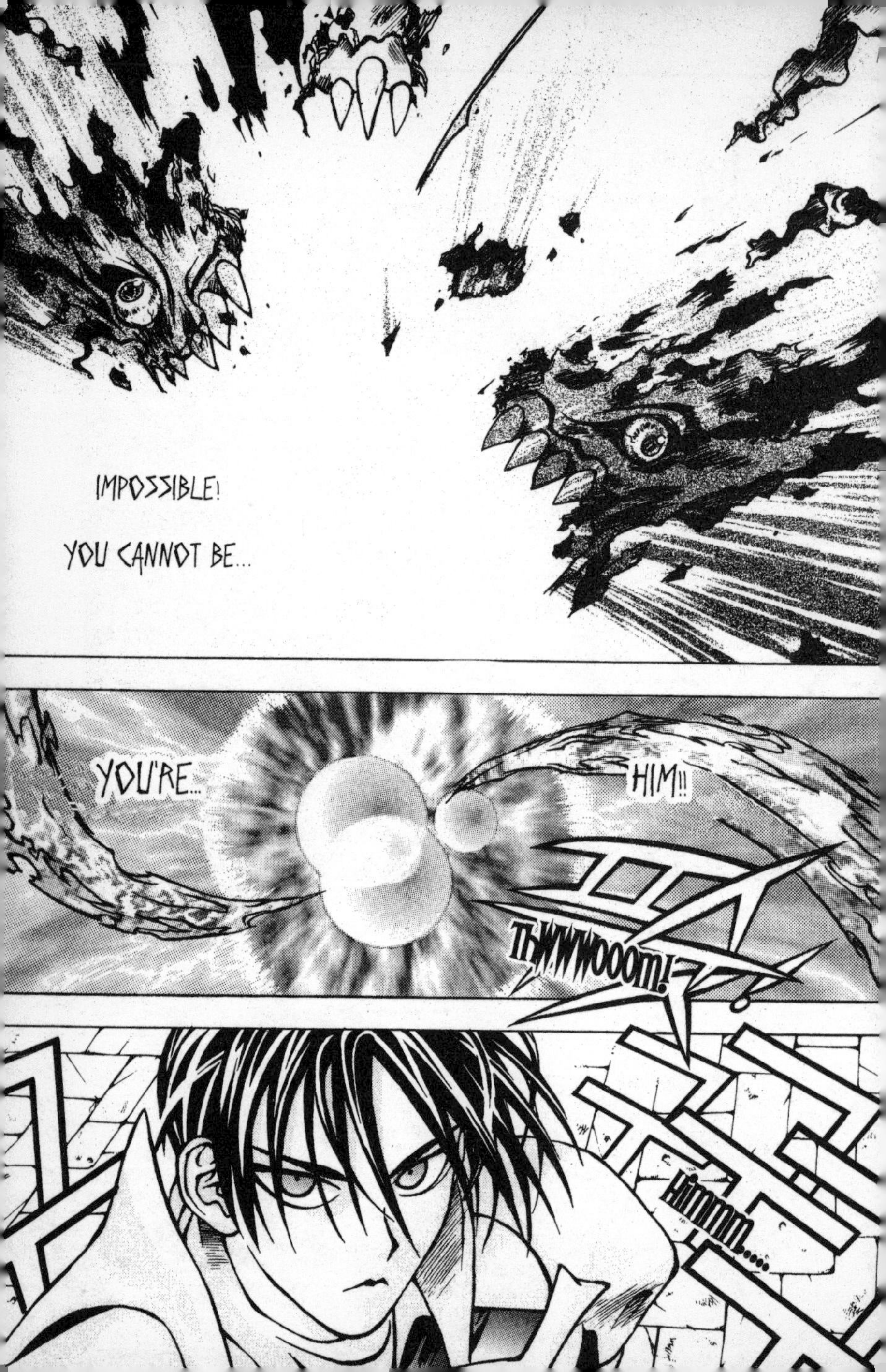
IMPOSSIBLE!
YOU CANNOT BE...
YOU'RE...
HIM!!
ThWWWOOOm!
Hmmmm.....

RAGNAROK
라그나로크
IN TO THE ABYSS

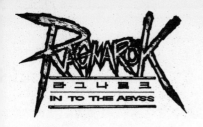

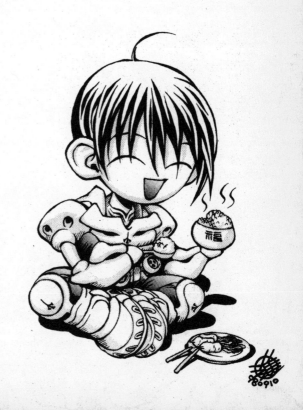

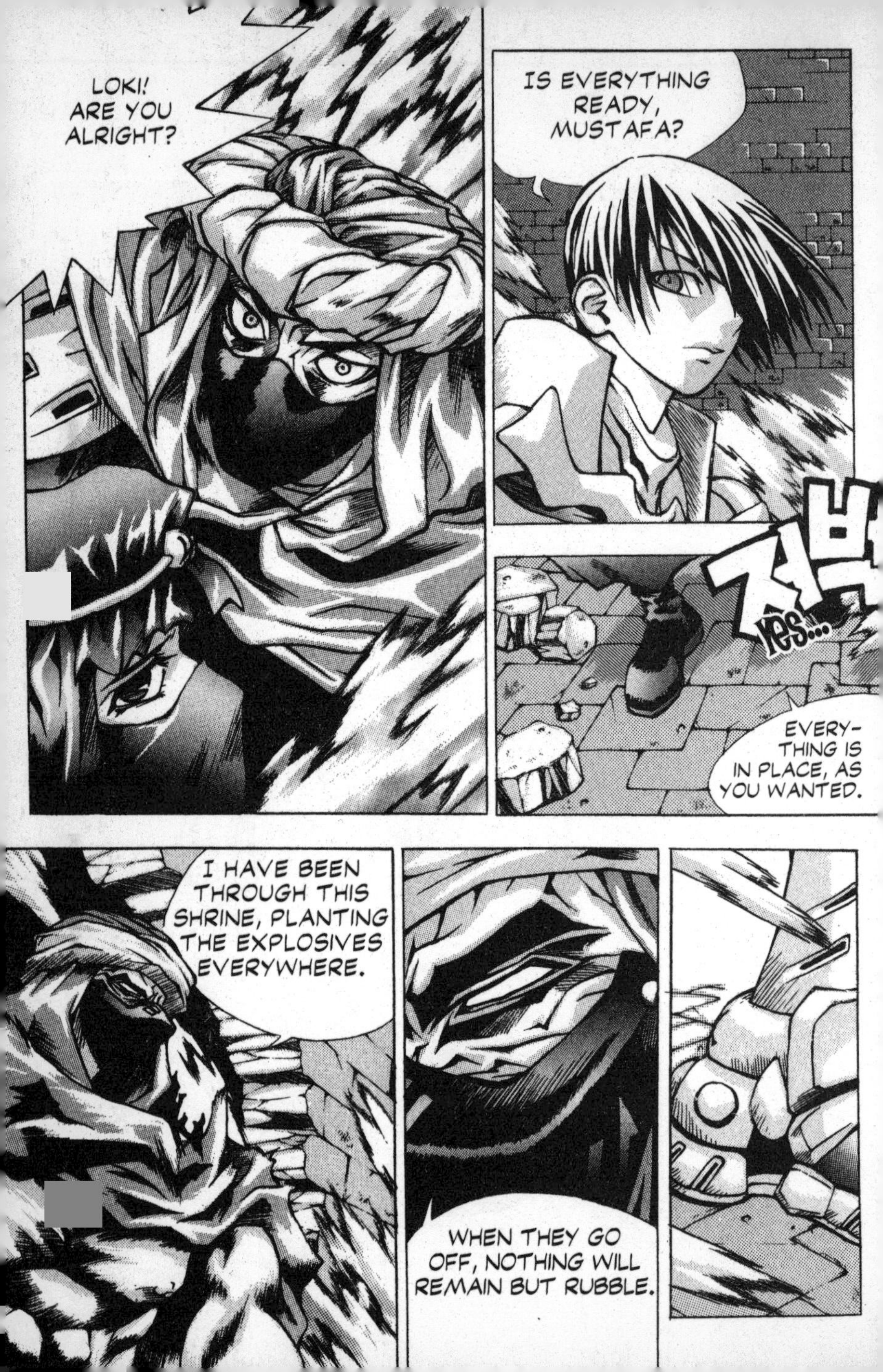
LOKI! ARE YOU ALRIGHT?
IS EVERYTHING READY, MUSTAFA?
저벅
YES...
EVERY-THING IS IN PLACE, AS YOU WANTED.
I HAVE BEEN THROUGH THIS SHRINE, PLANTING THE EXPLOSIVES EVERYWHERE.
WHEN THEY GO OFF, NOTHING WILL REMAIN BUT RUBBLE.

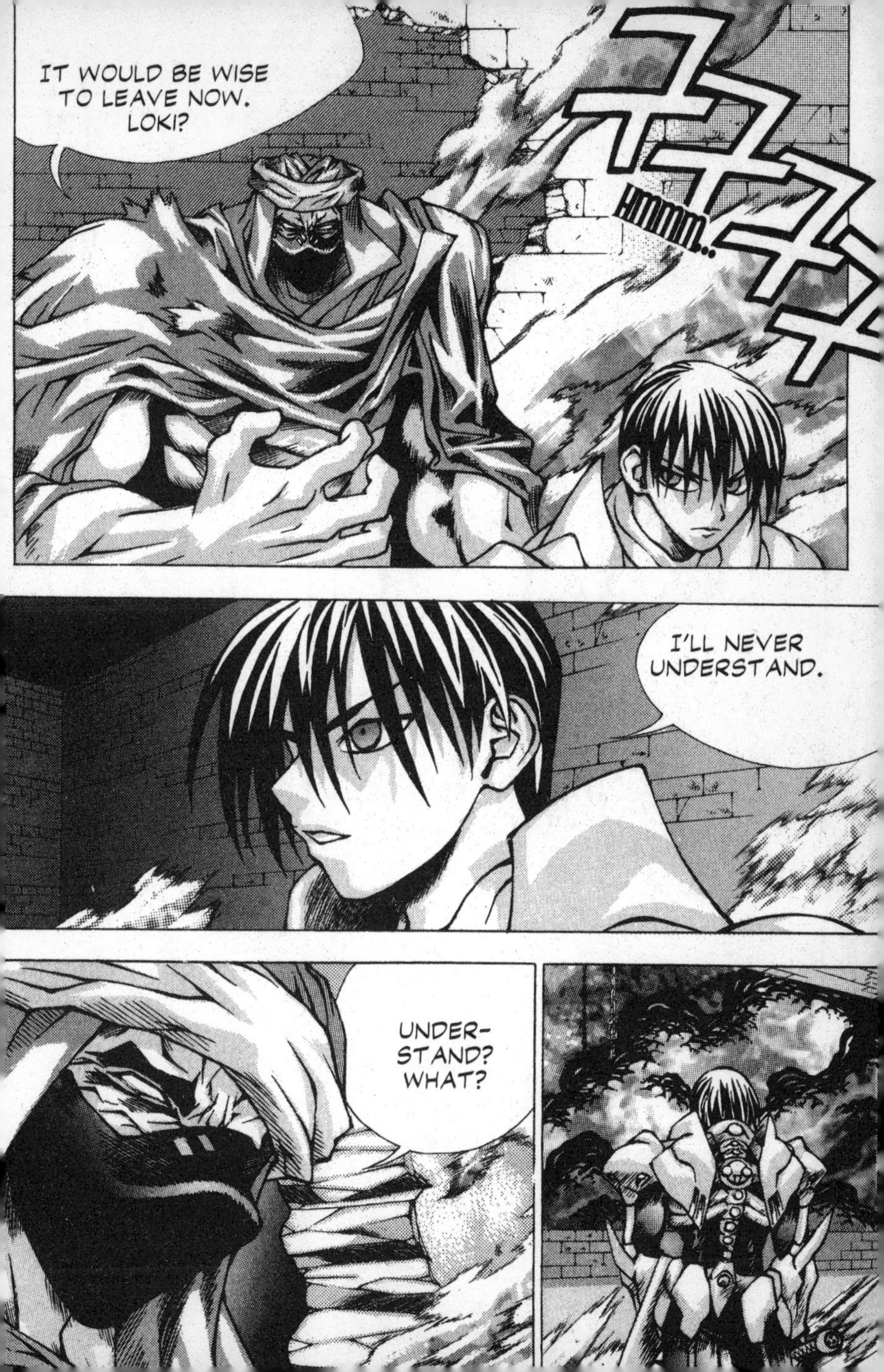
IT WOULD BE WISE TO LEAVE NOW. LOKI?
HMMM..
I'LL NEVER UNDERSTAND.
UNDER-STAND? WHAT?

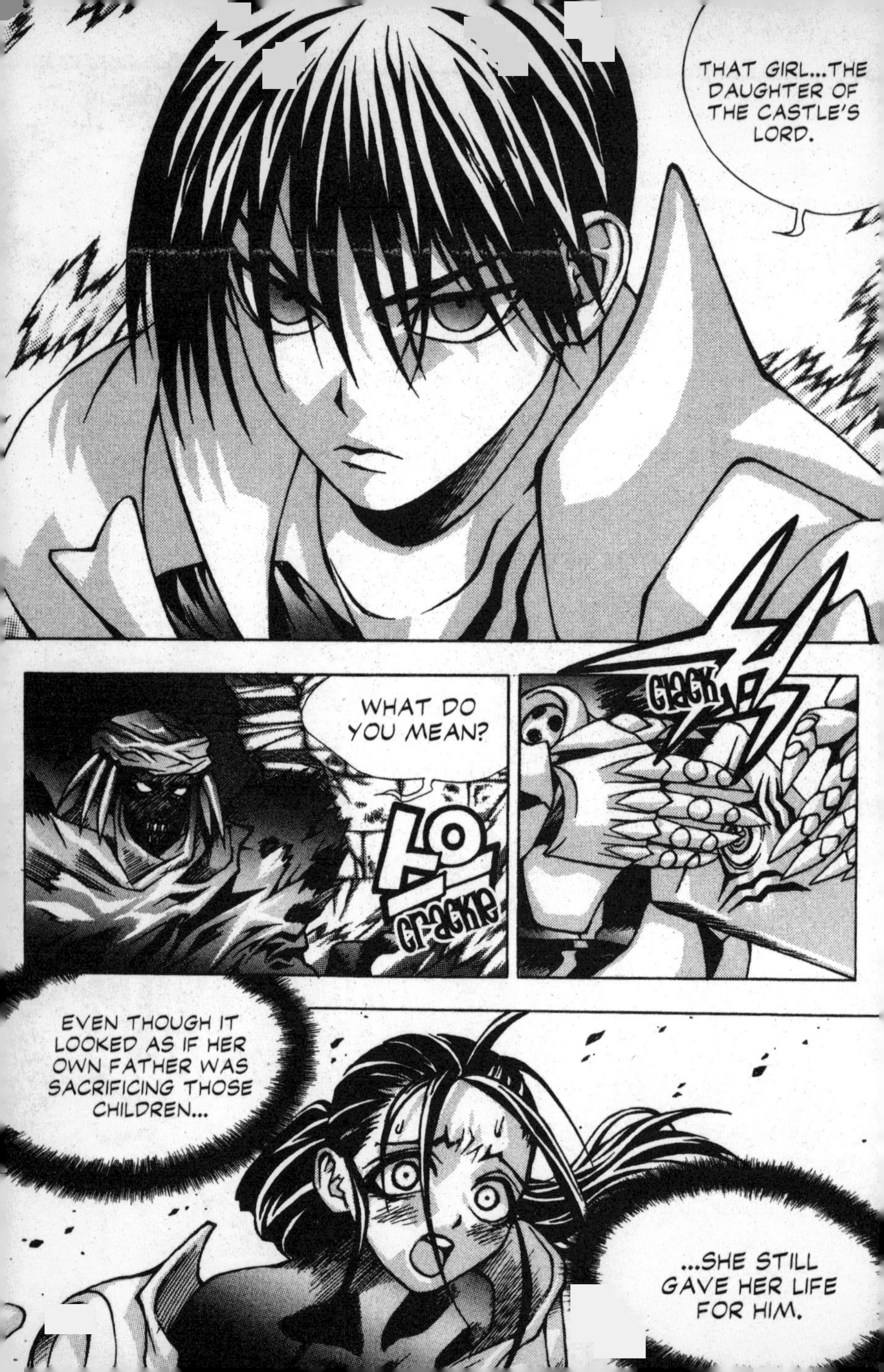
THAT GIRL...THE DAUGHTER OF THE CASTLE'S LORD.
WHAT DO YOU MEAN?
CRACKLE
CLACK
EVEN THOUGH IT LOOKED AS IF HER OWN FATHER WAS SACRIFICING THOSE CHILDREN...
...SHE STILL GAVE HER LIFE FOR HIM.

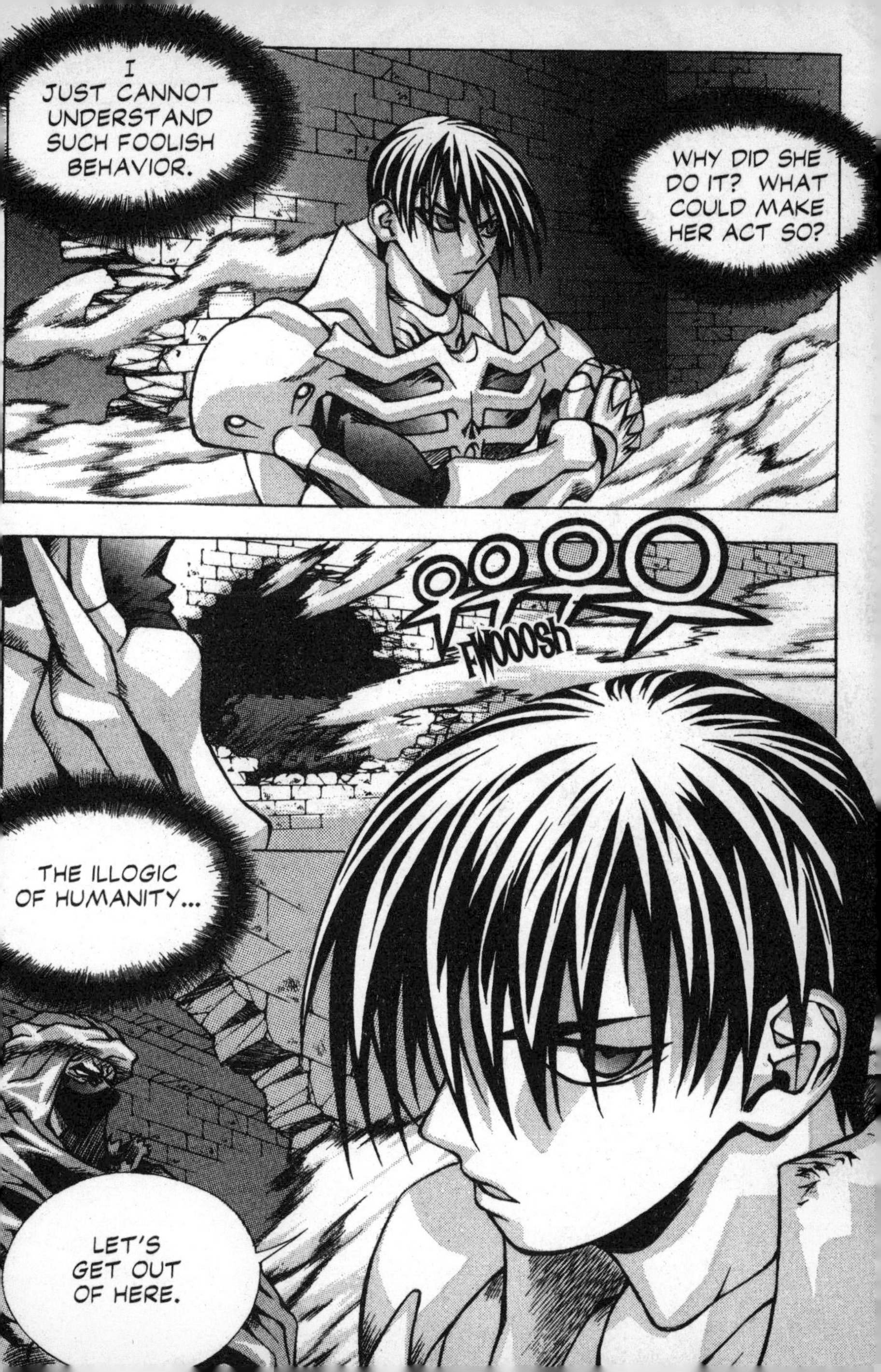
I JUST CANNOT UNDERSTAND SUCH FOOLISH BEHAVIOR.
WHY DID SHE DO IT? WHAT COULD MAKE HER ACT SO?
FWOOOSH
THE ILLOGIC OF HUMANITY...
LET'S GET OUT OF HERE.

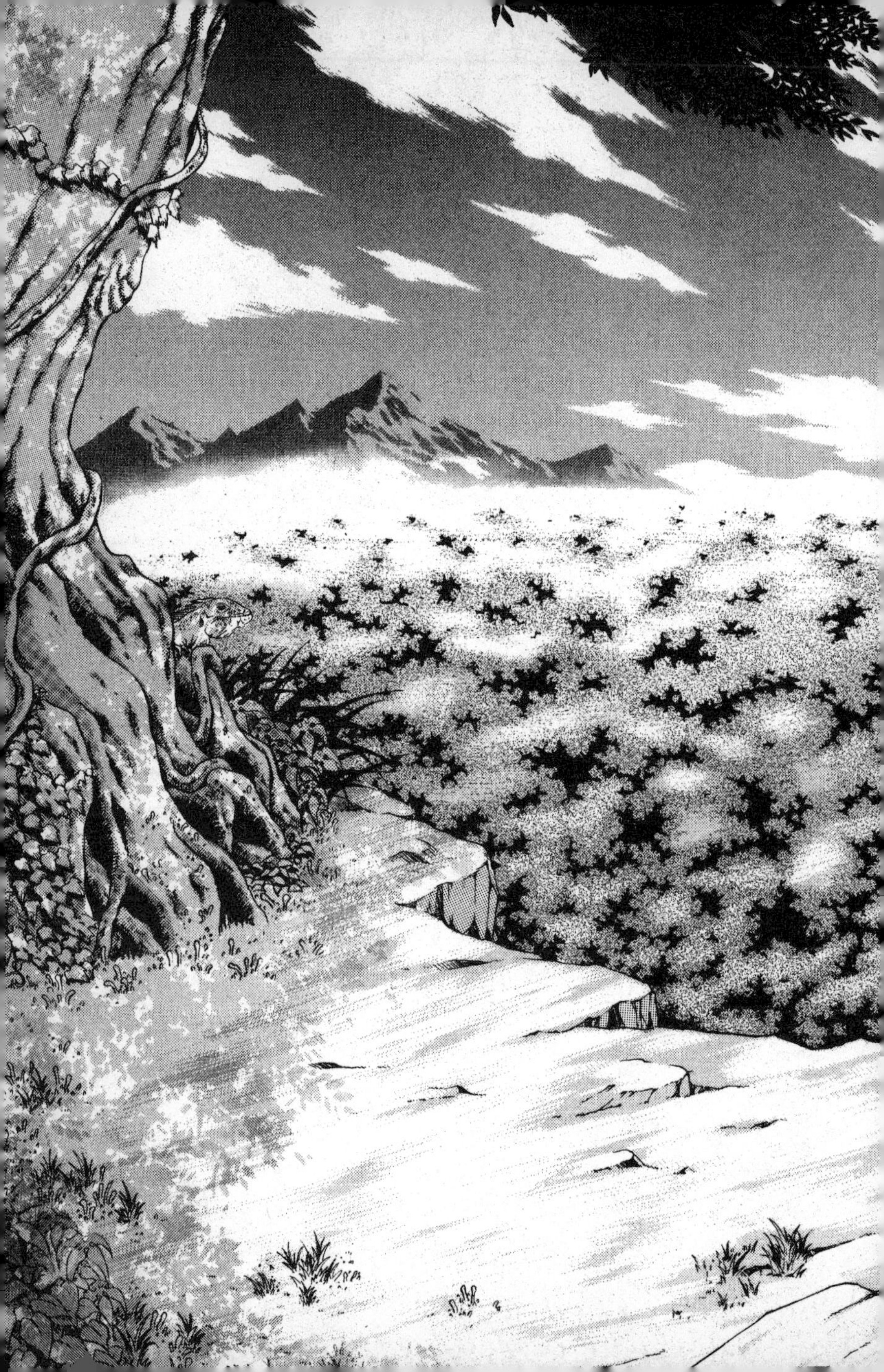

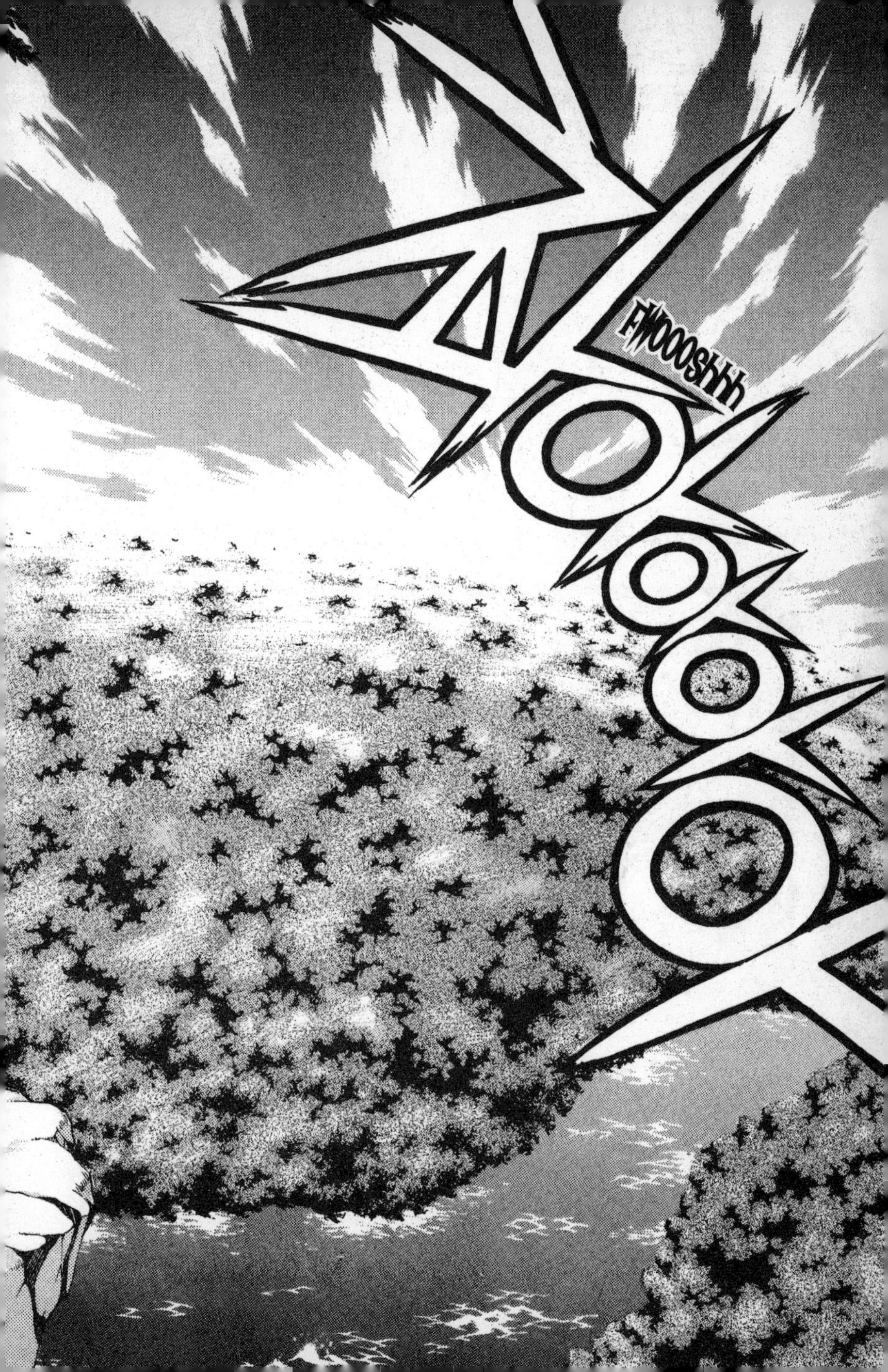
FWOOOSHhh

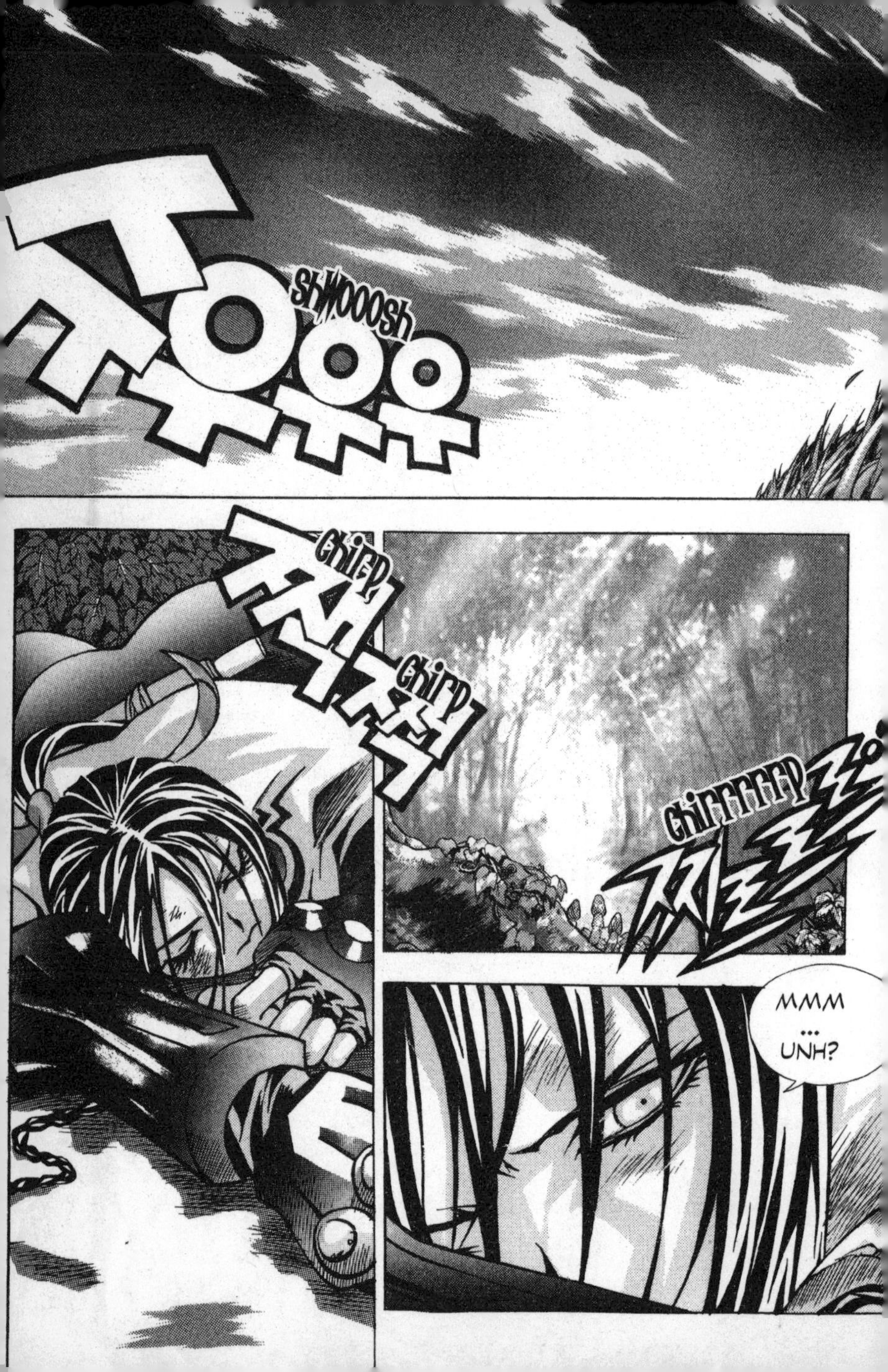
shwooosh
chirp
chirp
chirrrrrp
MMM ... UNH?

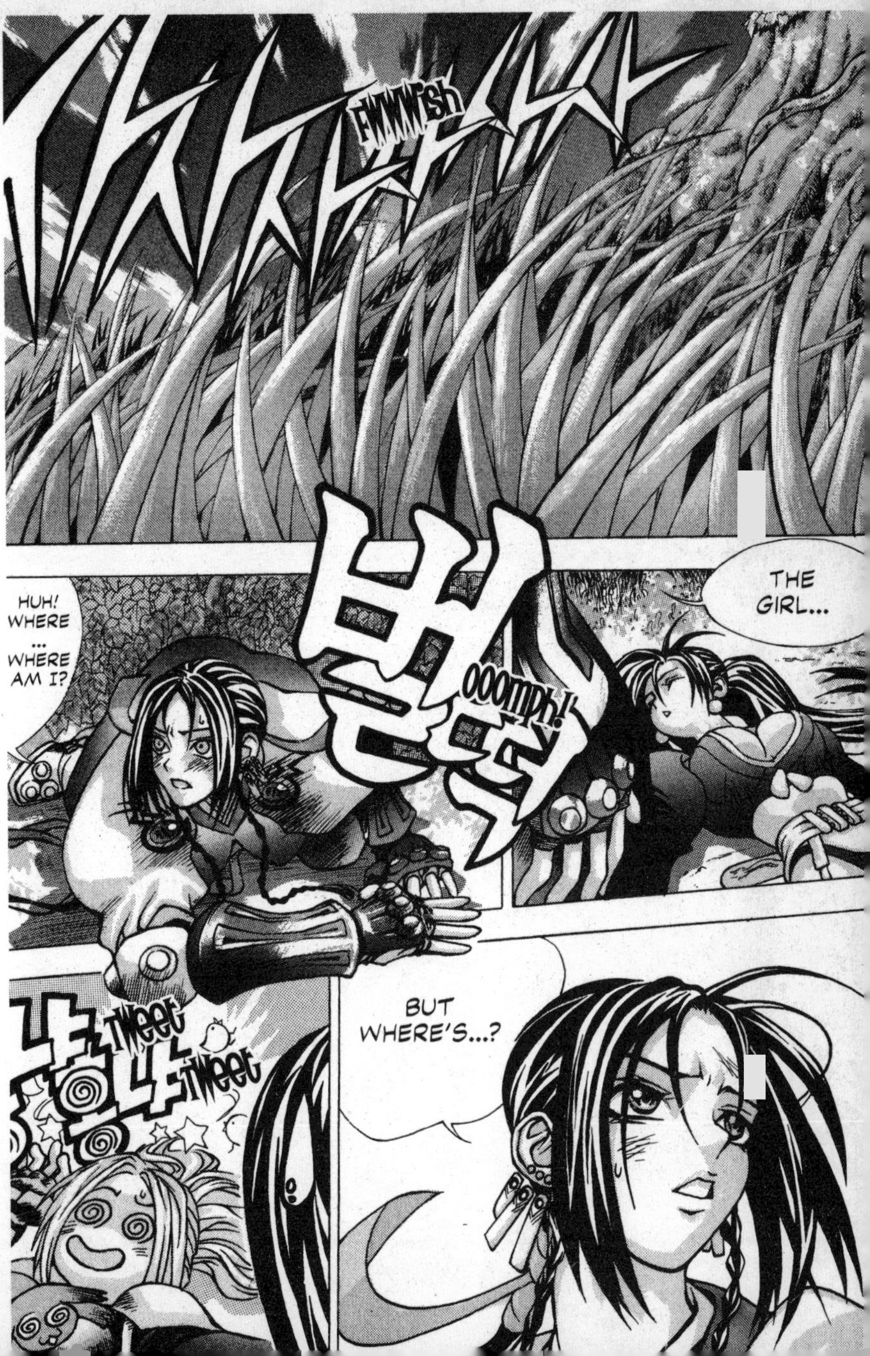
FWWWISH
HUH! WHERE ... WHERE AM I?
OOOMPH!
THE GIRL...
TWEET
TWEET
BUT WHERE'S...?

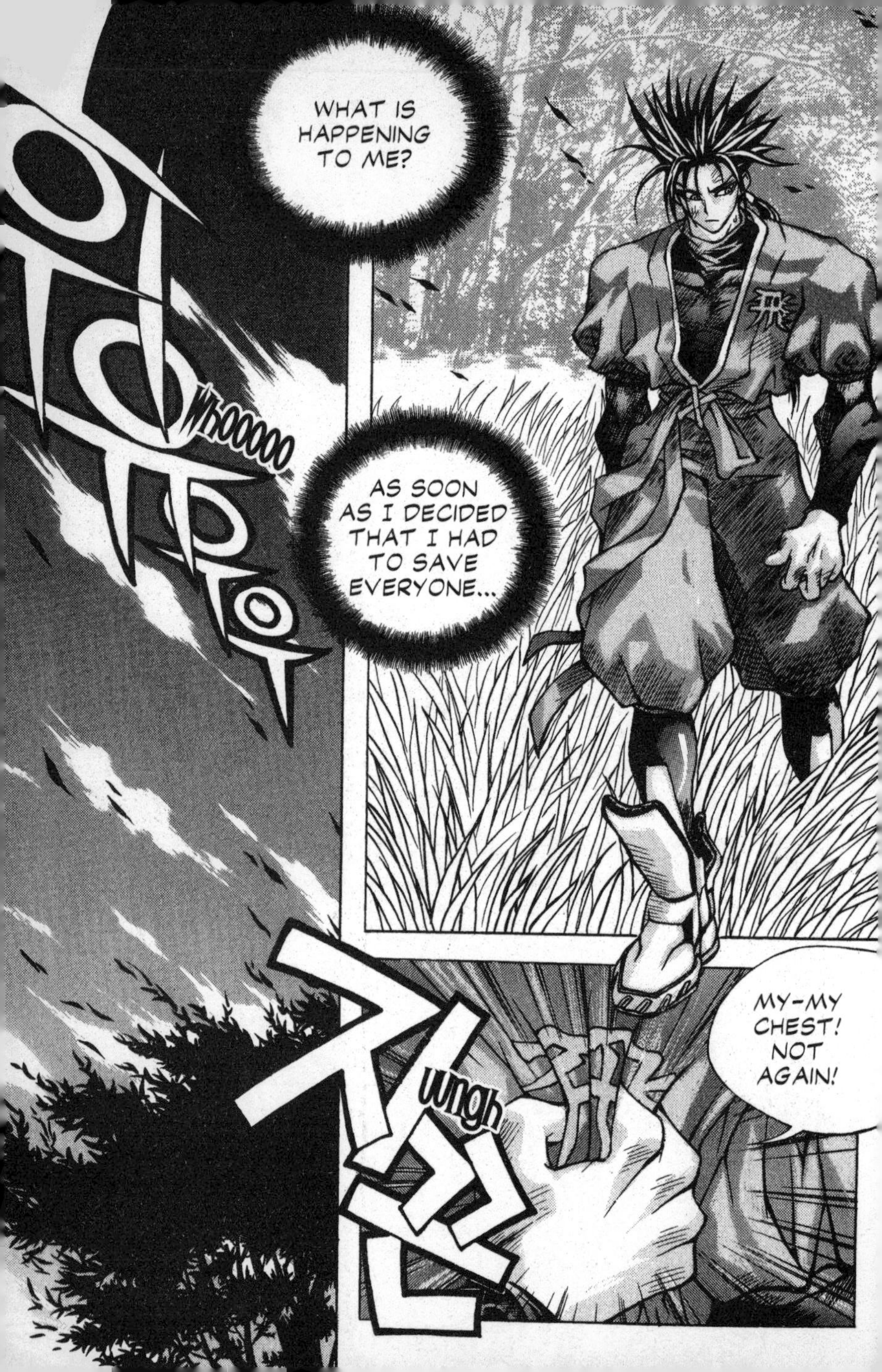
WHAT IS HAPPENING TO ME?
WHOOOOOO
AS SOON AS I DECIDED THAT I HAD TO SAVE EVERYONE...
MY-MY CHEST! NOT AGAIN!
UUNGH

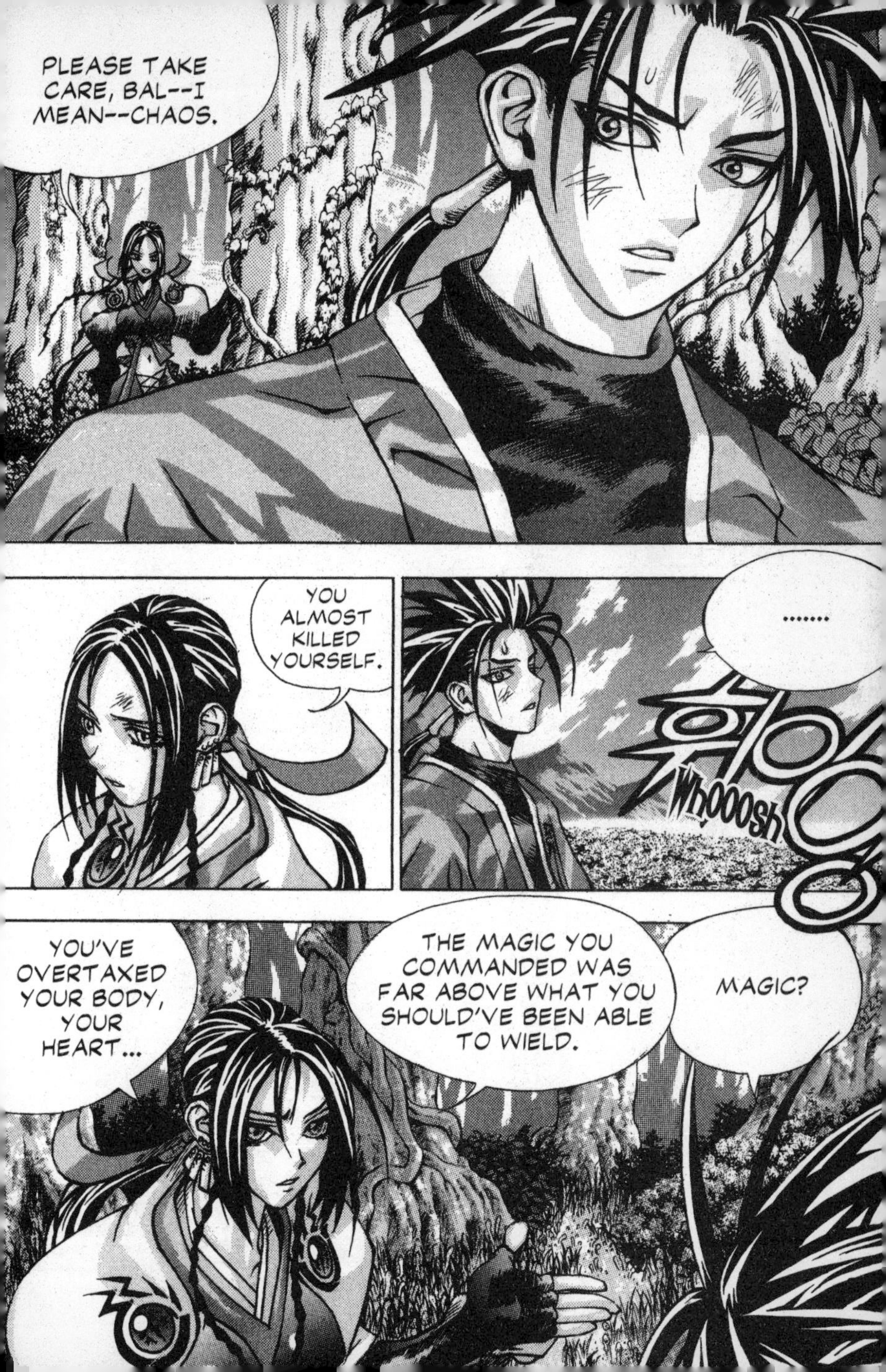
PLEASE TAKE CARE, BAL--I MEAN--CHAOS.
YOU ALMOST KILLED YOURSELF.
....
Whooosh
YOU'VE OVERTAXED YOUR BODY, YOUR HEART...
THE MAGIC YOU COMMANDED WAS FAR ABOVE WHAT YOU SHOULD'VE BEEN ABLE TO WIELD.
MAGIC?

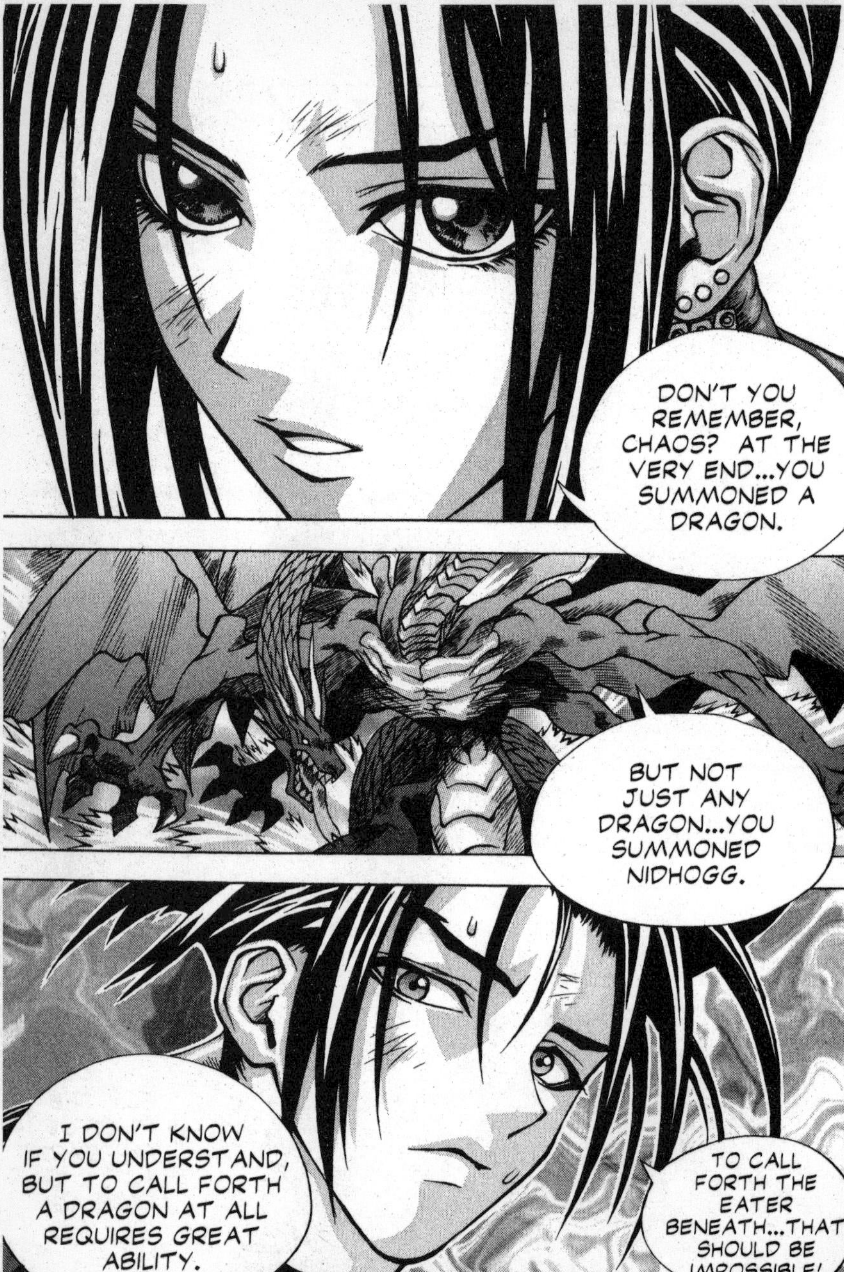
DON'T YOU REMEMBER, CHAOS? AT THE VERY END...YOU SUMMONED A DRAGON.
BUT NOT JUST ANY DRAGON...YOU SUMMONED NIDHOGG.
I DON'T KNOW IF YOU UNDERSTAND, BUT TO CALL FORTH A DRAGON AT ALL REQUIRES GREAT ABILITY.
TO CALL FORTH THE EATER BENEATH...THAT SHOULD BE IMPOSSIBLE!

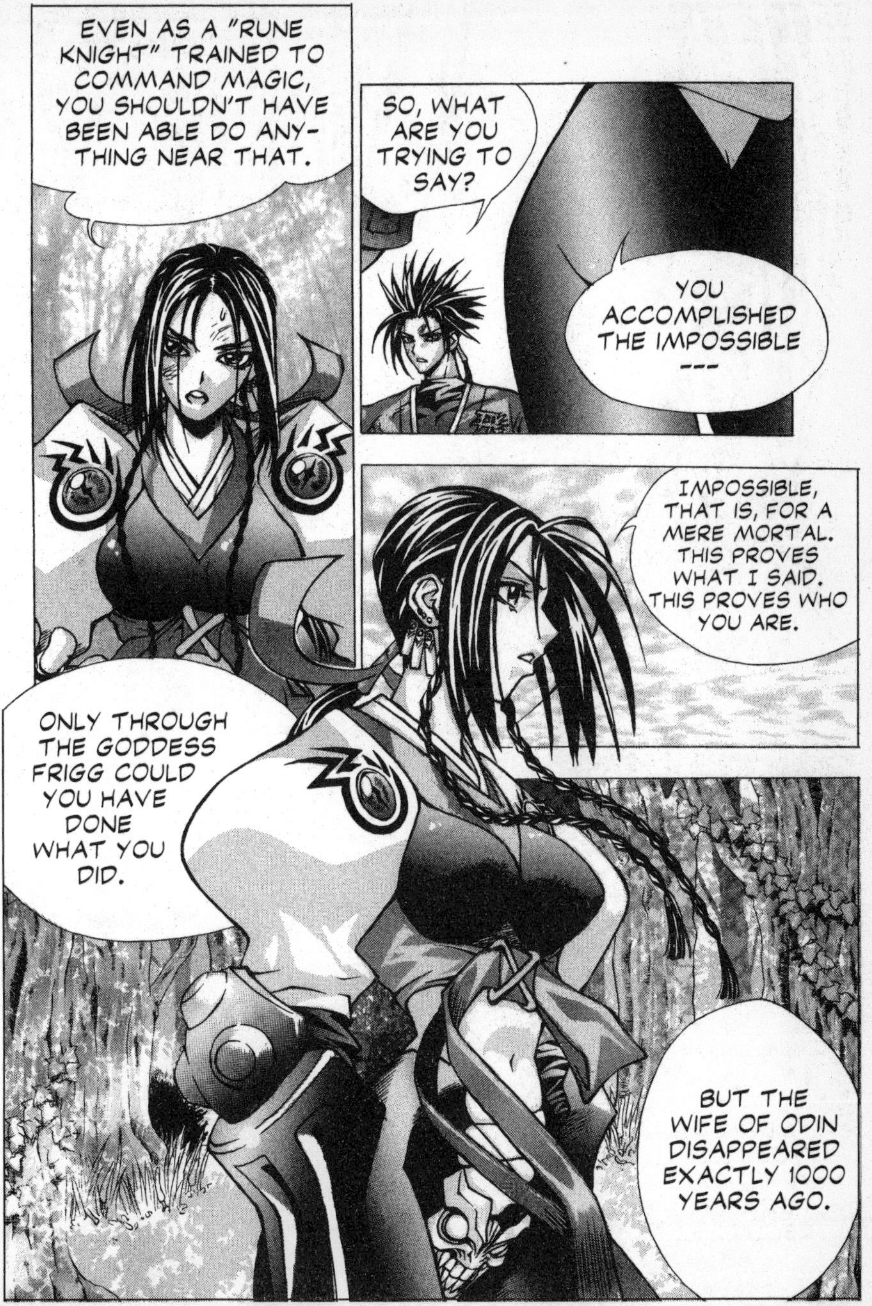
EVEN AS A "RUNE KNIGHT" TRAINED TO COMMAND MAGIC, YOU SHOULDN'T HAVE BEEN ABLE DO ANYTHING NEAR THAT.
SO, WHAT ARE YOU TRYING TO SAY?
YOU ACCOMPLISHED THE IMPOSSIBLE ---
IMPOSSIBLE, THAT IS, FOR A MERE MORTAL. THIS PROVES WHAT I SAID. THIS PROVES WHO YOU ARE.
ONLY THROUGH THE GODDESS FRIGG COULD YOU HAVE DONE WHAT YOU DID.
BUT THE WIFE OF ODIN DISAPPEARED EXACTLY 1000 YEARS AGO.

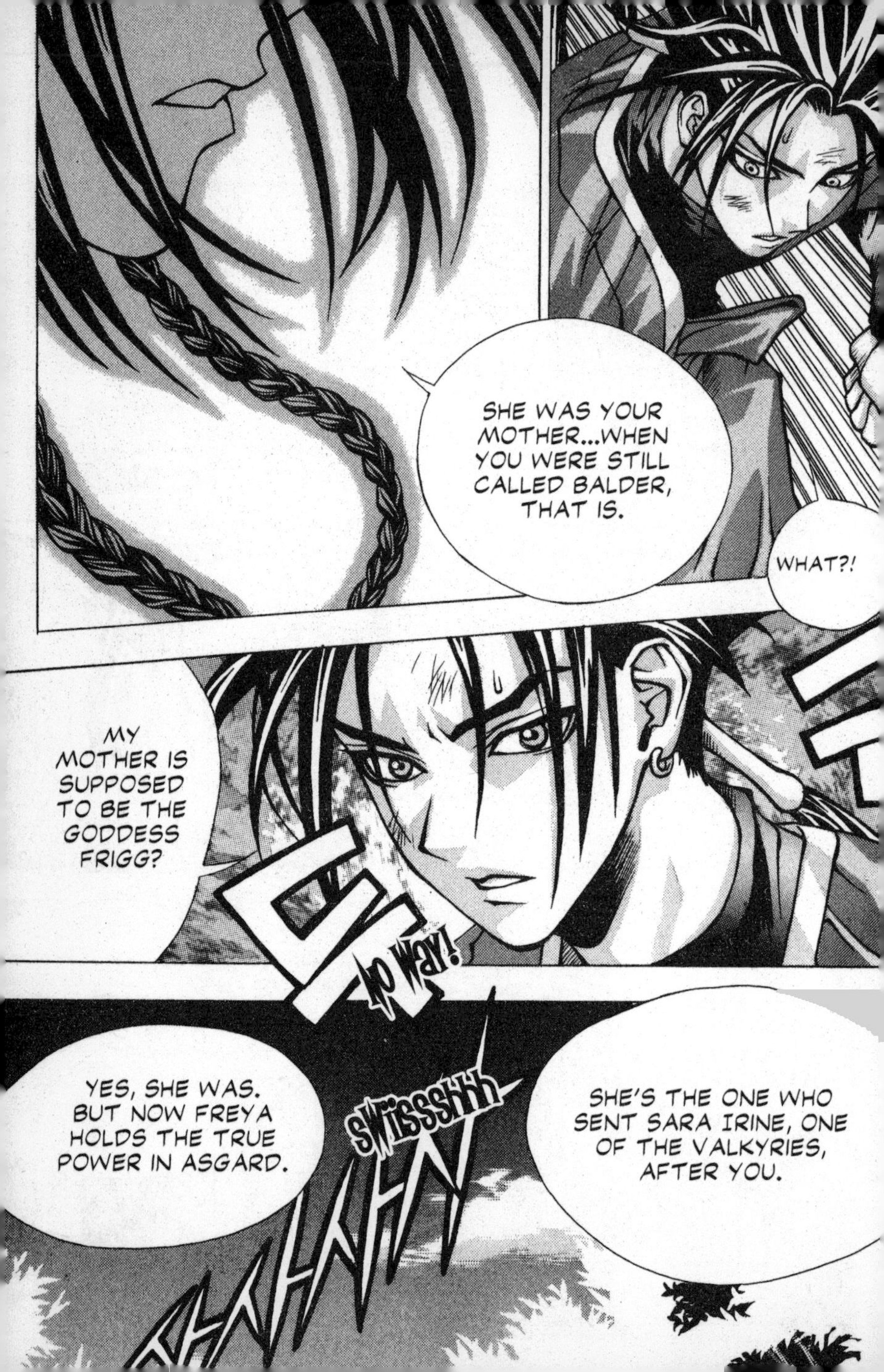

SHE WAS YOUR MOTHER...WHEN YOU WERE STILL CALLED BALDER, THAT IS.
WHAT?!
MY MOTHER IS SUPPOSED TO BE THE GODDESS FRIGG?
NO WAY!
YES, SHE WAS. BUT NOW FREYA HOLDS THE TRUE POWER IN ASGARD.
SWISSSHHH
SHE'S THE ONE WHO SENT SARA IRINE, ONE OF THE VALKYRIES, AFTER YOU.

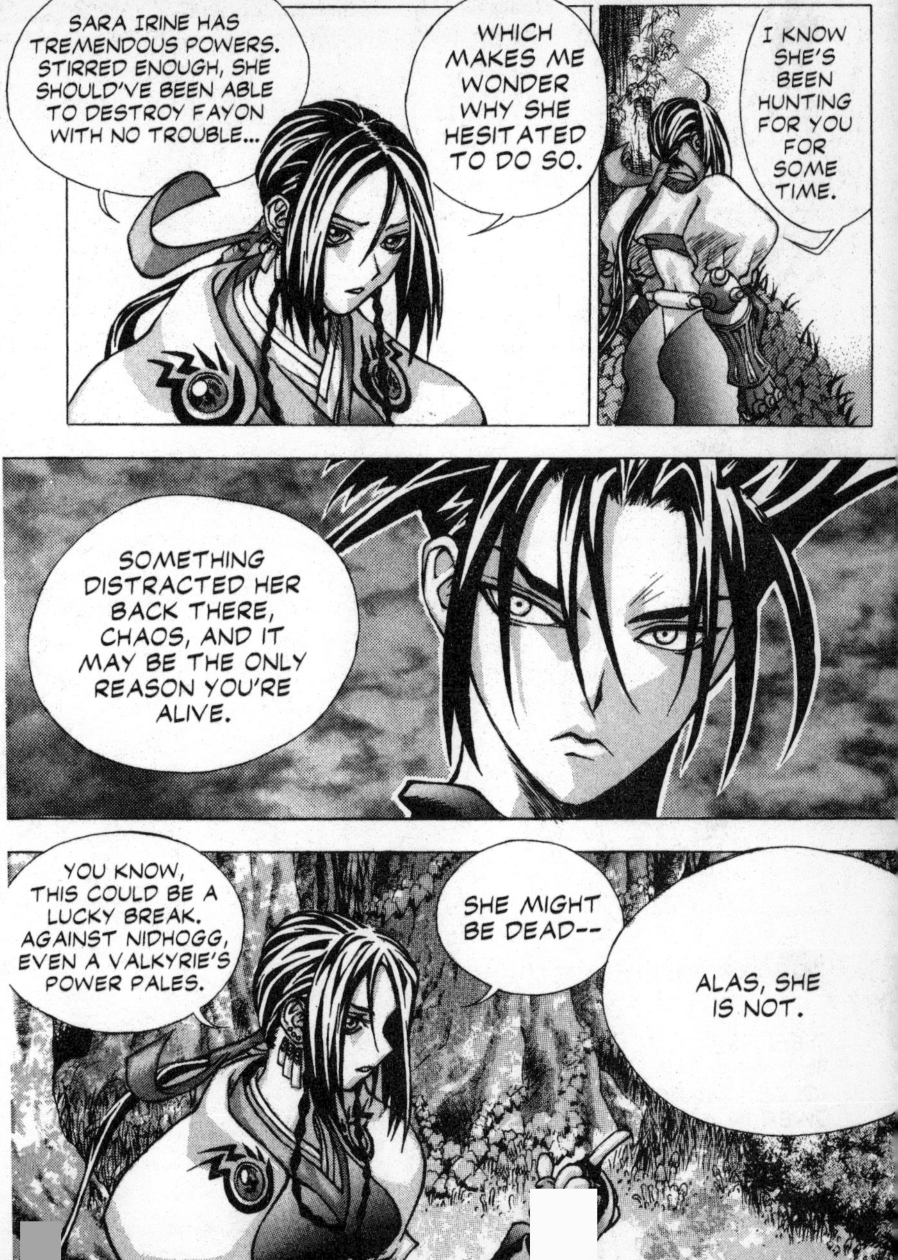
SARA IRINE HAS TREMENDOUS POWERS. STIRRED ENOUGH, SHE SHOULD'VE BEEN ABLE TO DESTROY FAYON WITH NO TROUBLE...
WHICH MAKES ME WONDER WHY SHE HESITATED TO DO SO.
I KNOW SHE'S BEEN HUNTING FOR YOU FOR SOME TIME.
SOMETHING DISTRACTED HER BACK THERE, CHAOS, AND IT MAY BE THE ONLY REASON YOU'RE ALIVE.
YOU KNOW, THIS COULD BE A LUCKY BREAK. AGAINST NIDHOGG, EVEN A VALKYRIE'S POWER PALES.
SHE MIGHT BE DEAD--
ALAS, SHE IS NOT.

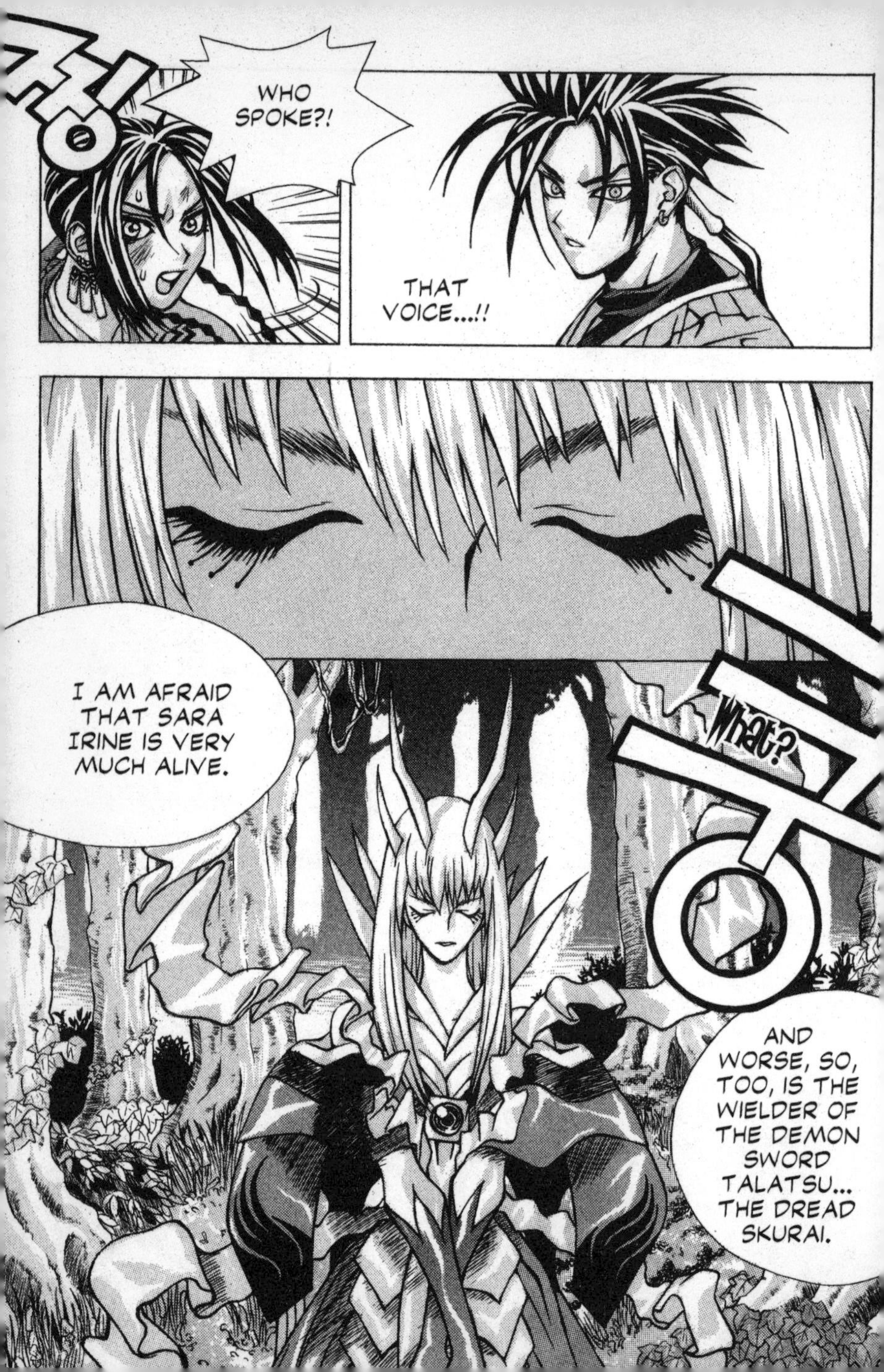
WHO SPOKE?!
THAT VOICE...!!
I AM AFRAID THAT SARA IRINE IS VERY MUCH ALIVE.
What?
AND WORSE, SO, TOO, IS THE WIELDER OF THE DEMON SWORD TALATSU... THE DREAD SKURAI.

RAGNAROK
라그나로크
IN TO THE ABYSS

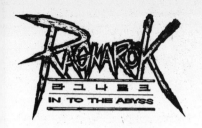

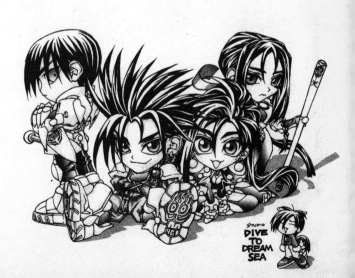

STUDIO
DIVE
TO
DREAM
SEA

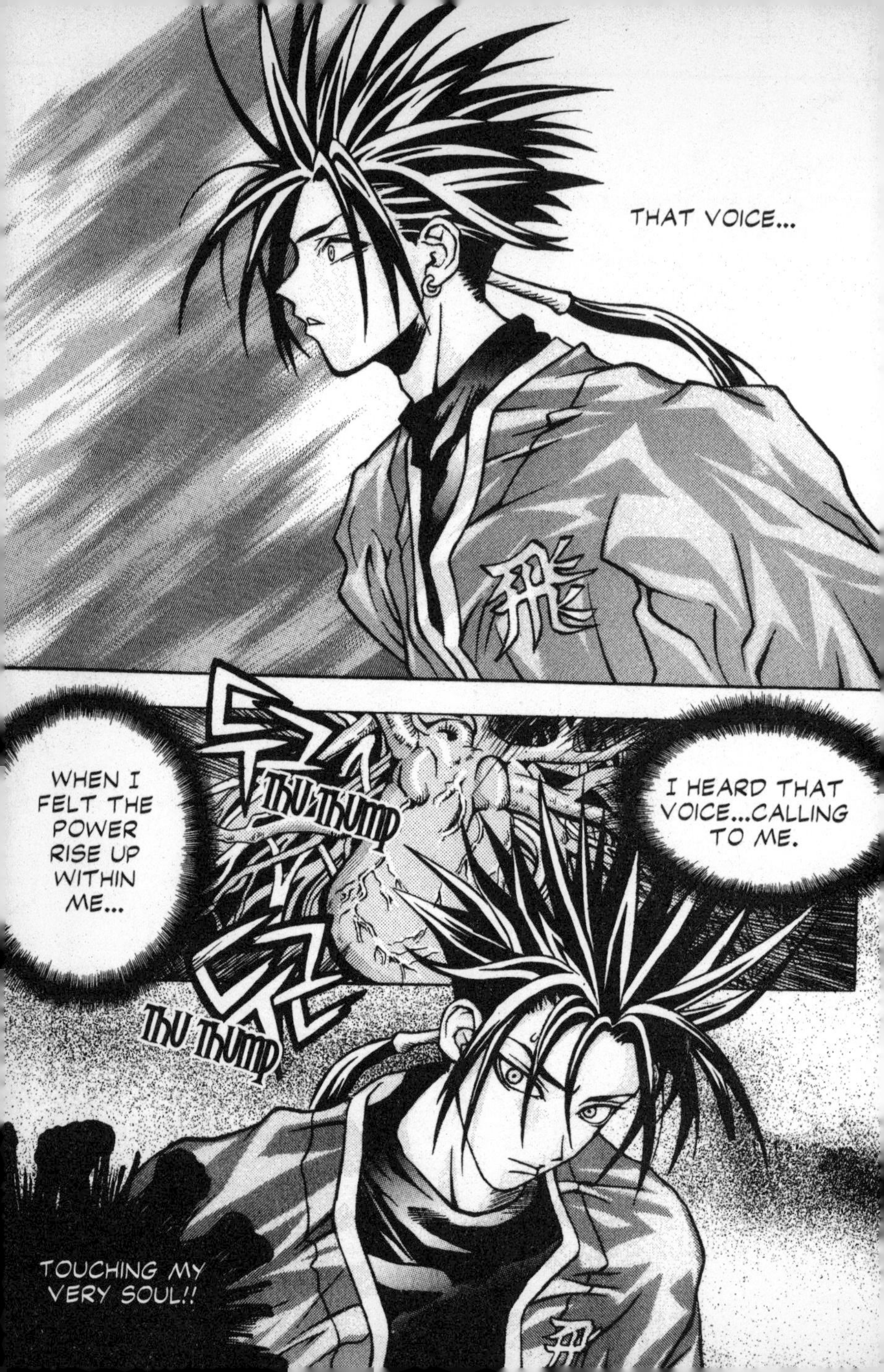
THAT VOICE...
THU THUMP
WHEN I FELT THE POWER RISE UP WITHIN ME...
I HEARD THAT VOICE...CALLING TO ME.
THU THUMP
TOUCHING MY VERY SOUL!!

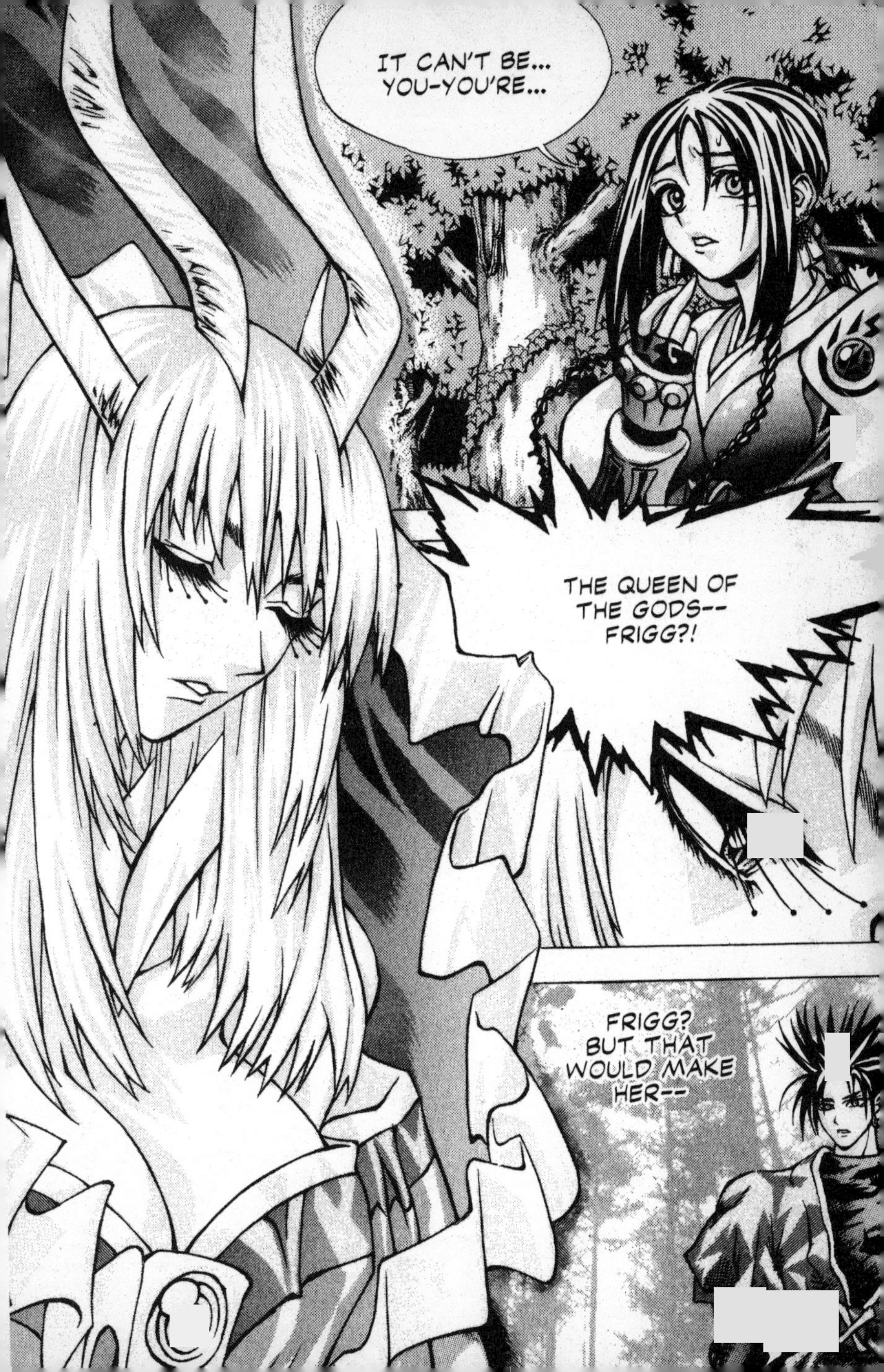
IT CAN'T BE... YOU-YOU'RE...
THE QUEEN OF THE GODS--FRIGG?!
FRIGG? BUT THAT WOULD MAKE HER--

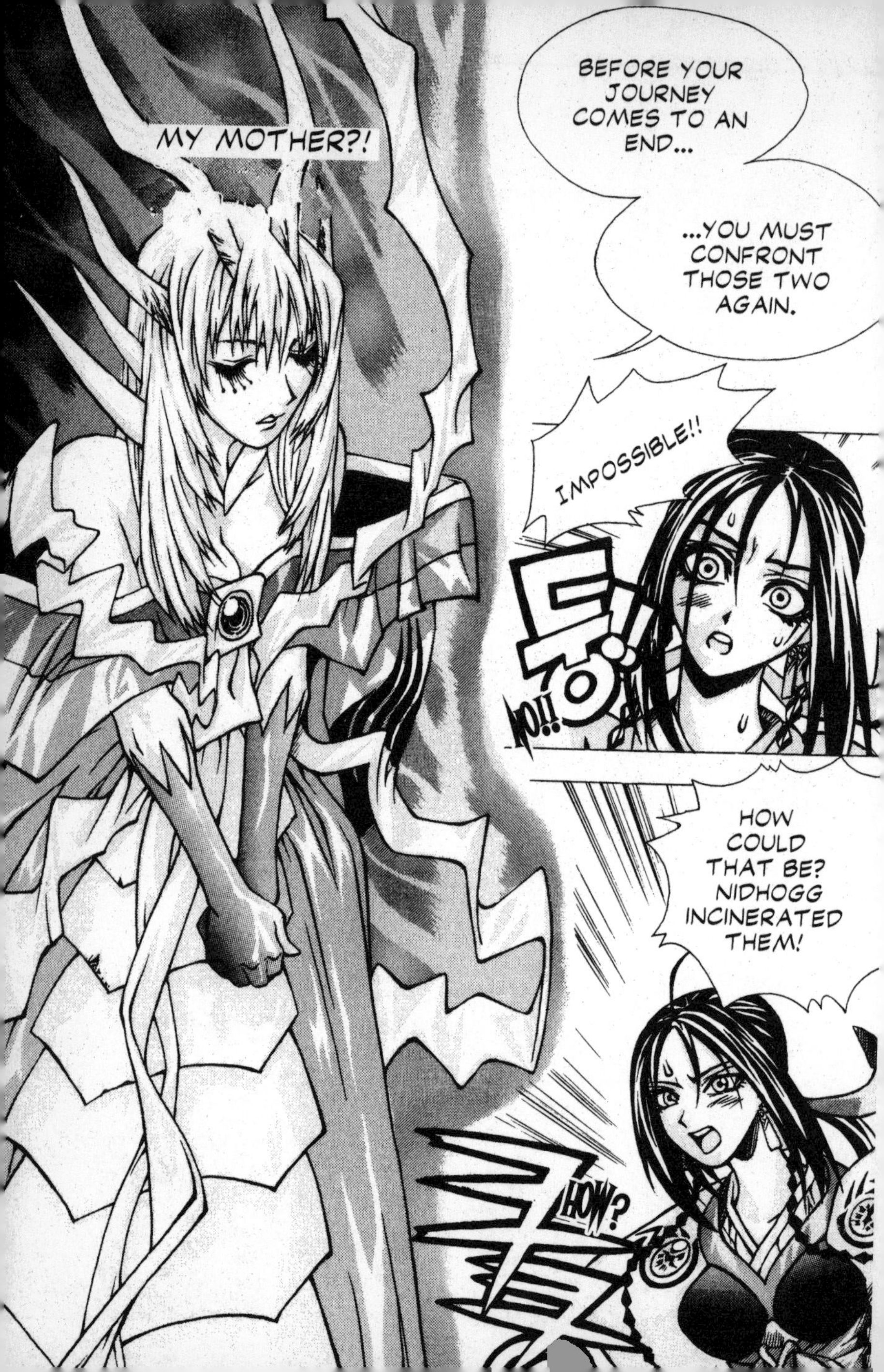
MY MOTHER?!
BEFORE YOUR JOURNEY COMES TO AN END...
...YOU MUST CONFRONT THOSE TWO AGAIN.
IMPOSSIBLE!!
NO!!
HOW COULD THAT BE? NIDHOGG INCINERATED THEM!
HOW?

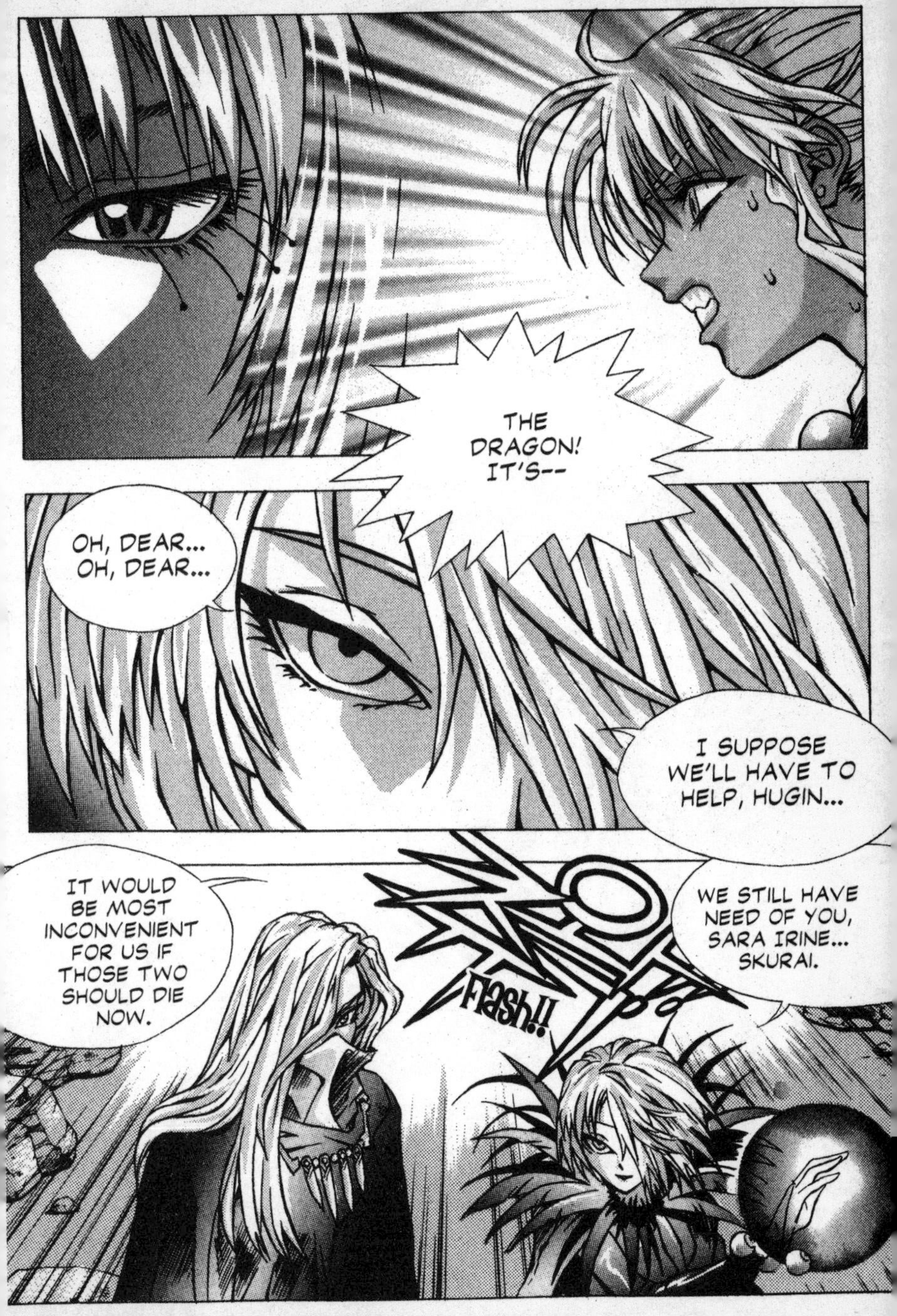
THE DRAGON! IT'S--
OH, DEAR... OH, DEAR...
I SUPPOSE WE'LL HAVE TO HELP, HUGIN...
IT WOULD BE MOST INCONVENIENT FOR US IF THOSE TWO SHOULD DIE NOW.
FLASH!!
WE STILL HAVE NEED OF YOU, SARA IRINE... SKURAI.

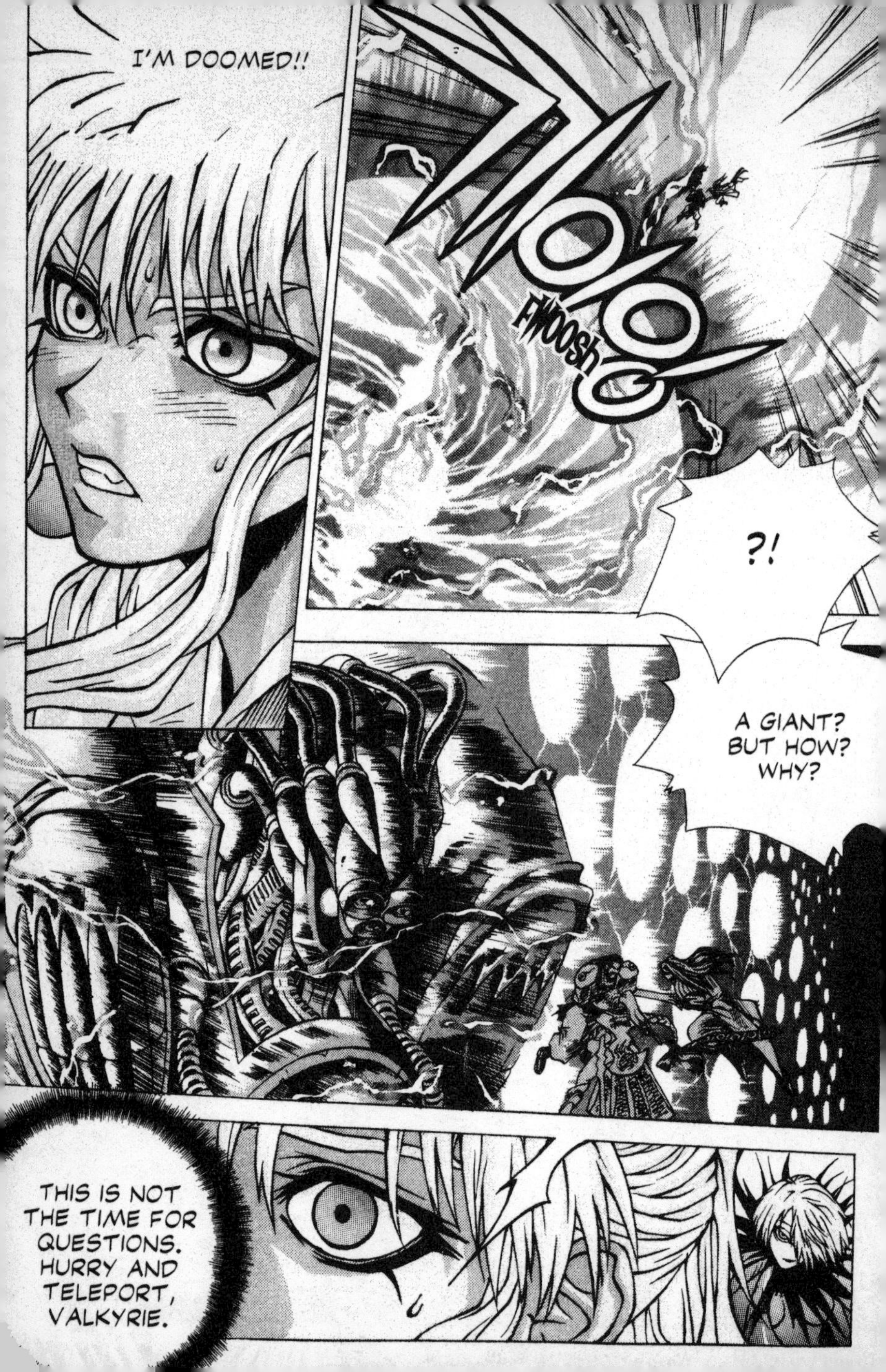
I'M DOOMED!!
FWOOSH
?!
A GIANT? BUT HOW? WHY?
THIS IS NOT THE TIME FOR QUESTIONS. HURRY AND TELEPORT, VALKYRIE.

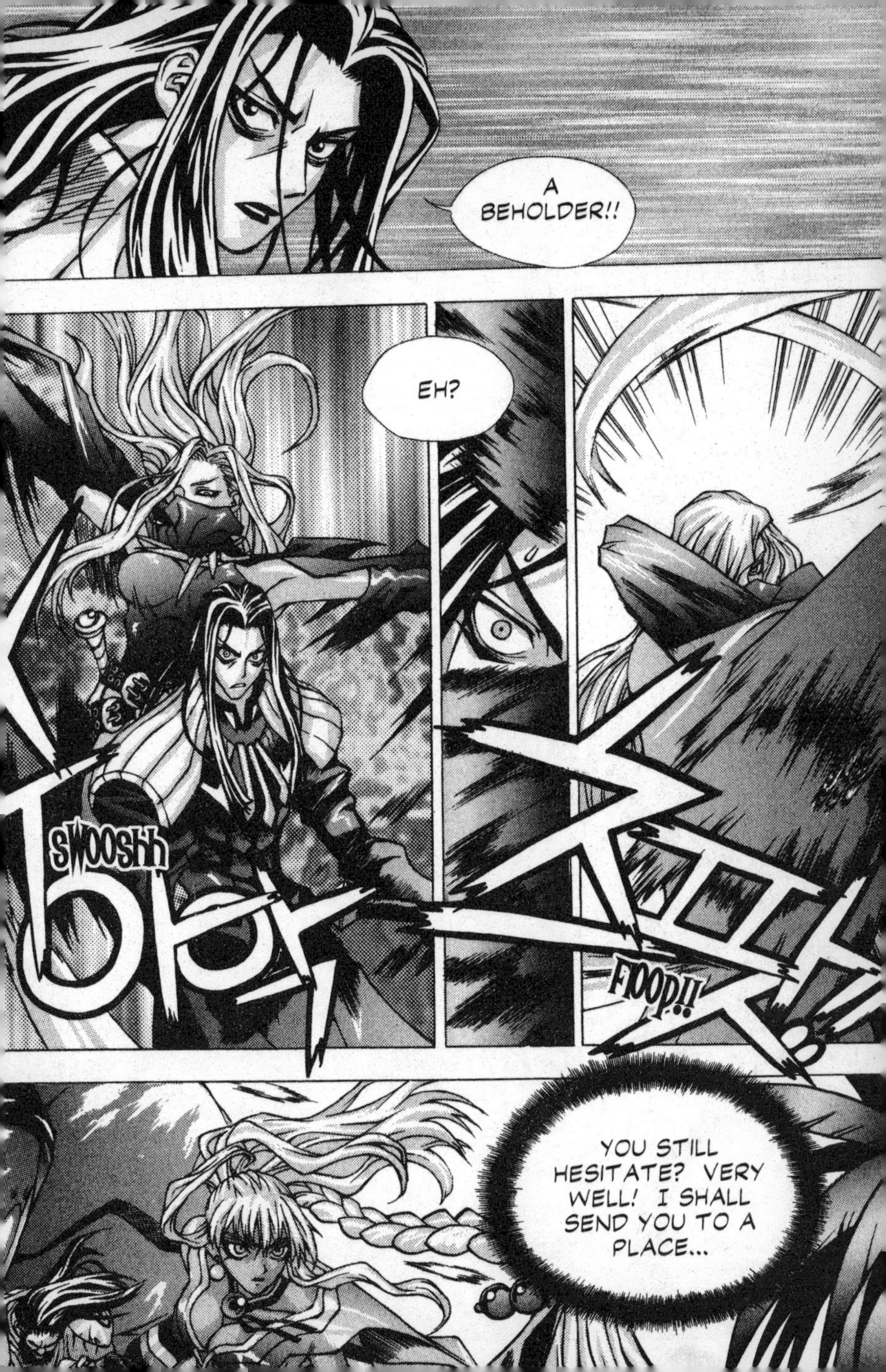
A BEHOLDER!!
EH?
SWOOSHH
FLOOP!!
YOU STILL HESITATE? VERY WELL! I SHALL SEND YOU TO A PLACE...

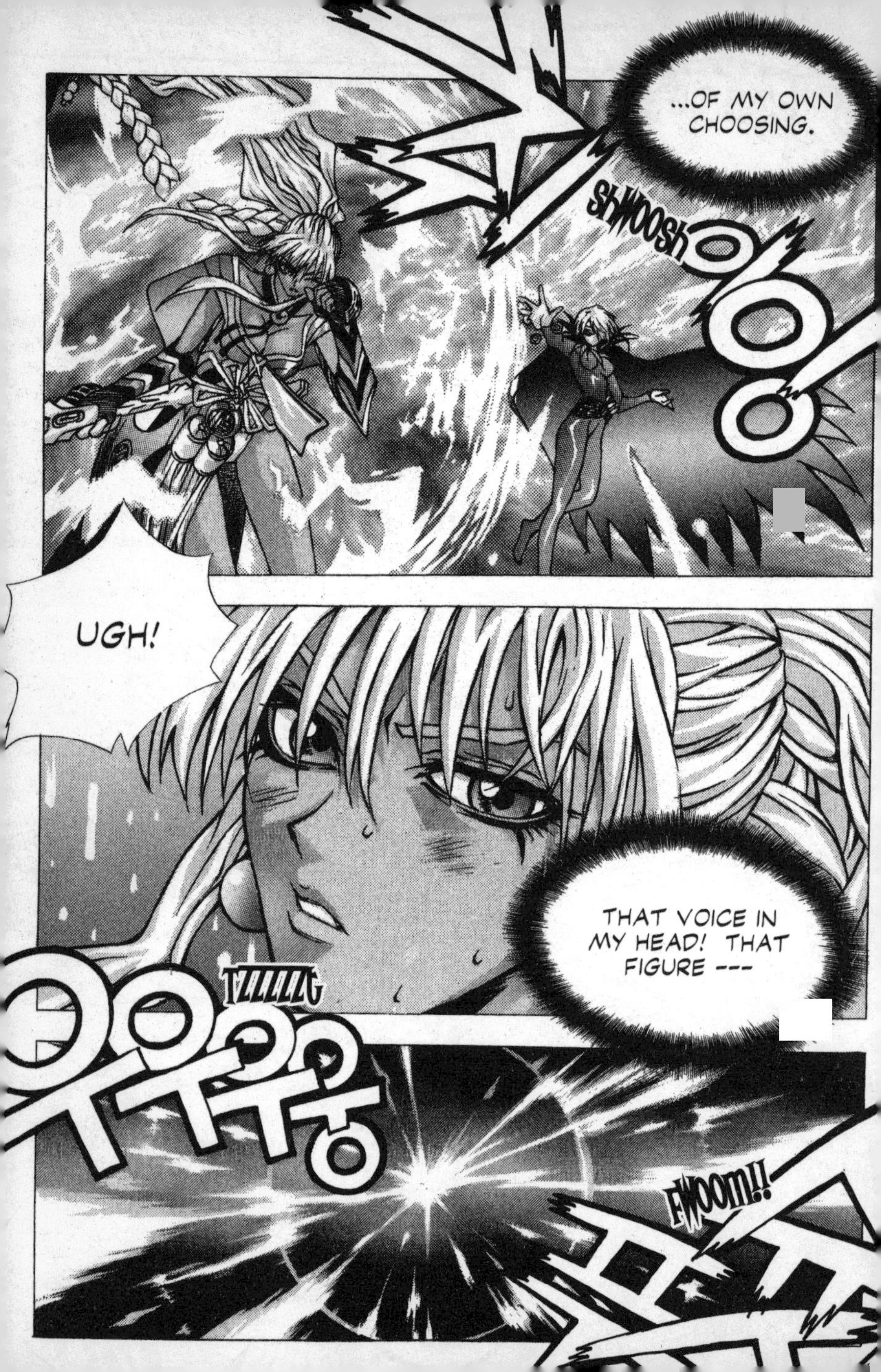
...OF MY OWN CHOOSING.
SHWOOSH
UGH!
THAT VOICE IN MY HEAD! THAT FIGURE ---
TZZZZZG
FWOOM!!

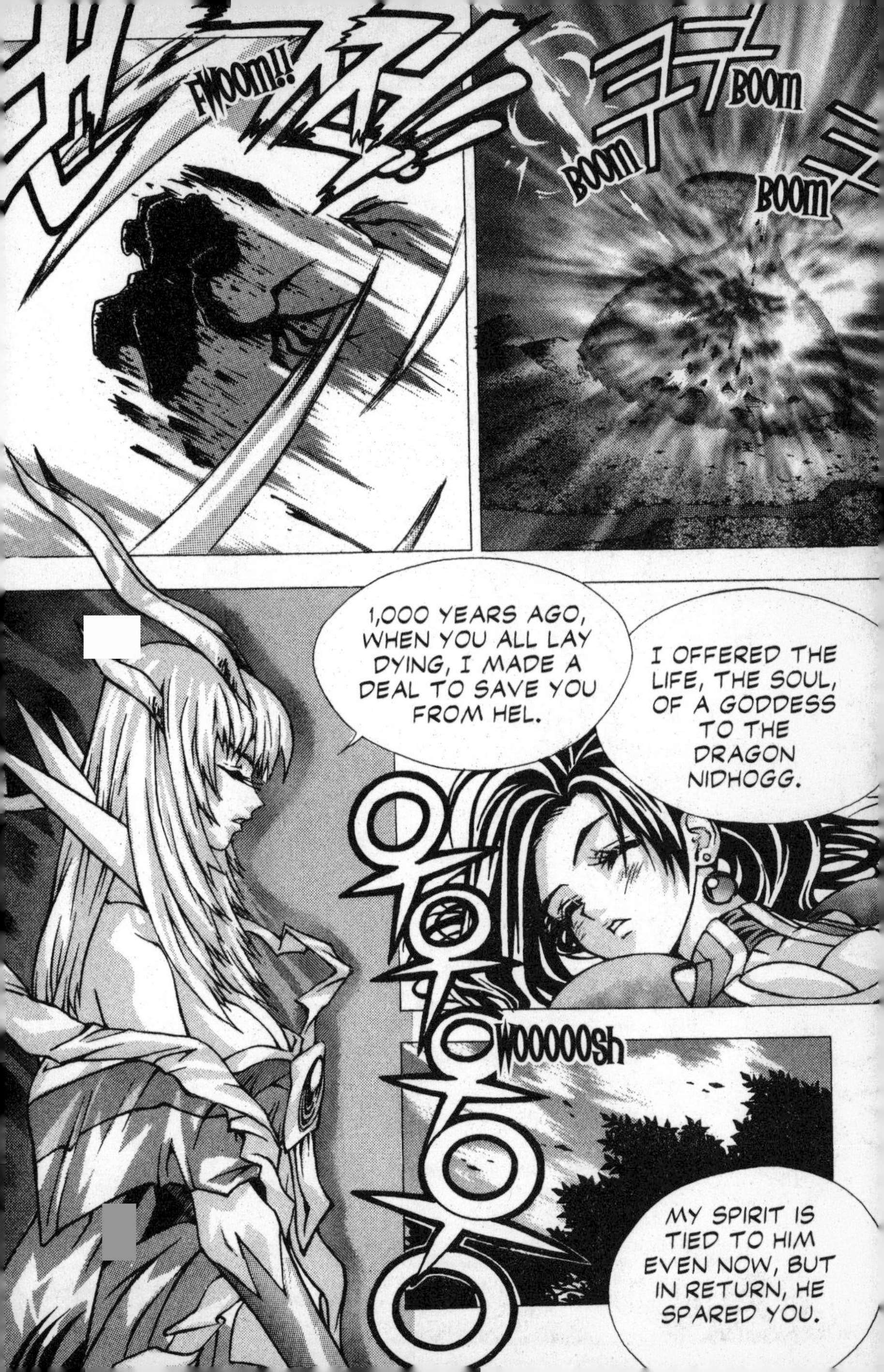
FWOOM!!
BOOM
BOOM
BOOM
1,000 YEARS AGO, WHEN YOU ALL LAY DYING, I MADE A DEAL TO SAVE YOU FROM HEL.
I OFFERED THE LIFE, THE SOUL, OF A GODDESS TO THE DRAGON NIDHOGG.
WOOOOOSh
MY SPIRIT IS TIED TO HIM EVEN NOW, BUT IN RETURN, HE SPARED YOU.

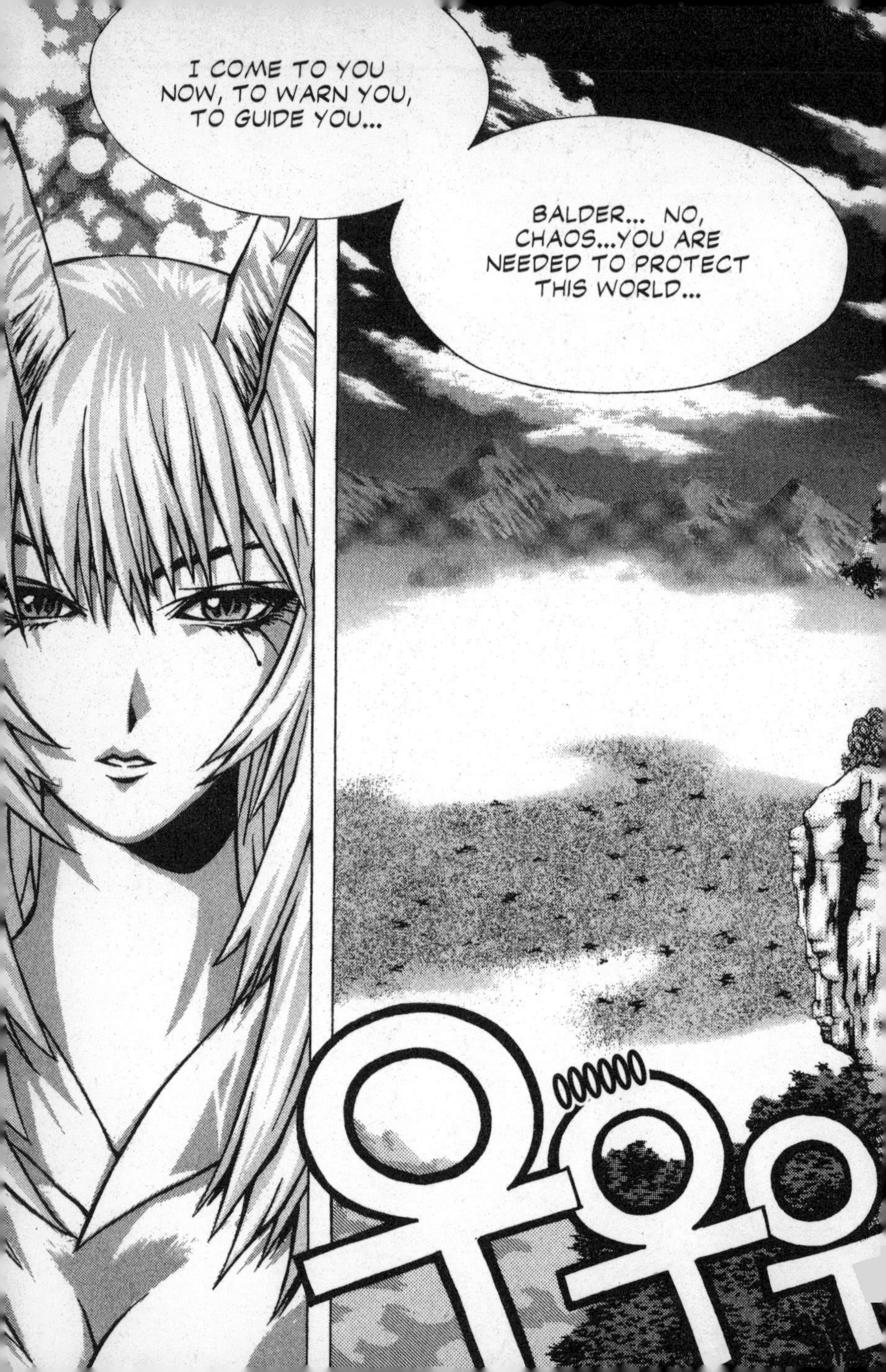
I COME TO YOU NOW, TO WARN YOU, TO GUIDE YOU...
BALDER... NO, CHAOS...YOU ARE NEEDED TO PROTECT THIS WORLD...
OOOOOO

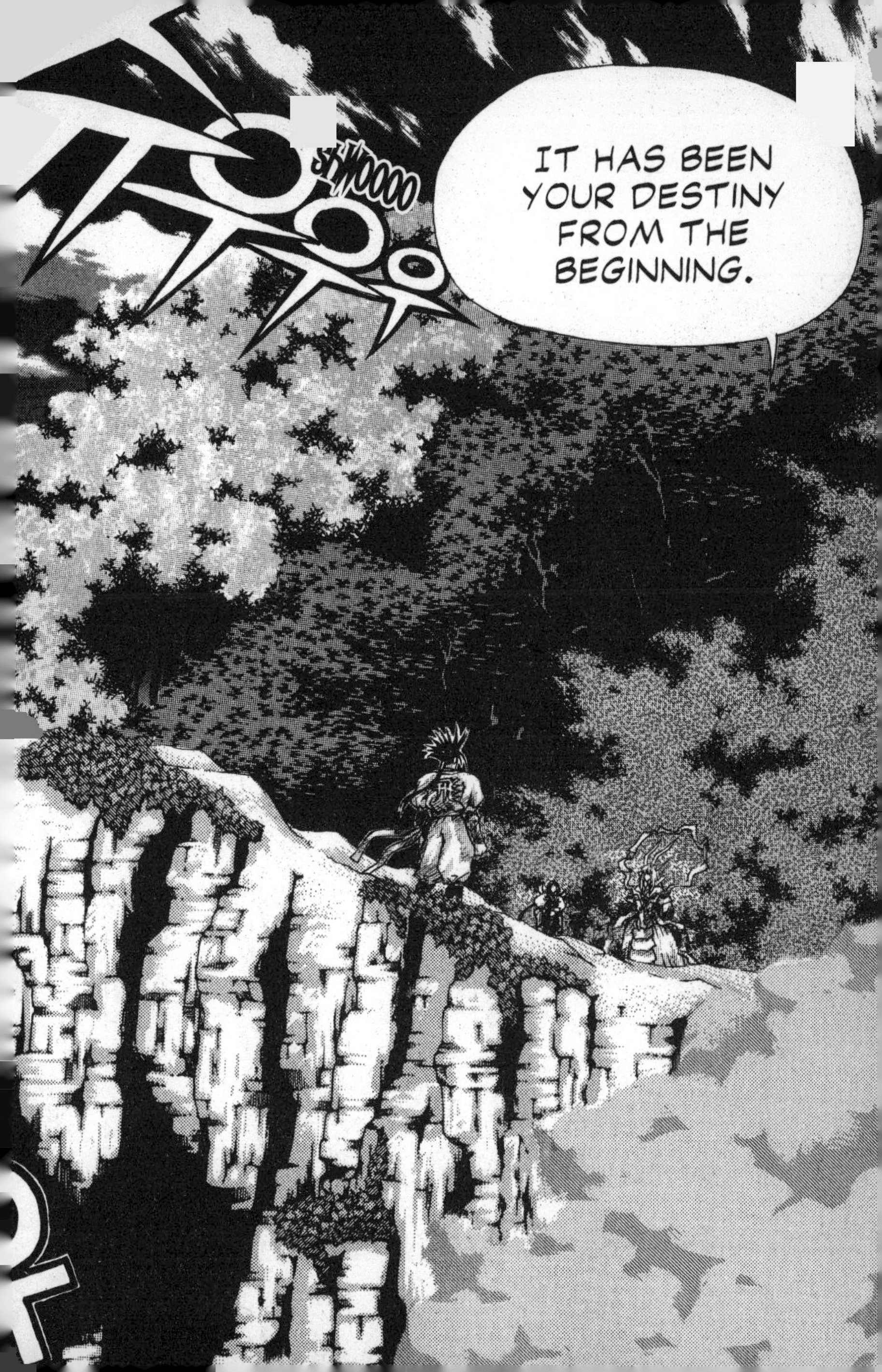
SHWOOOO
IT HAS BEEN YOUR DESTINY FROM THE BEGINNING.

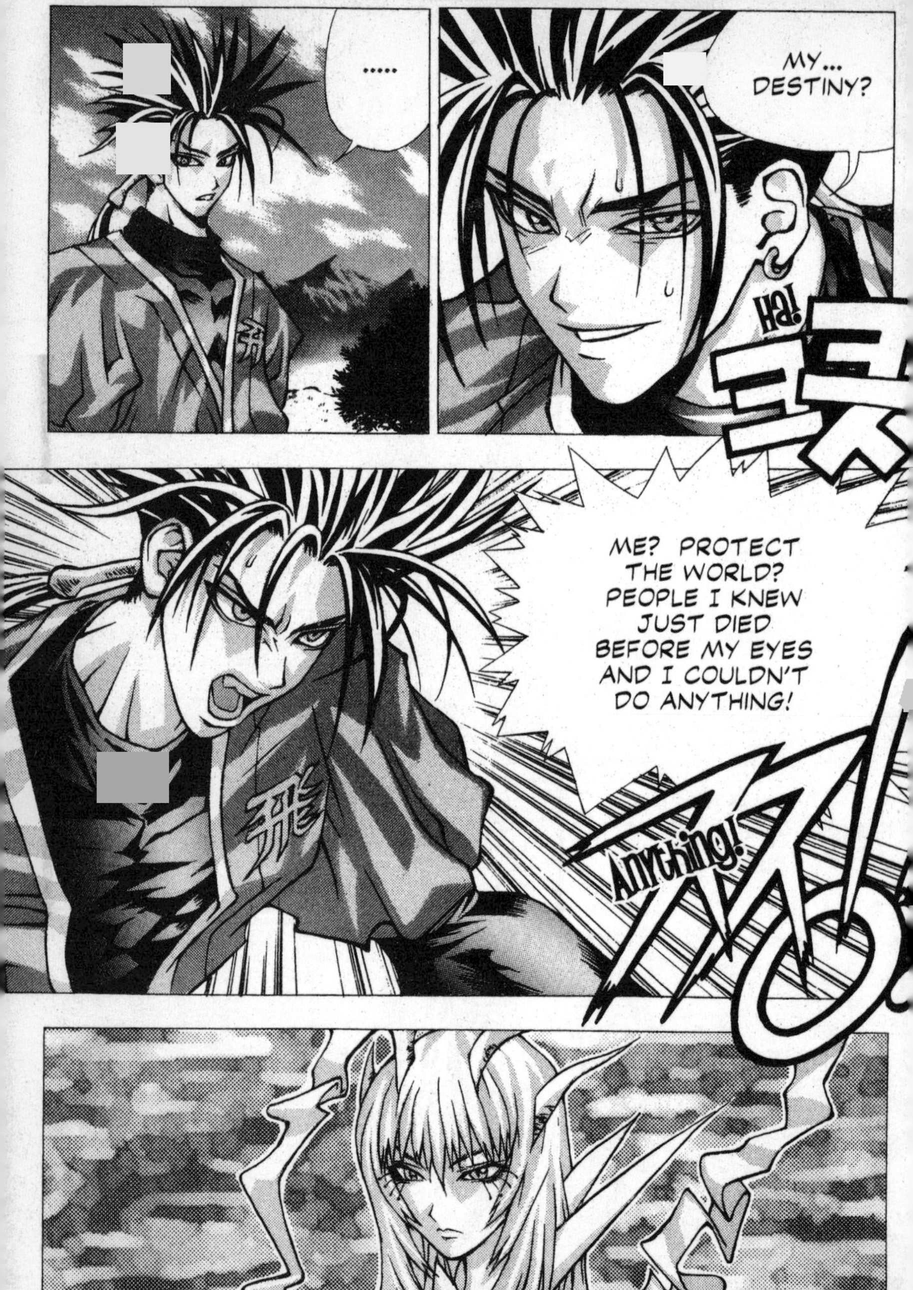
.....
MY... DESTINY?
HA!
ME? PROTECT THE WORLD? PEOPLE I KNEW JUST DIED BEFORE MY EYES AND I COULDN'T DO ANYTHING!
Anything!

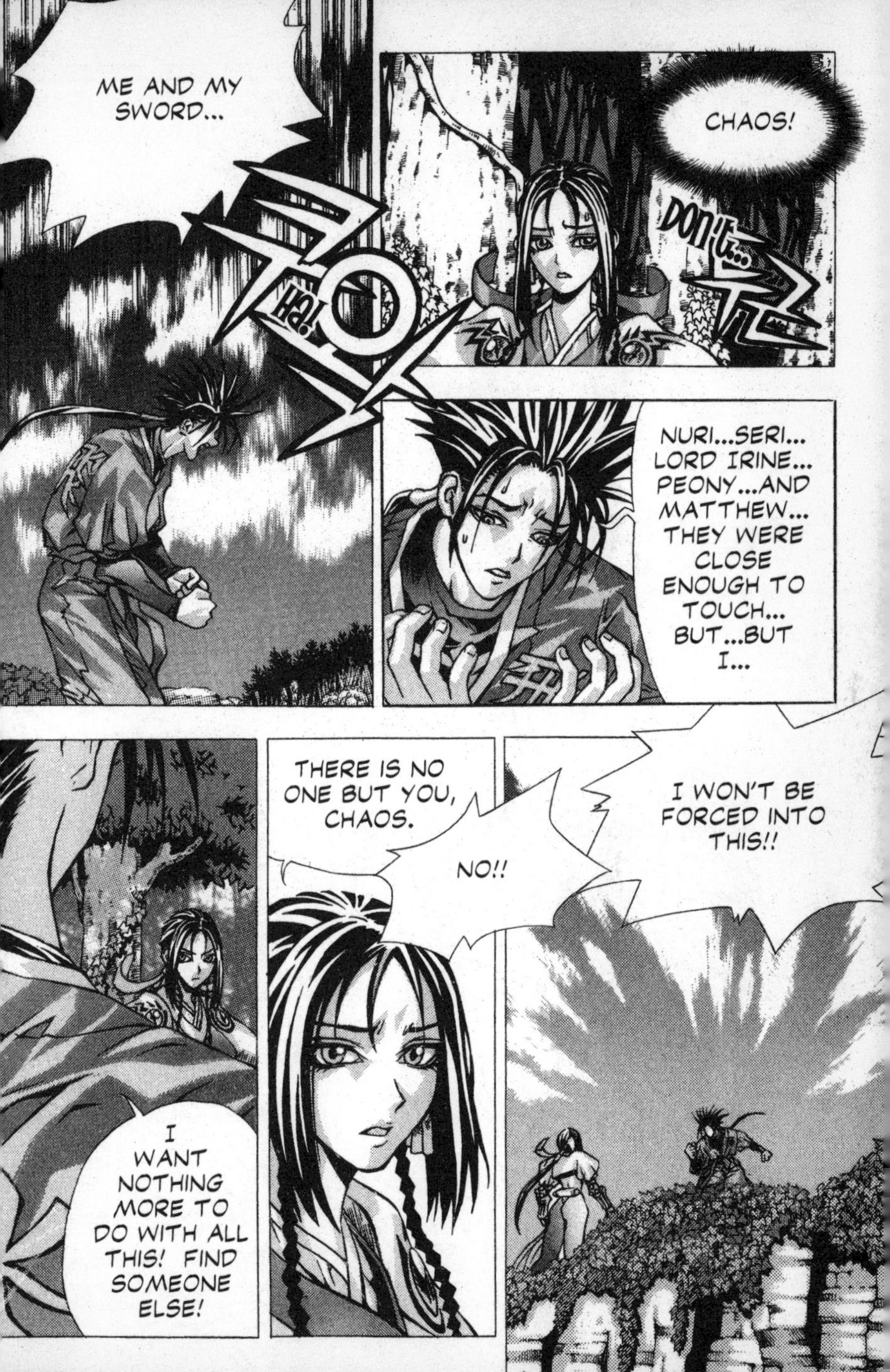
ME AND MY SWORD...
CHAOS!
DON'T...
NURI...SERI... LORD IRINE... PEONY...AND MATTHEW... THEY WERE CLOSE ENOUGH TO TOUCH... BUT...BUT I...
I WANT NOTHING MORE TO DO WITH ALL THIS! FIND SOMEONE ELSE!
THERE IS NO ONE BUT YOU, CHAOS.
NO!!
I WON'T BE FORCED INTO THIS!!

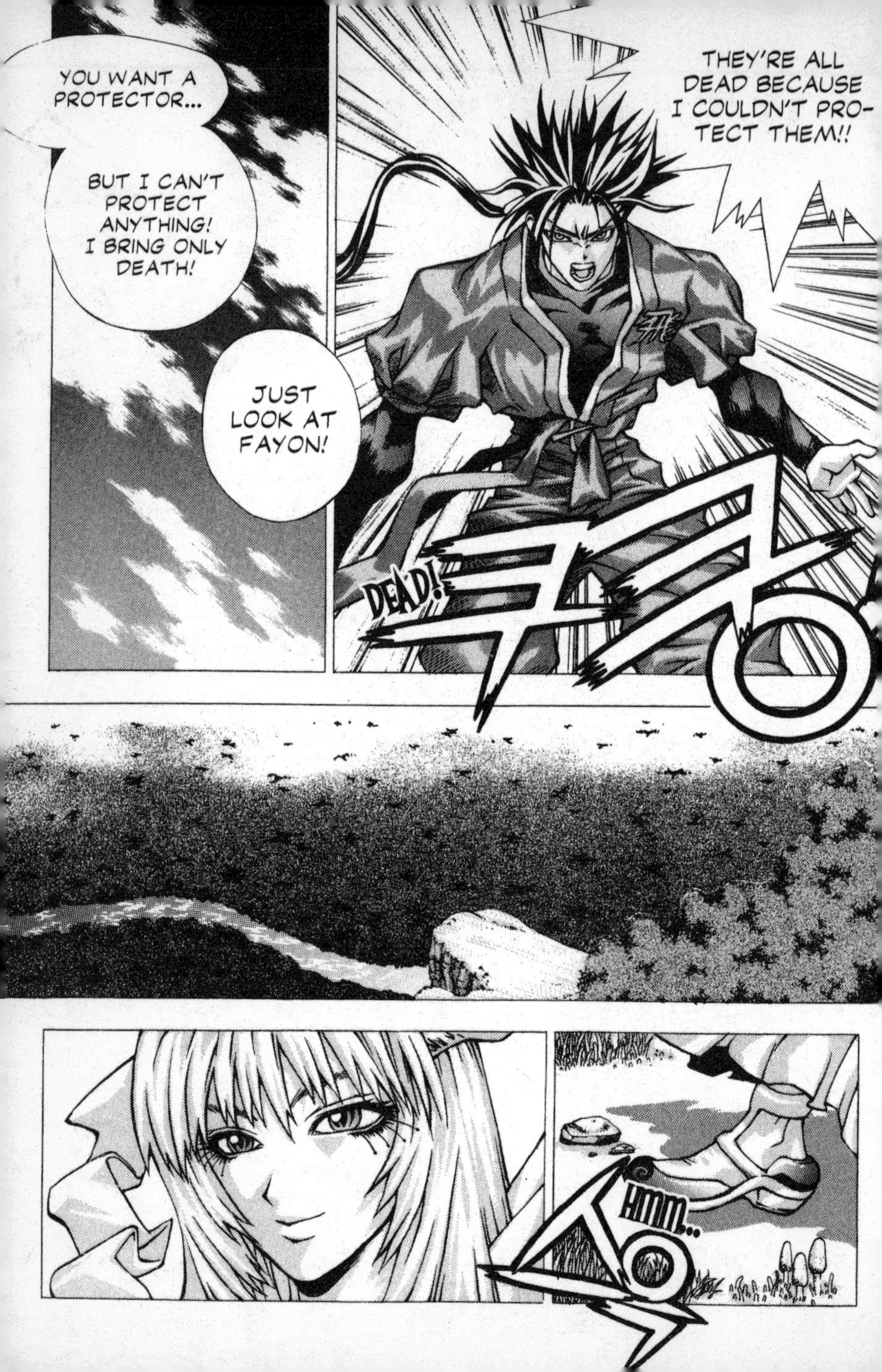
YOU WANT A PROTECTOR...
BUT I CAN'T PROTECT ANYTHING! I BRING ONLY DEATH!
JUST LOOK AT FAYON!
THEY'RE ALL DEAD BECAUSE I COULDN'T PRO-TECT THEM!!
DEAD!
HMM..

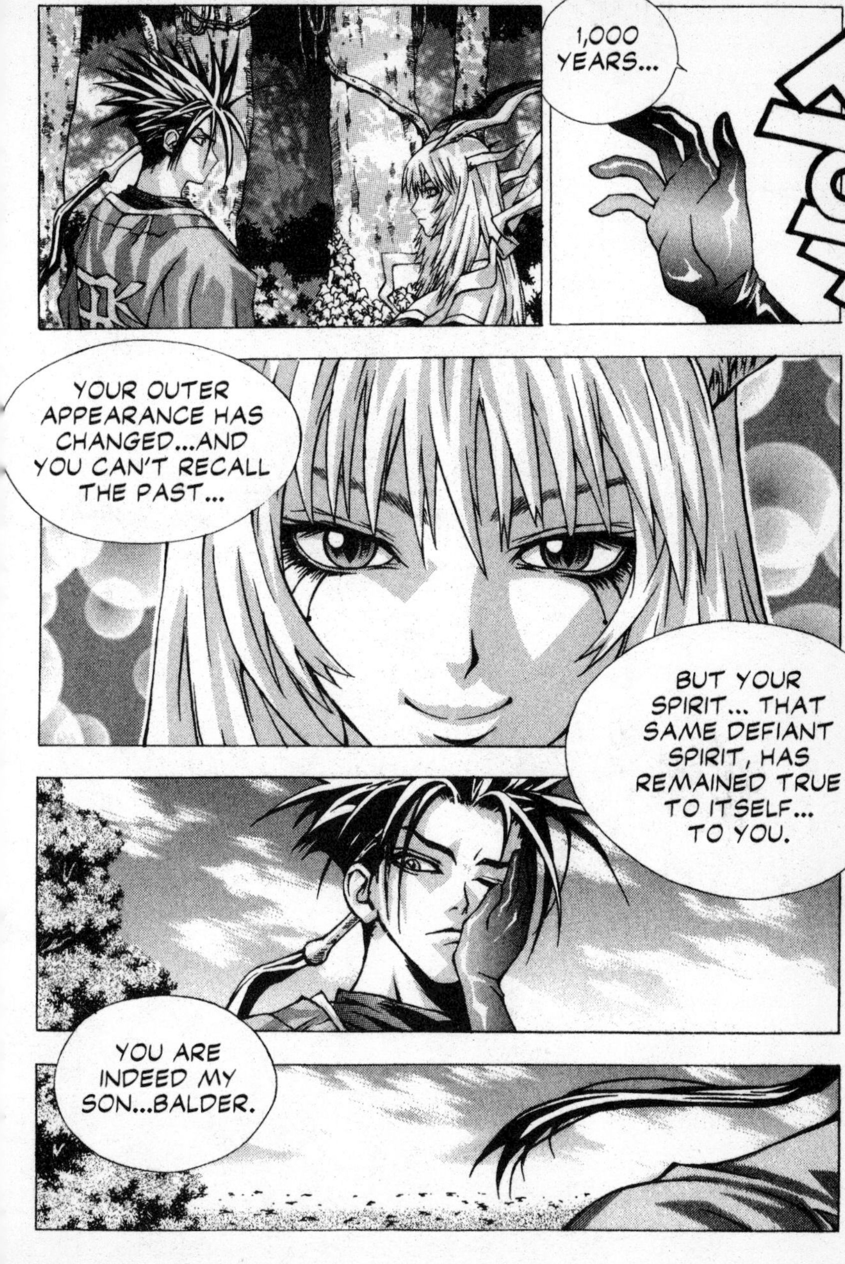
1,000 YEARS...
YOUR OUTER APPEARANCE HAS CHANGED...AND YOU CAN'T RECALL THE PAST...
BUT YOUR SPIRIT... THAT SAME DEFIANT SPIRIT, HAS REMAINED TRUE TO ITSELF... TO YOU.
YOU ARE INDEED MY SON...BALDER.

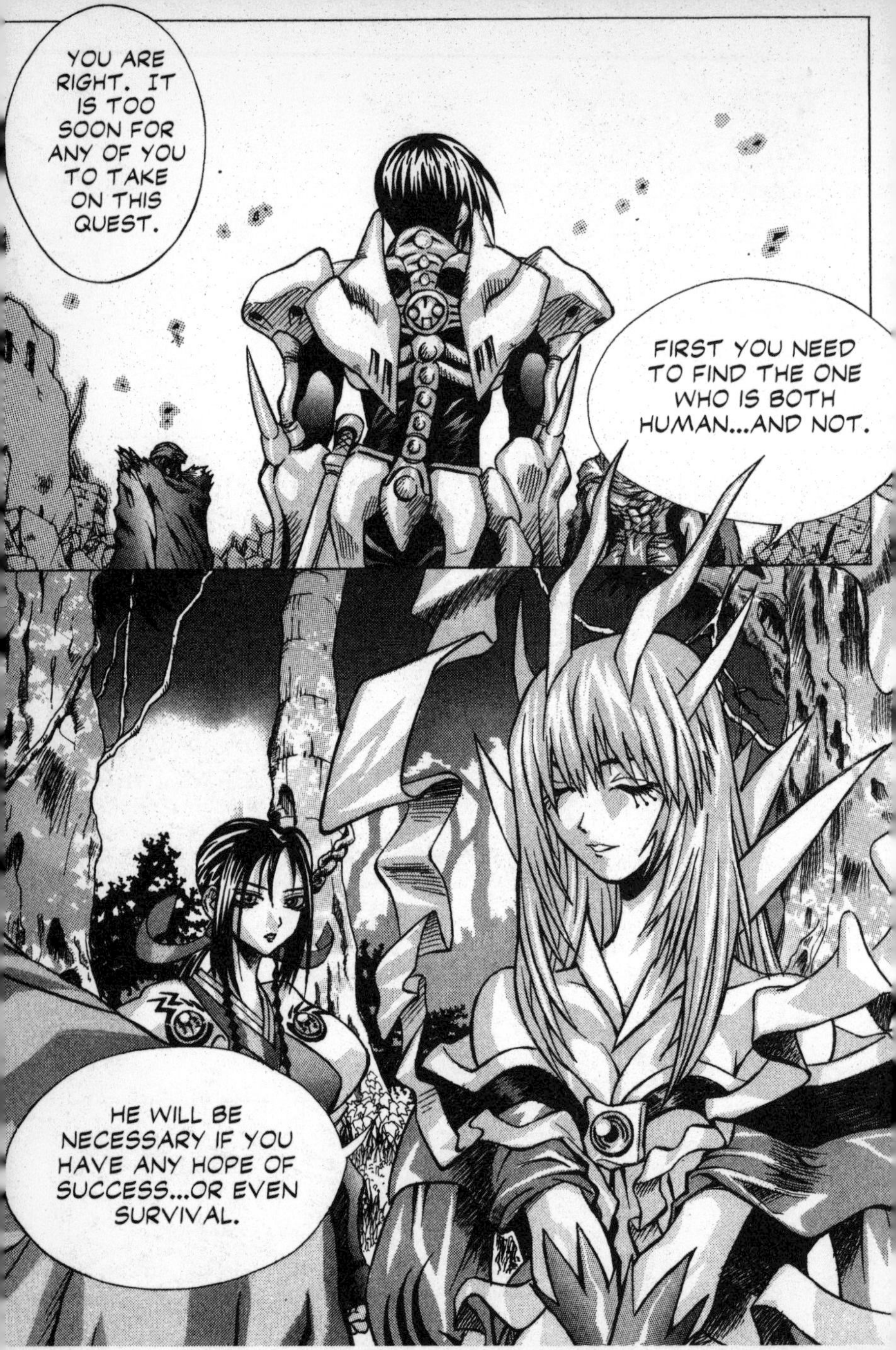
YOU ARE RIGHT. IT IS TOO SOON FOR ANY OF YOU TO TAKE ON THIS QUEST.
FIRST YOU NEED TO FIND THE ONE WHO IS BOTH HUMAN...AND NOT.
HE WILL BE NECESSARY IF YOU HAVE ANY HOPE OF SUCCESS...OR EVEN SURVIVAL.

RAGNAROK
라그나로크
IN TO THE ABYSS

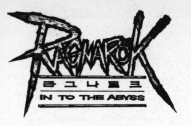

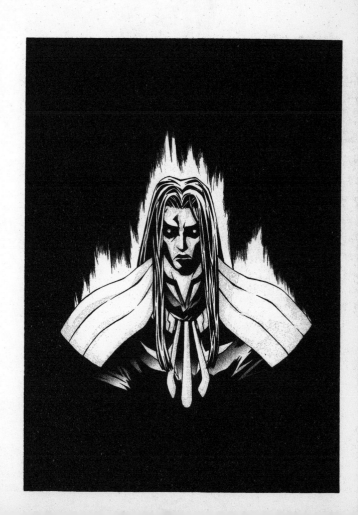

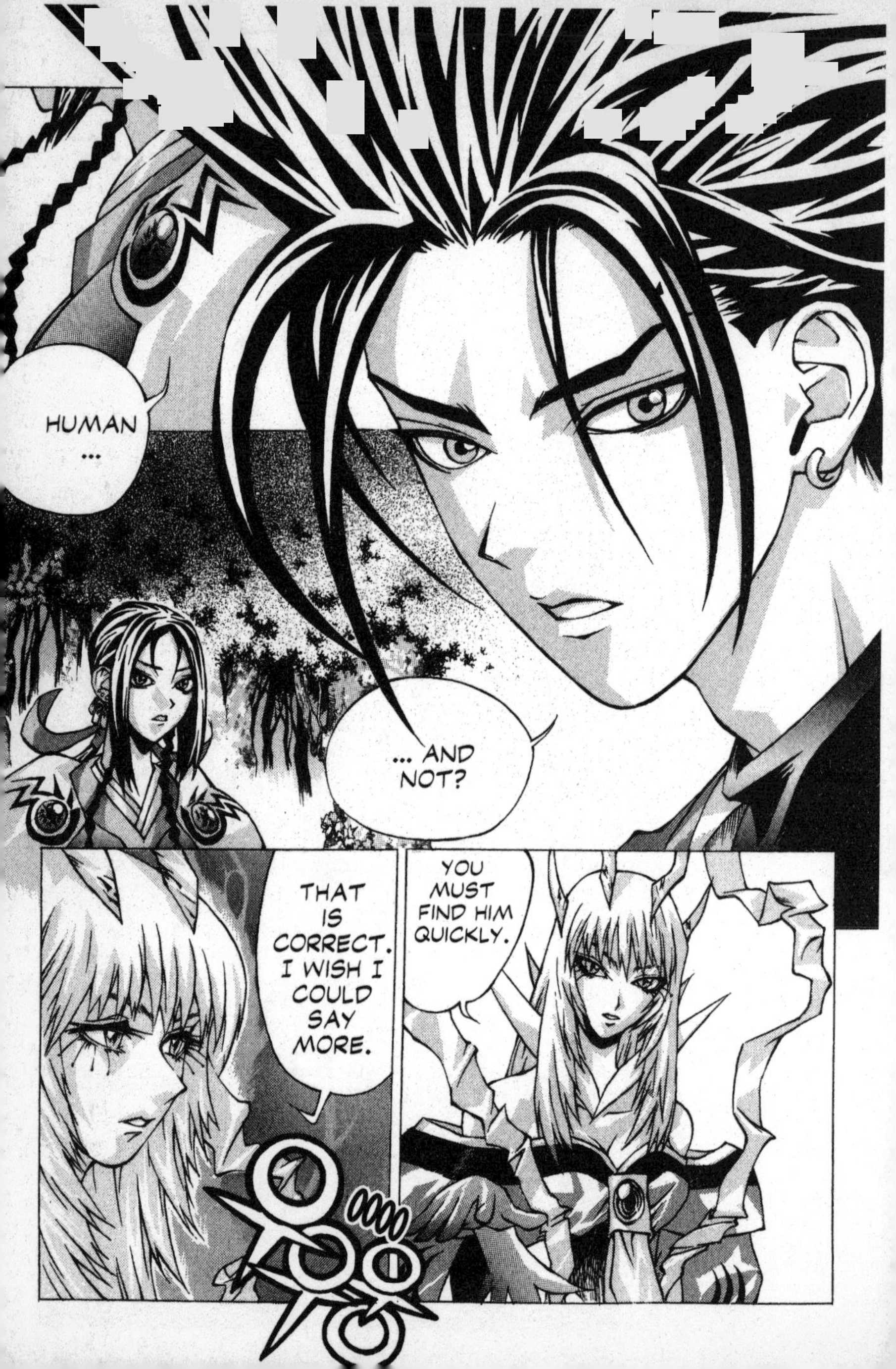
HUMAN ...
... AND NOT?
THAT IS CORRECT. I WISH I COULD SAY MORE.
YOU MUST FIND HIM QUICKLY.
OOOO

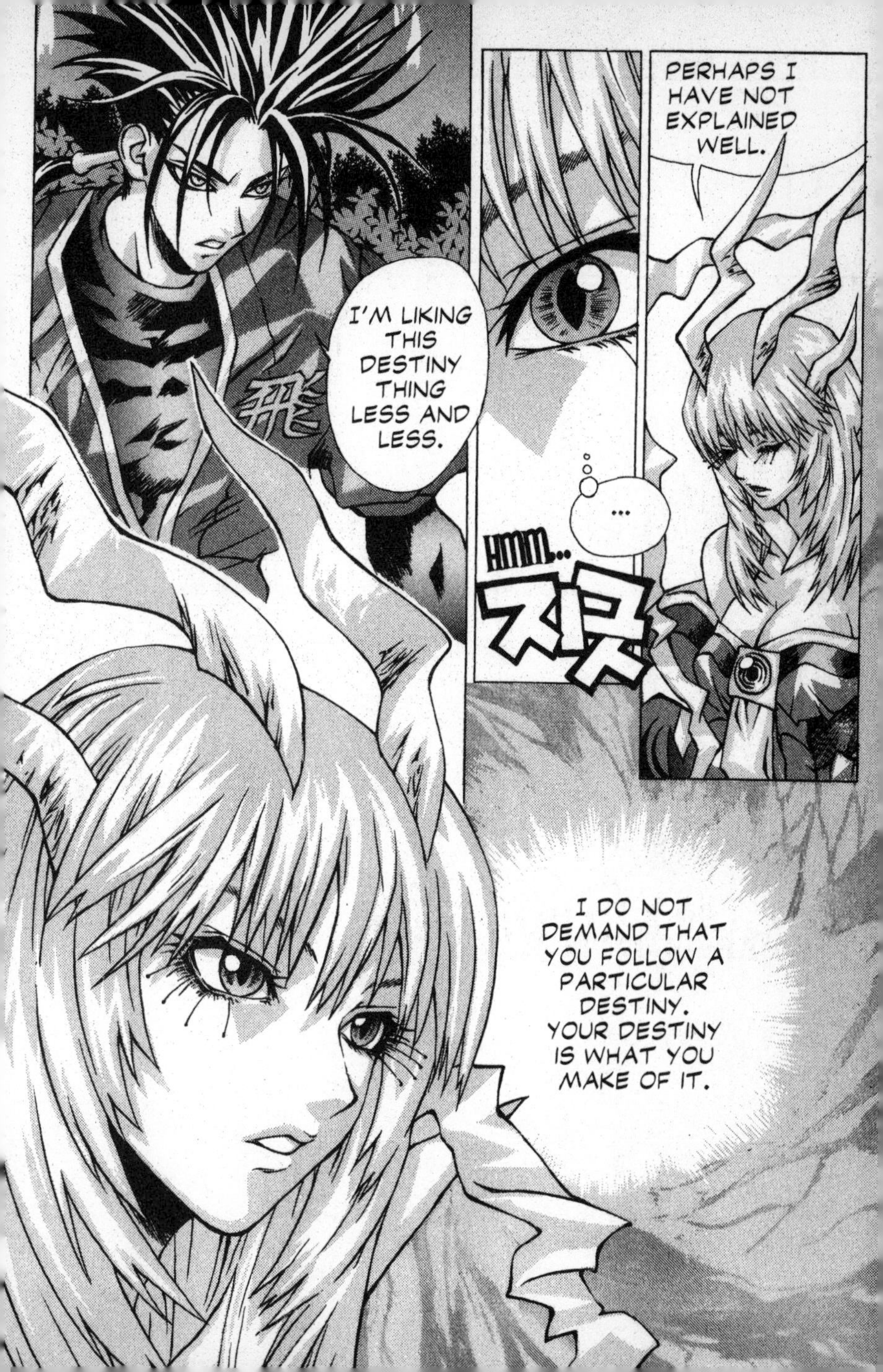
I'M LIKING THIS DESTINY THING LESS AND LESS.
PERHAPS I HAVE NOT EXPLAINED WELL.
...
HMM...
I DO NOT DEMAND THAT YOU FOLLOW A PARTICULAR DESTINY. YOUR DESTINY IS WHAT YOU MAKE OF IT.

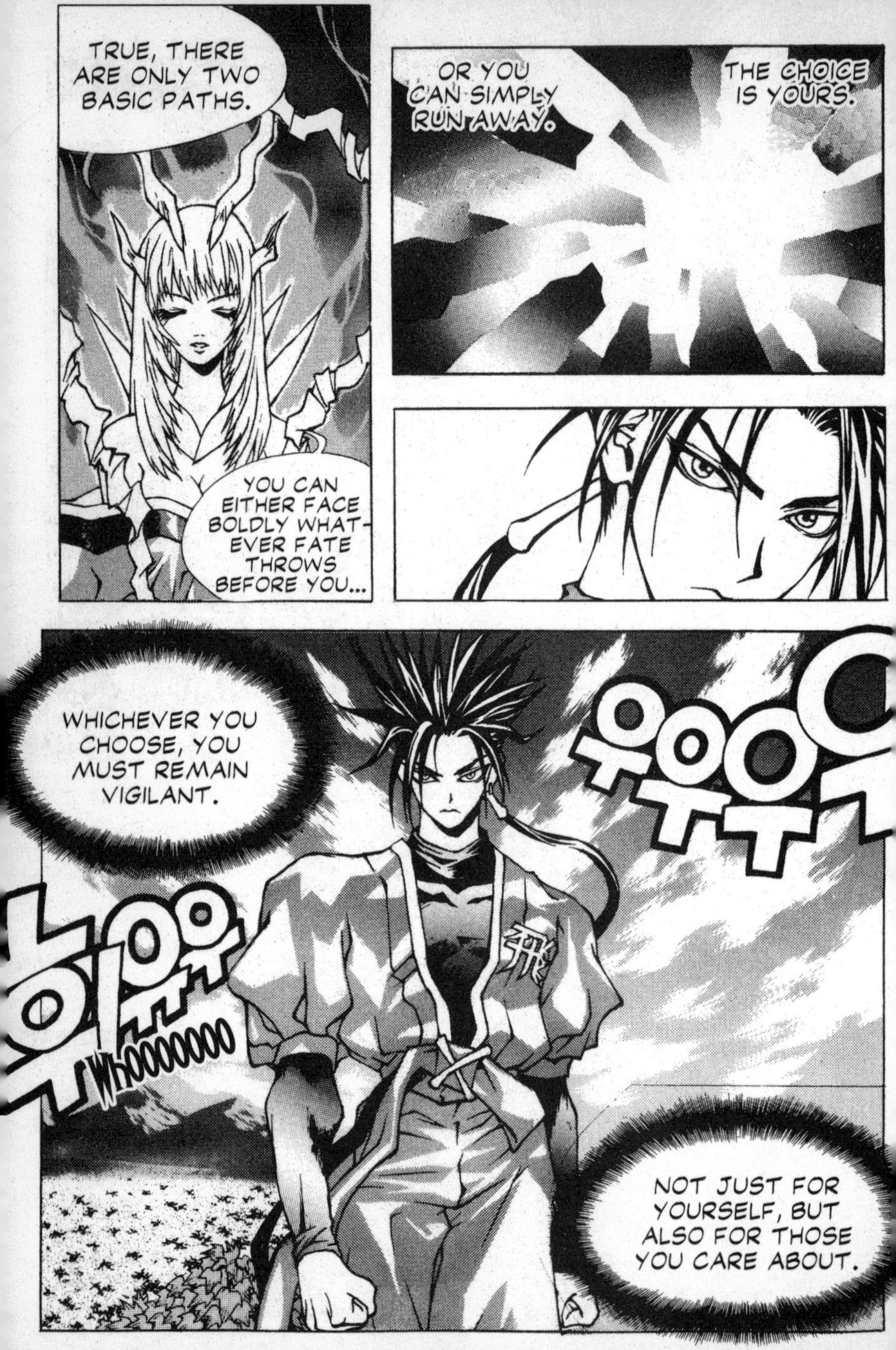
TRUE, THERE ARE ONLY TWO BASIC PATHS.
YOU CAN EITHER FACE BOLDLY WHAT-EVER FATE THROWS BEFORE YOU...
OR YOU CAN SIMPLY RUN AWAY.
THE CHOICE IS YOURS.
WHICHEVER YOU CHOOSE, YOU MUST REMAIN VIGILANT.
WhOOOOOOO
NOT JUST FOR YOURSELF, BUT ALSO FOR THOSE YOU CARE ABOUT.

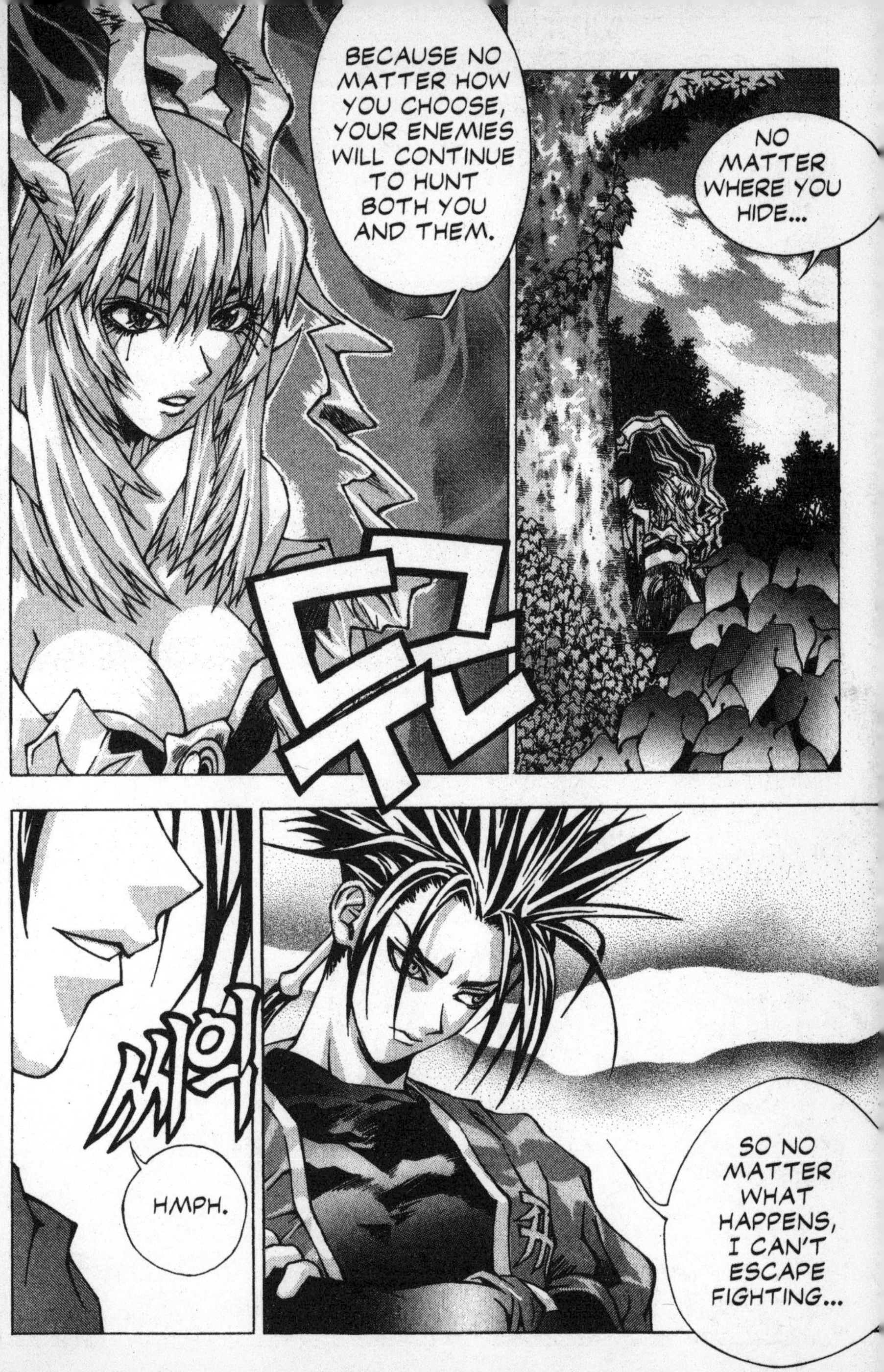
BECAUSE NO MATTER HOW YOU CHOOSE, YOUR ENEMIES WILL CONTINUE TO HUNT BOTH YOU AND THEM.
NO MATTER WHERE YOU HIDE...
두근
씨익
HMPH.
SO NO MATTER WHAT HAPPENS, I CAN'T ESCAPE FIGHTING...

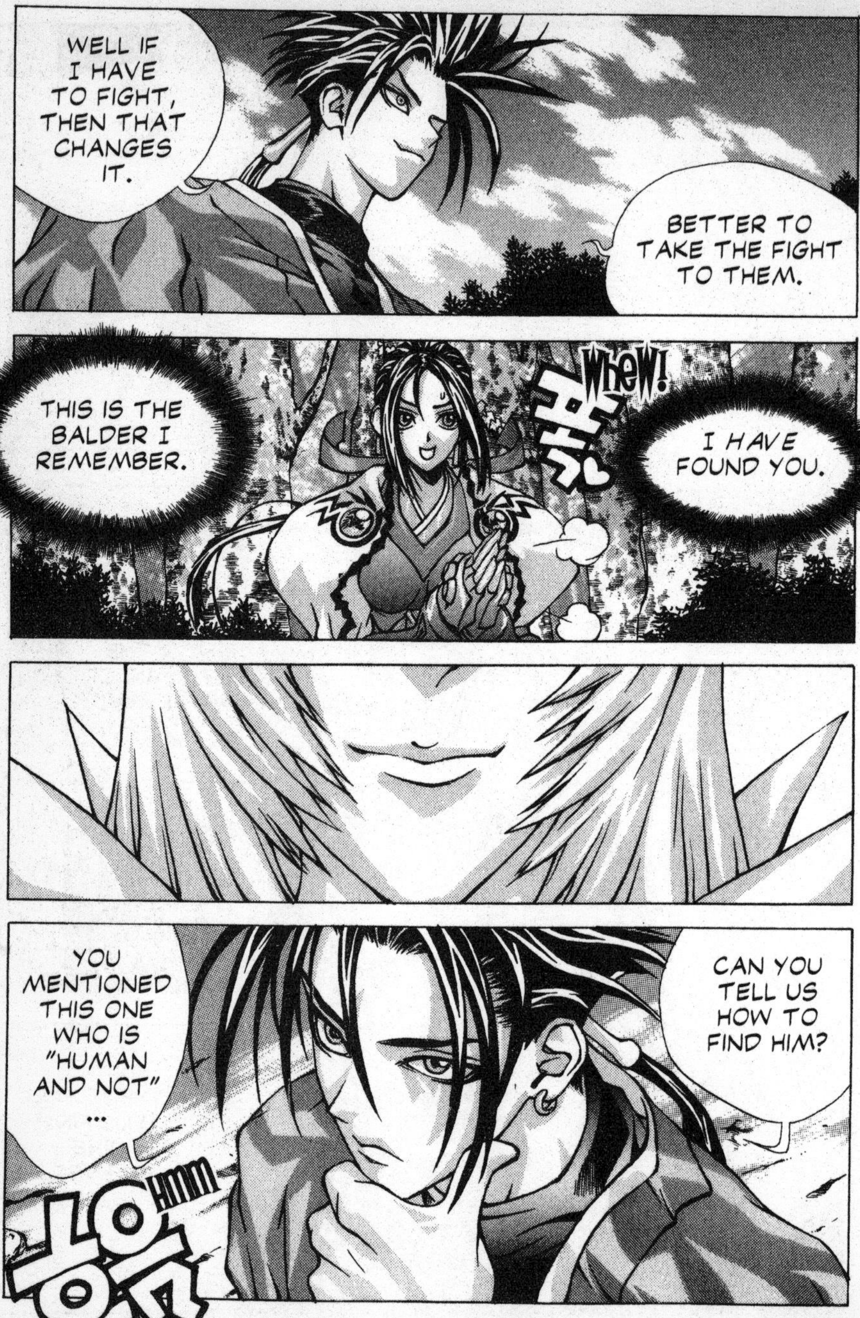
WELL IF I HAVE TO FIGHT, THEN THAT CHANGES IT.
BETTER TO TAKE THE FIGHT TO THEM.
THIS IS THE BALDER I REMEMBER.
WHEW!
I HAVE FOUND YOU.
YOU MENTIONED THIS ONE WHO IS "HUMAN AND NOT"...
CAN YOU TELL US HOW TO FIND HIM?
HMM

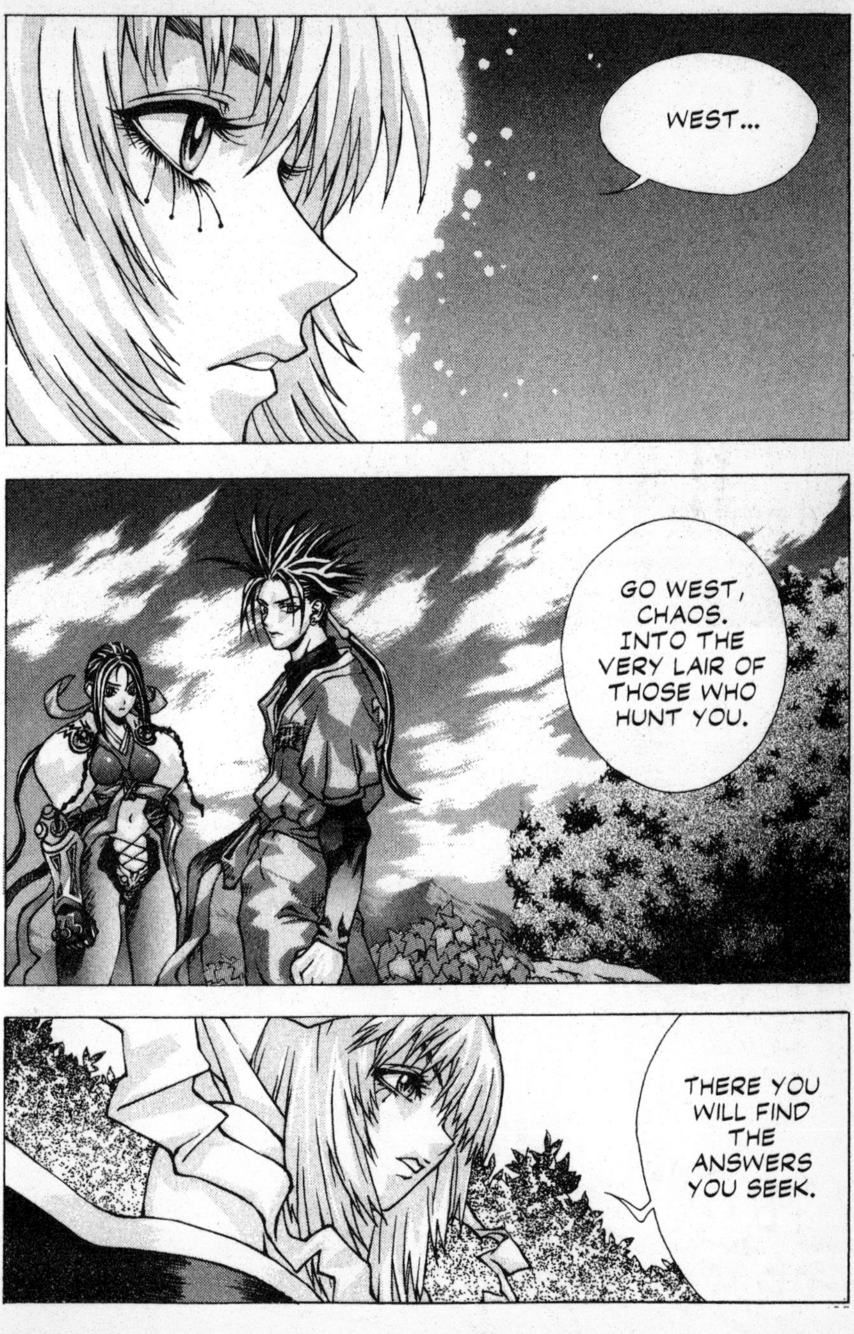
WEST...
GO WEST, CHAOS. INTO THE VERY LAIR OF THOSE WHO HUNT YOU.
THERE YOU WILL FIND THE ANSWERS YOU SEEK.

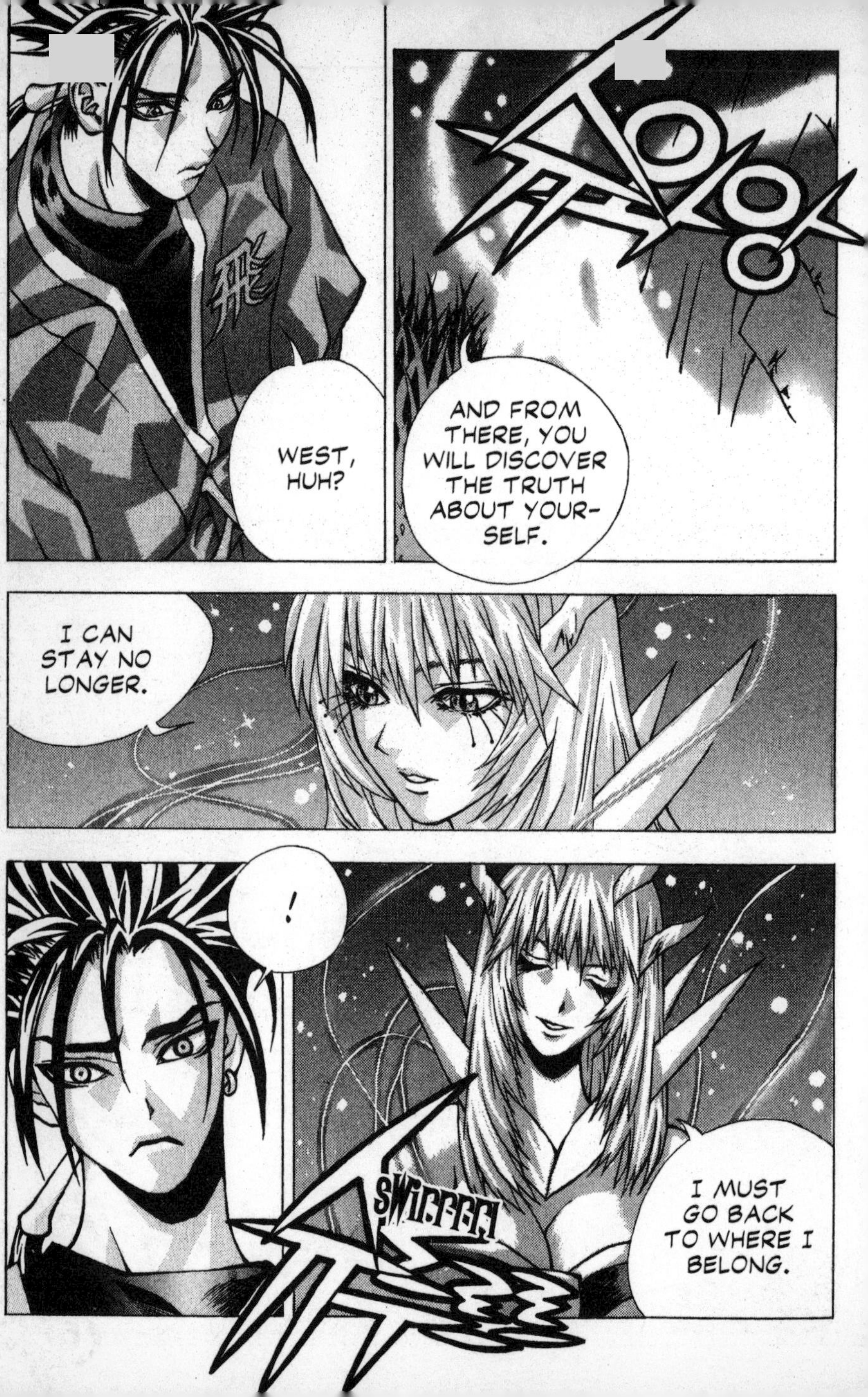

WEST, HUH?
TOOOO
AND FROM THERE, YOU WILL DISCOVER THE TRUTH ABOUT YOUR-SELF.
I CAN STAY NO LONGER.
!
SWIRRR
I MUST GO BACK TO WHERE I BELONG.

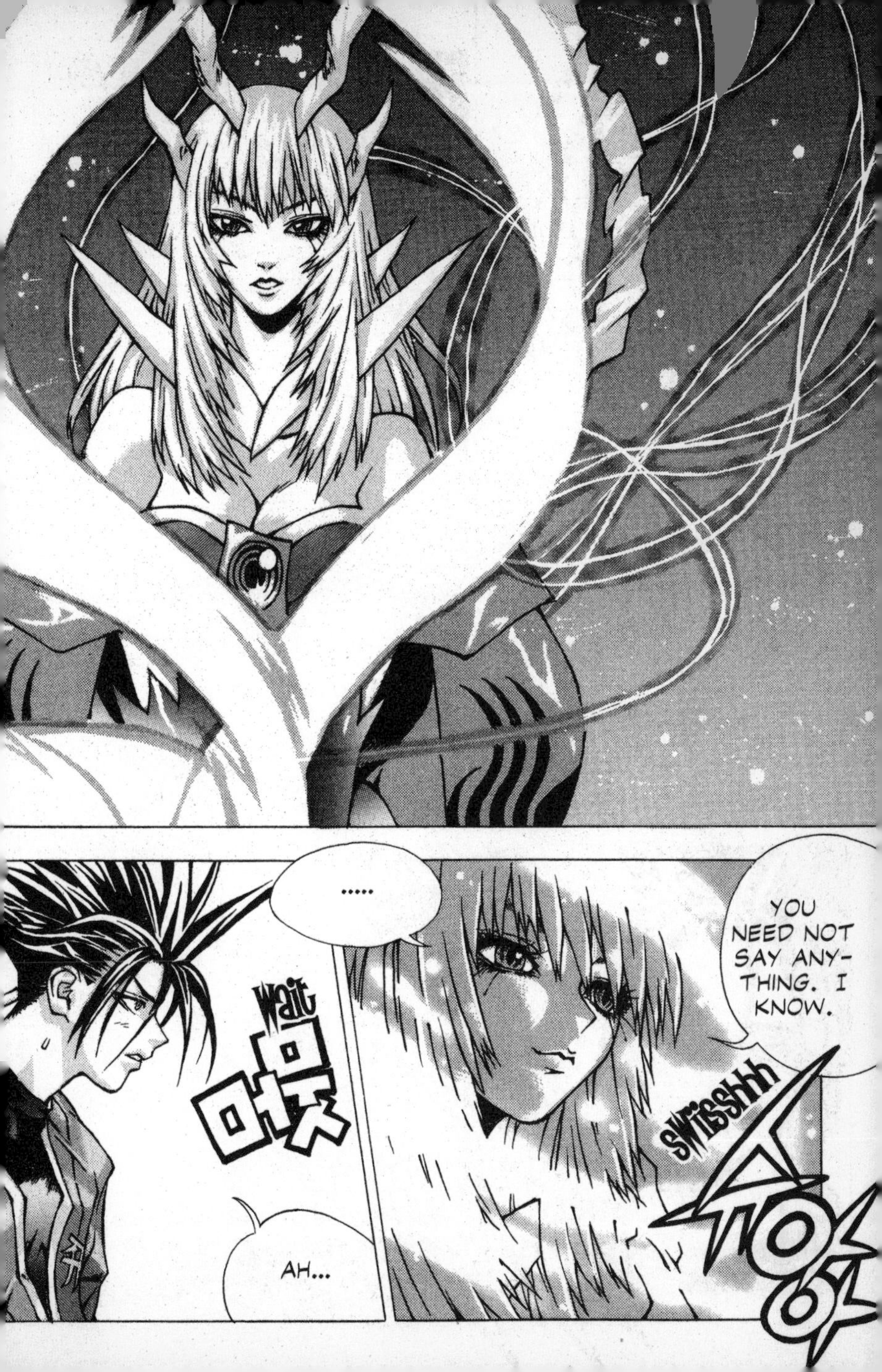
......
WAIT
AH...
YOU NEED NOT SAY ANY-THING. I KNOW.
SWISSHHH

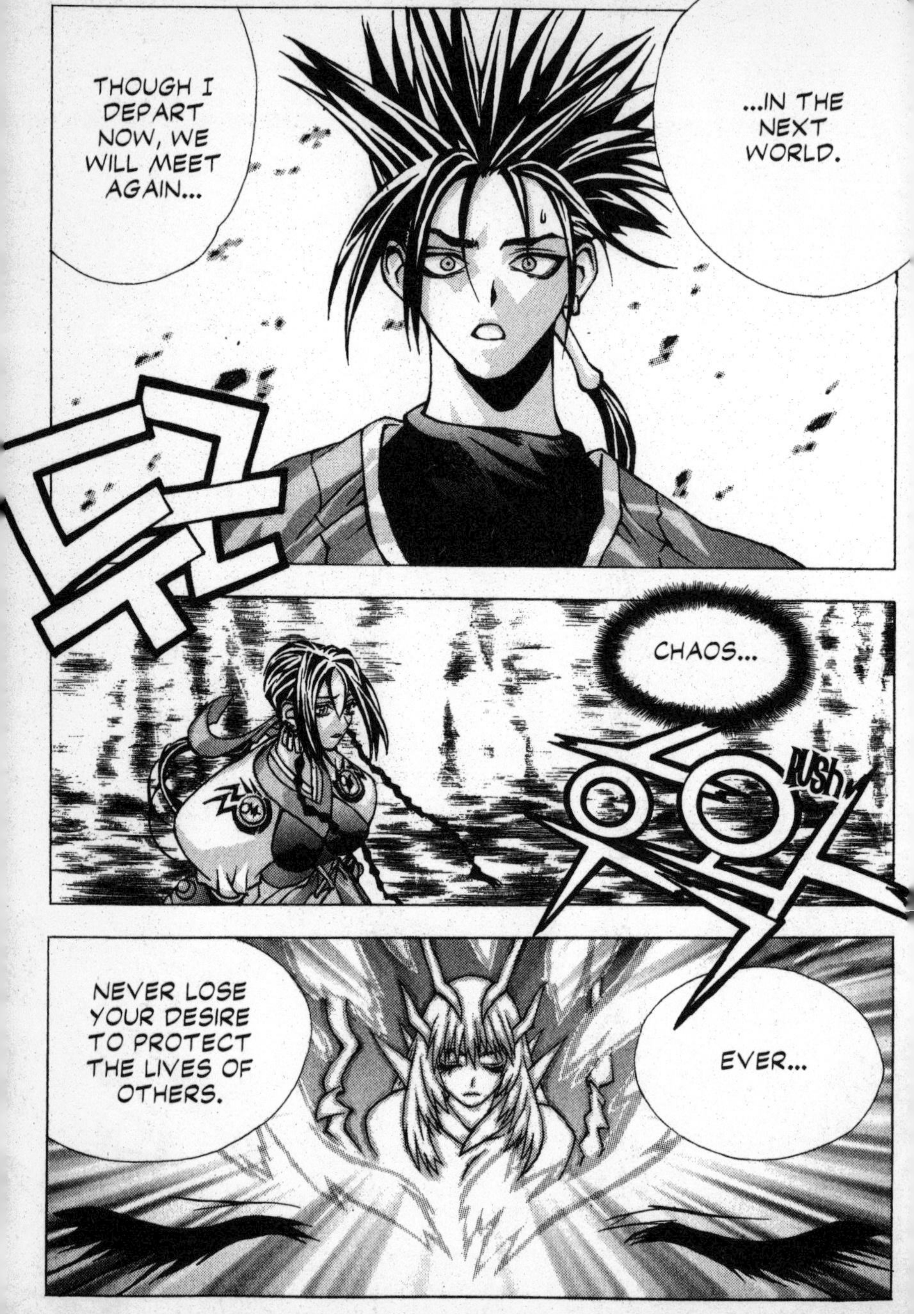
THOUGH I DEPART NOW, WE WILL MEET AGAIN...
...IN THE NEXT WORLD.
CHAOS...
RUSH
NEVER LOSE YOUR DESIRE TO PROTECT THE LIVES OF OTHERS.
EVER...

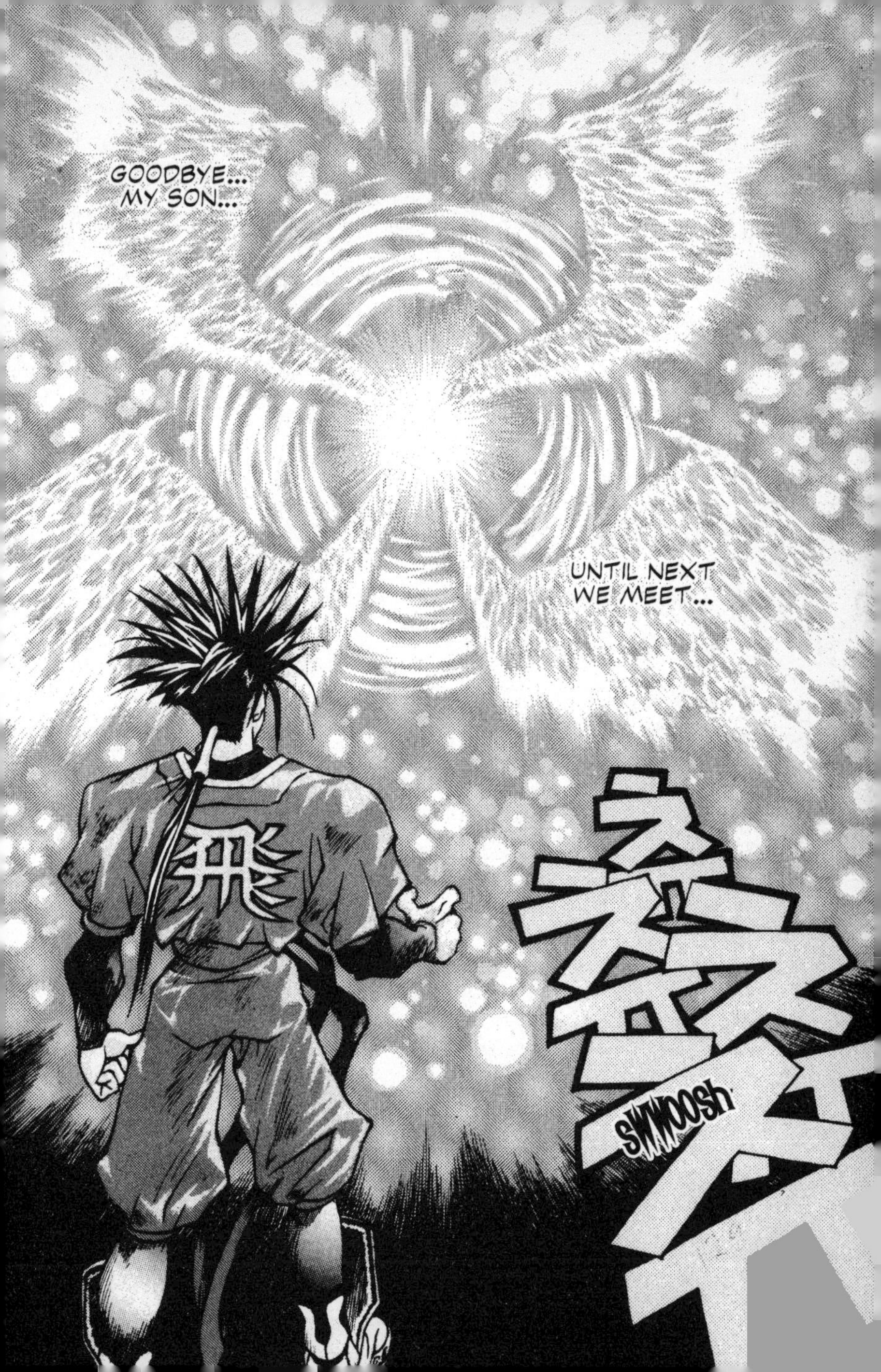
GOODBYE... MY SON...
UNTIL NEXT WE MEET...
ネス
SWOOSH

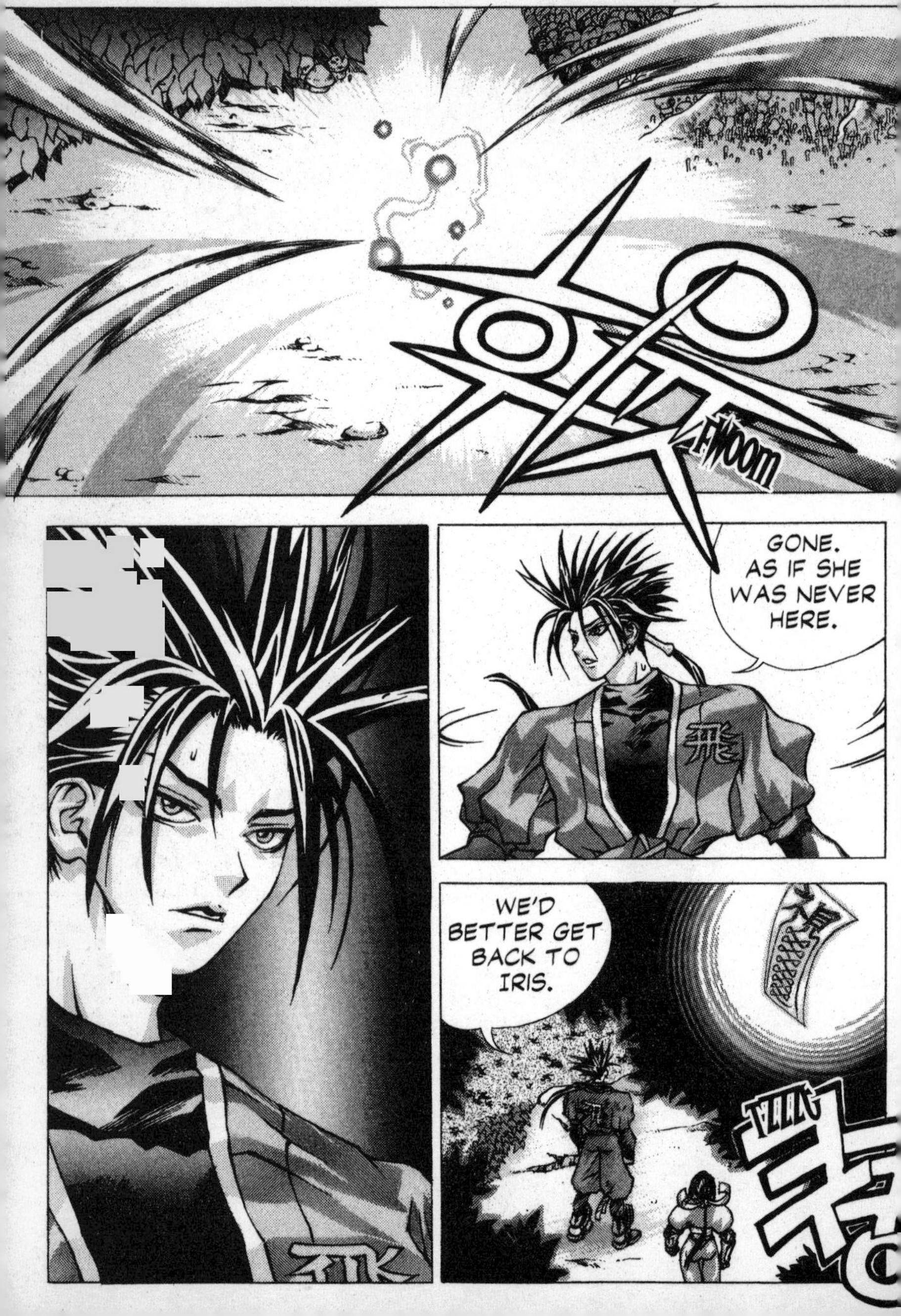
FWOOM
GONE. AS IF SHE WAS NEVER HERE.
WE'D BETTER GET BACK TO IRIS.

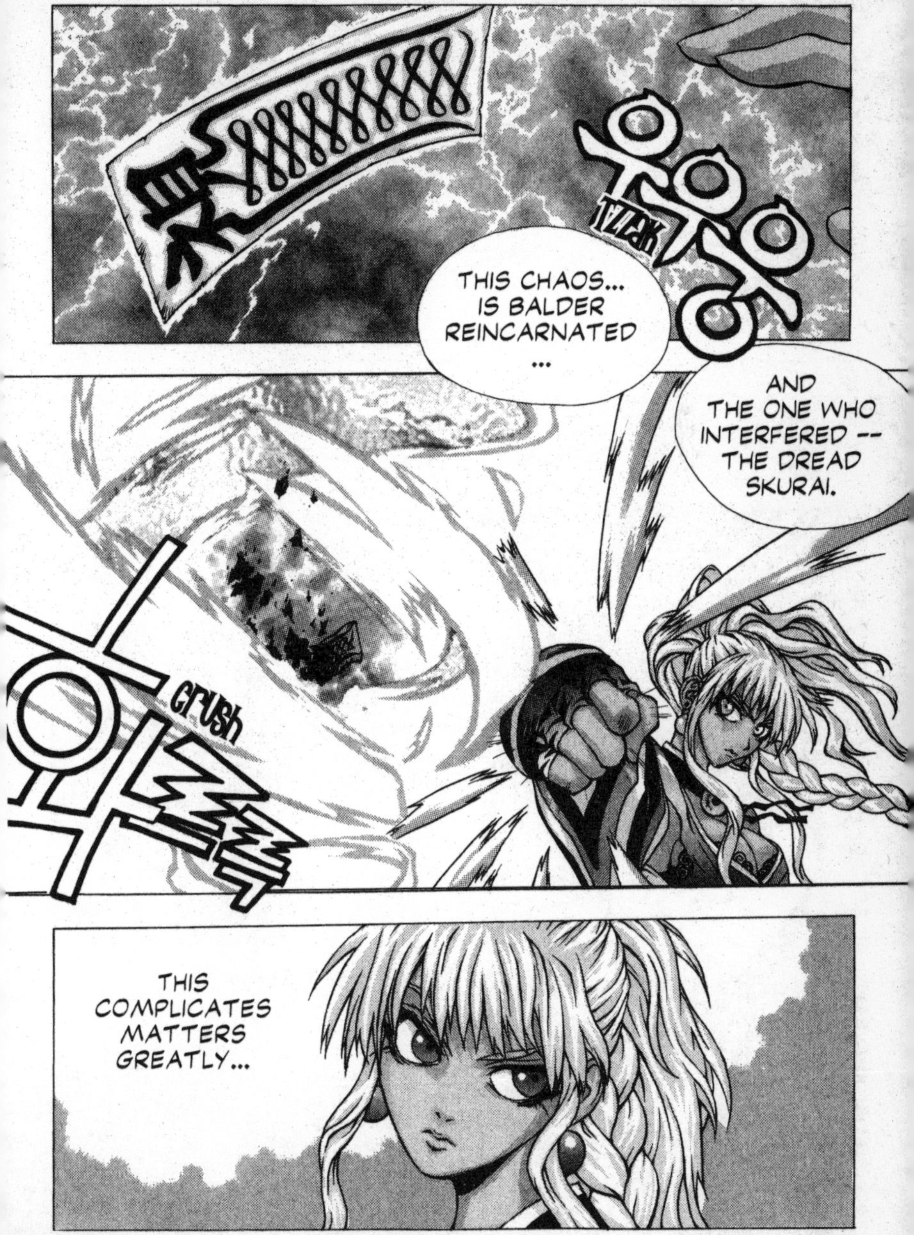
우웅웅
TZZAK
THIS CHAOS... IS BALDER REINCARNATED ...
AND THE ONE WHO INTERFERED -- THE DREAD SKURAI.
crush
THIS COMPLICATES MATTERS GREATLY...

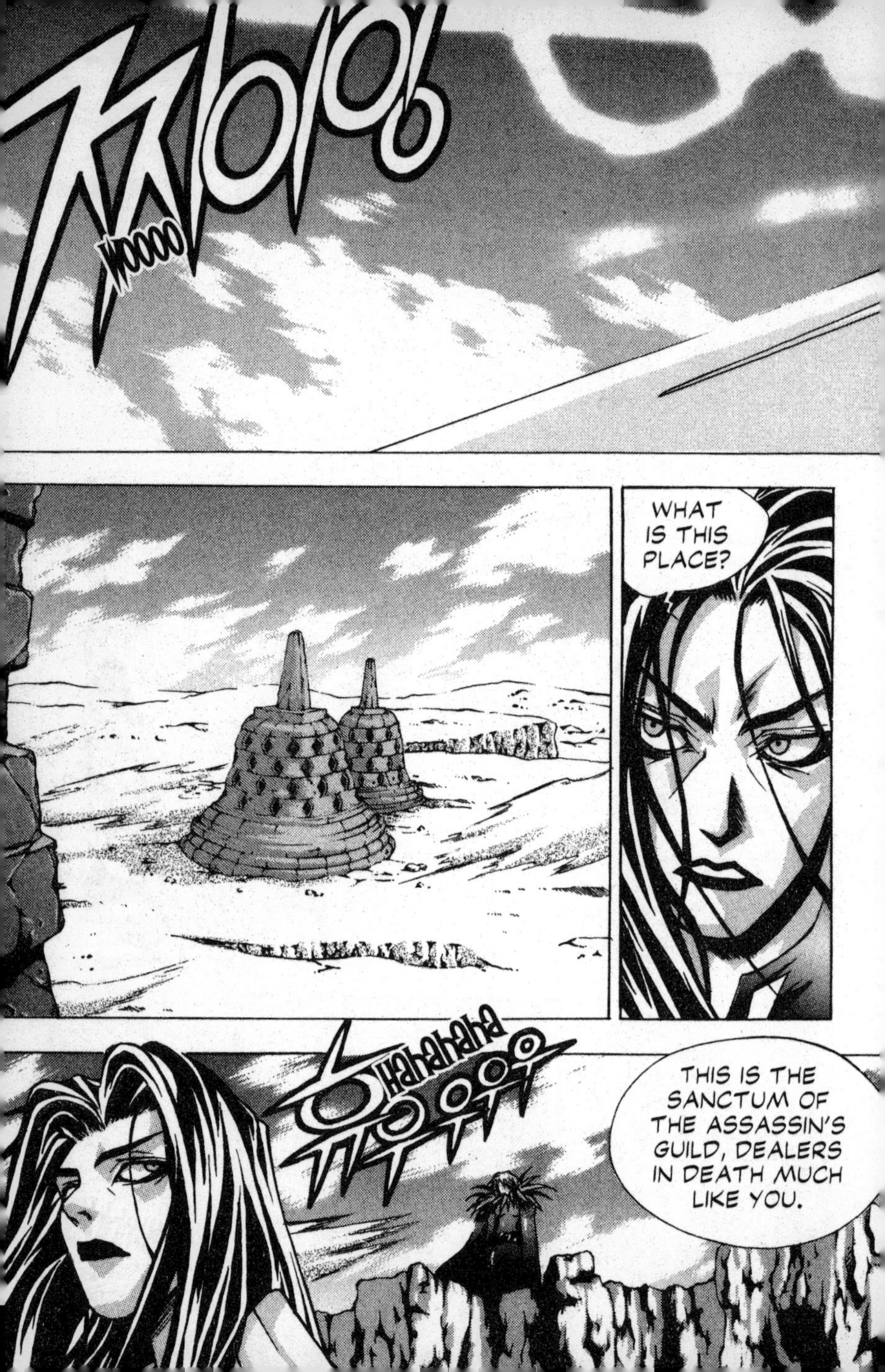
WOOOO
WHAT IS THIS PLACE?
HAHAHAHA
THIS IS THE SANCTUM OF THE ASSASSIN'S GUILD, DEALERS IN DEATH MUCH LIKE YOU.

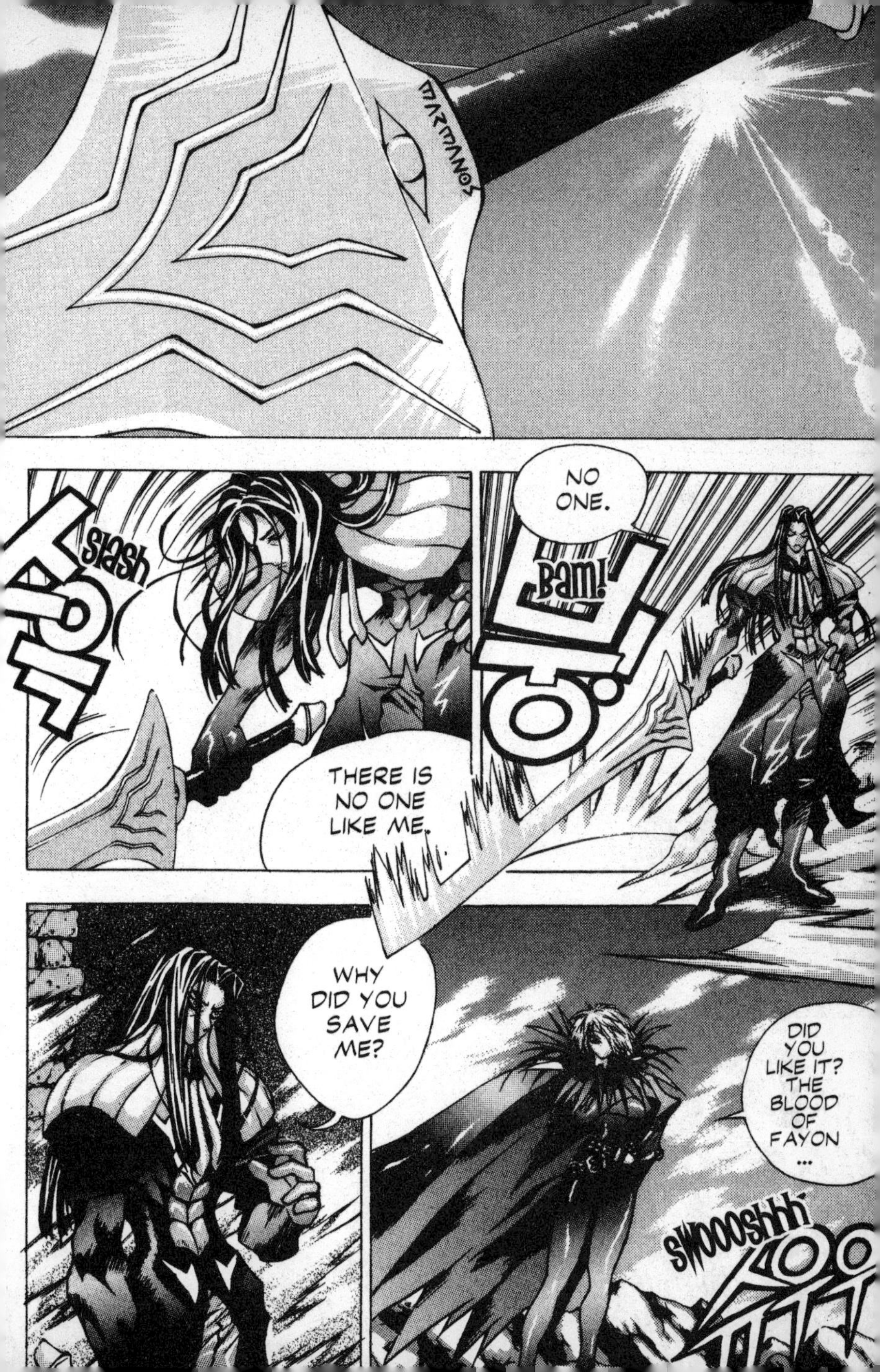
slash
THERE IS NO ONE LIKE ME.
NO ONE.
BAM!
WHY DID YOU SAVE ME?
DID YOU LIKE IT? THE BLOOD OF FAYON ...
SWOOOSHHH

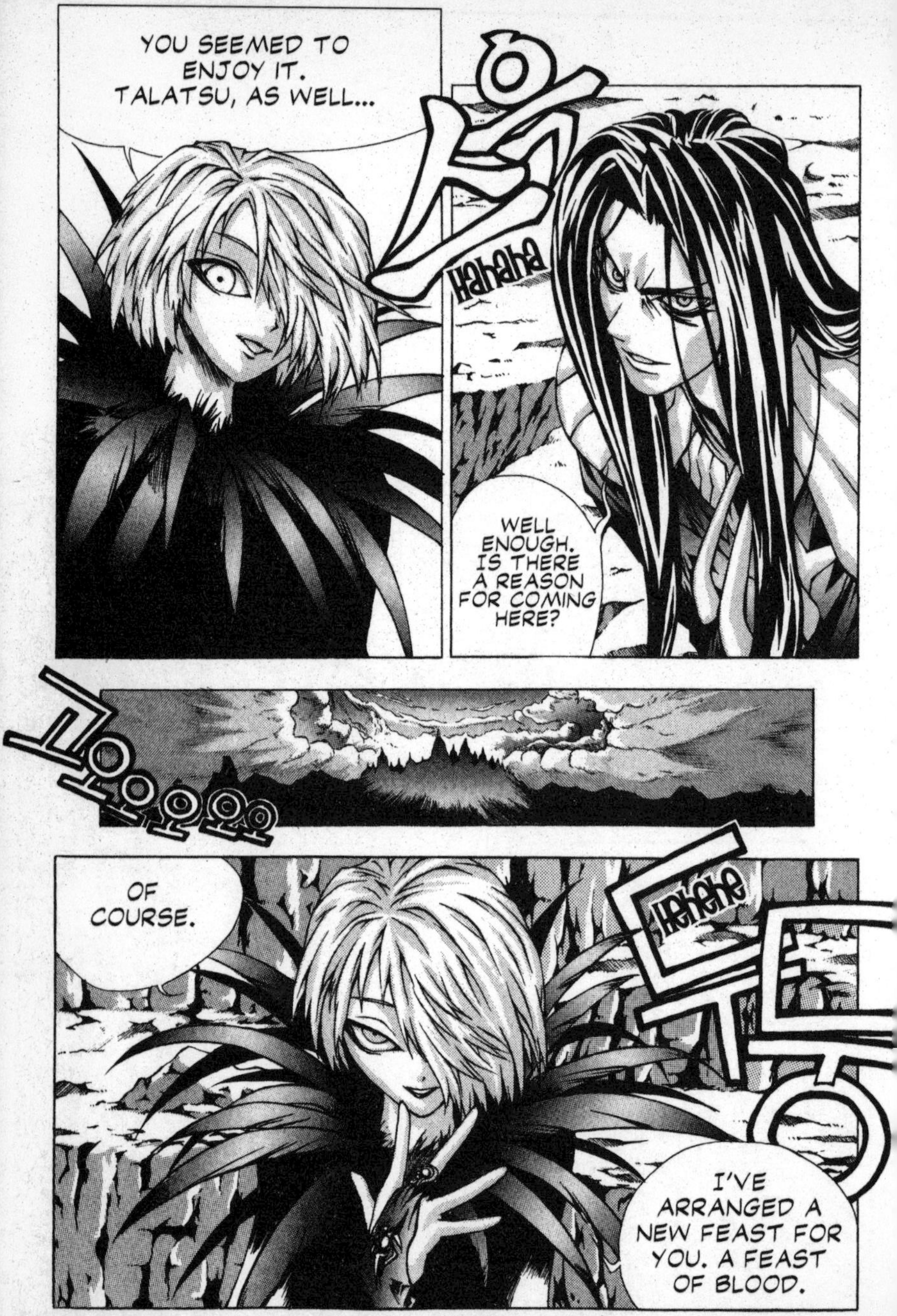
YOU SEEMED TO ENJOY IT. TALATSU, AS WELL...
Hahaha
WELL ENOUGH. IS THERE A REASON FOR COMING HERE?
OF COURSE.
Hehehe
I'VE ARRANGED A NEW FEAST FOR YOU. A FEAST OF BLOOD.

RAGNAROK
라그나로크
IN TO THE ABYSS

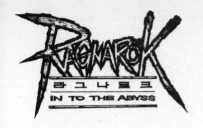

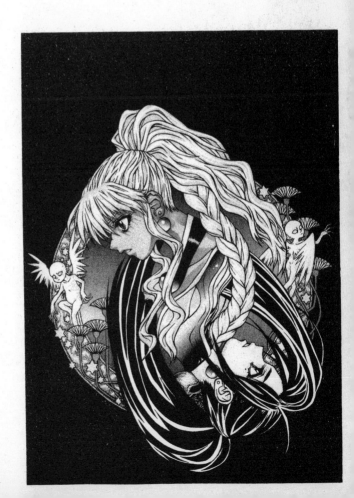

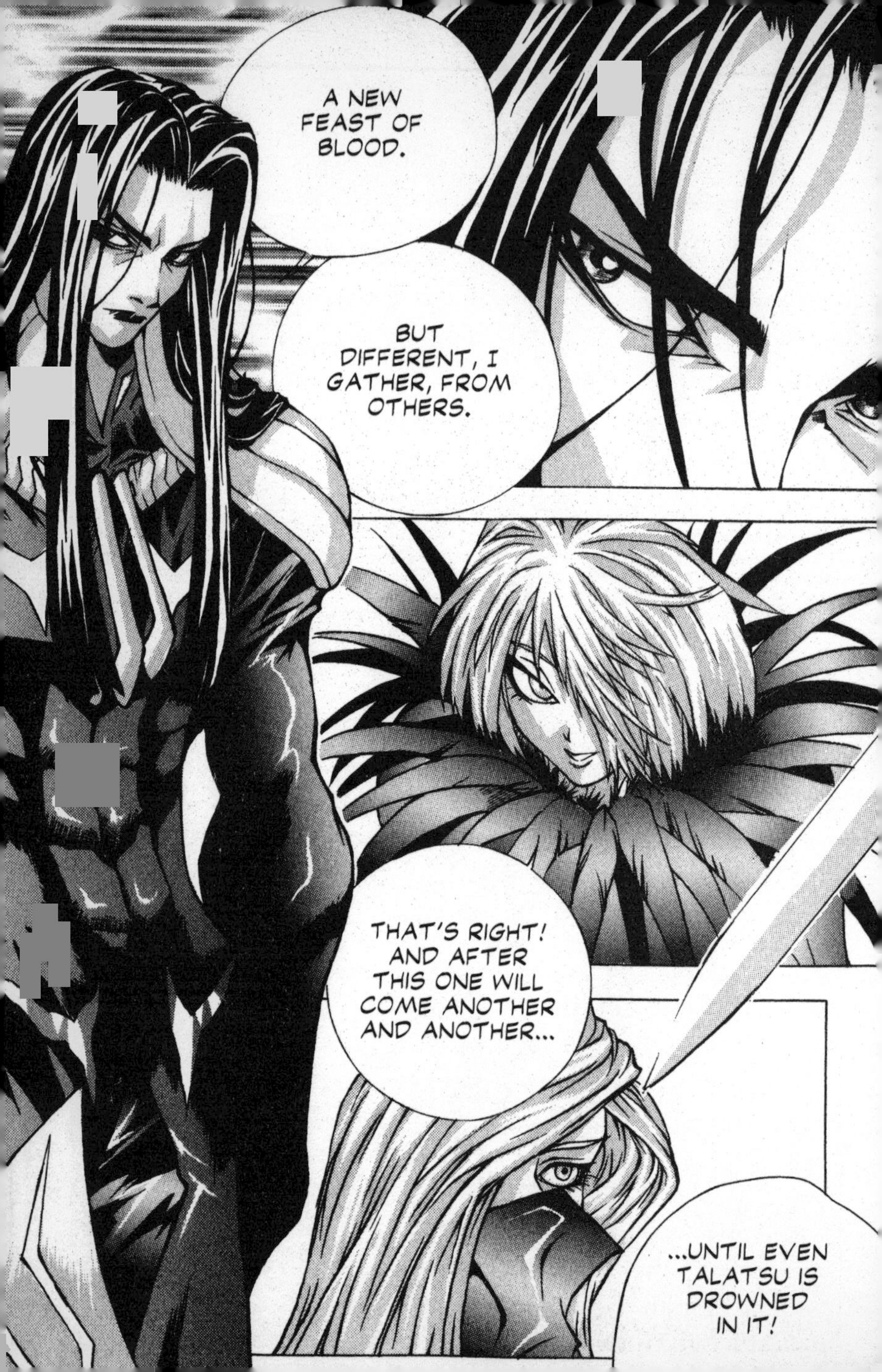
A NEW FEAST OF BLOOD.
BUT DIFFERENT, I GATHER, FROM OTHERS.
THAT'S RIGHT! AND AFTER THIS ONE WILL COME ANOTHER AND ANOTHER...
...UNTIL EVEN TALATSU IS DROWNED IN IT!

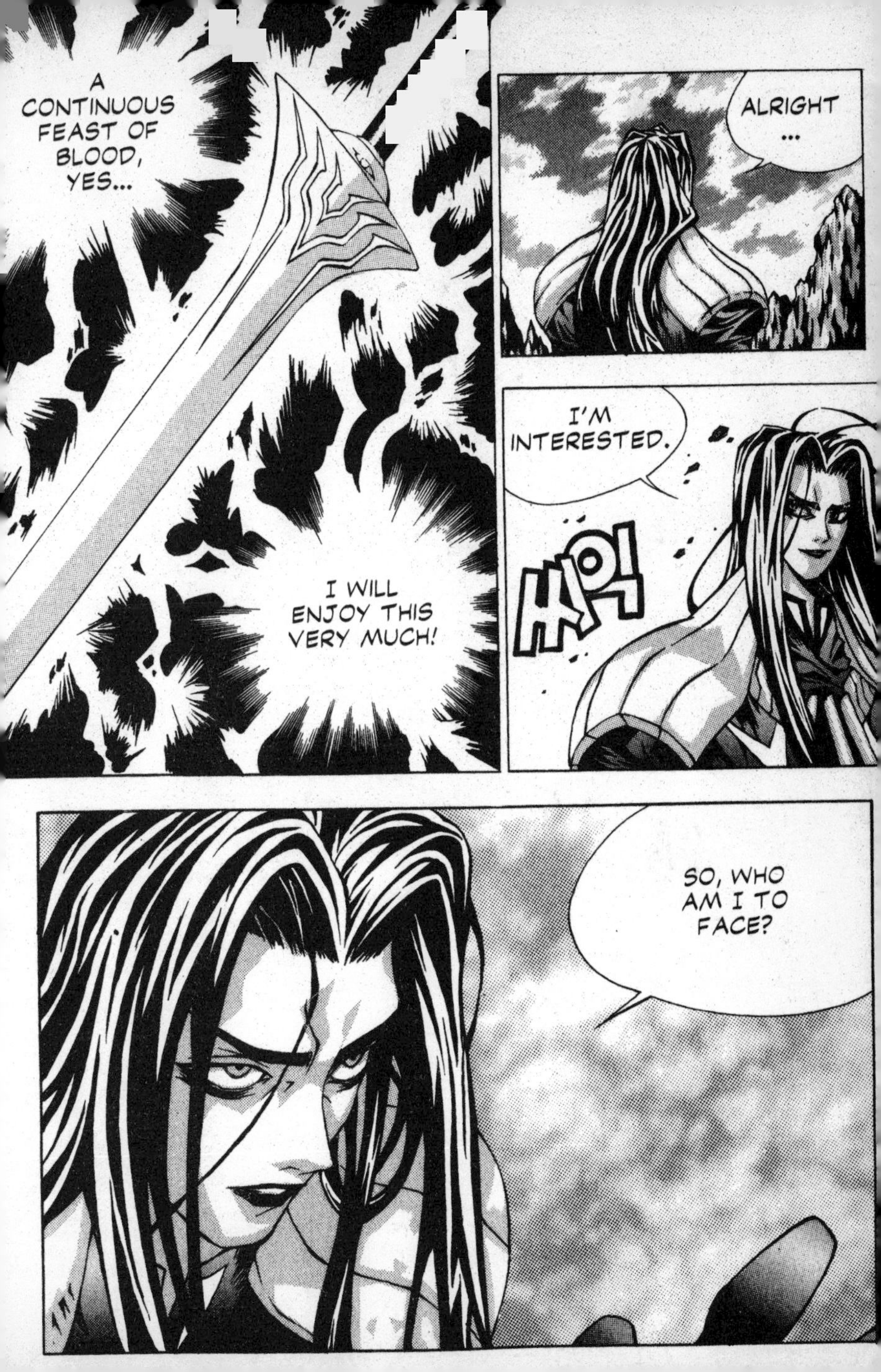
A CONTINUOUS FEAST OF BLOOD, YES...
I WILL ENJOY THIS VERY MUCH!
ALRIGHT ...
I'M INTERESTED.
SO, WHO AM I TO FACE?

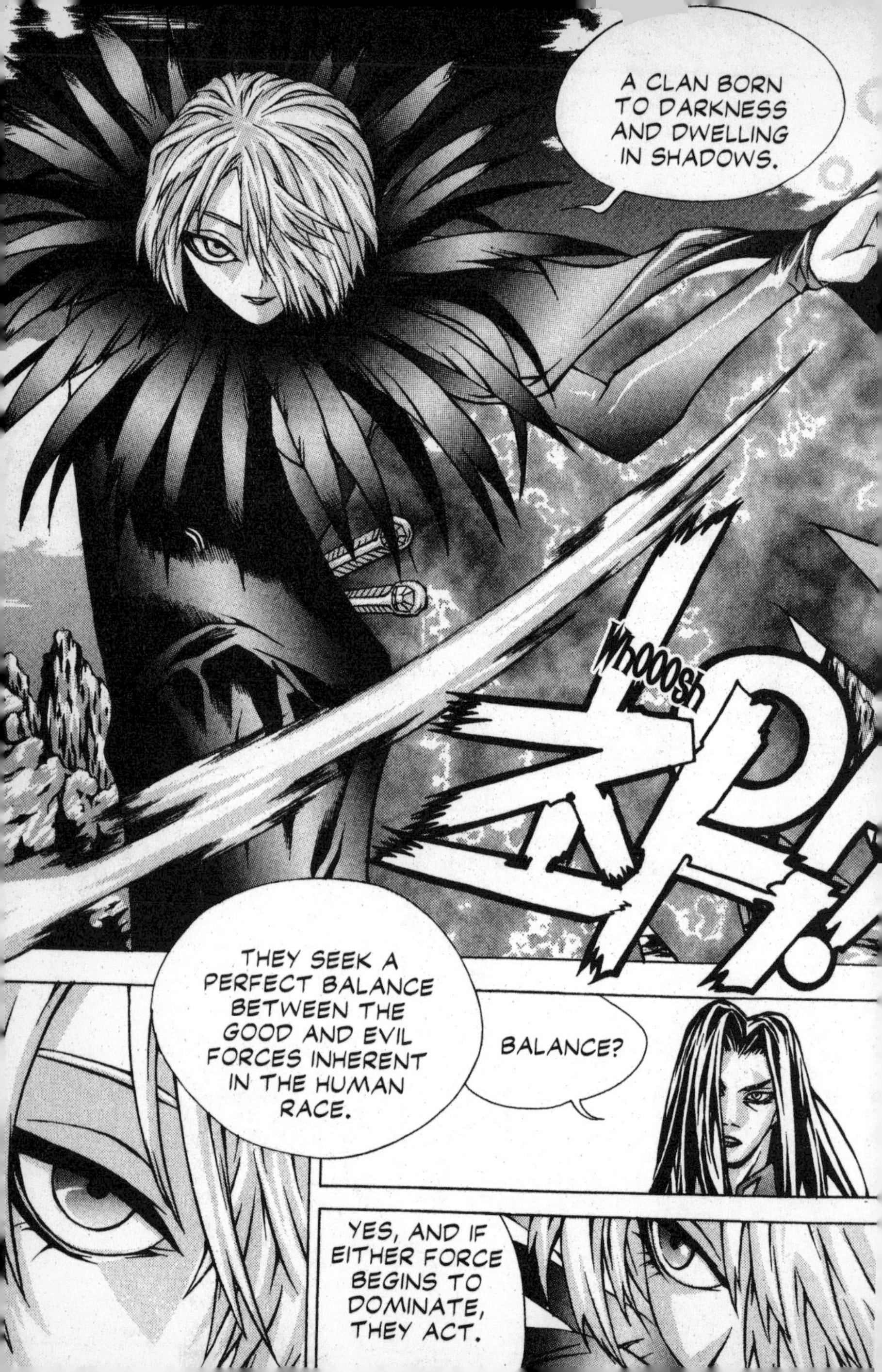
A CLAN BORN TO DARKNESS AND DWELLING IN SHADOWS.
Whooosh
THEY SEEK A PERFECT BALANCE BETWEEN THE GOOD AND EVIL FORCES INHERENT IN THE HUMAN RACE.
BALANCE?
YES, AND IF EITHER FORCE BEGINS TO DOMINATE, THEY ACT.

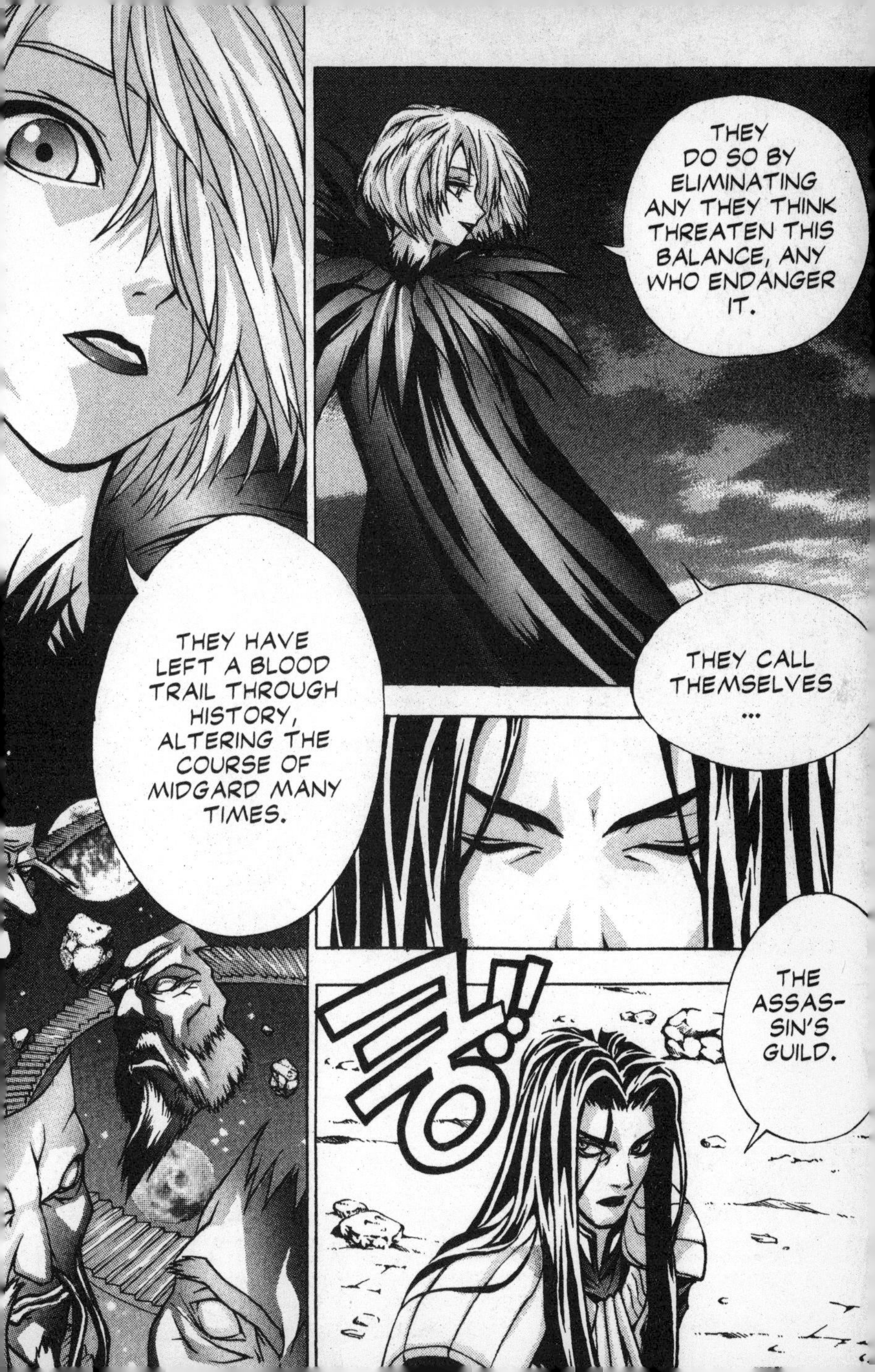
THEY DO SO BY ELIMINATING ANY THEY THINK THREATEN THIS BALANCE, ANY WHO ENDANGER IT.
THEY HAVE LEFT A BLOOD TRAIL THROUGH HISTORY, ALTERING THE COURSE OF MIDGARD MANY TIMES.
THEY CALL THEMSELVES ...
THE ASSAS-SIN'S GUILD.

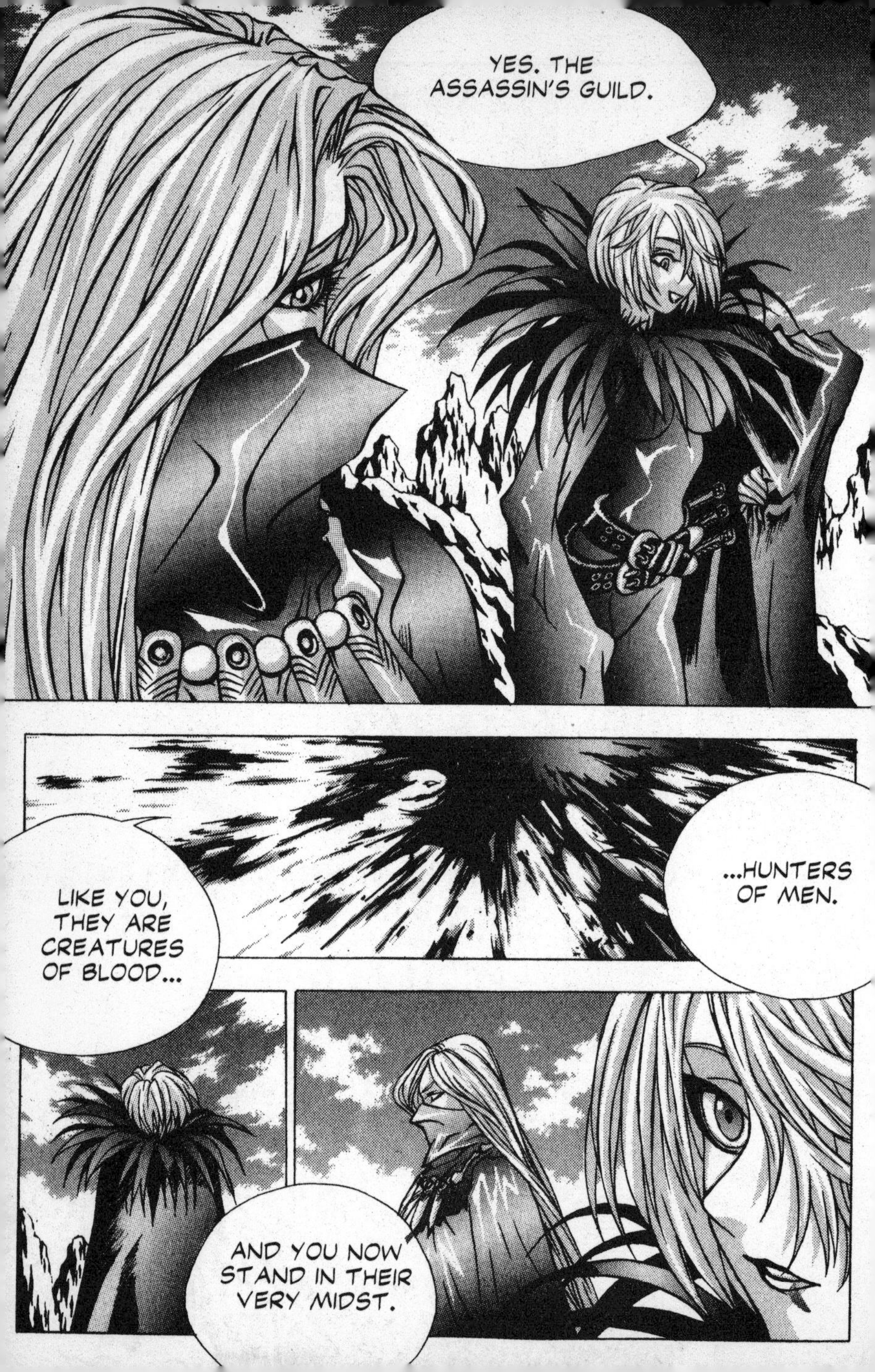
YES. THE ASSASSIN'S GUILD.
LIKE YOU, THEY ARE CREATURES OF BLOOD...
...HUNTERS OF MEN.
AND YOU NOW STAND IN THEIR VERY MIDST.

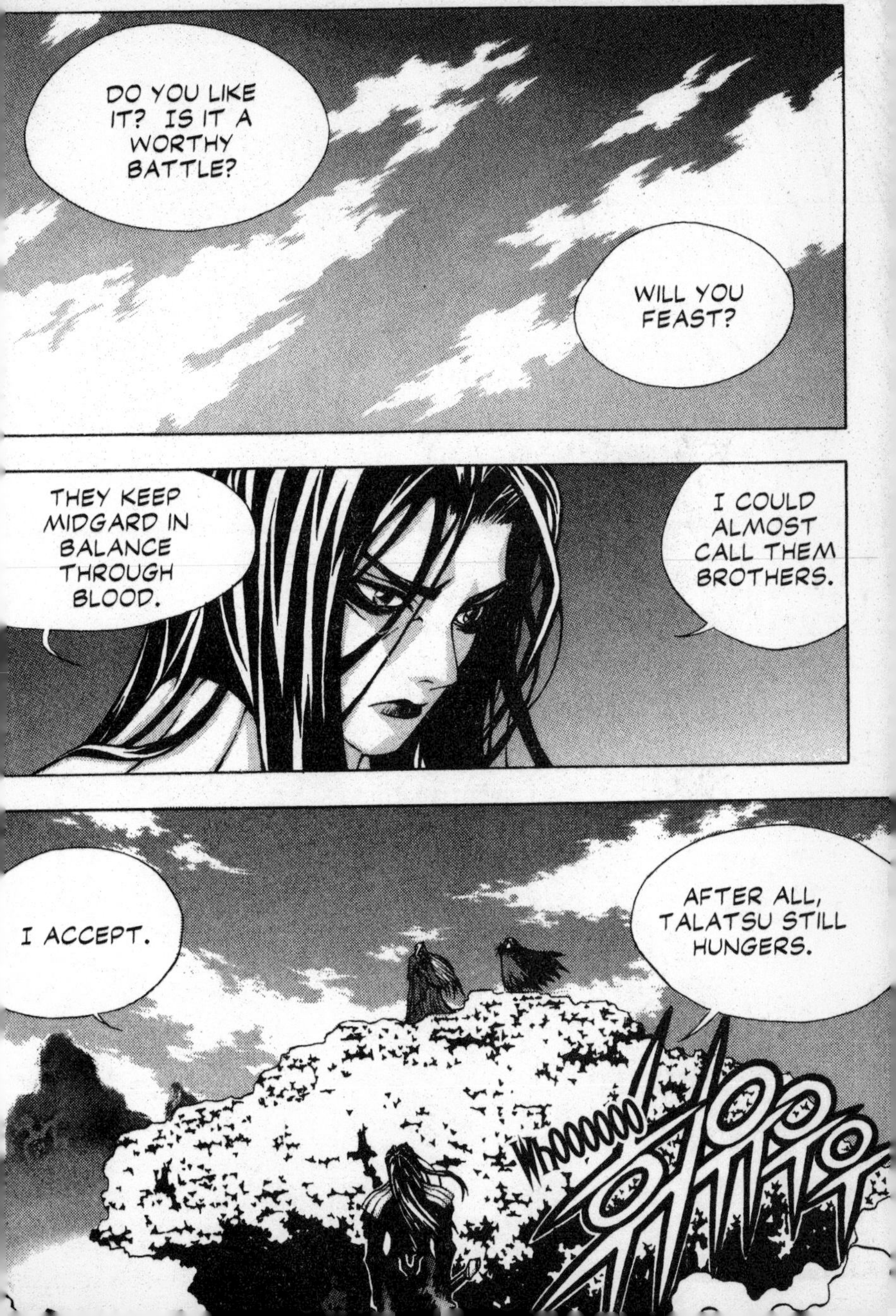
DO YOU LIKE IT? IS IT A WORTHY BATTLE?
WILL YOU FEAST?
THEY KEEP MIDGARD IN BALANCE THROUGH BLOOD.
I COULD ALMOST CALL THEM BROTHERS.
I ACCEPT.
AFTER ALL, TALATSU STILL HUNGERS.
WHOOOOOO

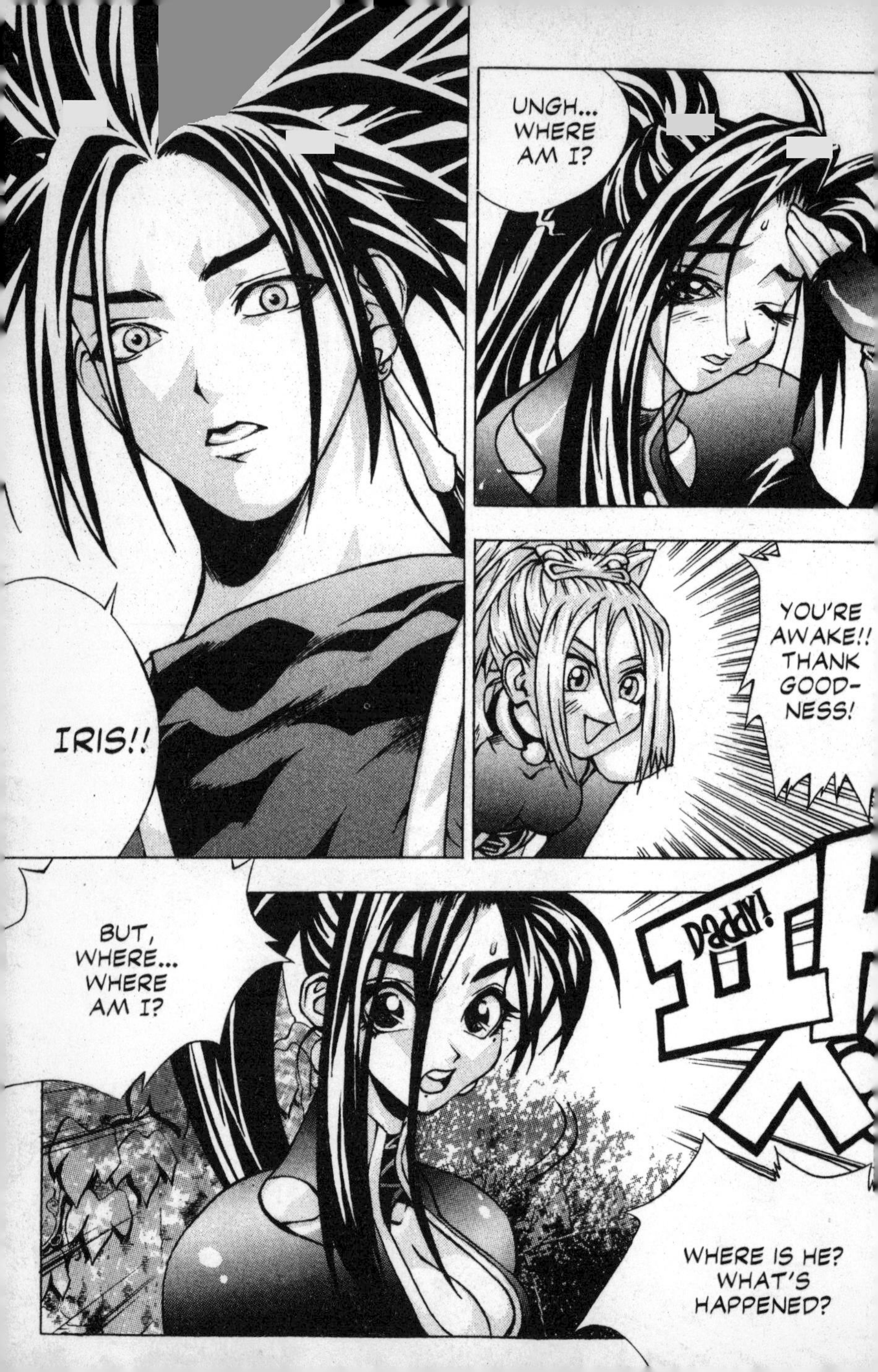
IRIS!!
UNGH... WHERE AM I?
YOU'RE AWAKE!! THANK GOODNESS!
BUT, WHERE... WHERE AM I?
DADDY!
WHERE IS HE? WHAT'S HAPPENED?

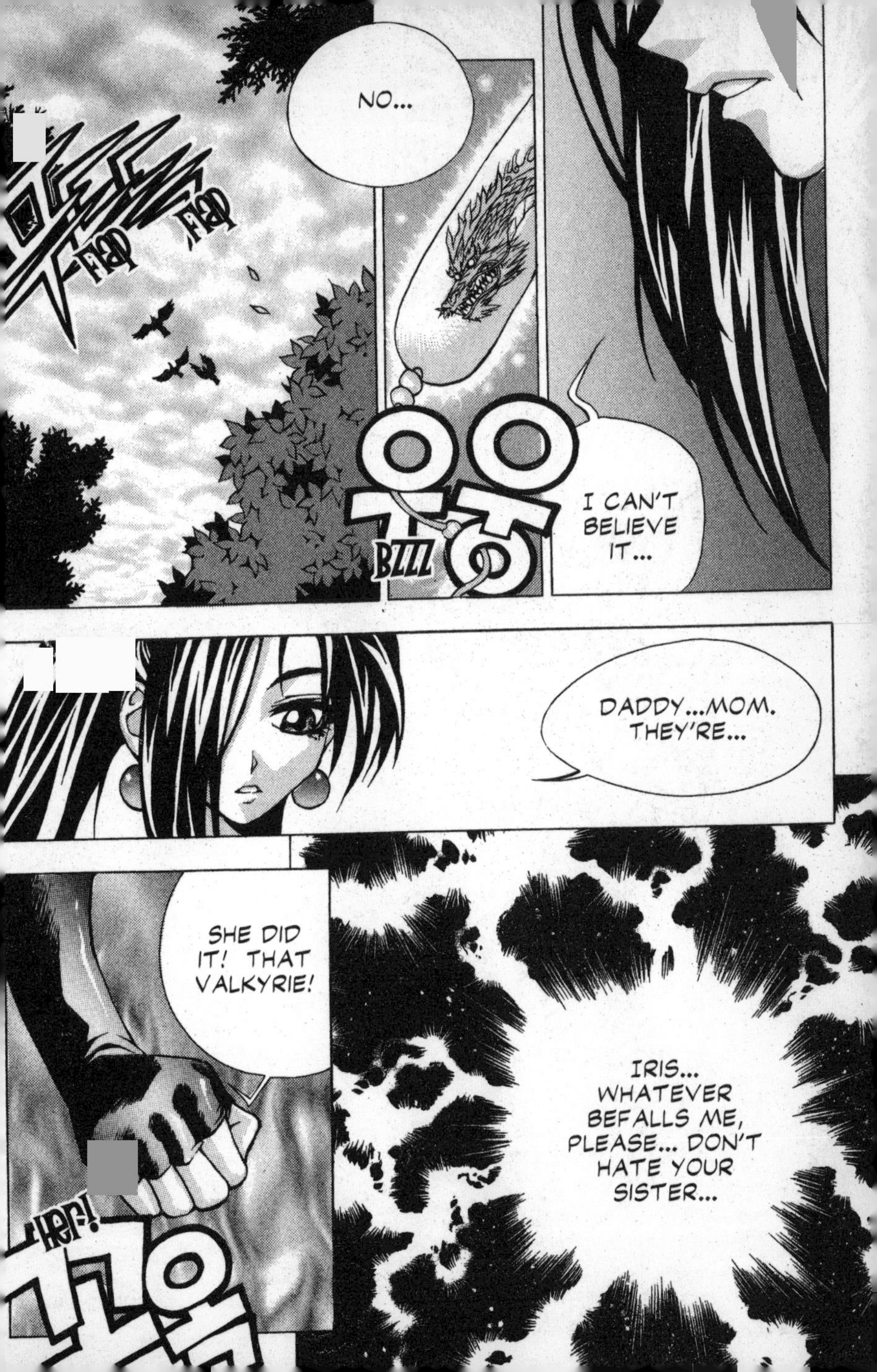
FLAP
FLAP
NO...
BZZZ
I CAN'T BELIEVE IT...
DADDY...MOM. THEY'RE...
SHE DID IT! THAT VALKYRIE!
Heh!
IRIS... WHATEVER BEFALLS ME, PLEASE... DON'T HATE YOUR SISTER...

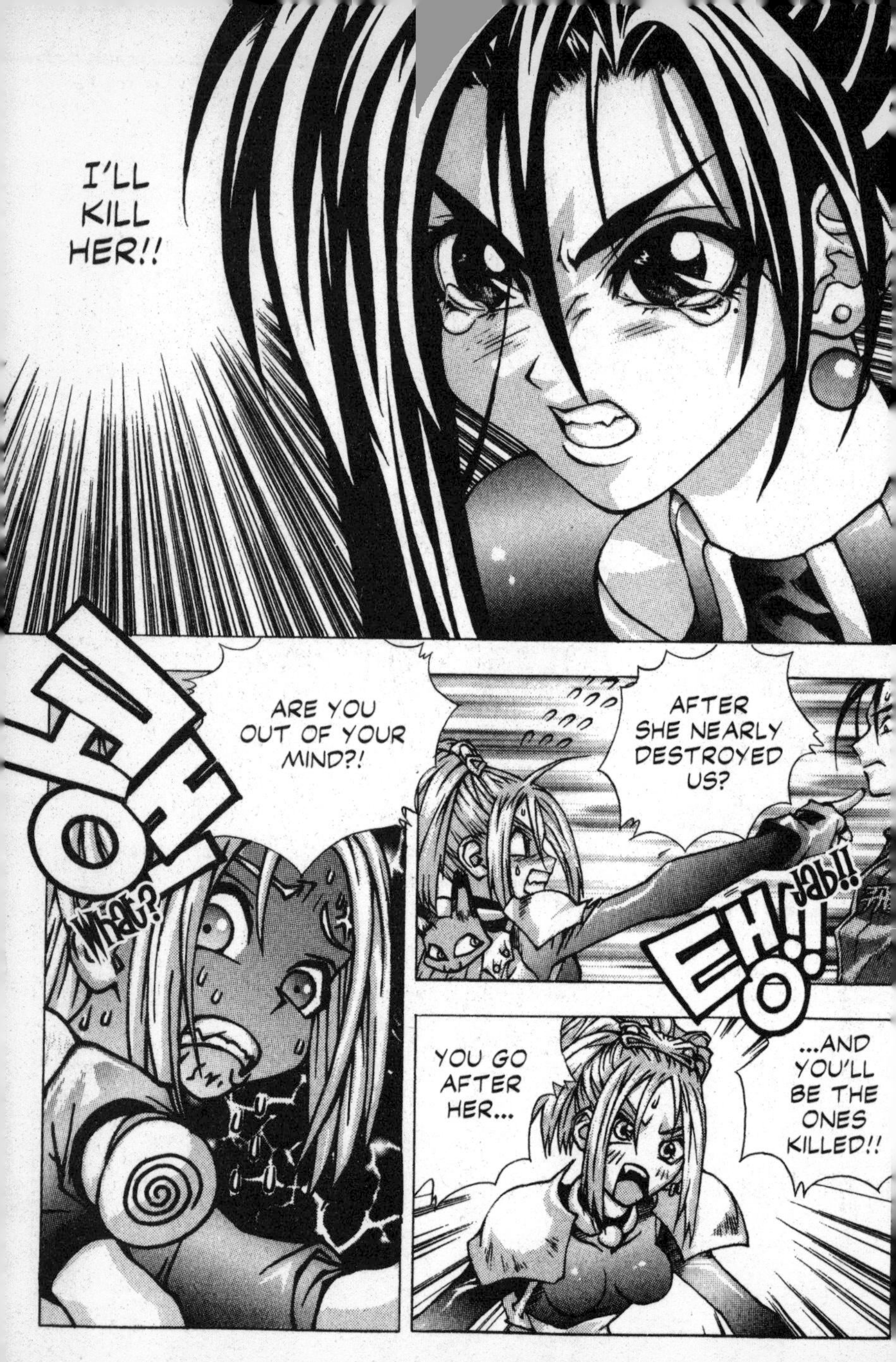
I'LL KILL HER!!
What?!
ARE YOU OUT OF YOUR MIND?!
AFTER SHE NEARLY DESTROYED US?
JAB!!
EH...!!
YOU GO AFTER HER...
...AND YOU'LL BE THE ONES KILLED!!

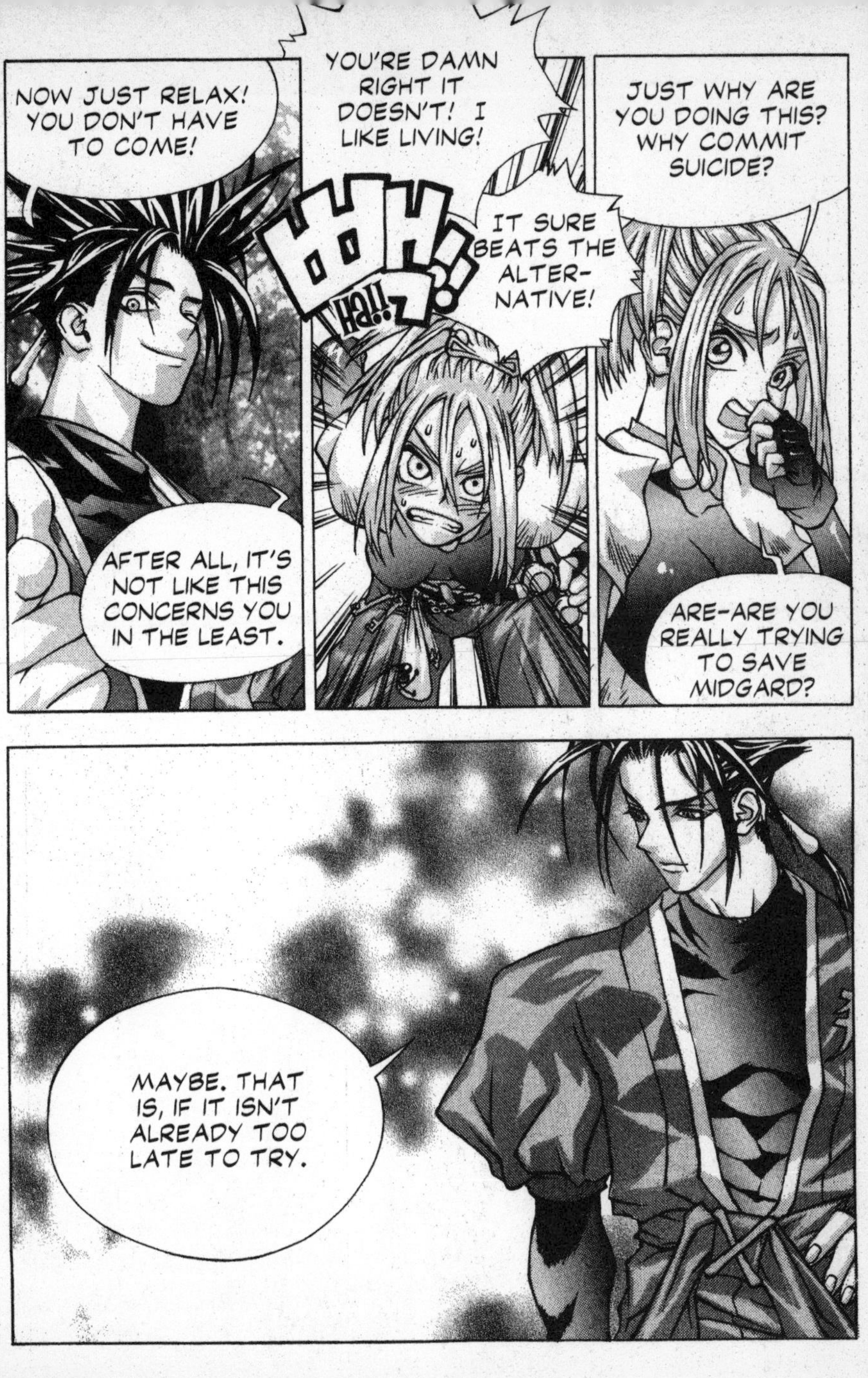
NOW JUST RELAX! YOU DON'T HAVE TO COME!
AFTER ALL, IT'S NOT LIKE THIS CONCERNS YOU IN THE LEAST.
YOU'RE DAMN RIGHT IT DOESN'T! I LIKE LIVING!
IT SURE BEATS THE ALTER-NATIVE!
JUST WHY ARE YOU DOING THIS? WHY COMMIT SUICIDE?
ARE-ARE YOU REALLY TRYING TO SAVE MIDGARD?
MAYBE. THAT IS, IF IT ISN'T ALREADY TOO LATE TO TRY.

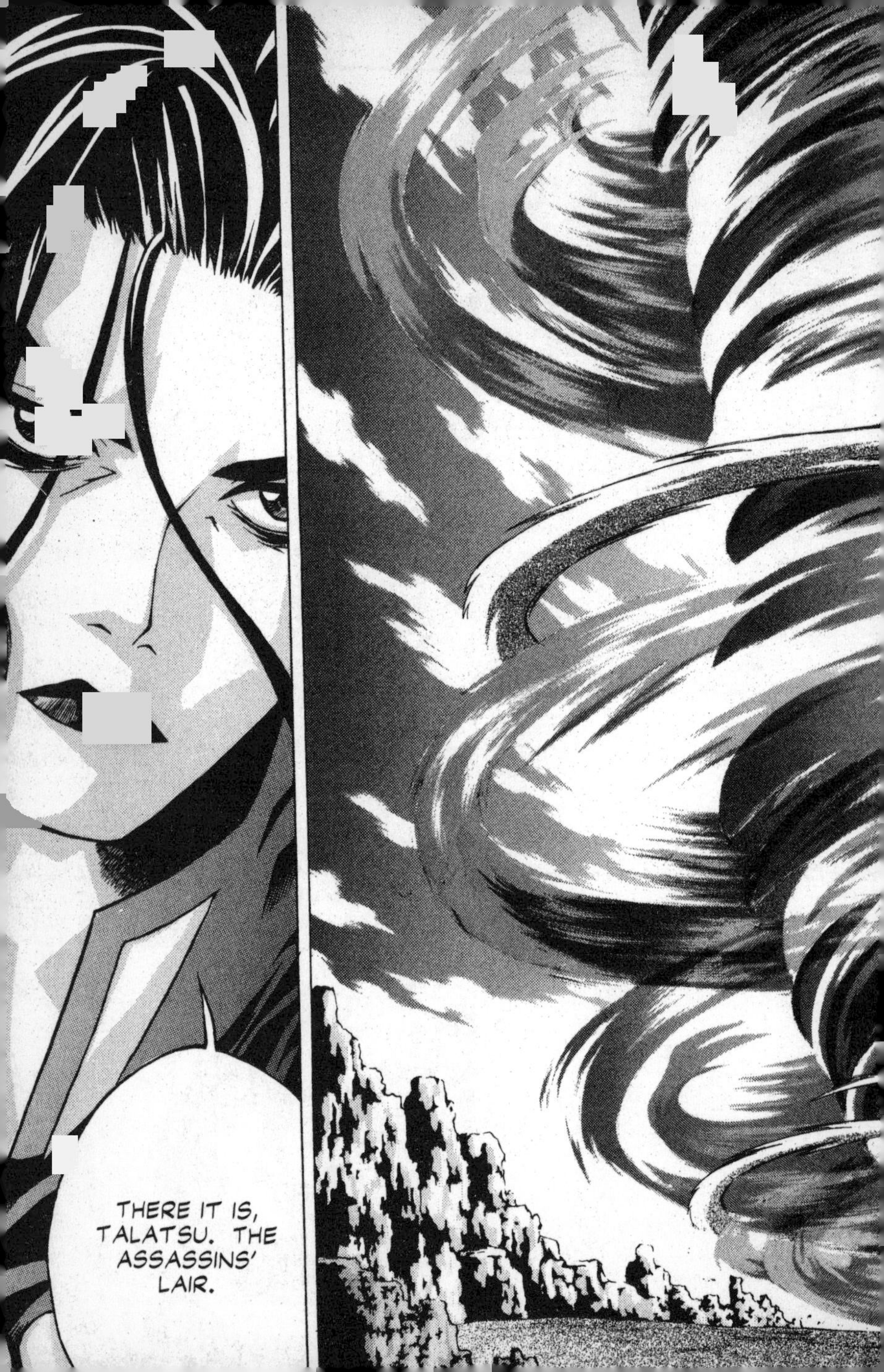
THERE IT IS,
TALATSU. THE
ASSASSINS'
LAIR.

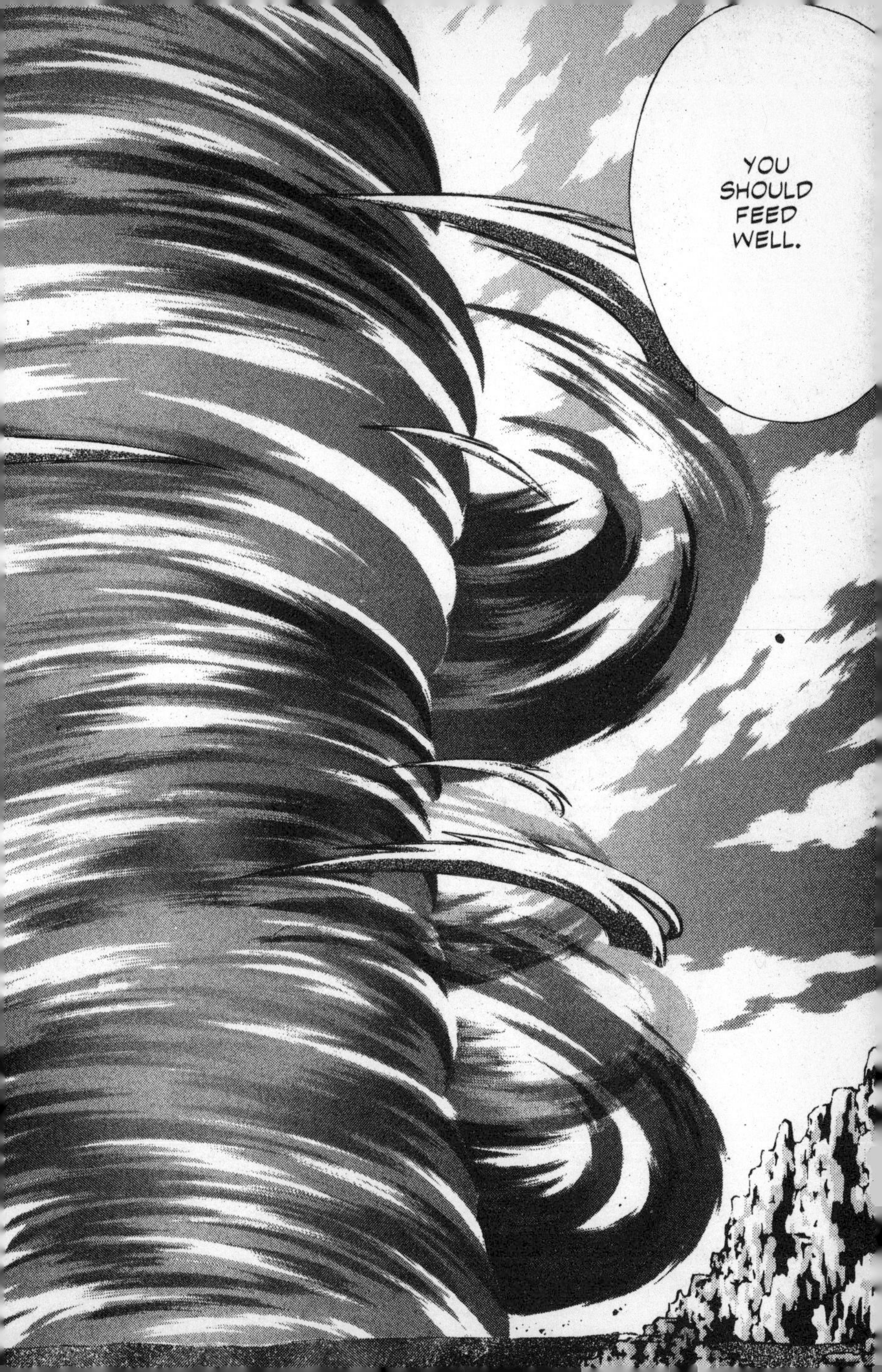
YOU SHOULD FEED WELL.

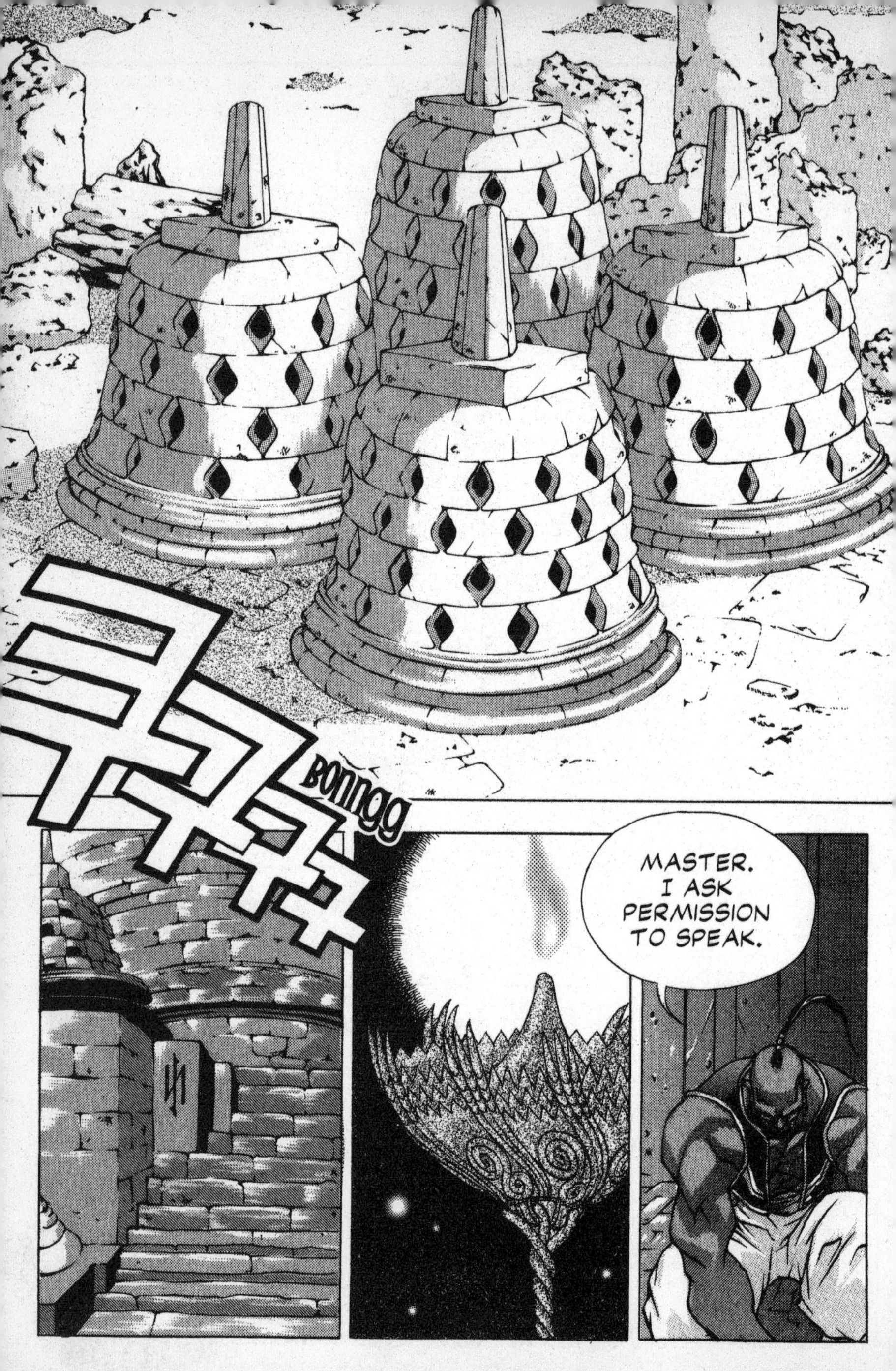
BONNGG
MASTER. I ASK PERMISSION TO SPEAK.

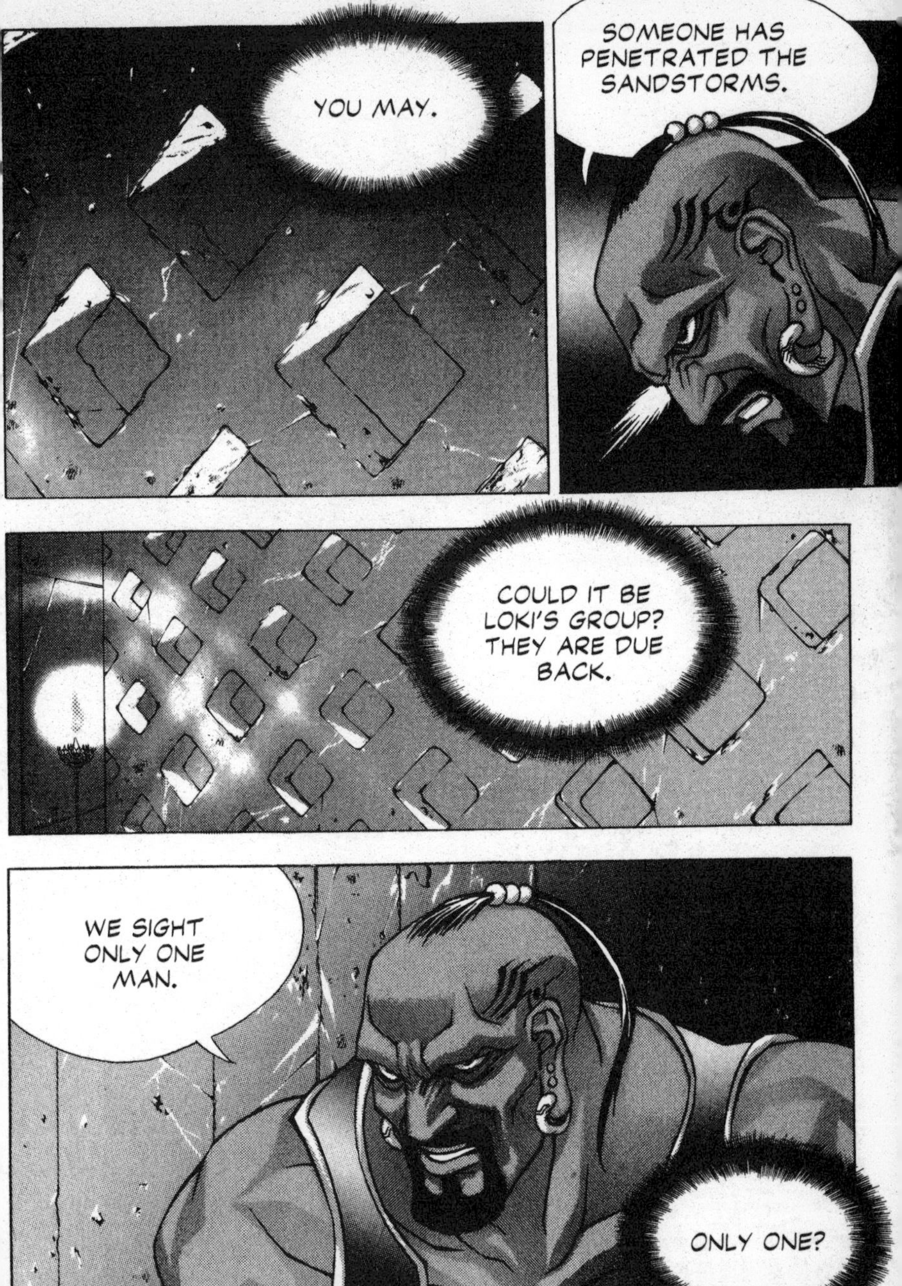
YOU MAY.
SOMEONE HAS PENETRATED THE SANDSTORMS.
COULD IT BE LOKI'S GROUP? THEY ARE DUE BACK.
WE SIGHT ONLY ONE MAN.
ONLY ONE?

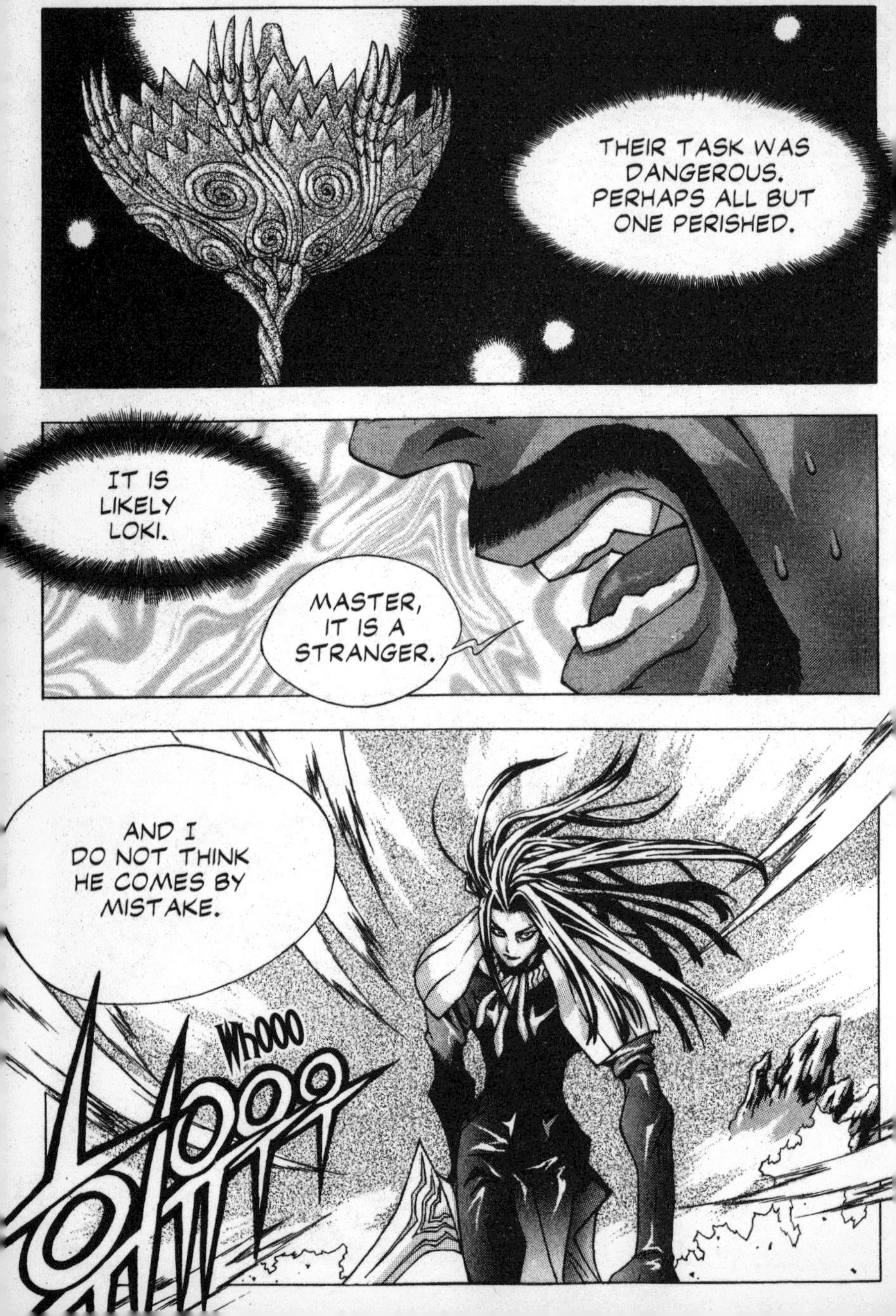
THEIR TASK WAS DANGEROUS. PERHAPS ALL BUT ONE PERISHED.
IT IS LIKELY LOKI.
MASTER, IT IS A STRANGER.
AND I DO NOT THINK HE COMES BY MISTAKE.
WhOOO
WOOO

RAGNAROK
라그나로크
IN TO THE ABYSS

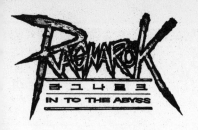

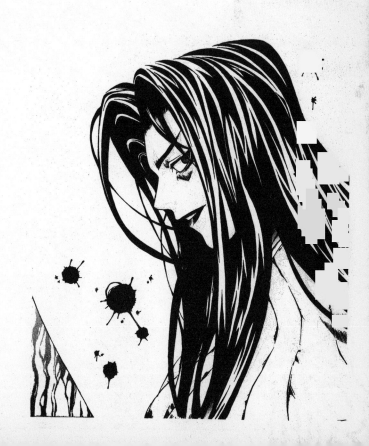

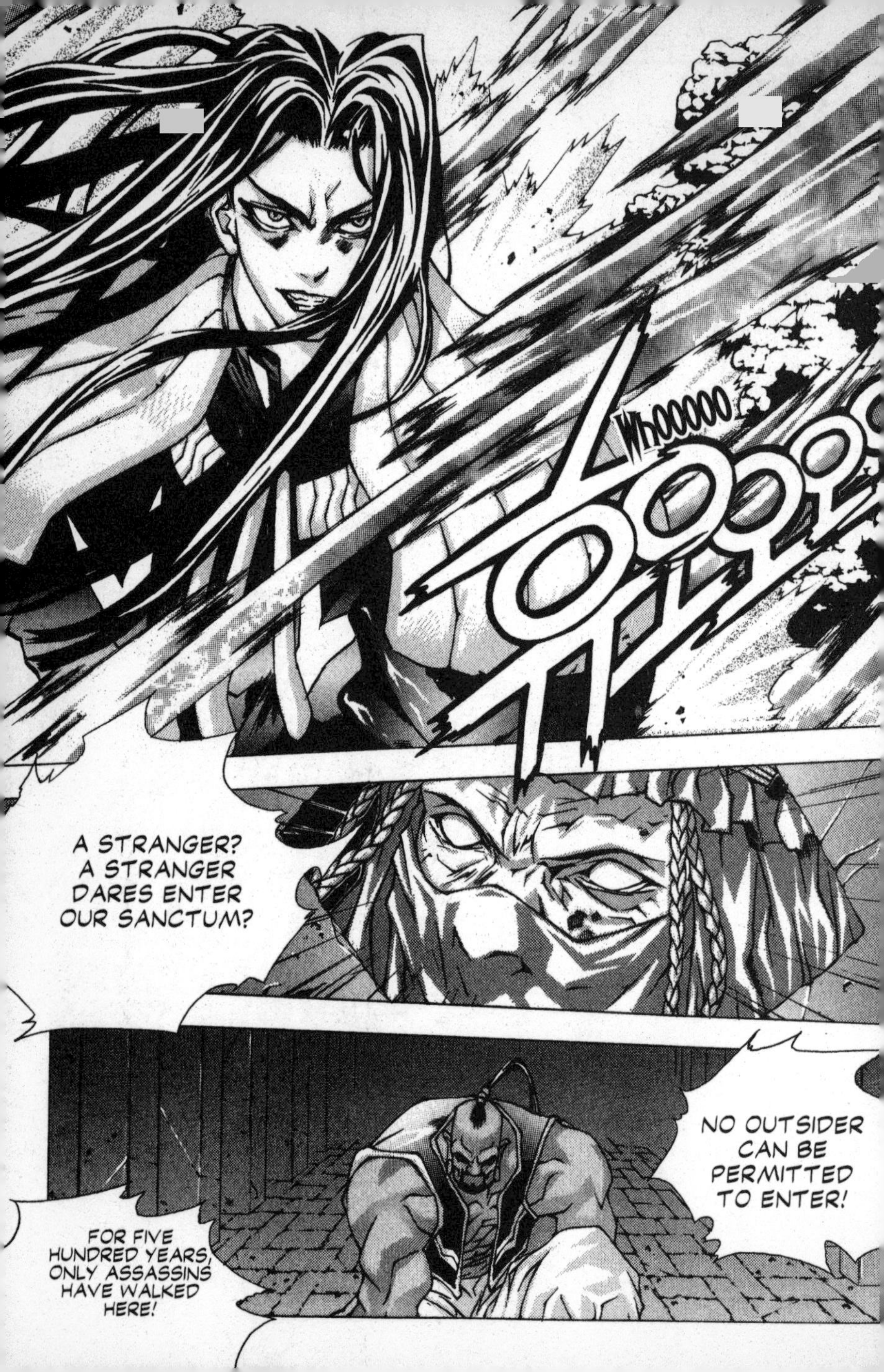
WHOOOOO
OOOO
A STRANGER? A STRANGER DARES ENTER OUR SANCTUM?
FOR FIVE HUNDRED YEARS, ONLY ASSASSINS HAVE WALKED HERE!
NO OUTSIDER CAN BE PERMITTED TO ENTER!

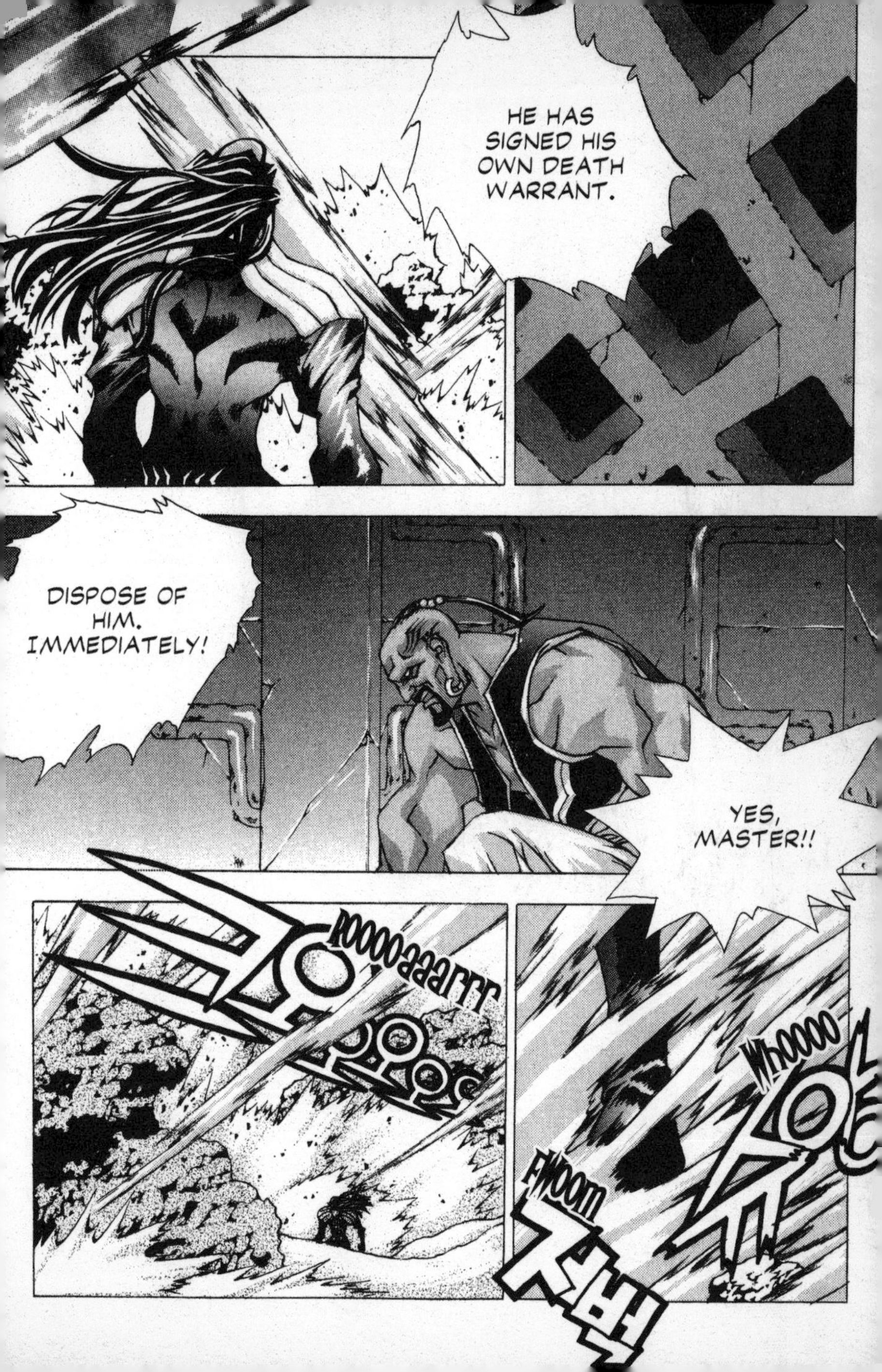
HE HAS SIGNED HIS OWN DEATH WARRANT.
DISPOSE OF HIM. IMMEDIATELY!
YES, MASTER!!
ROOOOaaarrrr
WHOOOO
FWOOM

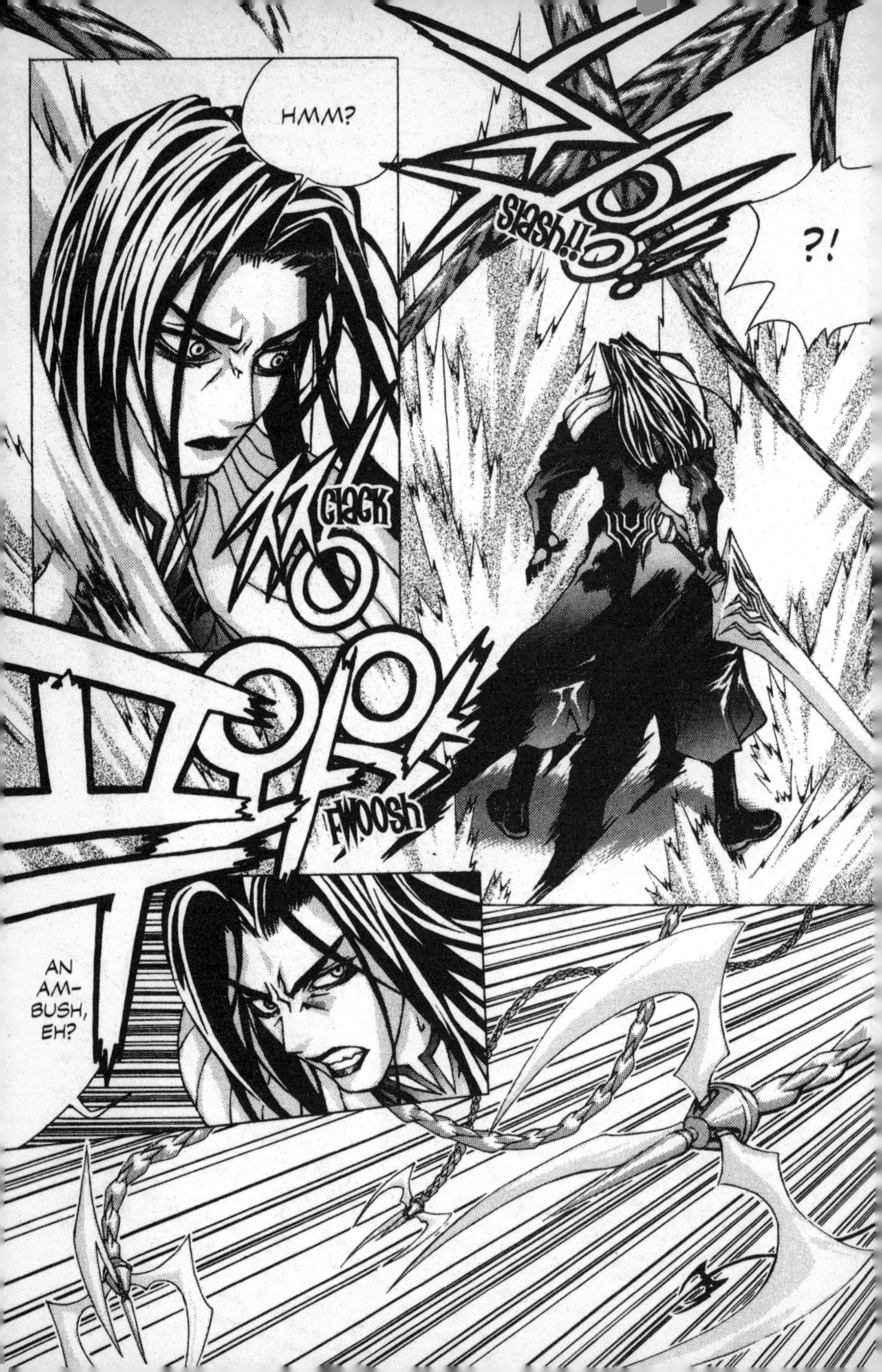
HMM?
CLACK
SLASH!!
?!
FWOOSH
AN AM-BUSH, EH?

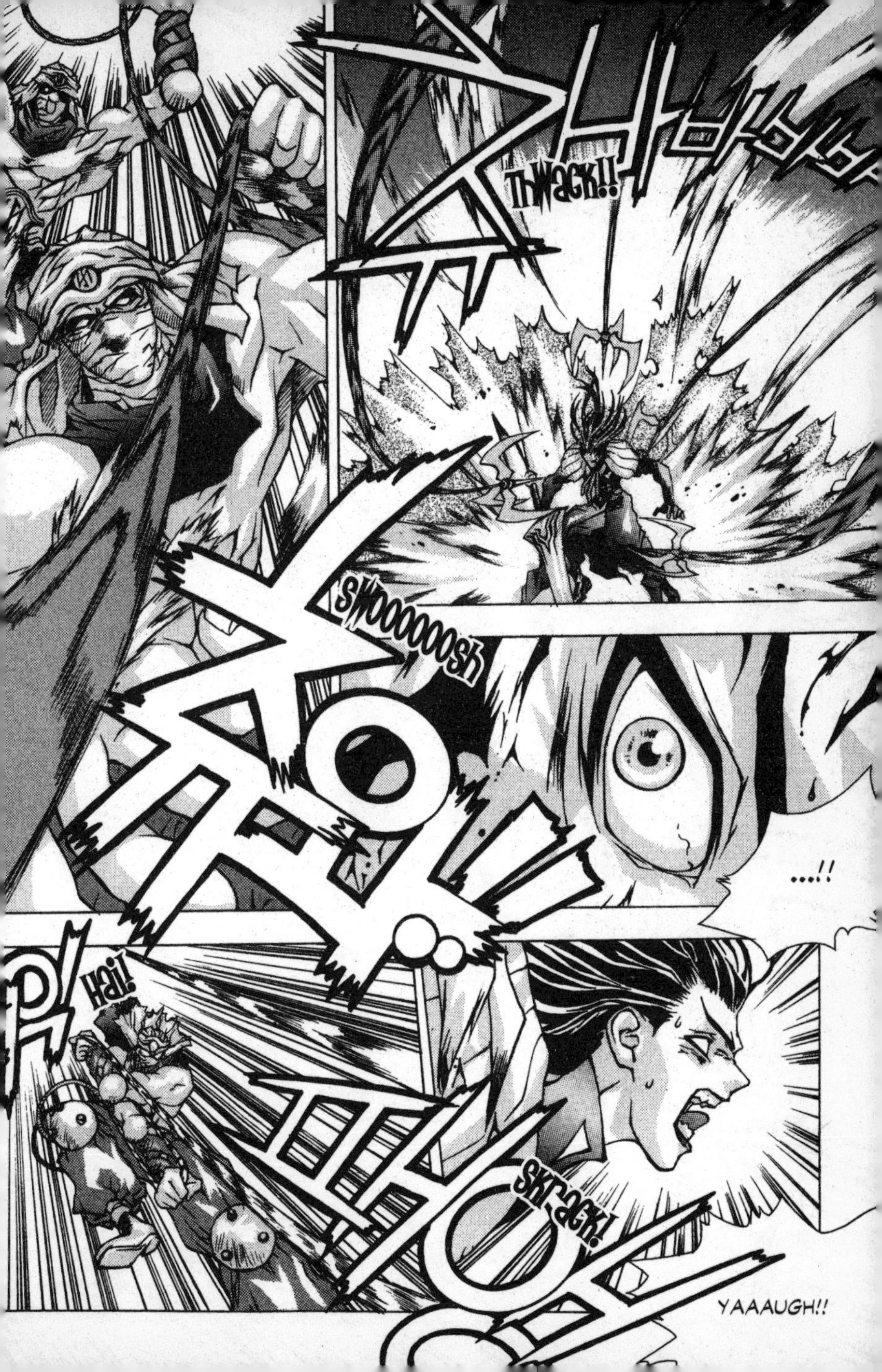
THWACK!!
SWOOOOOOOSH
...!!
HAI!
SKRACK!
YAAAUGH!!

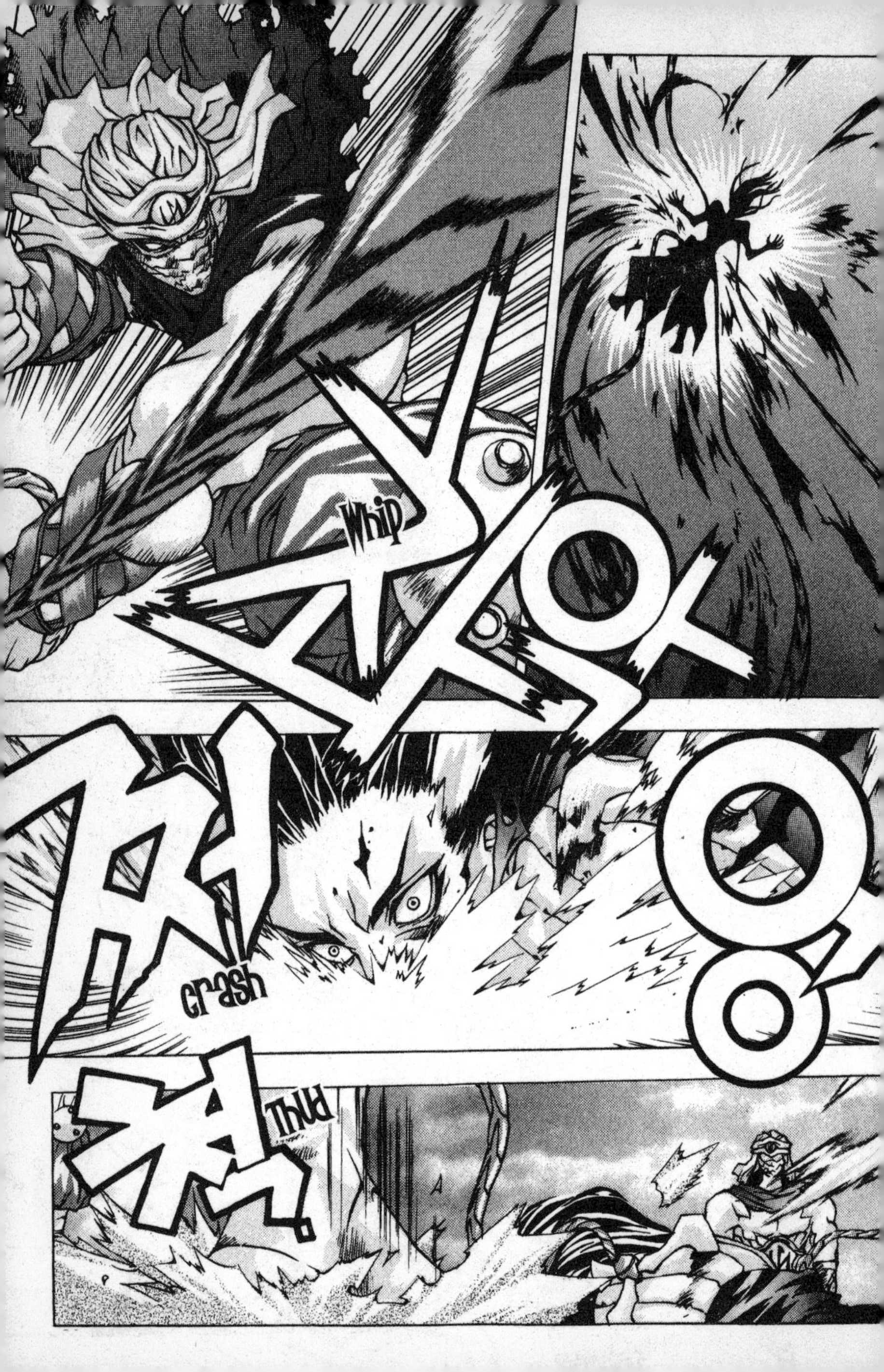
Whip
crash
Thud

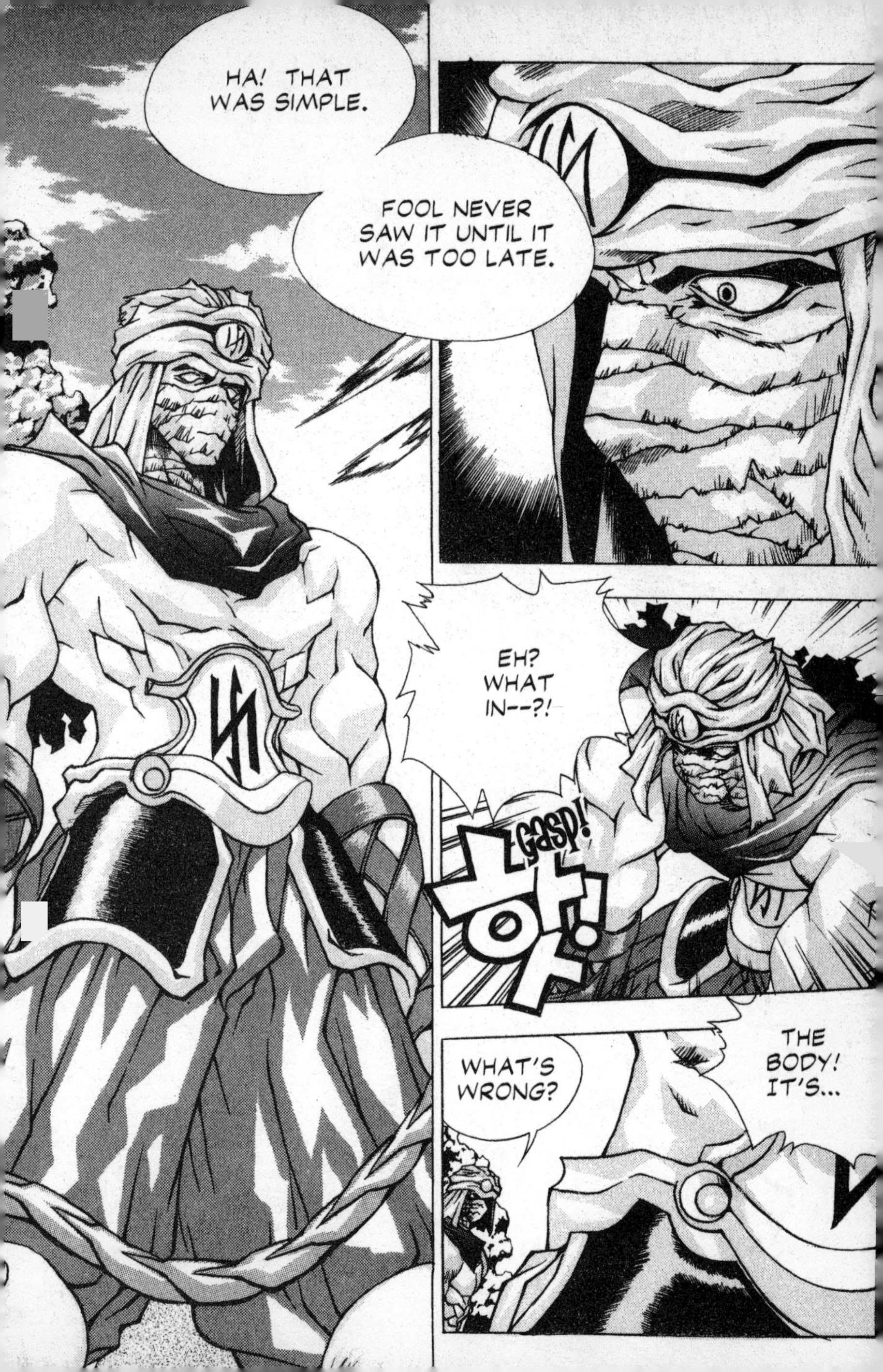
HA! THAT WAS SIMPLE.
FOOL NEVER SAW IT UNTIL IT WAS TOO LATE.
EH? WHAT IN--?!
GASP!
WHAT'S WRONG?
THE BODY! IT'S...

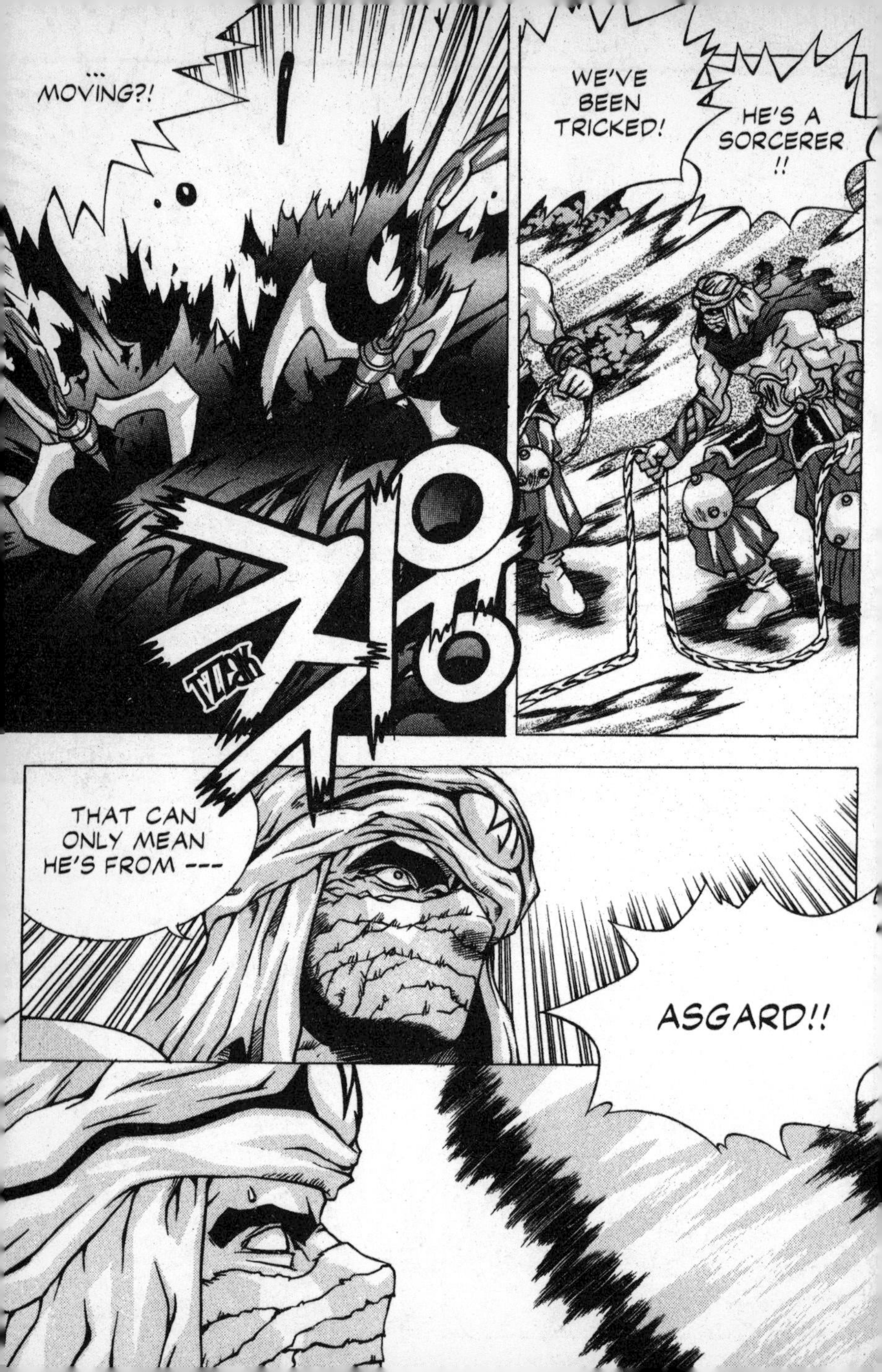

... MOVING?!
WE'VE BEEN TRICKED!
HE'S A SORCERER !!
THAT CAN ONLY MEAN HE'S FROM ---
ASGARD!!

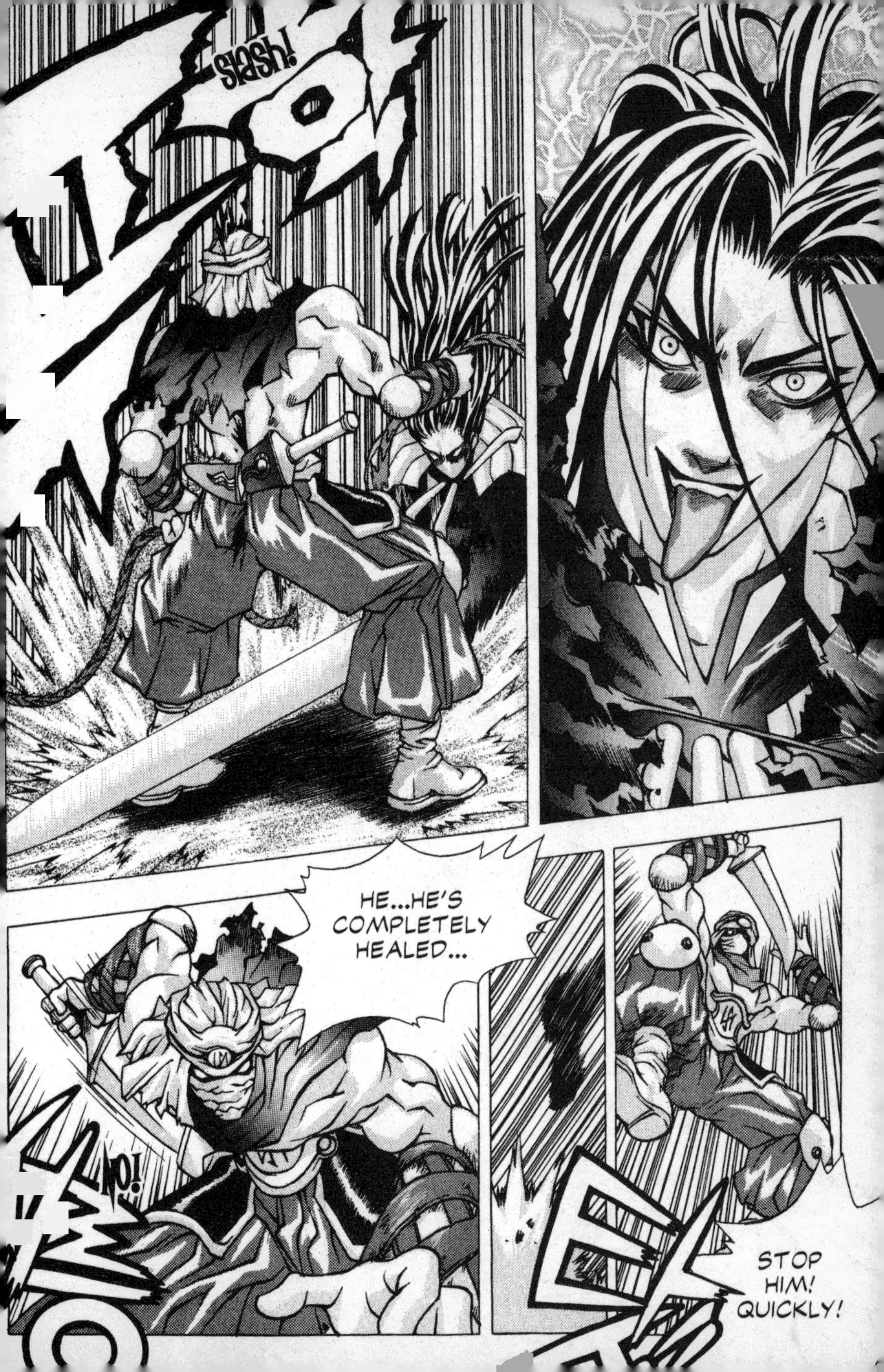

SLASH!
HE...HE'S COMPLETELY HEALED...
NO!
STOP HIM! QUICKLY!

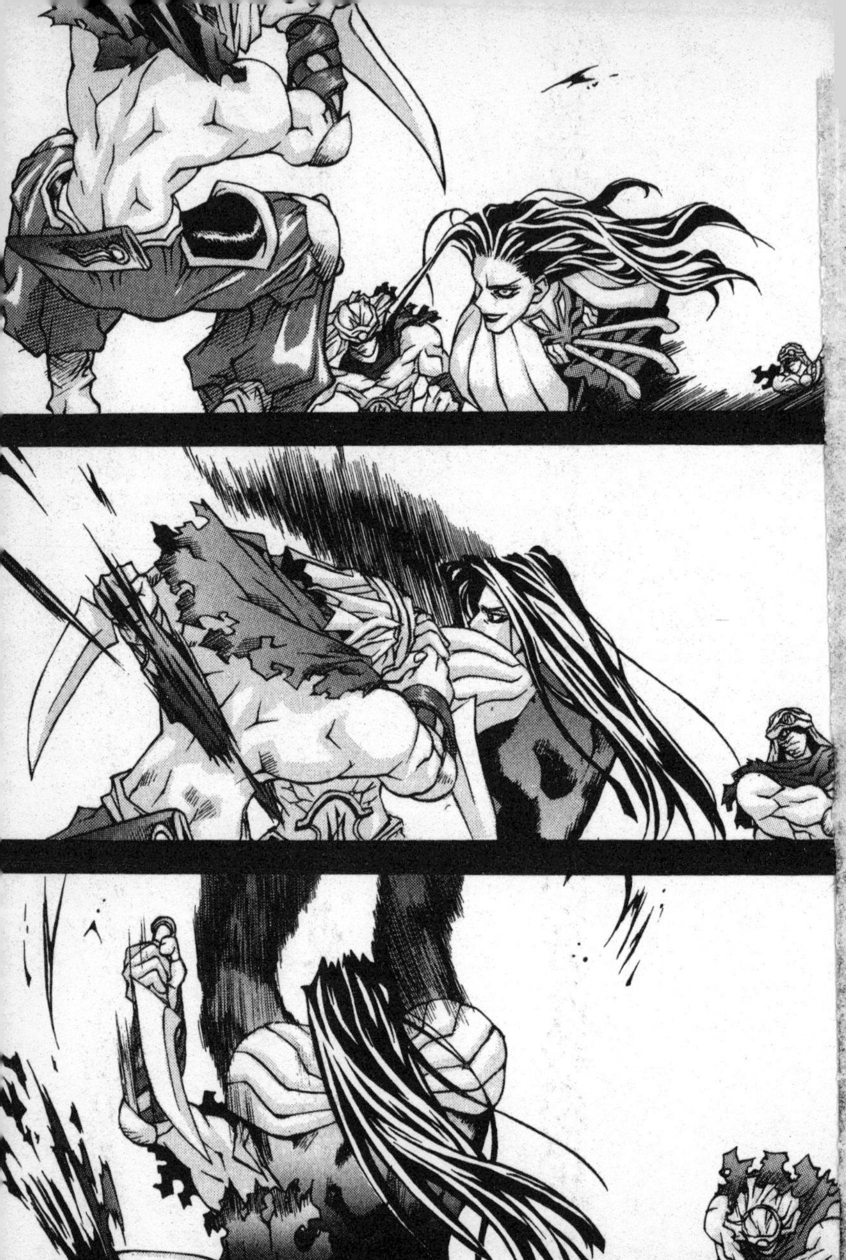

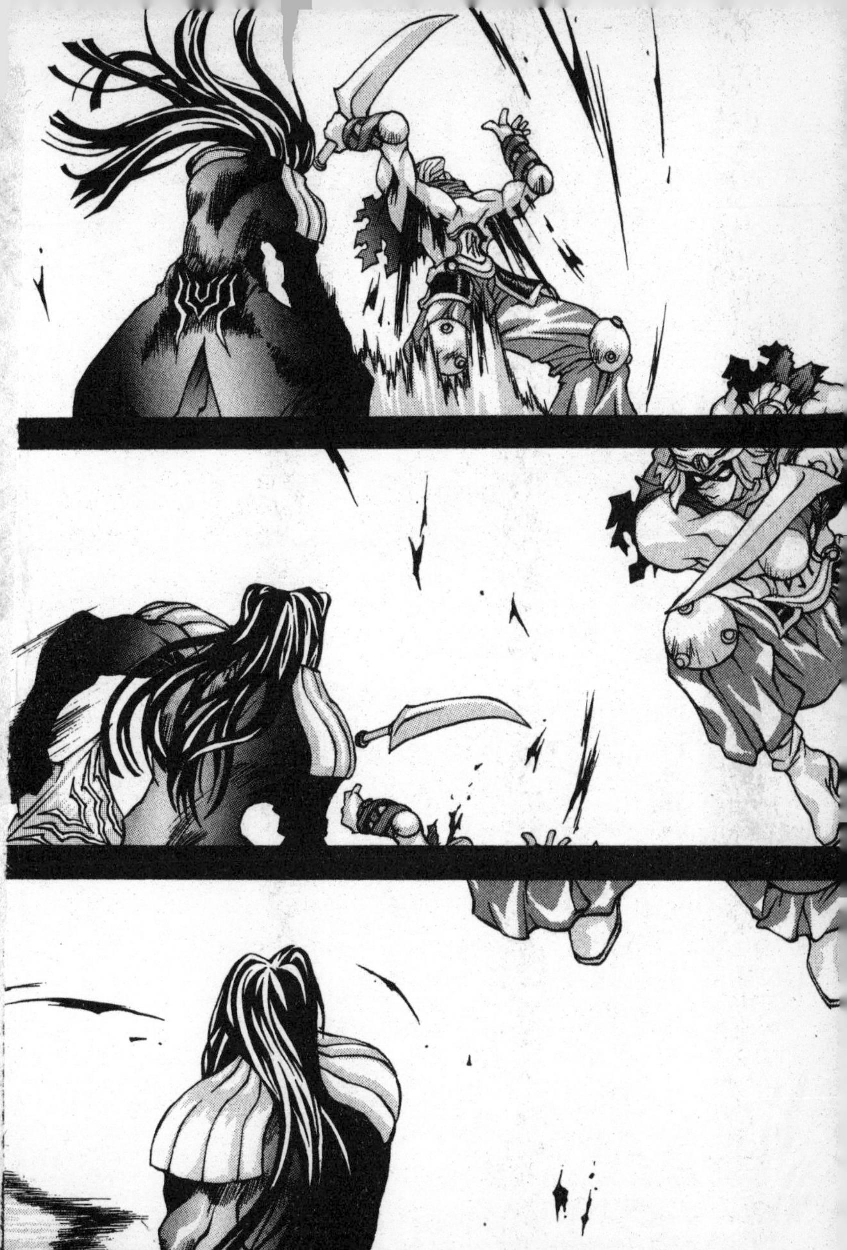

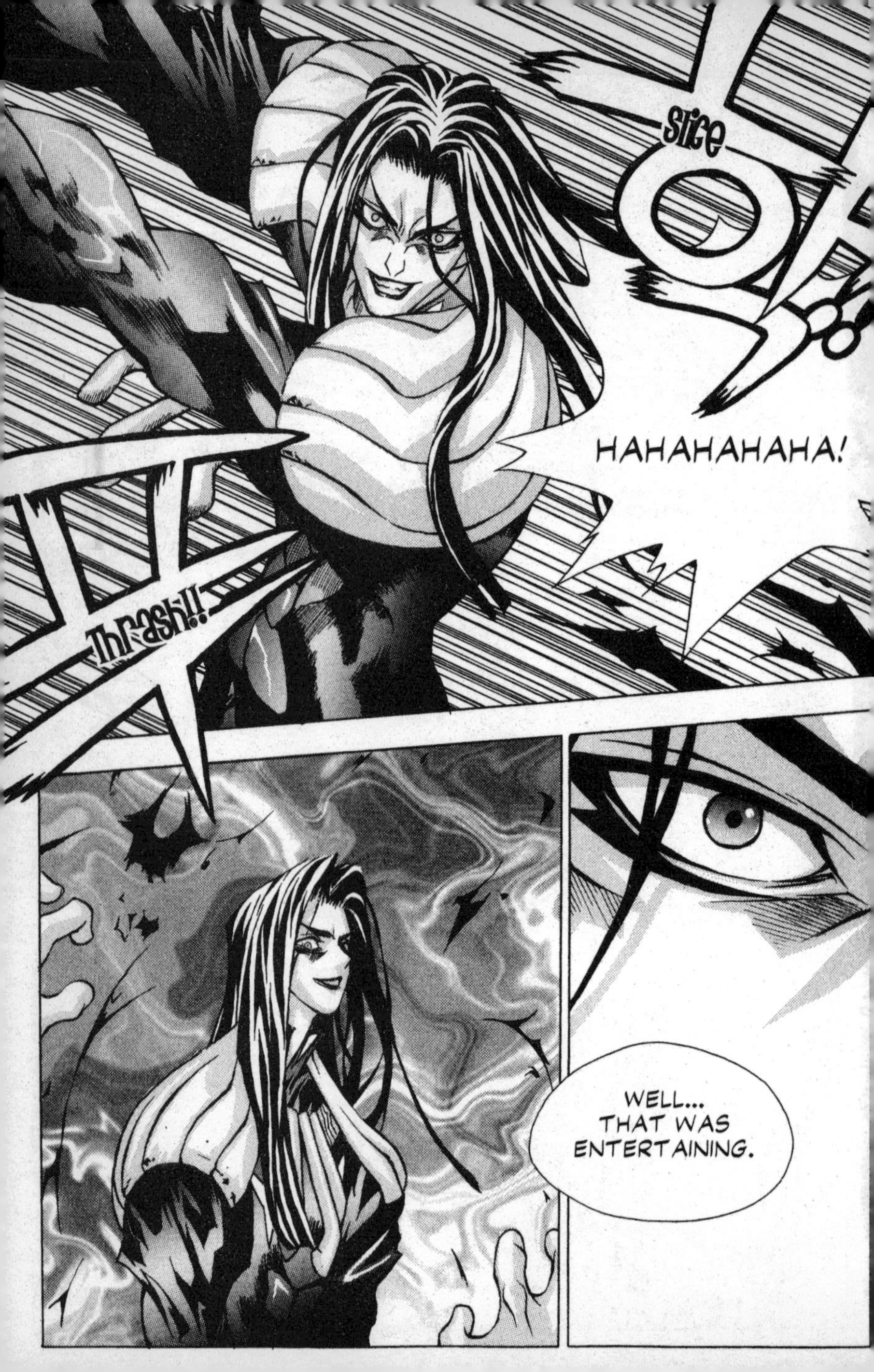
SLICE
THRASH!!
HAHAHAHAHA!
WELL... THAT WAS ENTERTAINING.

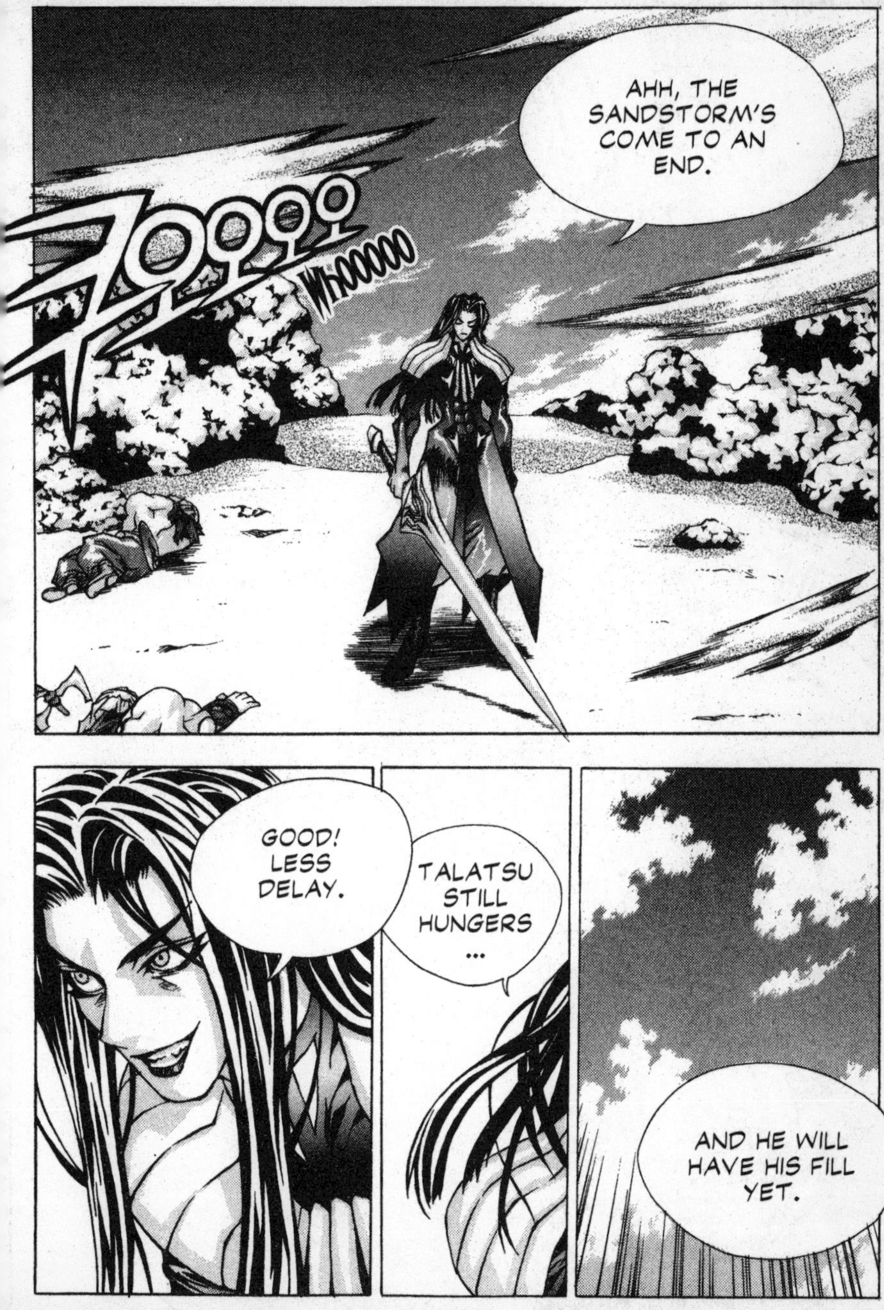
AHH, THE SANDSTORM'S COME TO AN END.
ZOOOOO
WHOOOOO
GOOD! LESS DELAY.
TALATSU STILL HUNGERS ...
AND HE WILL HAVE HIS FILL YET.

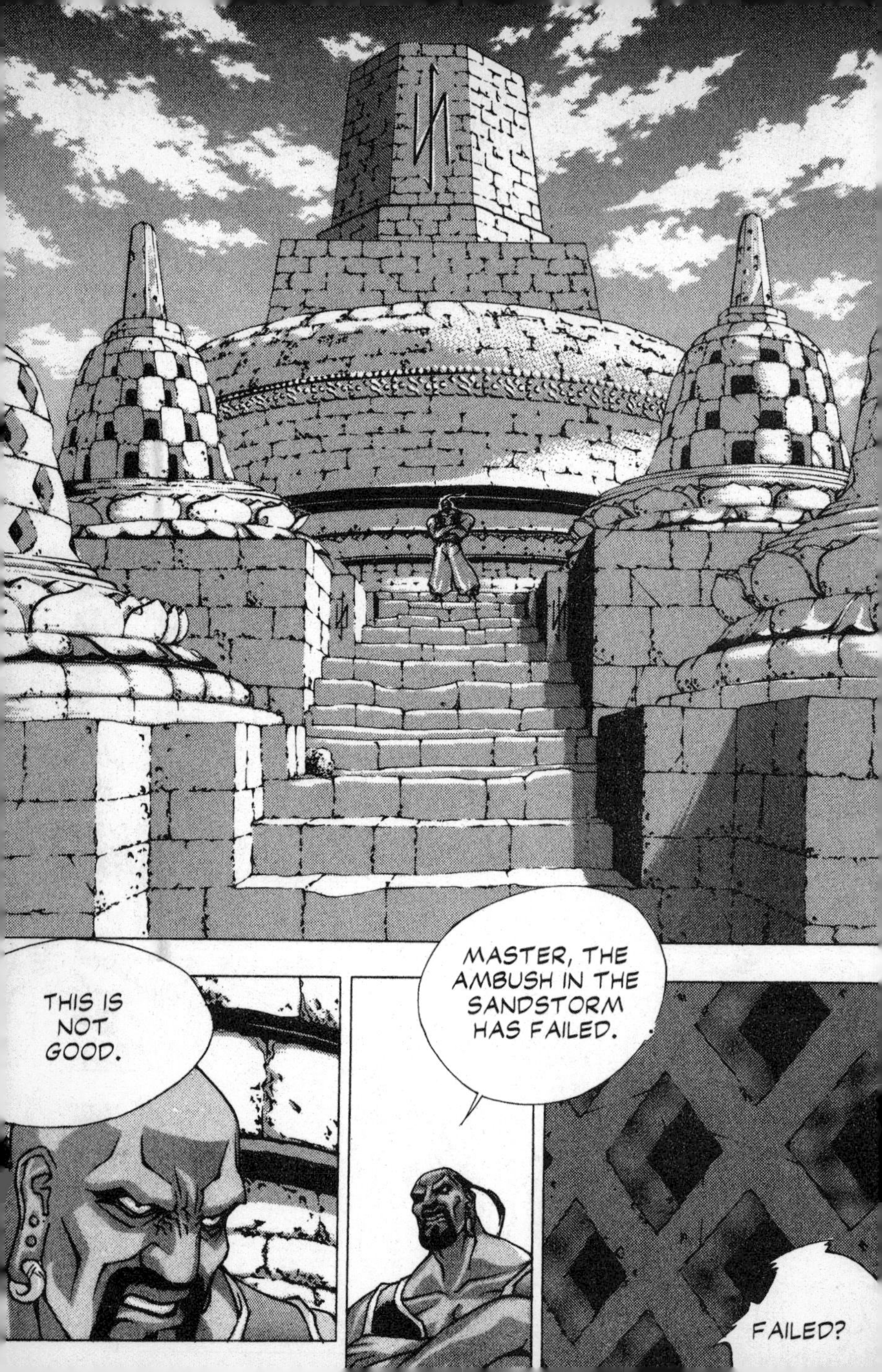
THIS IS NOT GOOD.
MASTER, THE AMBUSH IN THE SANDSTORM HAS FAILED.
FAILED?

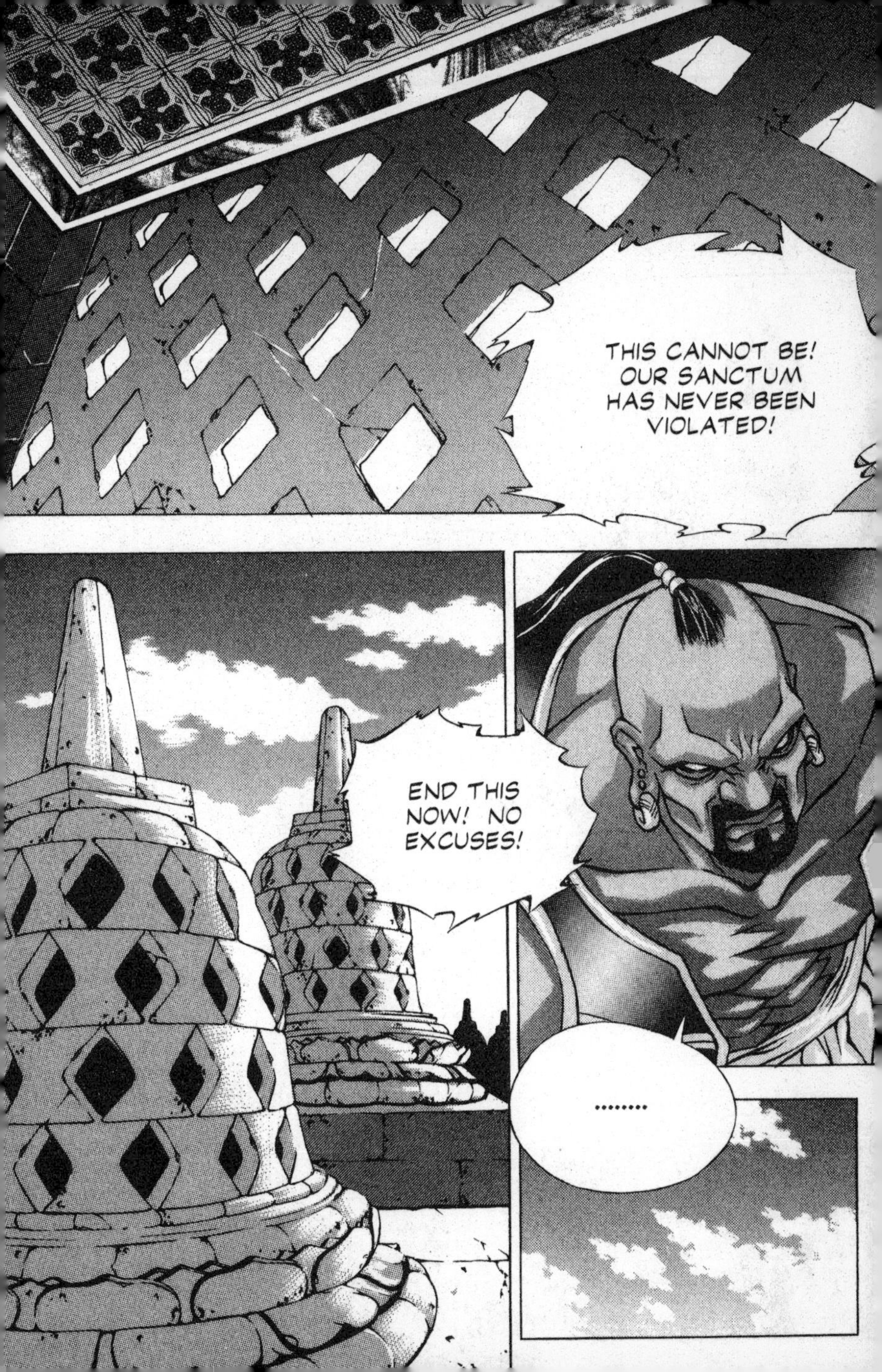
THIS CANNOT BE! OUR SANCTUM HAS NEVER BEEN VIOLATED!
END THIS NOW! NO EXCUSES!
....

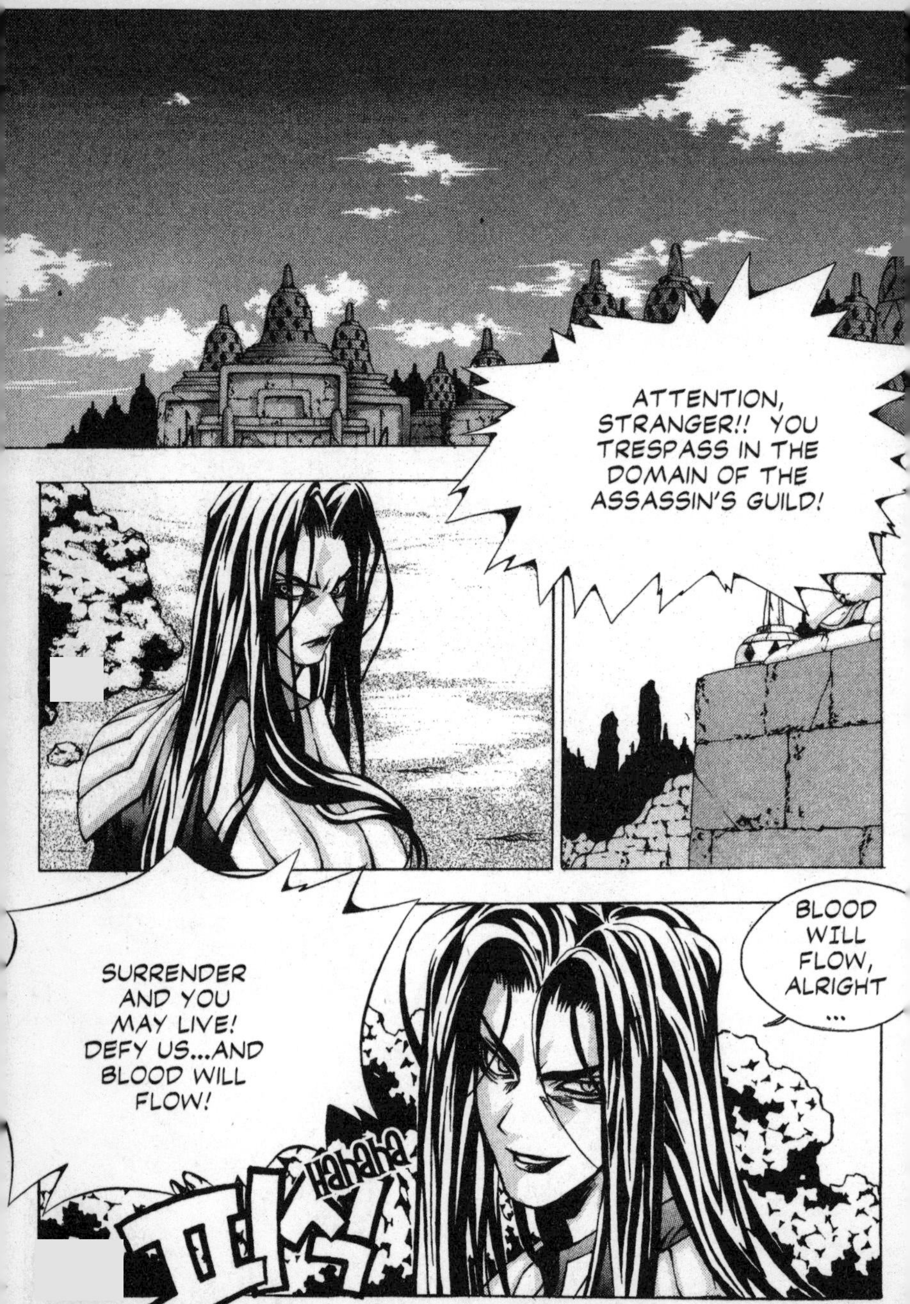
ATTENTION, STRANGER!! YOU TRESPASS IN THE DOMAIN OF THE ASSASSIN'S GUILD!
SURRENDER AND YOU MAY LIVE! DEFY US...AND BLOOD WILL FLOW!
BLOOD WILL FLOW, ALRIGHT ...
Hahaha

RAGNAROK
라그나로크
IN TO THE ABYSS

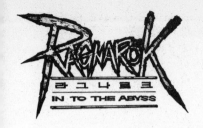

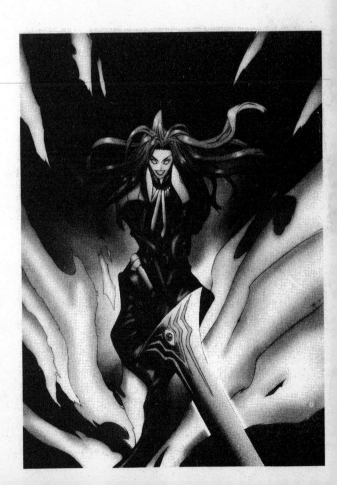

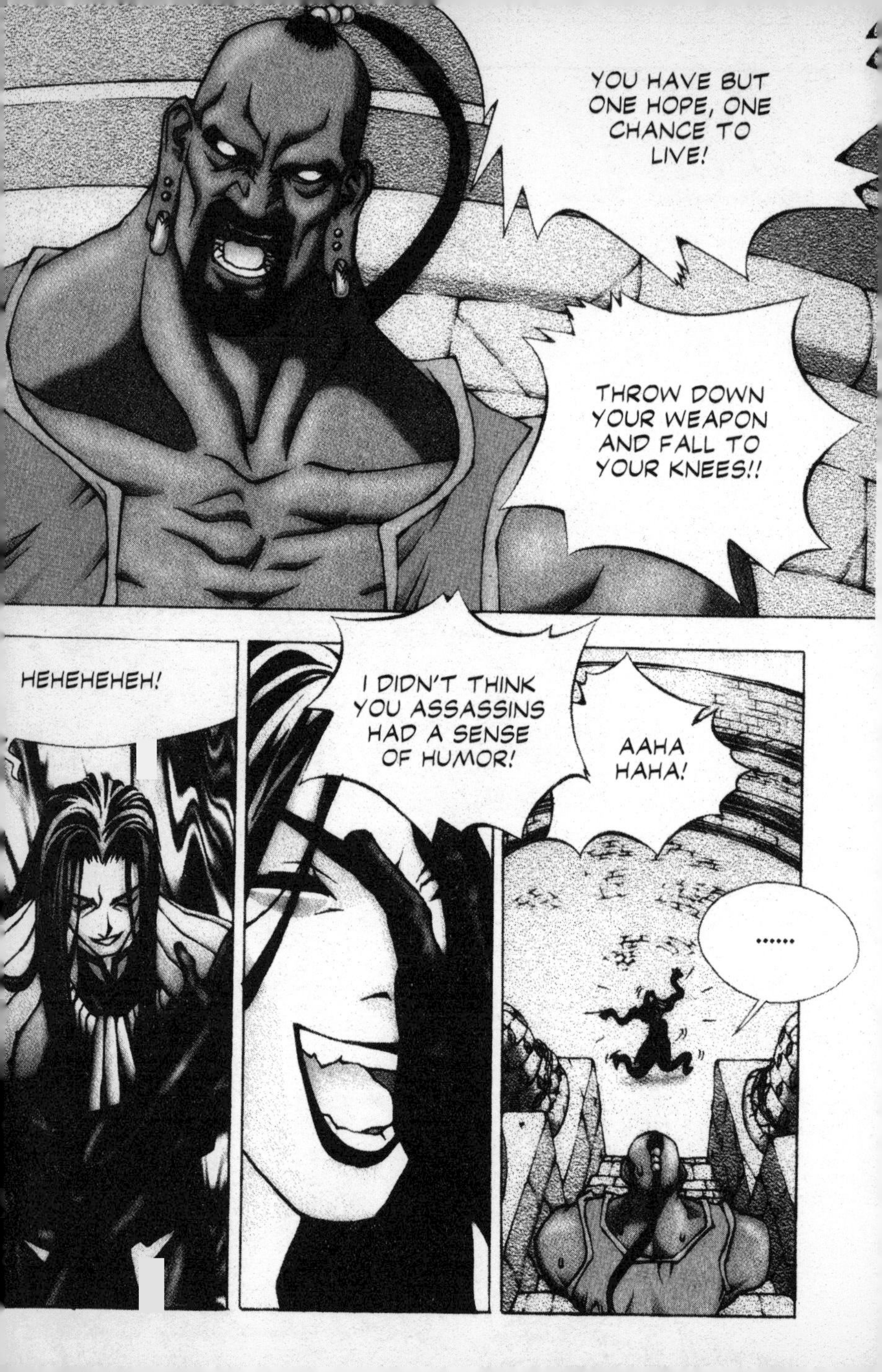
YOU HAVE BUT ONE HOPE, ONE CHANCE TO LIVE!
THROW DOWN YOUR WEAPON AND FALL TO YOUR KNEES!!
HEHEHEHEH!
I DIDN'T THINK YOU ASSASSINS HAD A SENSE OF HUMOR!
AAHA HAHA!
......

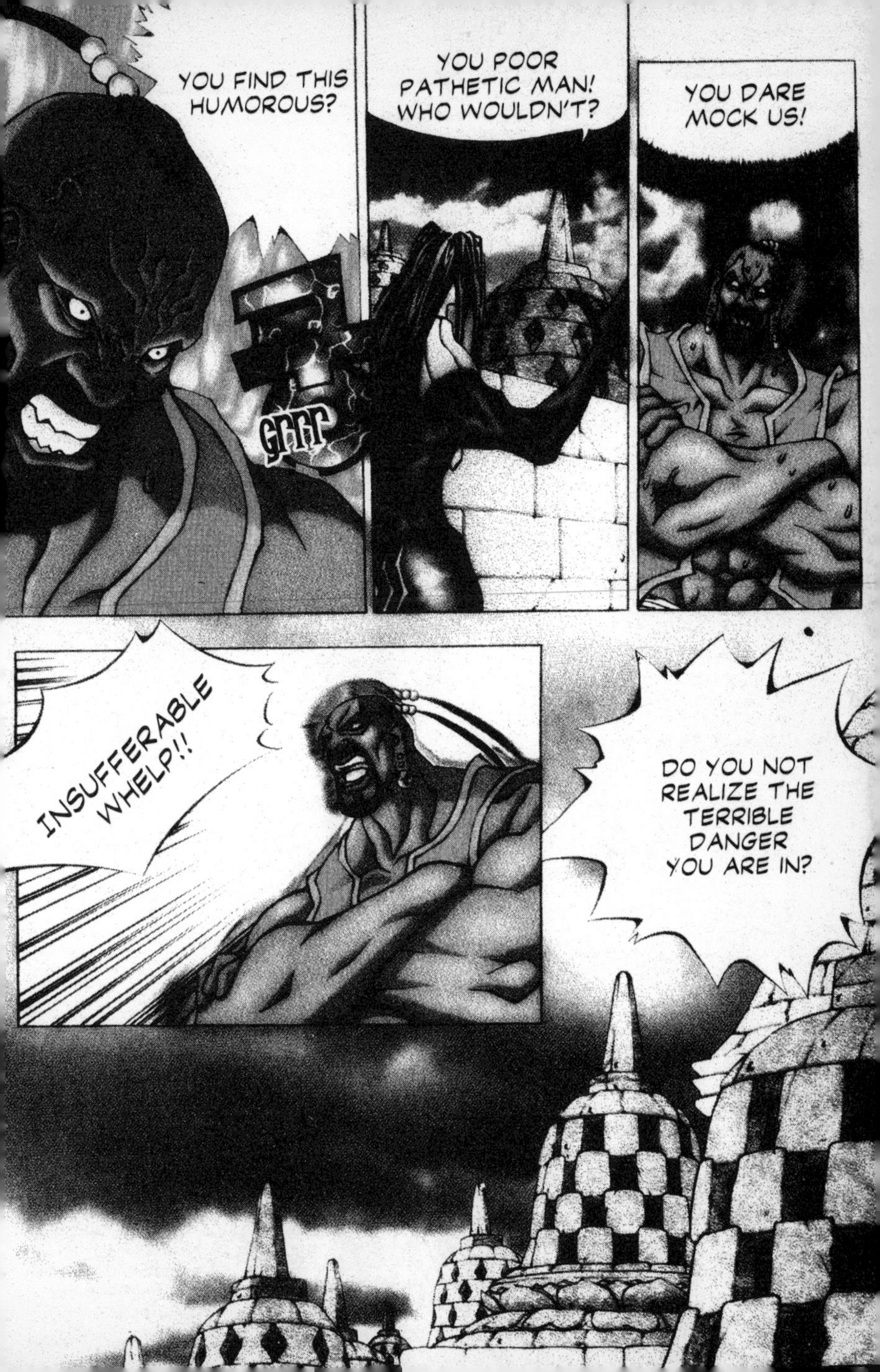
YOU FIND THIS HUMOROUS?
GRRR
YOU POOR PATHETIC MAN! WHO WOULDN'T?
YOU DARE MOCK US!
INSUFFERABLE WHELP!!
DO YOU NOT REALIZE THE TERRIBLE DANGER YOU ARE IN?

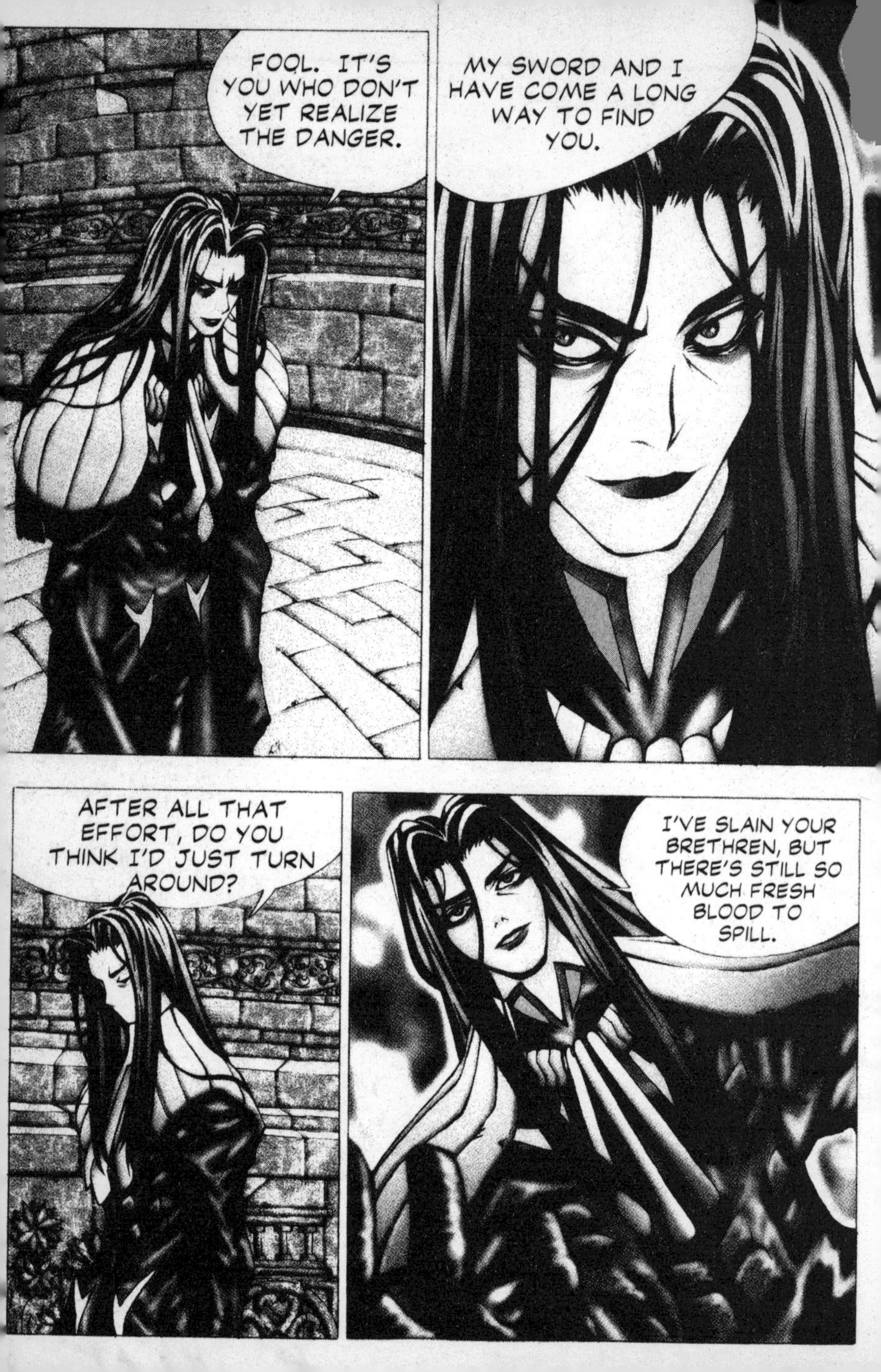
FOOL. IT'S YOU WHO DON'T YET REALIZE THE DANGER.
MY SWORD AND I HAVE COME A LONG WAY TO FIND YOU.
AFTER ALL THAT EFFORT, DO YOU THINK I'D JUST TURN AROUND?
I'VE SLAIN YOUR BRETHREN, BUT THERE'S STILL SO MUCH FRESH BLOOD TO SPILL.

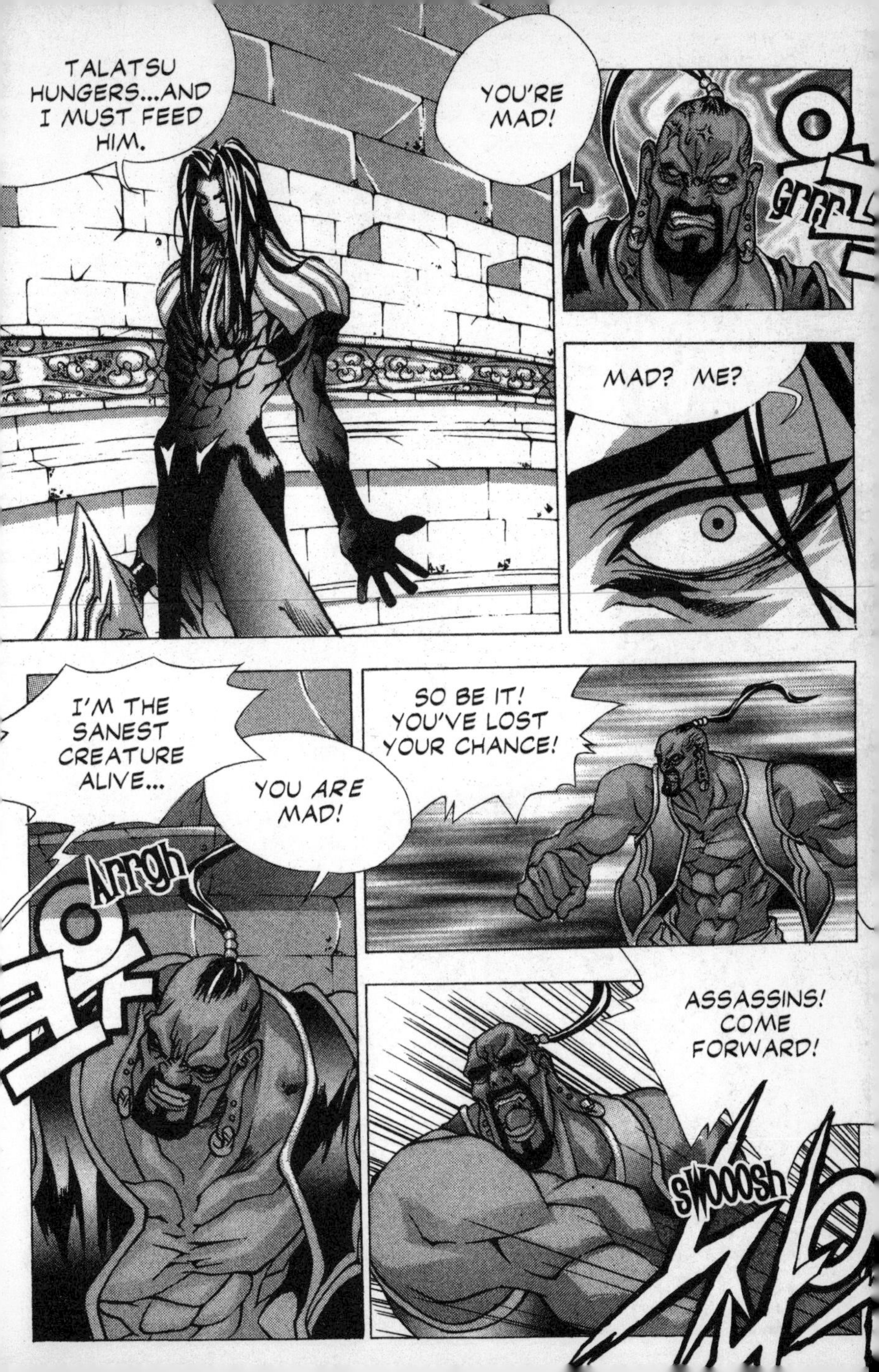
TALATSU HUNGERS...AND I MUST FEED HIM.
YOU'RE MAD!
Grrr
MAD? ME?
I'M THE SANEST CREATURE ALIVE...
YOU ARE MAD!
Arrgh
SO BE IT! YOU'VE LOST YOUR CHANCE!
ASSASSINS! COME FORWARD!
SWOOOSh

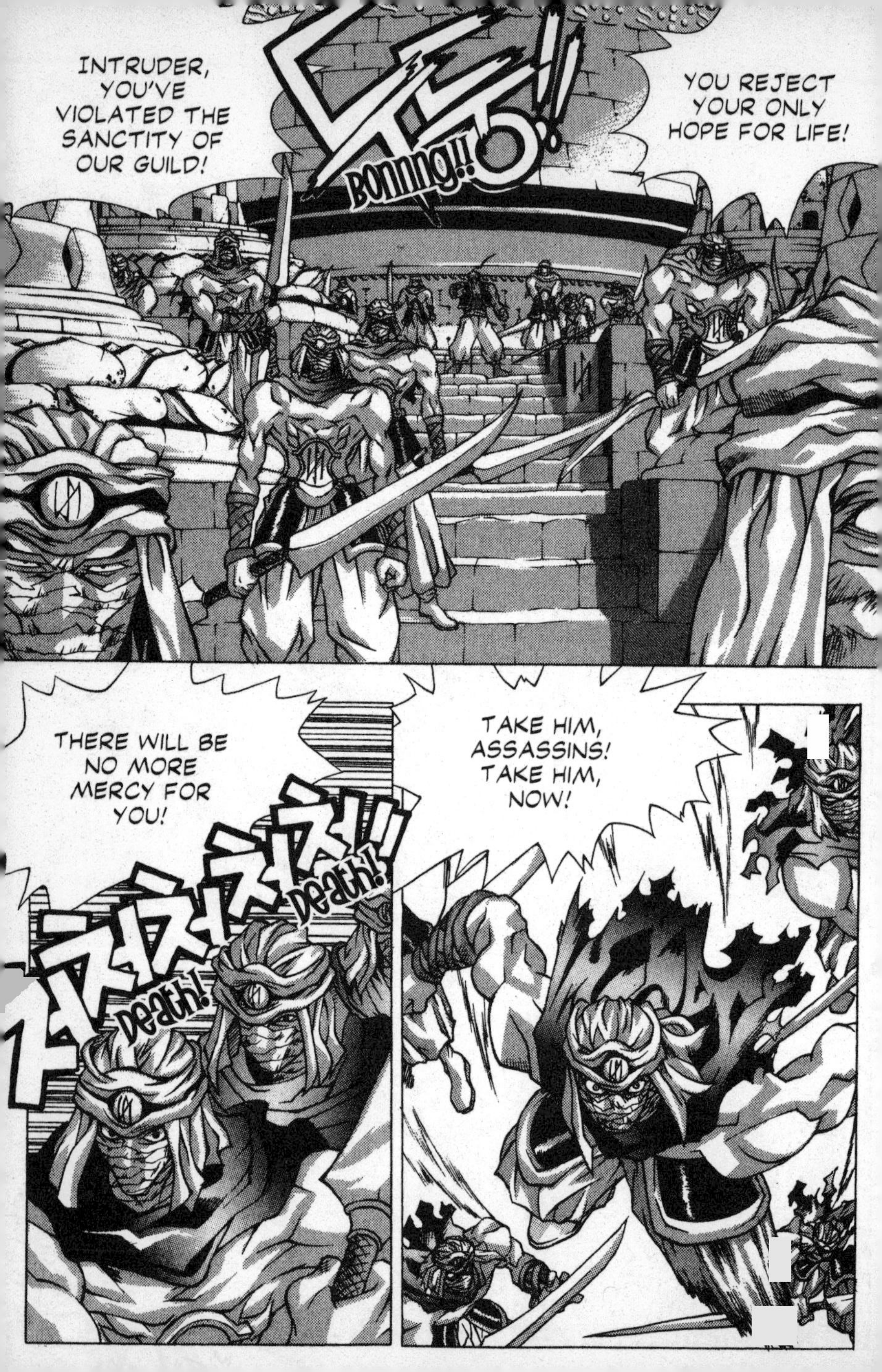

INTRUDER, YOU'VE VIOLATED THE SANCTITY OF OUR GUILD!
BONNNG!!
YOU REJECT YOUR ONLY HOPE FOR LIFE!
THERE WILL BE NO MORE MERCY FOR YOU!
Death!
Death!
TAKE HIM, ASSASSINS! TAKE HIM, NOW!

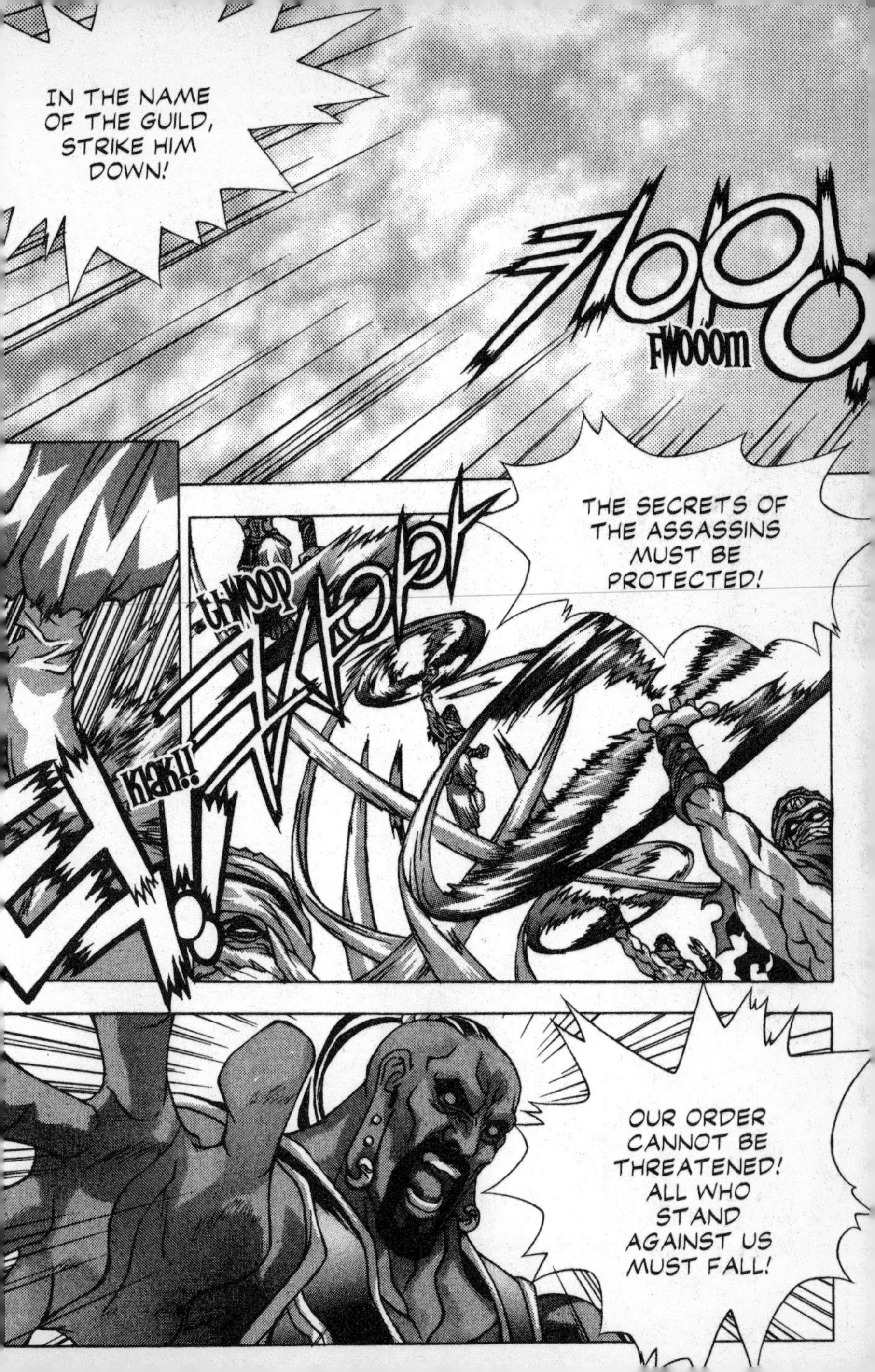
IN THE NAME OF THE GUILD, STRIKE HIM DOWN!
FWOOOM
THWOOP
KLAK!!
THE SECRETS OF THE ASSASSINS MUST BE PROTECTED!
OUR ORDER CANNOT BE THREATENED! ALL WHO STAND AGAINST US MUST FALL!

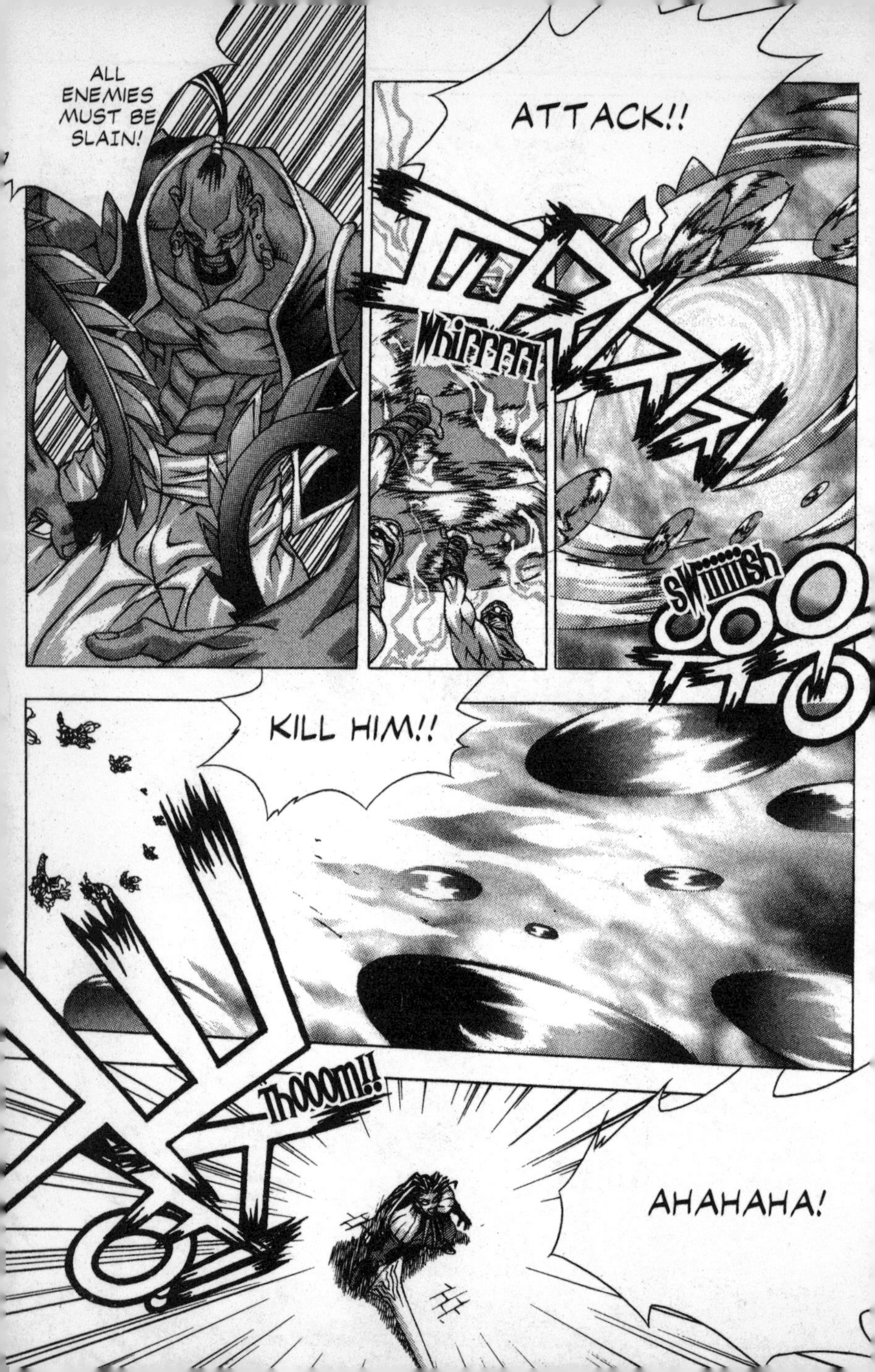
ALL ENEMIES MUST BE SLAIN!
ATTACK!!
Whirrrrr
Swiiiiiish
KILL HIM!!
Thooom!!
AHAHAHA!

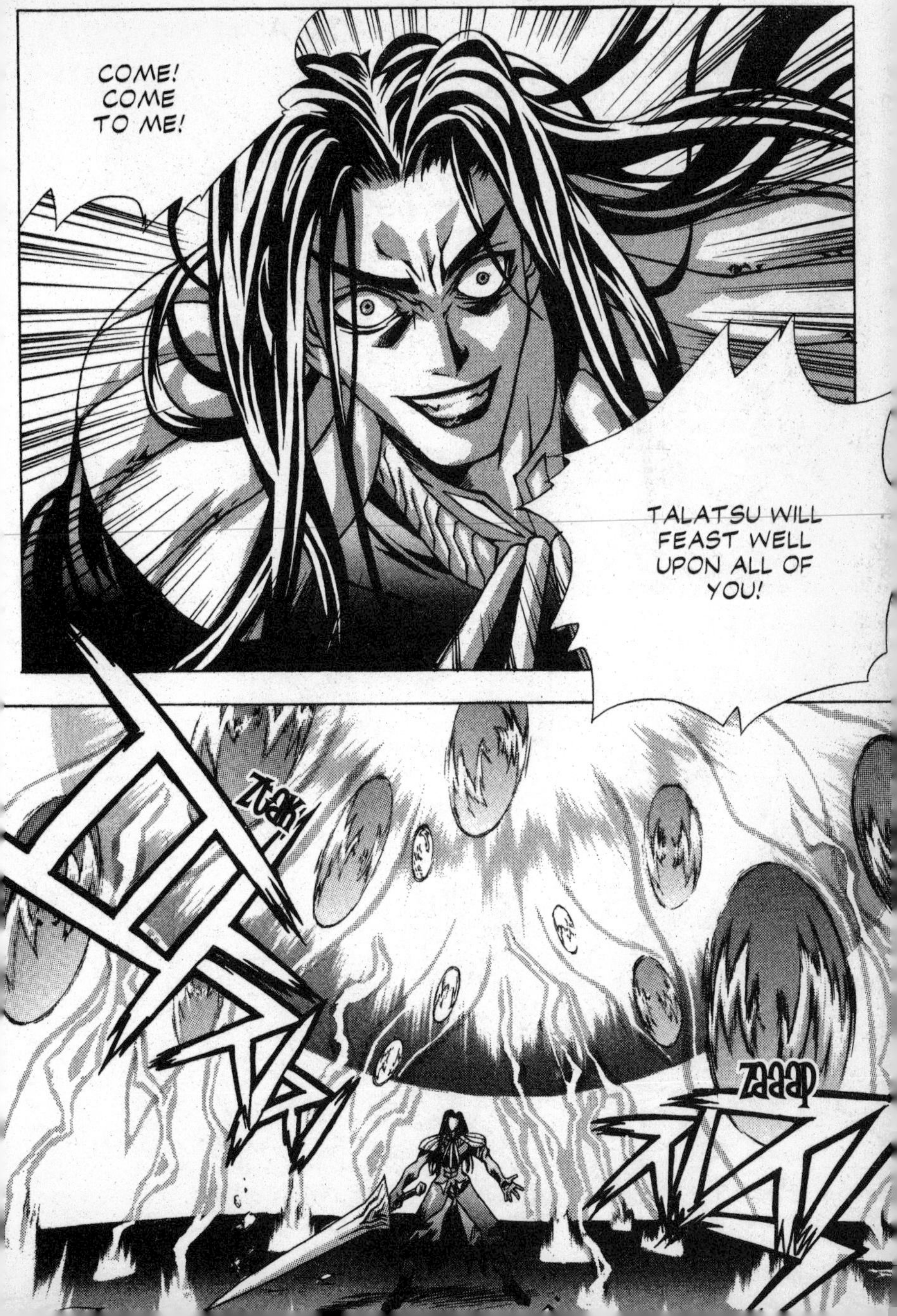
COME! COME TO ME!
TALATSU WILL FEAST WELL UPON ALL OF YOU!
ZGAK!
ZAAAP

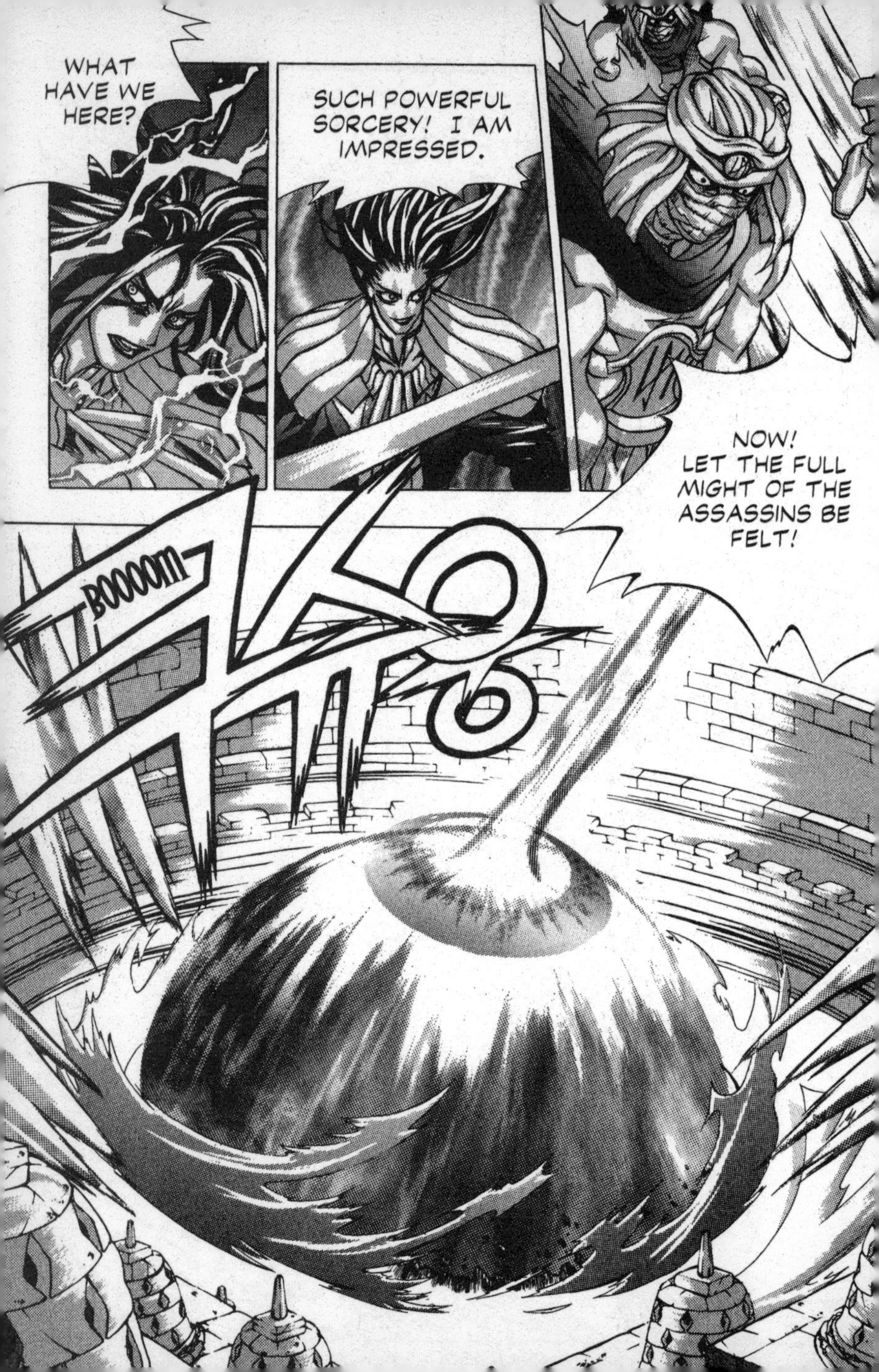
WHAT HAVE WE HERE?
SUCH POWERFUL SORCERY! I AM IMPRESSED.
NOW! LET THE FULL MIGHT OF THE ASSASSINS BE FELT!
BOOOOM

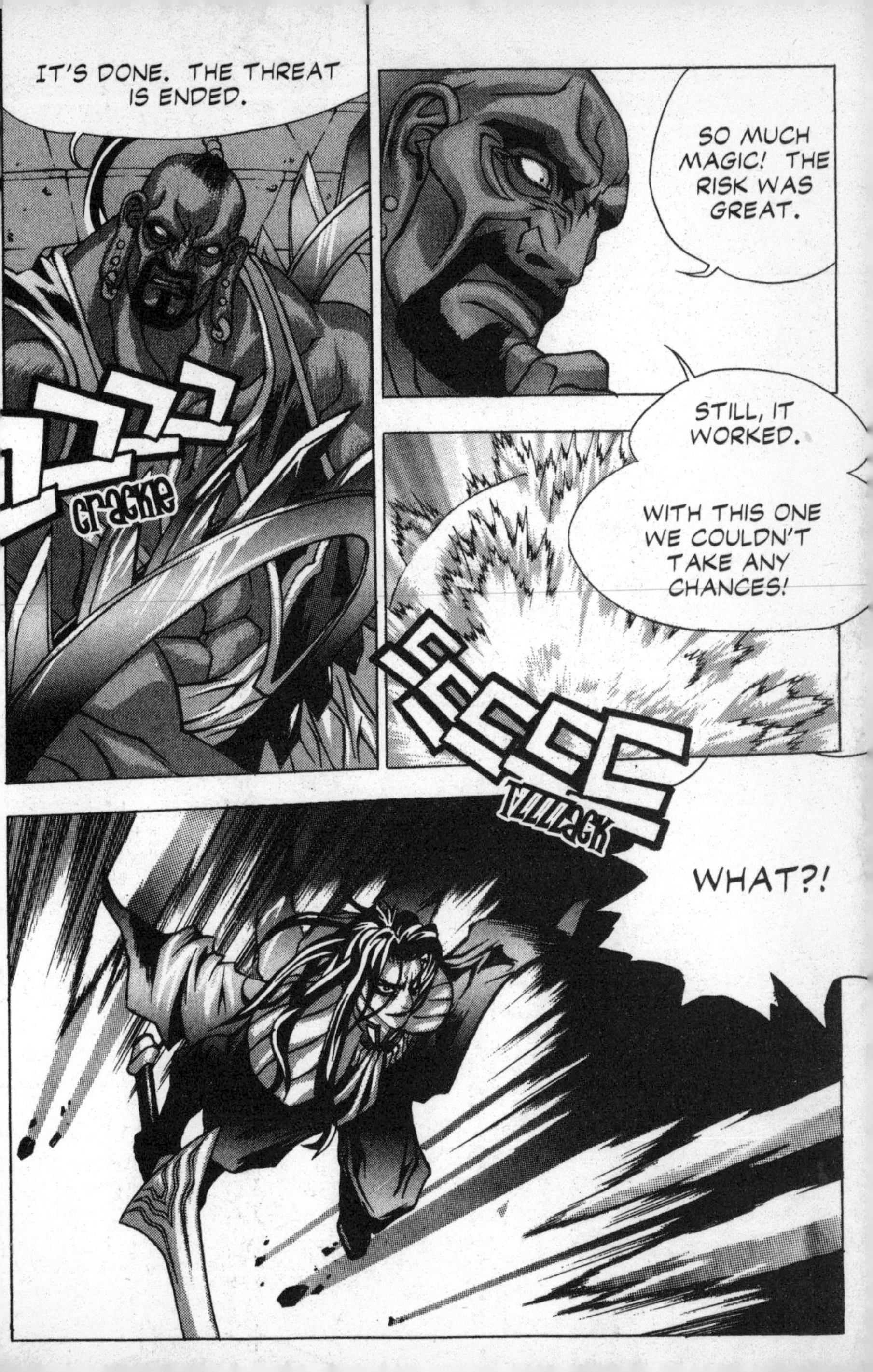
IT'S DONE. THE THREAT IS ENDED.
crackle
SO MUCH MAGIC! THE RISK WAS GREAT.
STILL, IT WORKED.
WITH THIS ONE WE COULDN'T TAKE ANY CHANCES!
tzzzack
WHAT?!

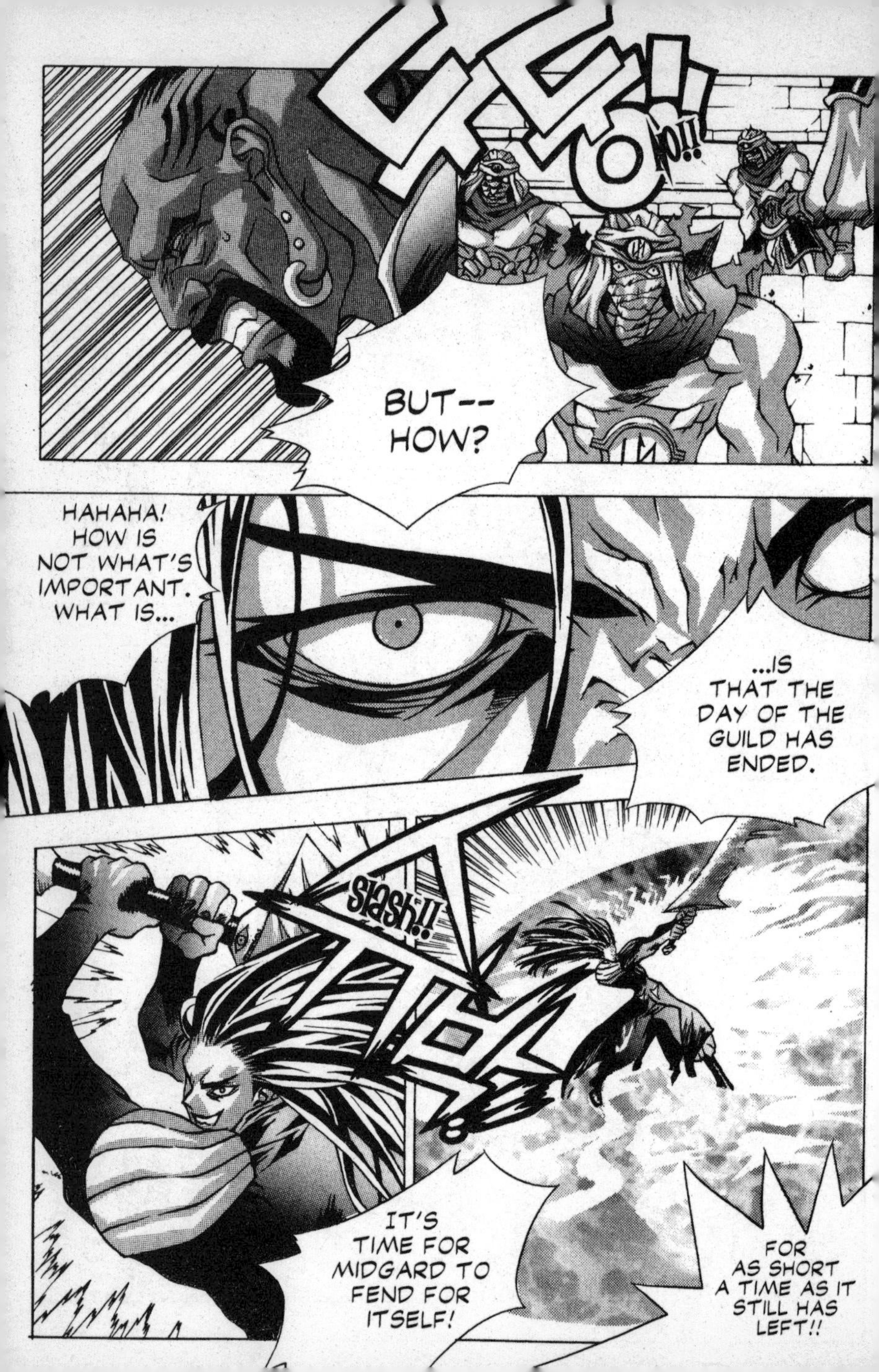

BUT-- HOW?
HAHAHA! HOW IS NOT WHAT'S IMPORTANT. WHAT IS...
...IS THAT THE DAY OF THE GUILD HAS ENDED.
slash!!
IT'S TIME FOR MIDGARD TO FEND FOR ITSELF!
FOR AS SHORT A TIME AS IT STILL HAS LEFT!!

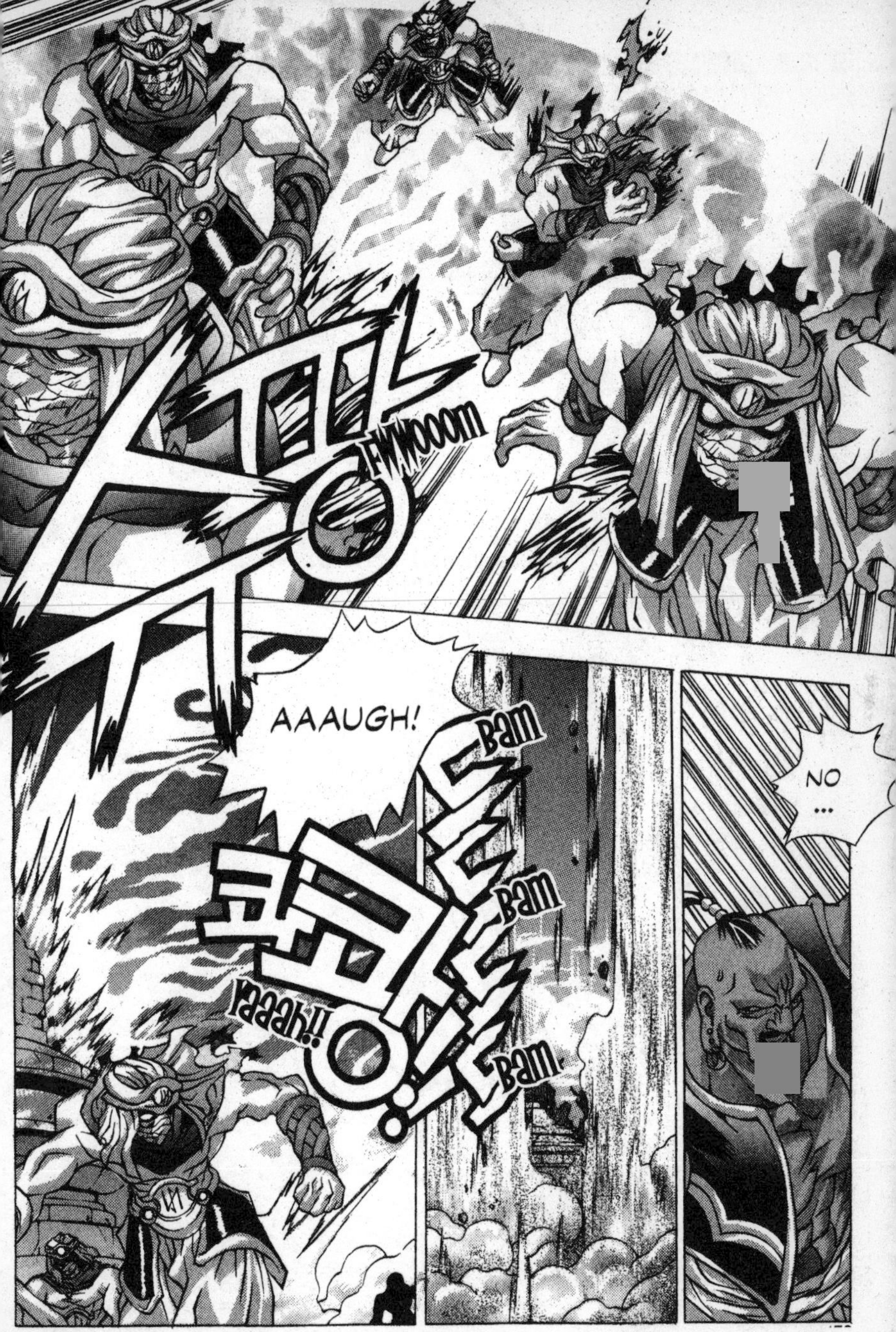
FWWOOOM
AAAUGH!
YAAAH!!
Bam
Bam
Bam
NO ...

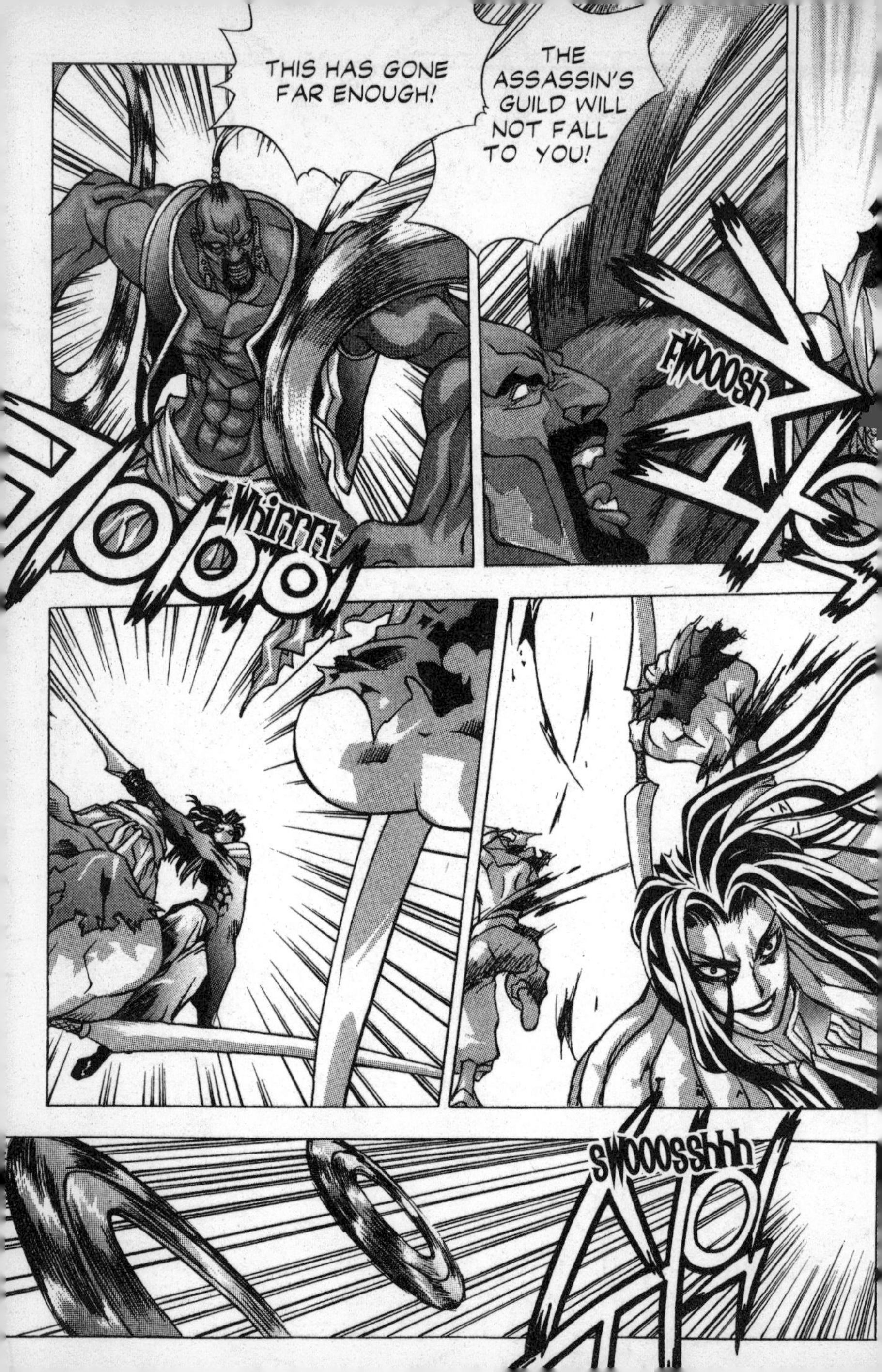
THIS HAS GONE FAR ENOUGH!
THE ASSASSIN'S GUILD WILL NOT FALL TO YOU!
Whirrr
FWOOOSh
SWOOOSShhh

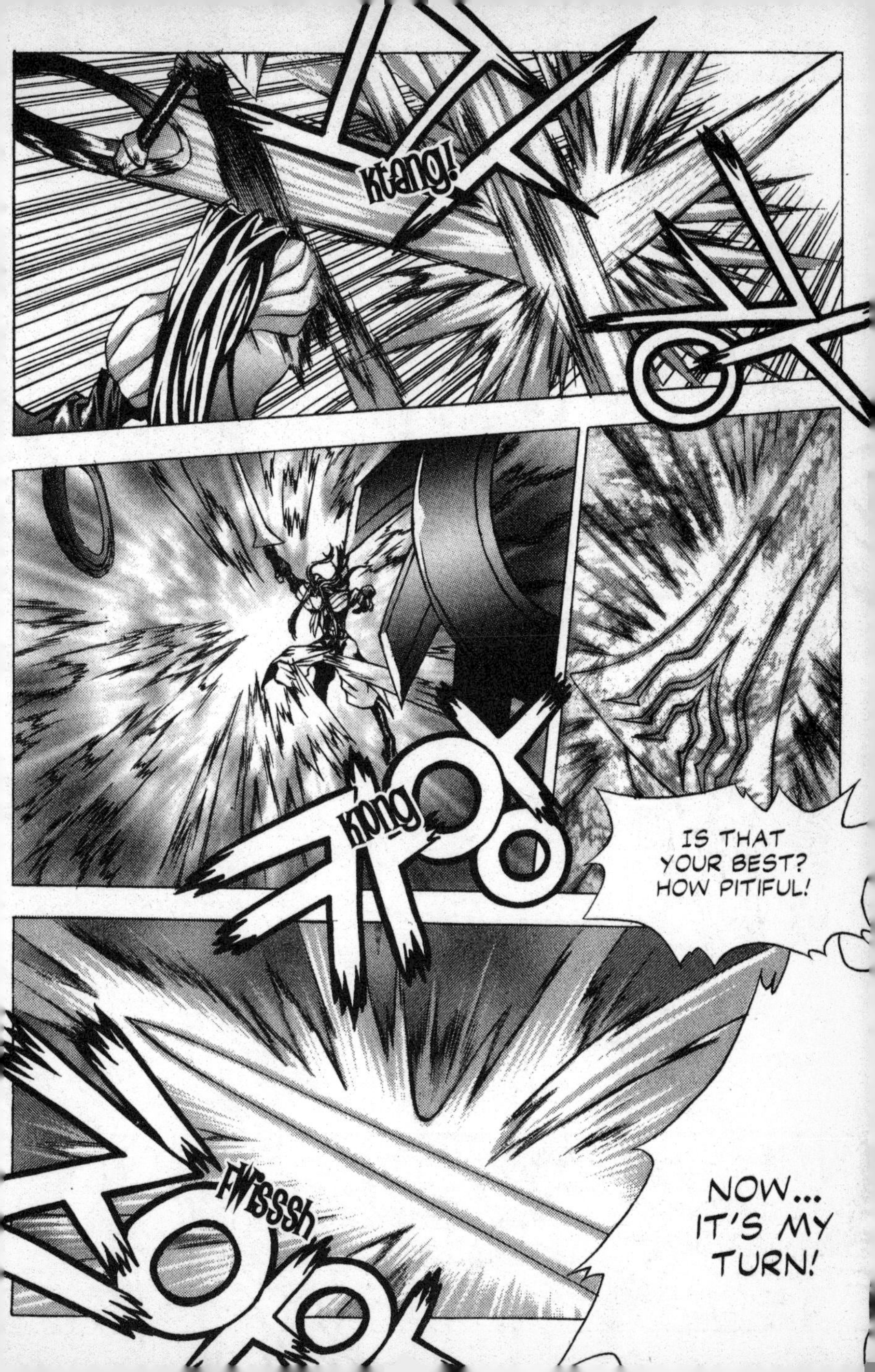
Ktang!
Kpng
IS THAT YOUR BEST? HOW PITIFUL!
FWisssh
NOW... IT'S MY TURN!

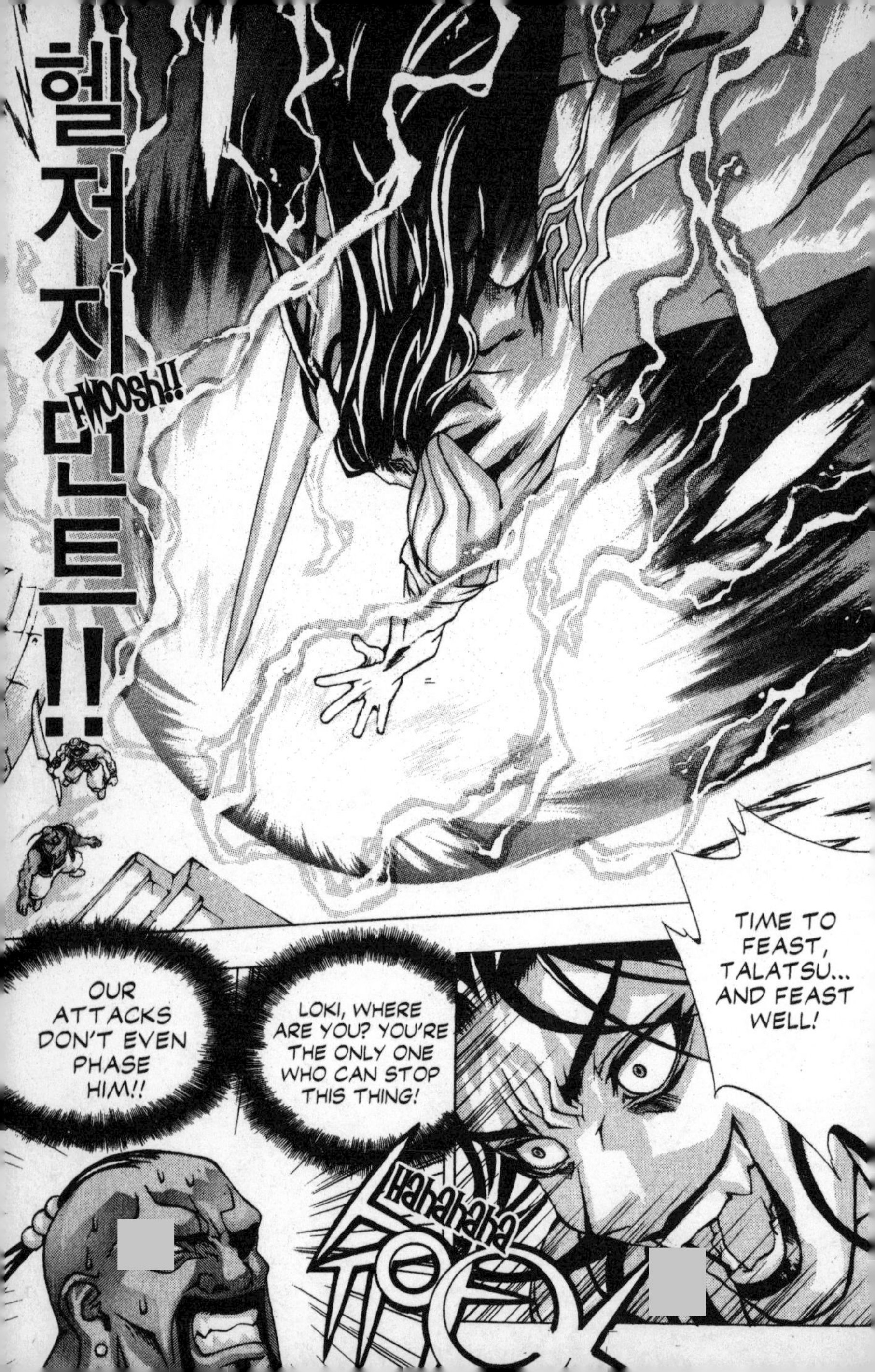
헬저지먼트!!
FWOOSH!!
OUR ATTACKS DON'T EVEN PHASE HIM!!
LOKI, WHERE ARE YOU? YOU'RE THE ONLY ONE WHO CAN STOP THIS THING!
TIME TO FEAST, TALATSU... AND FEAST WELL!
HAHAHAHA